Our Frontier Is the World

A VOLUME IN THE SERIES

THE UNITED STATES IN THE WORLD

Edited by Mark Philip Bradley, David C. Engerman,
Amy S. Greenberg, and Paul A. Kramer

A list of titles in this series is available at cornellpress.cornell.edu.

Our Frontier Is the World

The Boy Scouts in the Age of
American Ascendancy

Mischa Honeck

Cornell University Press
Ithaca and London

First published 2018 by Cornell University Press

Printed in the United States of America

Library of Congress Cataloging-in-Publication Data

Names: Honeck, Mischa, 1976– author.
   Title: Our frontier is the world : the Boy Scouts in the age of American ascendancy / Mischa Honeck.
   Description: Ithaca : Cornell University Press, 2018. | Series: The United States in the world | Includes bibliographical references and index.
   Identifiers: LCCN 2017040107 (print) | LCCN 2017043855 (ebook) | ISBN 9781501716195 (epub/mobi) | ISBN 9781501716201 (pdf) | ISBN 9781501716188 (cloth : alk. paper)
   Subjects: LCSH: Boy Scouts of America—History. | Scouting (Youth activity)—Political aspects—United States. | Imperialism—Social aspects—United States—History.
   Classification: LCC HS3313 (ebook) | LCC HS3313 .H66 2018 (print) | DDC 369.430973—dc23
   LC record available at https://lccn.loc.gov/2017040107

Cornell University Press strives to use environmentally responsible suppliers and materials to the fullest extent possible in the publishing of its books. Such materials include vegetable-based, low-VOC inks and acid-free papers that are recycled, totally chlorine-free, or partly composed of nonwood fibers. For further information, visit our website at cornellpress.cornell.edu.

Keen, clean face of the embryo man . . .
Conquer the world, as you will and can!
We dip the flag to your world-long file
And the whimsical vim of your Boy Scout smile.
                    —Edmund Vance Cooke, *Salute the Boy Scouts*, 1919

Boy Scouts of America are all over the world. Kind of like the army,
everybody has heard of it.
                    —Fourteen-year-old Boy Scout dropout, 1968

To Elena, Nikita, and Vera,
who light my way

Contents

Illustrations

Acknowledgments

The historian and the Scout have much in common. Both veer off well-trodden paths and reconnoiter unknown territory, both blaze trails that others are supposed to follow, and both are respected for sharing with a broader audience the knowledge they have gained from exploring faraway countries or presumably distant pasts. Yet more often than not, what people like to think of as a solitary effort is actually the product of teamwork. Since this truism certainly applies to the pages that follow, I cannot but profess that this book is not entirely my own. It belongs to my family, who has sustained and keeps sustaining me. It belongs to my teachers, colleagues, students, and countless interlocutors who have drawn my attention to things both big and small as I was forging ahead. And it belongs to the innumerable helping hands in the archives that have opened their doors to me as well as to the institutions that have employed me over the years.

Even though this book is chiefly about youth, I would like to honor the adage "Respect thy elders" and begin by thanking my four academic mentors who created the conditions that allowed this project to flourish. Manfred Berg, who counseled me when I was working on my dissertation, has gone from a trusted tutor to a wonderful companion. Detlef Junker, the founding director of the Heidelberg Center for American Studies, pulled me into thought-provoking discussions about the value of embarking on a project about the Boy Scouts and U.S. international relations. I am indebted to Hartmut Berghoff, who hired me as a research fellow at the German Historical Institute (GHI) and believed in the project when it was still in its infancy. Simone Lässig, who assumed the GHI's directorship in 2015 and remains a wellspring of good advice, helped to shepherd the study to a successful conclusion.

I am happy to acknowledge the many fine colleagues who have sharpened my thinking and enriched my analysis with their interventions at various stages of the research and writing process. Martin Klimke, Sebastian Jobs, Joshua Clark Davis, Jan Logemann, Clelia Caruso, Gabriel N. Rosenberg, Emily Swafford, Mario Daniels, Kristine Alexander, James Marten, Britta Waldschmidt-Nelson, Benjamin Jordan, Uwe Spiekermann, and Simone Müller deserve special mention in this regard. I owe even more gratitude to my fellow researchers at the GHI, Elisabeth Engel, Jan C. Jansen, and Anne Schenderlein, who read parts of the manuscript and provided precious feedback on earlier drafts. Without Casey Sutcliffe, David Lazar, and Mark Stoneman, my prose would be much duller. Let me also harken back to the stimulating discussions my project generated at venues ranging from the more intimate research colloquia in Berlin, Augsburg, Jena, Germany, and Alexandria, Virginia, to the more crowded forums of the American Historical Association, the Organization of American Historians, and the Society for the History of Childhood and Youth. Although their names go unsung, the people who quizzed me at these events in a manner that was always collegial and constructive broadened my understanding of pertinent methodological and empirical issues and helped me avoid analytical pitfalls.

As I was piling up sources, I benefited in no small measure from the tremendous support of an amazing group of students who devoted much time and energy to helping me locate and organize archival material for this study. Among the young historians who assisted me with sifting through sources while interning at the GHI, Merle Ingenfeld, Sascha Brünig, Julie Davis, Christoph Nitschke, Kevin Hall, Andre Algermissen, and Paul Schweitzer-Martin provided the most valuable contributions. I feel fortunate to have met numerous former Scouts during the research and writing process. Our conversations have enriched my understanding of the subject in ways too plentiful to mention, and I am grateful that many agreed to answer questions that became the basis of a small but insightful oral history compilation. To Ken Badgett, a passionate collector and Boy Scout historian in his own right, I owe a special debt. I am afraid that our exchanges were a lopsided trade—without Ken's generosity, many rare sources on African American and Filipino Scouting would never have come my way.

The professionalism exhibited by the people working at Cornell University Press has been nothing short of amazing. Our alliance started more than seven years ago during the annual meeting of the American Historical Association in

Boston. A casual but fateful conversation ensued between Michael McGandy and me. Michael's instant enthusiasm for the project was contagious, and he never tired of supporting it from start to finish. His unswerving loyalty gave me the assurance I needed to complete a study that will hopefully appeal to a broad readership. Ange Romeo-Hall competently oversaw the book's production. Michelle Witkowski and her team of copyeditors were a pleasure to work with. Dave Prout compiled the index. I am satisfied to see this book included in the United States in the World series and want to thank the series editors, Mark Bradley, David Engerman, Paul Kramer, and Amy Greenberg, for accommodating a study on the Boy Scouts. I hope they can take delight in the pages that follow.

There are no words sufficient to thank those closest to me. My sisters Jasmin, Natalie, and Jessica as well as my uncle Leander and his wife Ulla are an infinite source of emotional comfort. I am a better person for the kindness and hospitality provided by my in-laws, Sergei Matveev and Valentina Matveeva, as well as my sister-in-law, Irina, all of whom have lifted and continue to lift us up with their unconditional support. While I was working on this project, my son Nikita and my daughter Vera were born. Had it not been for Elena, the love of my life, I doubt that I would have been able to operate halfway properly in both the private and professional realms. Elena deserves the greatest praise of all. My wife and children are the pillars of my world. With all my love, I dedicate this book to them.

Abbreviations

AYC	American Youth Congress
BDP	Bund Deutscher Pfadfinder (Federation of German Scouts)
BRS	British Scout Association
BSA	Boy Scouts of America
BSIB	Boy Scouts International Bureau (1920–68)
BSJ	Boy Scouts of Japan
BSP	Boy Scouts of the Philippines
CCC	Civilian Conservation Corps
CFR	BSA Committee on Foreign Relations
DPs	Displaced Persons
FCDA	Federal Civil Defense Administration
FDJ	Freie Deutsche Jugend (Free German Youth)
GAB	German-American Bund
GSA	Girl Scouts of America
GYA	German Youth Activities
IRS	BSA Inter-Racial Service
ISC	International Scout Conference
IWO	International Workers' Order
KKK	Ku Klux Klan
NAACP	National Association for the Advancement of Colored People
NARA	National Archives and Records Administration
NASA	National Aeronautics and Space Administration
NYA	National Youth Administration

OCD   Office of Civil Defense
OMGUS   Office of Military Government, United States
UN   United Nations
UNESCO   United Nations Educational, Scientific and Cultural
           Organization
UNRRA   United Nations Relief and Rehabilitation Administration
WAGGGS   World Association of Girl Guides and Girl Scouts
WCTU   Woman's Christian Temperance Union
WFF   World Friendship Fund
WRA   War Relocation Authority
WSB   World Scout Bureau (1968–today)
YCL   Young Communist League
YMCA   Young Men's Christian Association
YPA   Young Pioneers of America

Our Frontier Is the World

Introduction

The White Boy's Burden

Waging war in Afghanistan and Iraq, U.S. Secretary of Defense Robert M. Gates rarely got a chance to relive the lighter days of his youth. One such moment came on July 28, 2010—a day of celebration at Fort A.P. Hill in Virginia. The year marked the one-hundredth birthday of the Boy Scouts of America (BSA), and Gates's keynote address set the tone for a big patriotic show featuring flags, paratroopers, antiaircraft cannons firing blank shots, and a flyover of F-16 jets. Despite the jubilant occasion, the Pentagon chief had not come to spin campfire yarn. Amid the cheers of almost fifty thousand Scouts gathered at the army installation, Gates, an Eagle Scout from 1958, reaffirmed the movement's intergenerational contract that promised a relationship of mutual allegiance between boys and men. "I believe that today, as for the past 100 years, there is no finer program for preparing American boys for citizenship and leadership than the Boy Scouts of America." Reciting the themes of crisis, anxiety, and salvation that supporters of the nation's foremost youth organization had evoked since its founding, Gates extolled scouting as the best remedy for an America "where the young are increasingly physically unfit and society as a whole languishes in ignoble moral ease." While many youths had degenerated into "couch potatoes," the BSA continued to make men and leaders, men of "integrity and decency . . . moral courage" and "strong character—the kind of person who built this country and made it into the greatest democracy and the greatest economic powerhouse in the history of the world." More was at stake than the fate of the nation. "The future of the world itself," said Gates, depended on the "kind of citizens our young people" would become. Only with the sort of leaders molded by scouting would America remain "the beacon of hope and decency and justice for the rest of the world."[1]

Admittedly, these snippets from Gates's centennial speech do not capture the full scope of values espoused by America's major boyhood institution. In the BSA's 108-year history, nearly 120 million boys and men—among them future generals, ambassadors, business magnates, and presidents—have donned the uniform of an organization that continues to be embroiled in debates over what constitutes proper boyhood and manhood. Over the years, pacifists, socialists, atheists, feminists, gay rights activists, and pedophile watchdog groups have lambasted the BSA as detrimental to the development of young males.[2] For its defenders, the BSA has always been a big tent, bringing together knot tiers and flag wavers, accommodating the outdoorsman and nature enthusiast as much as the lover of uniforms and military pageantry. Gates's globe-spanning oratory may surprise those more familiar with scouting as an icon of small-town America, neatly nested among its churches, schools, and tight-knit families. Individual troops in which Scouts earned their merit badges in community projects and summer camps may have recognized the authority of national headquarters but certainly hiked their own local trails to manhood and citizenship. Yet contrary to personal memory and public nostalgia, scouting in the United States was never simply about home and country.[3] When Bob Gates spoke at Fort A.P. Hill, former Scouts were advancing U.S. interests as soldiers, politicians, and aid workers from Boston to Baghdad and from Kansas City to Kabul. The nation's top scouter had a point. Throughout its history, the BSA has always relied on wider spaces to construct the ideal man and citizen. The world has been its final frontier.

This book charts the BSA's shifting global frontiers from the Progressive Era to the countercultural rebellions of the second half of the twentieth century. During this period, the United States experienced intense social conflict and economic turmoil but also ascended from a continental power to the undisputed hegemon of the Western world. The term "frontier" is used purposefully to suggest different relevant meanings: first, as a geographic borderland where different people and cultures meet; second, as a sociopolitical frontier that separates people into groups with unequal privileges; third, as a zone of initiation where boys and men fashion their masculinities in a matrix of play and adventure; and fourth, as a national myth that shapes Americans' encounter with the world.[4] Geographically, this book traces physical and imaginary border crossings across several generations. It connects various moments, events, and places inside the United States as well as in other countries where scouting has brought Americans, young and adult, into contact with people of different origins. Across these historical moments, I examine the making and remaking of young imperial masculinities, a category equally applicable to the realms of ideological aspiration and social practice.[5]

Let me state the rationale of this book clearly: by prioritizing a point of view that is mindful of but not bound by national developments, I show that the dual agenda promoted by the BSA—the making of men and of citizens—was closely tied to the changing international fortunes of the modern United States. Most accounts of America's chief boy organization suggest that the BSA turned into a domestic institution with purely domestic interests, that it looked inward rather than outward, and that its members negotiated the meaning of boyhood and manhood among themselves on American terms, not in conversation with the outside world. As a result, the powerful links that connected the evolution of scouting for boys in the United States to larger global trends have receded from sight.

Our Frontier Is the World is an exercise in deprovincialization. It shows, in Amy Kaplan's words, how "cultural phenomena we think of as domestic or particularly national are forged in a crucible of foreign relations."[6] Salvaging what we have missed does not require a radical paradigm shift. Rather, this book readjusts the relationship of key paradigms, treating the local, national, and global not as competing but as complementary frames of interpretation. Only by giving all three frames their due can we understand the history of scouting in the United States and beyond.

The Boy Scouts started as an Anglo-Saxon project launched in the early 1900s by men in England and the United States who feared that white Protestant middle-class masculinity was in decline. The movement's vision of re-masculinizing and rejuvenating societies through a return to nature, physical training, and ideals of robust citizenship spread rapidly beyond the English-speaking world. Scouting found adherents in old empires as well as in the new nationalist regimes of Europe, Asia, and Latin America, where governments sanctioned local adaptations of the movement or created ideological variations. Globally, the Boy Scouts encouraged international travel and spawned penpalships, even friendships, between boys from different countries. Within the first two decades of its existence, scouting erected its own transnational platforms with the Boy Scouts International Bureau (BSIB), the International Scout Conference (ISC), and its signature event—the multiday open-air festivals of global scouting that became known as the world jamborees. In the early twenty-first century, scouting functions as a rite of passage for over thirty-one million boys and girls in more than 216 countries and territories worldwide.[7]

Over time, I realized that my research would not only impel me to reinterpret past events but also to reflect on their enduring relevance. Perhaps most significantly, writing about the Boy Scouts opened my eyes to the political leverage of children, either assigned by adults or claimed by the young themselves. Children and adolescents were never simply a series of unfinished projects on which interested parties could impose their will. Without activating the initiative of young people, organizations such as the Boy Scouts and Girl Scouts would have remained hollow vessels, mere cardboard constructions that would have collapsed on their own. Scouting may have outlived its prime, but the movement's rich history demonstrates the complex connection between the supposedly carefree realm of childhood and the contentious arena of politics. Clashes over thorny issues of sexual orientation, religion and citizenship, and U.S. international engagement are bound to trigger stronger emotions when young people are involved. Whether we are confronted with an early twenty-first century image of a suffering refugee child or behold a mid-twentieth-century depiction of an American Boy Scout saluting the flag, it is hard not to acknowledge the multiple ways in which the very idea of youth—not to mention young people's own actions—structures how we feel, think, and respond to the messy and often incomprehensible realities that surround us. Pondering the roles children and youths have played, and continue to play, in shaping the relationship between America and the larger world leads to the heart of history, not to its margins.

The Vista of Open Spaces

Scouting advocates never grew tired of touting the romance of faraway places. As one BSA author mused during World War II, the word "Scout" conjures up "the vista of open spaces," where the boy "may find his highest joy" and see himself "as a frontiersman, an explorer."[8] When accounting for these spaces, historians of the modern era have offered at least three different, though related, approaches: the international, the transnational, and the imperial.[9] Traditional international histories and their concern for state-to-state relations have been enriched by investigations into the broad array of nonstate actors and phenomena such as migration, tourism, networks, civil organizations, sports, diseases, and social movements that populate the transnational narratives now en vogue in the historical profession. The analysis of empire, meanwhile, has proved particularly fruitful at the intersection of the international and transnational.

Young people were often the first to travel the global highways that made the world a smaller place. By the early twentieth century, few had been quicker to transcend the confines of the nation-state than the period's budding youth movements. Scouting grew out of a much larger field of organized youth that spanned immense geographical distances while serving the needs of particular cultures. Societies of all types planted their flags in the evolving landscape of youth work. The beginnings of the Young Men's Christian Association (YMCA) in England, the founding of the 4-H movement for rural youth in the United States, the Wandervogel in Imperial Germany, communist youth in Soviet Russia, and adaptations of several of these initiatives that took root in China, Japan, India, Latin America, and Africa represented different facets of a broader historical formation.[10] Despite national and ideological peculiarities, all these movements shared the same goal of revitalizing their societies by breeding strong, healthy, and morally sound citizens.

The identities of nation, gender, race, class, religion, and age forged in this process, however, cannot be explained with references to transnationalism alone. The characters assembled in this book never pursued a transnational utopia, and applying an analytical model preoccupied with liberating global flows would result in a distorted account of why the BSA acted in contexts smaller and larger than the nation. Scouting crossed borders without subscribing to an ideology of borderlessness, respecting and reinforcing all kinds of boundaries that separated nations, races, age groups, and sexes. Although the Boy Scout movement was rife with metaphors of travel and exploration, I argue that a border-crossing history of the BSA can shed more light on the sprawling and ambiguous processes of power formation—gendered, racialized, classed, and aged—across vast distances. These expanding webs of hierarchy and privilege can be scrutinized with greater rigor through the lens of the imperial. To say this is not to erect an insuperable wall between writing transnational and imperial histories. Both fields are, and have to be, closely connected, just as there is a reciprocal relationship between power and mobility and between the circuits of subordination and the routes of the subaltern.

This book illuminates why the United States, rather than Great Britain, became one of the main drivers and beneficiaries of the globalization of scouting. Population growth, efficient leadership, government backing, corporate funding, and transnational networks all facilitated the BSA's remarkable development and longevity. Taken together, these factors reflect the ways in which scouting's playful enactment of self-reliance, patriotism, and male companionship came to serve a less readily acknowledged purpose. The Boy Scouts, I contend, soared to prominence in the United States because they provided a beguiling solution to America's imperial dilemma, furnishing a template for doing empire in a nation notoriously invested in negating its own imperiality.

Oscillating between transnational cooperation and imperial influence, scouting enabled American boys and men to forge cross-border ties while bolstering the idea that the United States, by virtue of its youth, could retain the luxury of innocence as it was accumulating greater power.

Modern empires rarely referred to themselves as such after great powers had begun to appropriate the language of democracy and self-determination. This is particularly true of the United States, where talk of an "American Empire" has been considered anathema to the nation's self-image. The degree to which calling America an empire arouses controversy obviously depends on what one means by the term. Among historians, there is no consensus on the subject, although the literature on U.S. empire is capacious. There are those who favor a broad understanding of empire to account for the range of coercive and non-coercive means employed by the United States to create an international order, the protection of which became its raison d'être.[11] The works by these historians show that empires are not just the domains of statesmen and generals but multilayered systems of power upheld through long-distance connections that penetrate nearly every aspect of human existence. Then there are those who claim that except for maybe a brief moment at the turn of the twentieth century, Americans have never actively sought to build an empire. The long list of euphemisms invented to explain away a complex and sometimes dis-comforting imperial reality ranges from phrases such as "the indispensable nation" and "the leader of the free world" to the wordplay of an author who likened America's role in international relations to an "umpire," a benign en-forcer of universally accepted norms of conduct between sovereign nations.[12] These neo-exceptionalist historians tend to claim that only state-directed op-erations of conquering and colonizing foreign territory count as evidence of empire. In adopting this stance, they conveniently ignore how nonstate actors working in tandem with the state or apart from it formed networks of influ-ence for the sake of aligning people and markets at home and abroad with their interests. Established to direct and monitor cross-border currents of cap-ital, commodities, and knowledge, these networks were deeply enmeshed in the exercise of imperial authority in ways both formal and informal. That the state maintained a relatively low profile in their operations made them no less effective and no less imperial.[13]

Following Paul A. Kramer, I see the imperial as something to "think with more than think about," not as a signifier for a monolithic political behemoth but as a lens through which to track the multiplicity of actors, power asym-metries, and unequal transformations within large geographic realms shaped by various patterns of domination and exchange.[14] This widened perspective, informed by a "new imperial history" that focuses more on language, society, and culture than on hard economic or political structures, helps to overcome the traditional fixation on the state as the locus of imperial might. As such, it discloses the ways in which civil institutions and networks—churches, businesses, fraternal organizations, and so on—have wielded a commanding influence over people inside as well as outside the boundaries of the state. Internal social stratification and international involvement are reciprocally tied together in an imperial framework, which posits that domestic and foreign power struggles have been linked through entangled discourses of race, gender, class, religion, and age.[15] This book, thus, embeds the emphatic youthfulness, boyish masculinities, and frontier narratives that converge in the BSA in an "interconnected world . . . wrought in hierarchy and power, even as that power is bounded and contested."[16]

The aversion to taking stock of the role of empire in U.S. history may explain the lopsidedness in the historiography on the Boy Scouts on both sides of the Atlantic. In the scholarship on Great Britain, there is little denial that the emergence of scouting shaped, and was shaped by, a commitment to empire. Historians have linked the popularity of the movement's self-acclaimed founder, Robert Baden-Powell, an imperial officer and veteran of the Second Boer War, to longings for a revitalized British role in global affairs. Initiated in 1907, Baden-Powell's program to toughen boyhood through the promotion of outdoor vigor and male camaraderie won approval from imperial elites for internal as well as external reasons. Internally, Boy Scouting was supposed to roll back the forces of industrialization, urbanization, and feminization that had allegedly made young men soft, degenerate, and incapable of taking up what Rudyard Kipling had famously called "the white man's burden."[17] Externally, it was supposed to fasten the bonds of imperial affection between the metropole and the colonies by kindling fraternal feelings among different youths living under the Union Jack.[18]

Curiously, while the first domestic rationalization has been thickly applied to the often-invoked "crisis of masculinity" in the United States and other industrialized nations at the turn of the century, the second international one is glaringly absent from historical accounts of the BSA. For all their lucid findings, authors who have studied the BSA in order to offer insight into processes of Americanization, the construction of masculine gender roles, youth culture, mass leisure, and environmentalism have all remained trapped in a nation-centered paradigm. As a result, they have perpetuated the myth of a nonimperial United States. If the transnational or imperial is mentioned at all in their storylines, the solution these historians offer is to speak of the nationalization of scouting as a British import. Too often, they disregard parallels to and connections with organized youth elsewhere, and barely look "back out" again.[19] Only by bridging the artificial divide between national and global histories can we discover that scouting constituted a transnational hub of interimperial exchange that brought the United States in proximity to other great powers.

Our Frontier Is the World takes this broader view. It combines the analytical tools of age and gender to illuminate how the BSA operated as a vehicle of American empire, and how scouting repackaged U.S. global expansion as a playful and unimpeachable yet serious masculine adventure. This book examines the horizontal and vertical projection of power without failing to address its limitations. Imperial practices and ideologies were never simply applied by a governing center or an obedient periphery. Rather, they were composed among rulers and ruled, adults and youths, by means of coercion, persuasion, and subversion. Contrary to the familiar Americanization-of-the-world narrative, placing the history of scouting in the United States in broader spatial contexts can add to our understanding of how the movement changed people's lives across cultures. I see culture as a coalescing enterprise in which the political, social, and cultural form mutually constitutive spheres. This means identifying concerns of power, structure, experience, agency, and (self)-representation as force fields that necessarily shape and support one another. The BSA's accounts of U.S. continental conquest and overseas intervention, its vision of white masculine authority, and the regimentation of male youth were received differently at various sites and were always subject to negotiation, appropriation, and rejection by a diverse group of historical actors.

More than the study of a youth organization, this book is a history of the reciprocities of youth, manhood, and empire in U.S. culture that is intergenerational and part of a larger interimperial history of the twentieth century. Of all the organized youth movements that breathed life into Kipling's panimperial masculine fantasy, the Boy Scouts fit the description best. Called on to enter the world's stage as the embodiments of empire and its simultaneous extenuation, they smoothed the rough edges of America's rise to global predominance in meaningful ways. Making the imperial work for a society without causing an affront to its nonimperial identity became, in essence, the white boy's burden.

Power and Innocence

The Scout is a familiar figure in the annals of Euro-American settler imperialism. His ability to gather information on the enemy and reconnoiter unknown territory made him a crucial player in the history of colonial expansion. Celebrated in popular fiction for his bravery and rugged individualism, the Scout epitomized a frontier masculinity that tied superior survival skills in the wild to the spread of white civilization. In the United States, the myths of nineteenth-century pathfinders and colonial mercenaries such as Daniel Boone, John C. Frémont, Kit Carson, Buffalo Bill, and Frederick Russell Burnham, who rode with Baden-Powell in South Africa, were canonized as instructional tales for young males to prevent their enfeeblement in an age of big cities and office buildings.[20]

Boys, on the other hand, are unlikely imperial actors (and prospective imperialists at best). Though primed to become men, boys are still children, and the immaturity and dependency associated with young age stand diametrically opposed to notions of imperial authority. If children and adolescents are assigned a role in the literature on empire, they usually appear as either its victims or its students. Scout organizers undoubtedly sought to instill in boys adult ideals of thought and behavior. Boy Scouts were to learn empire, not question it, thereby offering a sense of continuity in societies riddled with political, social, and generational conflict. Conceived as a staging ground for the responsibilities of citizenship, scouting not only provides insight into how children and youths function as objects of adult design. It also shows, to paraphrase historian Richard Ivan Jobs, how youth are turned into "an agreeable matrix" through which adults could contemplate their "past, present, and future."[21]

Adult interest in youth was twofold: it extended to young people as a social formation as well as to youth as a gendered idea that could be mined for cultural and political capital. "Youth" often stood in for young men, less so for young women. Charging youth with the task of shaping national and international futures lent extraordinary importance to the category of age, but the ubiquity of youth also made it an elastic concept that could be utilized for different purposes. Experiences of growing up varied according to institutional practices and cultural assumptions about youth in a given historical setting. Where childhood ends, youth begins, and adulthood beckons, moreover, is not determined by biology, because all three categories are ultimately social constructs.[22] So, too, are the rites of passage that mark the transitions from one age group to the next. Even older men, as will be shown, could pass as young if they were exuding qualities associated with youthfulness.

Documenting the evolution of modern definitions of youth and childhood reveals that they incorporated multiple understandings of modernity. Because these definitions often reflected metaphysical, almost suprapolitical concepts of progress and decline, they could serve as allegories for a variety of global developments. According to the cultural anthropologist Liisa Malkki, children occupied a central place in the modern internationalist imagination: as "embodiments of a basic human goodness (and symbols of world harmony); as sufferers; as seers of truth; as ambassadors of peace; and as embodiments of the future."[23] These futures could be liberal or conservative, religious or secular, socialist or capitalist. Ideologues from the revolutionary left and the radical right, too, fashioned a language of youth conducive to their agendas. Invoking the "new man" in communist and fascist propaganda did more than express a common belief in the malleability of youth; it presented politics in gendered and generational terms, contrasting able-bodied and idealistic young males (less so females) with old bourgeois elites portrayed as decadent, unprincipled, and weak.[24] With youth gaining visibility and political clout, age, as it intersected with other categories of difference, emerged as a productive mechanism of demarcation and grafted distinctions between old and young onto complex struggles for power and belonging.

Despite the relative absence of age in the historiography of empire, historians are well advised to pay closer attention to how the common but fluid category of age reveals contingencies of power and agency. A critical history of the Boy Scouts can illuminate how changing conceptions of boyhood, youth, and manhood are not only thoroughly embedded in social and cultural systems of authority but were also used to at once mask and bolster U.S. power in the world. Even as the meaning of age depends on time, place, and geography, the deceptive belief in the universality of various age stages tends to mitigate the very real differences that exist within each stage. Age does not operate independently of other social variables; yet at times the idea that individuals might share certain cross-cultural traits on account of their age became so powerful that it was employed to diminish or even disavow other distinctions that separated these individuals. At the very least, I dispute the notion that age-based constructs such as boyhood or youth are simply appendages to larger historical phenomena. These constructs, too, have the power to shape the cultural systems and social fabrics that envelop them.

The perennially vague meaning of youth aided the regeneration of empires in an age of virulent nationalism, competing internationalisms, and anticolonial movements.[25] Advocates of empire did not stand idly by as different parties crowded around the fountain of youth. Why should its waters not also reinvigorate settler societies plagued by the strife between capital and labor, racial and ethnic friction, and gender insecurities? The historian Frederick Jackson Turner was certain that the North American frontier had done just that, likening it to "a magic fountain of youth in which America continually bathed and was rejuvenated."[26] Thinking about familiar tropes related to youth—such as purity, innocence, and the promise of new beginnings—and their significance for the reproduction of imperial power invites reflection whether contemporary articulations of a crisis of masculinity actually betrayed a crisis of old age. Youthfulness became the dominant marker of manhood in modern societies in which expanding markets targeted young consumers, social movements advocated physical health and fortitude, and seniors lived longer but were also seen as frail and dependent.[27] The devaluation of old age, albeit not unique to the United States, was closely tied to the idea of American exceptionalism, which held that the nation possessed a special destiny because it had turned away from the settled ways of others.

Demographic changes amplified the desirability of youth over old age. Among the white middle and upper classes of industrialized nations, advances in medicine and female birth control led to fewer and healthier children, whose value as future citizens of the state rose as family sizes shrank. Declining birthrates, social conflict, and geopolitical rivalries bled into the conviction that men, nations, and empires lacking in vitality were bound for extinction.[28] To elude associations of aging with a decline in masculine authority, older men sought rejuvenation. In scouting, they found what they wanted: an institution and culture that imbued men with a boyishness that allowed them to immunize themselves against the emasculating effects of aging. It is here that the book inverts the typical causal narrative about gender and age in scouting: it was not just the adults who sought to masculinize their charges. The boys, too, acted as agents of transformation, if merely by proximity to the men who wanted to embody a fresher, more innocent version of themselves.

Studying the Boy Scouts in imperial contexts has to mean more than tracking the masculinization of boys. It also has to include tracking the boyification of men. With boyification, I do not mean men purposefully regressing into the dependencies of childhood. The concept describes a social performance employed to sustain existing power relations by shrouding them in the emotionally uplifting valences of youth. The Boy Scouts were the first mass incarnation of a modern boy-man culture devoted to the pursuit of perpetual boyhood without surrendering the prerogatives of manhood.[29] In scouting, masculinity was as much taught as it was drawn out of boys. "Boy-men" such as Baden-Powell in England, Daniel Carter Beard in the United States, and countless scoutmasters who followed their example tried to be fatherly tutors and boyish playmates at the same time.[30] With their penchant for wearing shorts, playing games, bonding with boys around the campfire, and shouting cowboy yells and Indian war whoops, they strove to recapture the purity and zest of youth, which shielded them from the debilitating ambiguities of modernity. The redemptive quality of boy-man-hood was crucial to what political theorist Jeanne Morefield has called "the politics of deflection," an avoidance strategy consciously employed by liberal empires that needed to convince themselves that they were not responsible for the ugly consequences of their actions.[31] Fostering father-son-like relationships in homosocial spaces inhabited by hobby pioneers, fake Zulu warriors, and fantasy Indians, scouting prepared boys for empire at the same time that it exonerated the men who had been complicit in its violent enlargement.

Like other fraternal organizations, the Boy Scouts promoted bonding activities between same-sex individuals that were at once intensely homosocial and professedly asexual. Boys were to be admired for their pluck and pliability. Their sexual maturation, on the other hand, was seen as something precarious, almost unwanted. This preference for the preadolescent asexual boy might well have arisen from fears about the possibility of child abuse. Still, as queer studies scholars have argued, and as the BSA's ongoing struggle against pedophiles in its midst has demonstrated, the lines separating homosocial, homoerotic, and homosexual desire are less clear-cut than they may seem.[32] Because male homosociality devoid of sexuality is such a fragile construction, its effectiveness depends on the repression of influences that could disrupt the illusion it peddles: the creation of chaste and chivalrous boy-men who stood outside the laws of biological aging and were neither fully juvenile nor mature. The exclusion of females and homosexuals became essential for this particular performance of homosociality to work. Actual sexual contact, be it between boys and girls or, worse, men and boys, was condemned since it would impede the quest to regain the curative innocence of boyhood.

Apart from desexualizing boyhood, the desire of men to turn their cluttered biographies into a youthful tabula rasa came to reflect the race and class preferences of adult scouters. It was no coincidence that an organization dominated by white middle-class Protestant males largely conceived of childhood innocence within the sociocultural parameters of their group. As bourgeois reformers built the child-saving movements of the late nineteenth and early twentieth centuries with the post-Enlightenment image of the guiltless and imperiled white child in mind, they also began rendering working-class youths and youths of color as more likely to exhibit delinquent behavior. Boyification never really resonated with nonwhites, who were infantilized because of their race. This was most clearly the case with African American men, for whom the term "boy" was fraught with racist connotations because it expressed the notion that blacks were mentally and physically inferior.[33] White men, in turn, were more inclined to see in boyification a tool to smooth the social and racial divisions of the adult world, partly because reconnecting with the carefree world of boyish play promised to make these divisions seem less sinister.

In explicating how innocence and purity became objects of male desire, at least one other major interpretation has to be considered. When pressed to explain the rise of scouting, most historians cling to an evolutionary logic promulgated by the educated classes of the late nineteenth and early twentieth centuries. In texts ranging from Mark Twain's *Huckleberry Finn* to Granville Stanley Hall's writings on developmental psychology, boys appear not as angelic beings but as little savages bent on conquering their worlds through ferocious play and an untamed appetite for adventure.[34] Adult longings to control and channel the wildness of boys, a desire resonant with colonial fantasies, have to be taken seriously, as they gendered narratives of imperial expansion and offered a rationale for marginalizing girls, who were depicted as fragile and frail. Yet picturing boys as possessing an archaic will to fight can also simplify and distort. The embrace of youth as a means of purifying manhood, by contrast, transcends accounts that have pictured brutal combat as vigorously rejuvenating.[35] Instead of limiting the history of organized youth to a history of masculine regeneration, this book probes the potential of organized youth to act as agents of moral purification.

Our Frontier Is the World details how BSA organizers deployed a specific concept of youth to sanitize the bloody work of empire and allay anxieties about the nation's future in a century marred by ideological conflict, war, depression, and the threat of nuclear annihilation. The Adamic myth of inhabiting a virgin continent gave the descendants of white settlers a strong understanding of their nation as innocent and energetic.[36] Asserting that scouting originated from the pristine vitality of the North American frontier, Americans furthered the exceptionalist story of a youthful United States and a tired old Europe. Adults, though, never enjoyed sole ownership of youth. The meaning of youth, like that of gender, was as dynamic and contested as the experiences of young people were varied: what connoted vigor and idealism in one instance could resonate with inexperience and manipulability in another. The categories of youth and childhood were so pliable that they could be claimed by nearly everyone, including the young themselves. Over the past decades, historians of youth and childhood have revealed the ways in which children and adolescents actively shaped historical events as students, laborers, consumers, and activists, demonstrating that the young have used their age as a bargaining chip in arguments with adults about their own place in society.[37] To treat the motivations of children and adolescents in scouting with the seriousness they deserve is to question presumptions of an intrinsically innocent childhood that deny children a say in their own history.

Putting the voices of the young on an equal footing with those of their elders, though, is easier said than done. For reasons common to historical research on subordinated groups, archival sources generated by minors are rare, and the few available letters, diaries, drawings, and oral histories that capture the Scouts' point of view fade in comparison with the volumes of material—press releases, official reports, private correspondence, moving images, memoirs—left behind by the organizers. Even as children are not fully subaltern since their state is transient, the power of the archive to exclude nonadult voices has prompted scholars of childhood and youth to wrestle with many of the same problems of representation and agency discussed in postcolonial theory.[38] Fortunately, children's voices have not been silenced so much as muffled by the conventions of archival preservation, and it is the scholar's task to make these voices audible again.

In light of the inadequacies of traditional methodologies and the limited literacies of young people, such an undertaking has to be eclectic and rely on a close reading of textual and nontextual sources created by youths and the adults interacting with them. If historians care to look hard enough, the fingerprints of the young start to shimmer on documents drafted by the architects of scouting. The voices of the young speak through adult confessions that while youth in the abstract was rich in symbolism, actual youths refused to be soft clay in the hands of their leaders. Historians often survey youth organizations for evidence of the "moral panics" that led to their creation. Yet studying a youth organization's textual, visual, and material records should also lead to an appreciation of its hybrid culture, which Jay Mechling located in the tacit struggle between "adult intentions and youth's desire to exercise as much autonomy and agency as possible."[39] Since young people possessed not only agency but what historian Alf Lüdtke called "Eigen-Sinn"—the ability to carve out semiautonomous spaces in a hierarchical environment—they also had the power, however limited, to pursue trajectories independent of adult will.[40]

The concern that boys would not fully submit to, or wholly reject, the disciplinary framework of scouting was deeply unsettling to adult organizers. This disquiet echoed the fear that youths socialized in modern surroundings would learn to think and act in ways detrimental to the preservation of order. Noncompliance might lead to idleness and delinquency—the archenemies of imperial regeneration. Resonant with stories of waywardness as old as Icarus's fatal flight too close to the sun, telling cautionary tales about unwanted youthful initiative helped the BSA position itself as the savior of youth and nation. This is not to suggest that young people's aspirations and search for belonging were necessarily at odds with the BSA's vision of masculine development. Most boys would never have filled the ranks of the movement had it not offered rich opportunities for youthful self-realization. Adult organizers touted the collectivist values of obedience and service to others, but a contradictory strand in the movement urging Boy Scouts to become self-reliant suggested there was more to life than following orders.

The volatility of adolescence, widely imagined as a life stage of sudden impulses and erratic reinventions, remained a source of apprehension. Inasmuch as youth produces a frontier of its own, a contact zone in which young and old people interact in frames of discipline and lines of escape, adults, according to cultural theorist Hans Arthur Skott-Myhre, hold "ambivalent feelings" toward the contributions of youth: they "want to valorize and preserve it while at the same time wanting to civilize it and make it more palatable."[41] From Robert Baden-Powell to Robert M. Gates, the uncertainties of youth threatened to subvert scouting's intergenerational contract, and each generation had to confront this radical indeterminacy anew. Precisely because they were dynamic and evolving historical actors who could outgrow the ideological constraints of their elders, youths bore the seeds of the reproduction of imperial ideology as well as those of its undoing.

Generations of Empire

The chapters of this book are organized chronologically and thematically. Capable of tracing developments over a long period of time, a chronological structure can elucidate continuities and ruptures in how the nexus of youth and empire was shaped by demographic shifts, economic swings, cultural transformations, and global ideological conflicts. Of course, the conventional lines drawn by chronology are just that, conventions, and the biographies of people and organizations routinely cut across standard periodizations. Rather than conceptualize my topic within a linear, quasi-teleological scheme, I like to think of the themes highlighted in this book as currents that flow forward in time but are crossing and overlapping one another as they are being broadened, narrowed, and redirected by big and small contingencies. I say this not only to underscore the unpredictability of U.S. attitudes toward youth and international involvement during the twentieth century, but also to draw attention to the fact that constructions of boyhood, manhood, and empire echoed from one generation of Boy Scouts to the next. In all this, intersecting notions of age and gender were constantly recalibrated to bridge the ever-changing distance between historical narratives of nineteenth-century continental expansion and twentieth-century global realities.

Chapter 1 lays the groundwork for all the succeeding chapters. It revisits the social, political, and cultural catalysts that led to the transnational flowering of organized youth after 1900. Unlike the default narrative, which emphasizes the British roots of the Boy Scouts, this chapter locates the movement's inception in uncertainties about the future of youth, old age, boyhood, and manhood that haunted white elites on both sides of the Atlantic. Chapter 2 explores how the BSA re-created the myth of the frontier outside the boundaries of the United States to combat the rise of a largely peer-regulated, frivolous, and sexualized youth culture in the 1920s. Organizing two major expeditions, one to Africa and one to Antarctica, the BSA sent four Eagle Scouts abroad in the hope that their age-appropriate and consumer-friendly enactments of a young frontier masculinity would stabilize dominant hierarchies of age and gender.

Internationalism provided another momentous frontier for U.S. Scouts eager to inscribe themselves in debates about America's global role in the interwar period. Covering the first two decades of the world jamboree movement, chapter 3 details how BSA delegates participated in the reconstruction of nations and empires at these international festivals. Although the world jamborees identified peace as a worthwhile pursuit for boys and men, the colorful parades of Boy Scouts from across the globe rejuvenated ideas of civilizational difference, and performances of universal brotherhood were curtailed by national loyalties and imperial rivalries. Focusing on the inequalities of race, chapter 4 probes how BSA organizers drew on universal tropes of boy development from the 1910s to the 1930s to justify bridging color lines while upholding the belief in racial differences. At the same time that BSA executives developed a cautious approach to making scouting available to domestic and colonial boys of color, Filipino, African American, and Native American boys wrestled with their subordinate status in the movement and, where possible, refashioned it to serve their own interests.

Chapter 5 analyzes the BSA's expansion before and during World War II by centering on its struggle with rival communist and fascist youth organizations.

Casting scouting as the last best hope of boyhood in a world assailed by dictators reinforced the boundaries of Americanness and un-Americanness while
obscuring the closeness of the BSA's scheme to mobilize boyhood for democracy with methods of regimenting youth on the far right and left. Chapter 6
carries the story forward into the era of the Cold War. As children were growing up to the sounds and images of a modern teen culture and a swelling civil
rights movement, the BSA, which tripled its membership with the influx of
the baby boomers, worked to marshal the rising generation around the project
of a liberal empire to help protect the "free world" from Soviet aggression
and the menace of a nuclear holocaust.

Chapter 7 details the foreign equivalent of the domestic drama of Cold War
mobilization. Starting in the early 1950s, Boy Scout troops sprang up on every
major American military base in Western Europe and East Asia, giving boys
the opportunity to enact both the goodwill and resolve of U.S. intervention.
Still, the ideals of a military masculinity and of young ambassadors projecting
amity and democracy did not go together easily, especially when paternalist
attitudes heightened already-existing anti-American sentiments among local
populations. The book's epilogue links the contraction of Boy Scouting in the
United States to the countercultural youth movements, the decline of traditional civic organizations, and the antiwar protests of the global sixties and seventies. The dramatic membership loss of the 1970s, however, invigorated both
the forces of reform and reentrenchment. Their struggle over the BSA's soul
persists to this day.

From its inception, the BSA has crafted boyish masculinities to sustain the
fantasy of a powerful yet innocent America. To that end, it forged alliances with
statesmen, business elites, religious leaders, educators, the military, ordinary
citizens, and millions of boys, even as the agency of young people continued
to expose the uneasy tension between adult norms and juvenile practice.
Foregrounding the imperial as a device to unpack the entangled processes of
masculinization and boyification that transcended the domestic-foreign binary
does not mean that this is the only viable lens through which to study the Boy
Scouts. But like a large artery running through a massive body, the imperial
supplied much of the organization's lifeblood. Thus, it can serve as a robust
analytical frame for making sense of the various cross-border interactions that
the BSA facilitated. If this premise is convincing, *Our Frontier Is the World* has
much to offer. It adds to the growing transnational scholarship on childhood
and youth and corrects a bias implicit in the literature that ascribes meaningful
historical action to nonconformist youth but not to their adult-organized

peers. It shows how boyhood became a potent symbol of America's imagined national and international destiny. It reveals how the frontiers of youth and manhood overlapped with the frontiers of empire, and how globalization and empire worked not only on young people but through them. Lastly, it promotes reflection on the extent to which boyish narratives of fun and fellowship, rather than hard military or economic might, spurred the evolution of an imperial America in the twentieth century.

Chapter 1

Brothers Together

Men, Boys, and the Rejuvenation of Empire

Albert Snoke's heart pounded with excitement. The Eagle Scout from Puyallup, Washington, was about to meet King Christian X of Denmark. The Danish king and other foreign dignitaries had gathered a few miles north of Copenhagen in August 1924 for a parade of Boy Scouts from thirty-four nations. Snoke climbed the staircase to the royal gallery and saluted Christian X. He then stood face to face with one of the most famous men of his time: Robert Baden-Powell, chief scout of the world. Snoke got "quite a kick" from his moment in the limelight. Baden-Powell shook his hand and gave him "a large box with a large silver shield inside," the award for winning the twenty-four-hour hike, one of fourteen contests held at the 1924 World Scout Jamboree in Denmark. The American troop had won the majority of the competitions, including contests in canoeing, diving, obstacle racing, and first aid. They had bested their Danish hosts and the great scouting nation of England, which made them "World Champions in Scouting." The young victors had their pictures taken and smiling faces put on film, images that would travel back with them across the Atlantic. "Oh boy it sure makes me feel good," Snoke rejoiced.[1]

The U.S. jamboree troop of 1924 foregrounded their boyish exuberance, but their success was a product of methodical preparation. National Scout leaders had selected fifty-six Scouts on the basis of rank, skill, and physical fitness to represent the United States in Denmark. The boys hailed from all four corners of the country. Even Hawaii, then still a colonial possession, sent one of its best: fifteen-year-old Tom Frazier. Reporters invited to the training camp in upstate New York praised the Scouts' mental and physical condition. One journalist gushed that the team the BSA dispatched to Europe consisted of "clear cut, capable, strong types of Scouthood and well nigh physically perfect specimens of American boyhood."[2] Shortly before setting sail, eagle scout Don Hawkins expressed the boys' determination to gain the "respect of the other countries for American Scouting."[3] Adolescents like Hawkins were who President Calvin Coolidge had in mind when he congratulated the Scouts for serving as "living examples" of the nation's youth and contributing to the "well-being, right-thinking, and true-living of the whole world."[4]

After U.S. athletes had rushed to gold at the Summer Olympics in Paris a couple weeks earlier, another mere sports spectacle would not have elicited this response from Coolidge. Yet the news of American boys outdoing their competitors and receiving awards from England's supreme scouter was rife with symbolism. For a moment, the twilight of an old empire, the British, and the dawn of a new one, the American, became palpable. In the global advance of this new empire, youth had become more than a metaphor. "At the present time," BSA Executive Director James E. West reminisced after the world jamboree in Denmark, "the hope and the future of the human race rests upon the youth of today. The world needs men of strong character, full of energy and good will." If evidence was needed that America had taken the lead in molding a new type of manhood, young men who were "capable of daring but [knew] how to sacrifice their own interests for the common welfare," West was certain that the U.S. Boy Scouts' performance on foreign soil had provided it.[5]

Saving Youth, Restoring Men

By asserting a basic relationship between "character" and "energy," between muscles and morals, West restated one of the central tenets of the Boy Scout movement. To be sure, Scout leaders were not the first educators to make that connection. Unlike nineteenth-century reformers who had focused on the soul, early twentieth-century boy workers centered on the body. Promulgating that Scout training made better boys, and thus better men, was West's job. But it was also a deeply personal affair. West had grown up as a frail and sickly orphan, battling the consequences of dilettantish surgery that left him half-crippled and unable to walk without a cane. When West reached his thirties, he found his calling in what turn-of-the-century urban middle-class reformers designated "boy work." Presumably to compensate for his childhood deficiencies,

West became an advocate of the playground movement, which focused on Americanizing immigrant children through supervised outdoor play, before he became the BSA's chief organizer in 1911.[6] Nature lovers criticized West's managerial style, but West always insisted that his businesslike approach served the paramount goal of turning boys into healthy young men and citizens.

West belonged to a small clique of men who gloried in their image as the founding fathers of scouting: Robert Baden-Powell in England, Jacques Guérin-Desjardins in France, Alexander Lion in Germany, Andrzej Malkowski in Poland, Pál Count Teleki in Hungary, and Daniel Carter Beard and Ernest Thompson Seton in the United States. Transnational movements, however, are rarely bred by individuals alone. The Boy Scouts crossed borders so quickly because the societies adopting them confronted similar challenges. Urbanization, industrialization, and mass migration chipped away at traditional forms of power and privilege. The arc of civilization no longer seemed to bend toward the secular millennium of material and social progress. Around 1900, European and North American elites began wondering whether the advancements in science and technology that had made their nations rich and powerful had not also made their people complacent. Men in leading positions saw their communities beset by crisis. They begrudged the rapid growth of big cities, where squalor, crime, and labor conflict appeared to run wild. They recoiled at the revolutionary speeches of plebeian radicals, whose demands for redistributing the wealth made the moneyed classes shudder. Treasuring childhood memories of bucolic landscapes, they lamented the gradual disappearance of their nostalgic visions of nature. Last, they feared the growing influx of ethnic and racial others, which posed a threat to the nationalist pursuit of homogeneity.

No expression in the Western world captured the racial and gender anxieties of the period's white upper- and middle-class men more dramatically than "race suicide." The term was coined in 1901 by the American sociologist Edward A. Ross, who augured that "the higher race quietly and unmurmuringly eliminates itself rather than to endure individually the bitter competition it has failed to ward off by collective action."[7] Ross's ideas inspired eugenic theories like those advocated in Madison Grant's 1916 book *The Passing of the Great Race*. The theories of Grant and his predecessors were amplified by Theodore Roosevelt, who declared the refusal of "well-to-do families" to procreate in greater numbers "the greatest problem of civilization."[8] "Race suicide" became the obsession of an entire generation of privileged white men who worried that "inferior" races would outbreed them. Concerns about reproduction galvanized social Darwinists, white supremacists, and liberal intellectuals on both sides of the Atlantic. Declining birthrates signaled extinction, and biology became the chief yardstick for discussions about race, sexuality, gender, citizenship, and national survival. All this prompted white middle-class men to actively search for and experiment with new masculine formulas appropriate for a modern industrial society and nascent transoceanic empire.[9]

Discomfort with national development was the great irony of empire. The ethnic and racial others that kept white Europeans and Americans awake at night were the same people that Western imperialists had set out to conquer. What remedies were available? Members of the ruling classes, speaking in the modern parlance of masculinity, reassured themselves that they could hold on to power by lashing out on several fronts. Some pushed for anti-immigration legislation, hoping to bar groups that they found undesirable—Hispanics, Asians, Jews—from infiltrating the body politic.[10] Some flung their racial animosities at domestic nonwhites, blacks in particular, using or condoning violence to bolster white male supremacy. Others went on a rampage against the "new woman," whose self-confident pursuit of public roles made her an easy target for conservatives declaring that being a wife and mother was a woman's foremost duty.[11] Still others found comfort in a "muscular Christianity" and enrolled in organizations such as the YMCA, which raised sports and physical exercise to the level of religion. For most, war reemerged as the supreme test of manhood.[12] The American soldiers who stormed San Juan Hill in 1898 fought an ocean apart from the British troops who cracked down on the South African Boers in 1902, but for Anglo-American commentators the Spanish-American War and the Second Boer War reflected the same longing to escape the routines of bourgeois conformism and ascend to the heights of rejuvenating heroic struggle.[13] Wealth, status, and memories of past glory, these new imperialists believed, would not suffice to ensure continued dominance. Only a new generation of "lusty youth," ready to gain maturity and masculinity through conquest, could do that.[14]

Likening the nation to a vigorous young man who needed growth meant that youth itself began to acquire more clout, both as an ideal and as a life stage. Two components stood out in modern constructions of youth—one political, the other scientific. Nineteenth-century revolutionaries and reformers cultivated a romantic imagery of youth around aspirations for national rebirth, which found expression in movements with the names of Young Italy, Young Germany, Young Poland, and Young America.[15] While these movements tied youth only loosely to age (Giuseppe Mazzini famously limited membership in the Young Italy movement to people under forty), the scientific invention of "adolescence" drew sharper distinctions. The American psychologist Granville

Stanley Hall revolutionized understandings of youth, infusing them with contemporary notions of physical education, race, civilization, empire, and manhood. In his study *Adolescence*, a monumental data-laden work published in 1904, Hall defined adolescence as an intermediate period bridging the gap between childhood and adulthood, an unstable life phase marked by extreme vitality and insecurity.[16] Where previous scholars had seen little more than a time of oscillation, Hall discovered a life stage that suspended a young person's passage into the adult world. With the scientization of adolescence, physicality and sexual maturation became defining characteristics of youth.[17]

Hall's ideas about adolescence were explicitly gendered. His famous recapitulation theory, which described the path to adulthood as a process that paralleled white society's evolution from barbarism to modernity, applied mainly to boys, not girls. Youth was preferably male, and its potentials and susceptibilities were expressed in the colonial tropes of savagery and civilization. For Hall, the work of raising white boys was akin to the work of uplifting nonwhite races. "Nearer to primitive man" than girls, boys should imitate the ways of hunters, bandits, and fighters before aspiring to gentlemanly conduct.[18] While Victorian educators frowned on rough and rowdy leisure activities, Hall found primitivism essential to a happy and healthy boyhood. Hall called for a more permissive attitude toward what he defended as the boy's natural urge to live out his savage instincts. He maintained that freewheeling play, and not formalized school curricula, built young men with strong bodies and superior morals. Taking the strenuous element out of a boy's upbringing, Hall warned, would leave him ill equipped for a world governed by Darwinist strife.[19]

Anglo-American fears that boys would grow up to be weaklings reached a crescendo during the Boer Wars and World War I. In 1904, the British government issued a report investigating signs of physical deterioration in Britain's armed forces that highlighted the bad health of many Boer War volunteers. Because 450,000 British soldiers were needed to defeat 40,000 Boers, imperialists linked the fact that roughly three out of every five British volunteers had failed to meet the requirements for military service to the debilitating effects of industrialization on childhood development. U.S. officials expressed similar concerns about the readiness of American soldiers when medical examinations of thousands of draftees in 1917 led physicians to conclude that the nation's young men were lacking in robustness.[20] Reminiscent of Hall's demand to promote physical education for boys, these worries corroborate that the fear of imperial and national decline was a powerful driving force in the formation of early youth movements.

Hall's gendered arguments resonated with white male reformers who agreed that women deserved a huge chunk of the blame for the increasing "sissification" of boys and, by extension, the emasculation of men. Raving about the physical aspects of youth and manhood sustained the belief in the fundamental dissimilarity of the sexes at a time when more women (and some men) were questioning this distinction. Male pedagogues voiced loud complaints about overprotective mothering and female teachers in public schools. Women, they fretted, had turned classrooms into sanctuaries of sentimentality, coddling and pampering boys and girls alike with their tales of spirits and sprites. If a boy was shy, one BSA manual stated, it was because he had been "brought up with his mother and sisters" and lacked "the touch of a man and a proper man's viewpoint."[21] Awakening young men's virile impulses, according to Hall, required going back to "reading the old bloody stories." Boys would like them, Hall found, for they were "healthy little savages."[22] To grow into manly citizens, boys needed to drink from the well of primitive masculinity.

Turn-of-the-century efforts to reverse the feminization of men fostered new techniques of manufacturing and restoring manhood. Men who sought to infuse public culture with a proper dose of masculinity advocated the reading of violent frontier novels, took their sons to baseball games and boxing bouts, and remasculinized church life.[23] Many were succumbing to a fraternal fever during which an estimated one out of every four adult men was flocking to one of the more than three hundred orders that existed at the time, including the Odd Fellows, the Freemasons, the Knights of Pythias, and the Red Men. Curiously, the effort to make men less feminine also made them more boyish. No longer seen as antagonistic to manhood, the boyish qualities of exuberance, playfulness, and impulsiveness acted out in these fraternal spaces shrunk the distance between boyhood and manhood and precipitated new relations between males of different generations.[24] Trying to make sons the natural allies of their fathers in order to remove the constraints placed on white middle-class manhood, men found themselves making common cause with their charges. Ideally, boys were to become the partners of men, not simply their successors. Reimagining their relationship as one between older and younger brothers, boys and men exceedingly emphasized gender over age differences. From this convergence of boyhood and manhood, it was only a small step toward arriving at the kind of boy-man-hood advanced by organizations such as the Sons of Daniel Boone, the Woodcraft Indians, and ultimately the Boy Scouts.

Nonetheless, if some started treating boys as miniature men, others still regarded them as children, worrying that they were getting too little or the wrong kind of attention. Child welfare became a cause célèbre for a coalition of male and female reformers on both sides of the Atlantic. Sociologists, psychologists, and clergymen pioneered a wave of research dealing with young people and their needs. States began passing laws to protect children from the excesses of industrial capitalism. Between 1903 and 1916, legislators in Britain, France, Germany, and the United States advanced the institutionalization of modern concepts of childhood as a sheltered space of existence.[25] They enacted a series of laws that regulated child labor, introduced school meals, launched infant care stations, and set up medical support for poor children. Humanitarianism as well as national interest guided these reformers.[26] When the Swedish feminist Ellen Key predicted that the twentieth century would become the "century of the child," she knew that it would be measured largely in terms of output—the extent to which nations would breed healthy, loyal, and productive citizens.[27] If children were left to rot in the gutter, societies would relinquish their most valuable resource. Adults of different political faiths began equating youth with an infinite spring of energy. "We may smother the divine fire of youth," Jane Addams wrote in 1909 "or we may feed it."[28]

Several institutional innovations reflected this newfound faith in the political productivity of youth. One legal novelty that came out of the United States was the juvenile court. First implemented in Illinois in 1899 and subsequently adopted by other states, the juvenile court system departed from punishing delinquent minors and locking them away, focusing instead on how to best reintegrate them into society. A new class of civil servants, probation officers, assessed whether felonious youths had achieved rehabilitation. Gender and race remained powerful categories of difference considering that boys were more often brought before the court for curfew violations or underage drinking, whereas girls were typically put into correction facilities for what was considered deviant sexual behavior. Nonwhite children experienced widespread segregation in the form of Native American boarding schools or separate educational institutions for blacks. Proclaiming youth and childhood national assets eroded parental monopoly over child rearing. As private- and state-run child welfare initiatives expanded, the surveillance of young bodies reached unprecedented levels.[29]

However, portraying youths as subjects of various interventions "from above" tells only half the story. Eager to shake off adult restraints, more and more young people began to discover a sense of themselves and their abilities *as* young people. Many of the burgeoning youth movements prior to World War I thrived on a feeling of generational difference, casting the world of their elders as materialistic and corrupt. The German Wandervogel, a coeducational middle-class youth movement that flourished in the 1910s, picked its own leaders and celebrated nature as the place where a purer, better life could be found.[30] In England, the Neo-Pagans, a group of young literati, dreamed of rustic simplicity and regeneration through poetry.[31] Youth's search for autonomous spaces free from adult interference gained momentum with the evolution of modern mass leisure and consumerism. Movie theaters, dance clubs, gambling halls, high school sports, and summer camps offered opportunities for adolescent bonding and self-expression.[32] That young people were rejecting the prolonged dependency intrinsic to modern notions of childhood by crafting their own gender and sexual identities through peer practices such as flirting and dating filled conservative educators with alarm, but it also demonstrated that youths were marching to a different drummer. Baden-Powell recognized youth's claim to sovereignty. "In the last thirty years," the British chief scout wrote in 1930, "the younger generation have emerged from the cocoon of Victorian discipline, which was applied from without, to the freer stage of regulating their own conduct by their own control from within."[33] Individually and collectively, young people were quite capable of developing their own visions of citizenship, which they defended in contentions with adults about their future.

Enter the Boy-Men

The same intergenerational forces that fastened the bonds between youth, gender, race, and empire also functioned as the midwives of scouting. Acknowledging the Boy Scouts' multiple origins helps unravel competing narratives about how and where the organization was hatched. For the British and American founders, vying for a central role in the invention of scouting was a matter of personal and national pride. The movement's global potential, its valorization of the boy-man, and a special Anglo-American relationship converged at a festive dinner at the Waldorf-Astoria Hotel in New York on September 23, 1910. Organized by the YMCA executive Edgar M. Robinson, a spokesperson of a fledgling association that bore the name Boy Scouts of America, the dinner attracted wealthy philanthropists, bankers, ministers, and educators who had pledged themselves to preparing American youth for future greatness. Between husky toasts and boisterous speeches, their attention centered on the main guests—men whose youth work epitomized the triple currents of national ambition, transnational cooperation, and imperial rivalry that brought the Boy Scouts to the United States. Close observers might have chuckled at the irony that the boy-men who were known for their dislike of rampant urbanism had traveled to its very heart, New York City, to advertise their cause. These

Figure 1.1. Robert Baden-Powell (seated), Ernest Thompson Seton (left), and Daniel Carter Beard (right) represented the boyish masculinity and youthful Anglo-Saxonism that converged in the early Boy Scout movement. (Courtesy of the Library of Congress, Prints and Photographs Division)

boy-men were Robert Baden-Powell, Ernest Thompson Seton, and Daniel Carter Beard.[34]

A decorated British cavalry officer and veteran of the Boer Wars, Baden-Powell exuded military flair and pluck. His name adorned the cover of the first official Boy Scout handbook, *Scouting for Boys*, which first appeared in London in 1908 and, until World War II, was the second best-selling book in the Anglophone world after the Bible.[35] By the time Baden-Powell arrived in New York, about one hundred thousand young Britons were already wearing the khaki-colored uniform of his movement. A popular media figure and charismatic self-promoter, Baden-Powell accepted the invitation to cross the Atlantic. Both sides reaped profits from what would flower into a lasting relationship. For the young BSA, the British scout leader's presence was a blessing. His endorsement helped elevate the young venture over rival organizations such as the American Boy Scouts, which was run by the jingoist publisher William Randolph Hearst. The BSA's overtures cemented Baden-Powell's reputation as the father of worldwide scouting, although his handbook was no work of originality. Rather, as Baden-Powell conceded in front of his American hosts, he had "cribbed a good deal from . . . books dealing with similar experiments."[36] The frontier stories of the globe-trotting American war scout Frederick Russell Burnham and William "Buffalo Bill" Cody's Wild West shows had left an indelible impression on Baden-Powell.[37] Anecdotes from the British imperial canon ranging from the Pocahontas myth to Rudyard Kipling's *Kim* added to the hodgepodge character of Baden-Powell's writing.[38] Moreover, the Englishman gleaned important insights from non-European warrior traditions, most notably from the Japanese Bushido code.[39]

As Anglo-American commentators were highlighting Baden-Powell's military prowess, they also ascribed to him a boyish charm that, as they believed, made him supremely qualified to be a leader of boys. He embodied the "eternal boy-man," one of his biographers wrote, always "joining in the Scout games and the Scout chorus, blowing the kudu horn," and bonding with young males instead of lecturing them. "Some men never grow up, so far as youthful thoughts and actions go, and if there ever was a boy who absolutely refused to do so, it is . . . Baden-Powell," remarked an American admirer, to whom the Englishman appeared "just as much in sympathy with boys and their ways, as he was when he was fifteen."[40] For many, Baden-Powell seemed almost immune to aging. His playful approach to questions of civic duty and religious morality put him refreshingly at odds with Victorian norms of education. As Baden-Powell insisted, "The Scoutmaster . . . must have the boy spirit in him." He "has got to put himself on the level of the older brother" and "must be able to place himself on a right plane with his boys."[41] If the Boy Scouts were to make men, they should be like their founder wanted them to be: spirited, buoyant, and full of unbridled curiosity—men who valued restless action more than academic rigor and staid decorum. Intertwining the masculine dream of regeneration with the promise of liberating play, Baden-Powell epitomized a growing disdain for older, more formalist models of masculine maturation. His boy-men would never lose touch with the unadulterated source of manhood, which they located in boys. They would go about remaking themselves and others in a spirit of "youthful" and "boyish" fun.[42]

Sitting next to Baden-Powell at the dinner at the Waldorf-Astoria was Ernest Thompson Seton, one of the authors whom the English officer had consulted while founding the Boy Scouts. Seton's life straddled the worlds of boy work in the United States and the British Empire. Seton's Scottish parents had moved to Toronto in 1866 when Ernest was six years old. In Canada and later in the United States, Seton took up the study of nature and animal life. A prolific artist and writer of children's fiction, Seton worried that city life was making young people decadent and immoral. His aspirations to imbue in youth a desire to return to the pastoral life of their ancestors and disavow "money grubbing, machine politics, degrading sports, cigarettes, [and] town life of the worst kind" inspired him to start the Woodcraft Indians in 1901.[43] Seton's hero was the Native American, a romanticized Indian who pointed the way to how humans could exist in harmony with nature. The boys who joined the Wood-craft Indians were to imitate Native Americans "in the fields of art, handicraft, woodcraft, agriculture, social life, health, and joy."[44] Seton presented Native Americans as primitive versions of his white self, not as people entitled to their own culture. Nature-study games, campfire lore, and Indian costumes, Seton claimed, built sturdy outdoor characters and held out the promise of a purified modernity.[45]

When Seton rose to address Baden-Powell at the Waldorf-Astoria, he had to swallow his pride. Three years earlier, while lecturing in England, Seton had met Baden-Powell and handed him a copy of his manual, *The Birch-Bark Roll of the Woodcraft Indians*. Admiration turned into annoyance after Seton accused Baden-Powell of lifting passages from his book and selling them as his own. Despite his irritation, Seton remained calm, knowing that he had more to gain than to lose from Baden-Powell's support. Seton's Woodcraft program had already begun to rouse suspicions among white nationalists, who wanted no connections to Native Americans, symbolic or real. Seton also lacked the money that the Carnegies and Rockefellers were pouring into scouting. Cognizant of his disadvantage, Seton joined the BSA and fought for his ideals from within. He was given the honorary title of "Chief Scout" and put in charge of drafting the first BSA handbook. Yet Seton remained a thorn in the side of his critics because of his opposition to a narrow patriotism and his idealization of Indianness, and because he was a British citizen at the head of an American organization.[46]

Seton's nemesis, Daniel Carter Beard, sat only a few chairs away. Like Seton, the U.S.-born Beard held that "over-refined civilization" turned boys into "mollycoddles" instead of young men.[47] Unlike the Canadian-American naturalist, Beard proposed remedies that were unabashedly nationalist. Although Beard felt that boys needed to reenact the frontier heroism of earlier decades to mature into strong and healthy citizens, his role model was the white pioneer. Beard had earned a place at the table as the founder of the Sons of Daniel Boone, a youth program that began in 1905 and emphasized outdoor proficiency and Wild West romance. Clad in the buckskin costume of the frontiersman, boys congregated in "forts" and received "notches" and "top notches" for achievements in camping, fire making, shooting, tomahawk throwing, knot tying, and tracking.[48] Beard made no secret of his distrust of reformers who wanted to import ideas into American boy work that he considered feminine or foreign. For the illustrator and writer from Ohio, true patriotism resided in the men who had conquered the West. Rather than playing old-world knights and monarchs, American boys should be animated to games that emulated "the old-fashioned virtues of American Knights in Buckskins."[49] Long after Baden-Powell had established himself as the global paragon of the Boy Scouts, Beard questioned the British credentials of the movement. Despite his belief in a shared Anglo-Saxon destiny, he maintained that the figure of the Scout "was essentially American, and not English." He considered reverence for nature and mastery of the wilderness expressions of an American national identity.[50] Seton's portrayal of Native Americans as role models struck Beard as naive and dangerous. Beard's Indians were not flora-and-fauna worshippers but barbarians whom history had selected for extinction. Seton's misrepresentations, Beard protested, betrayed his lack of immersion in U.S. culture and proved that it was irresponsible to put the stewardship of American boys in the hands of foreigners.[51]

What defused tensions between Beard and Seton was a shared admiration for boyish traits that had long been ridiculed as unmanly. Both youth leaders represented a class of men who, like their British companion, sought to reform white manhood not through intellectual refinement but by traveling back to the imagined days of boyhood, recapturing budding manhood at a developmental stage when it seemed pure and pliable. This nostalgic drift found expression in the frontier mythology Beard and Seton created, where imperial violence gave way to exhilarating play. Enthusiasm for camping and a chirpy survivalism are tied together in Seton's autobiographical novel *Two Little Savages* (1902), which tells the story of two poor white boys escaping the drab world of their fathers and becoming self-reliant through woodcraft.[52] Beard, too, embraced the curative potential of boyhood in the hope of restoring men who had degenerated into selfish and sarcastic beings without joy and imagination. Dreaming of men "who still retained some of the urge of boyhood," Beard sought to rid the world of "gray-headed philosophers" and "money-getting baldheads." His plan was to establish a brotherly pact between men and boys who "might get together" in the pristine outdoors "and make known their wants and ambitions."[53] For Beard and Seton, the Boy Scouts offered the ideal framework for this kind of familial relationship between young and old males. Turning boy-man-hood into a socially acceptable form of masculinity, Beard and Seton gave throngs of men who became scoutmasters reason to believe that there was nothing wrong with being "a boy with the boys."[54]

The uneasy alliance forged by Baden-Powell, Seton, Beard, and their sponsors at the Waldorf-Astoria in September 1910 demonstrates the hybrid forces that were at work when the BSA was in its infancy. Personal antagonisms and conflicting outlooks fired debates over how national, or how global, scouting should become. Regardless of their different blueprints for reform, pre–World War I boy workers grappled with the same problem: how to train boys and retrain men outside the feminized spheres of home, church, and school to avert masculine decline. The rejuvenation of manhood was an obsession that transcended national boundaries, even as many of scouting's supporters invested in it for narrower ends. Nowhere did the domestic voices striving for leadership in the new organization, as well as the echoes from abroad, merge more creatively than in the BSA's founding statements over what constituted the ideal American boy.

Building the American Boy

Chicago's Italian district on the Near West Side, a neighborhood teeming with new arrivals from overseas, had a reputation for being a Progressive Era laboratory for social improvement. The two youngsters who approached two Italian lads in a murky alley in the district, though, had little in common with the likes of Jane Addams or John Dewey. They were Boy Scouts whose body language spoke of a different kind of reform. In their khaki-green Scout uniforms—consisting of army-like knickers, jackets, and belts—they stood upright, speaking confidently to the young Italians over whom they towered. The immigrant boys, whom the Boy Scouts had come to recruit, by contrast, posed as archetypal slackers—little street roughs who, as they listened to the Scouts, leaned against the wall half-defiantly, conveying the image of youths who without proper guidance were bound to go astray.[55]

Rather than visualize a spontaneous encounter, this photograph from February 1915 was part of the BSA's early propaganda campaign that urged middle-class Americans to welcome scouting into their communities. Using various local and national media, Boy Scout officials made enticing claims about the possibilities for wholesome leisure that awaited men and boys who enrolled in the organization.[56] In a flurry of promotional material—handbooks, novels, pamphlets, posters, and films—the body emerged as the principal tool for building public trust and disseminating the organization's ideas regarding youth, gender, robust Americanization, and masculine citizenship. The goal was to establish the Boy Scouts as the one true organization capable of raising able-bodied men and citizens willing to serve the nation. The formula to achieve that goal was plain and simple: good social engineering starts with biological engineering.[57]

No radical eugenicists by early twentieth-century standards, the BSA's architects nonetheless held that biology and character were inextricably linked. The human body functioned as a gendered metaphor for national bodies, and vice versa. Clean, healthy, and upright male bodies reflected discipline, decency, and productivity. Constructing an ideal of masculine citizenship that was both moral and muscular, BSA leaders introduced an Americanized version of Baden-Powell's Scout oath in 1910. In addition to republicanizing the British pledge based on service to "God and the King," the American oath made young Scouts promise that they would keep themselves "physically strong, mentally awake, and morally straight."[58] The first BSA handbook, published one year later, placed special emphasis on personal hygiene, proper eating, and outdoor exercise. The *Handbook for Boys* played an important part in executive director James E. West's plan to carry through "the absolute adaption" of scouting "to American conditions."[59] Containing chapters on woodcraft, camping, merit badges, first aid, and patriotism, the manual also consisted of several sections written by experts from different U.S. youth agencies that spelled out the relationship between physical fitness, character, and good citizenship.

West's man for the handbook chapter "Health and Endurance" was George J. Fisher, the YMCA international secretary for physical education. Fisher, a medical doctor and advocate of team sports, infused into the Boy Scouts a careful dose of muscular Christianity. According to Fisher, the chief business of a boy was to grow. He advised a strict regimen to ensure that the young body gained "endurance, physical power, physical courage, and skill."[60] The handbook recommended that boys exercise outdoors for at least two hours per day to offset the physical disadvantages that resulted from lingering at home or sitting still at school. Scouts should exert themselves in cross-country running and hiking but also play games such as baseball and tennis. They should attend summer camp to breathe fresh air. Daily gymnastics would "cure round shoulders" and teach boys to walk with an erect carriage. Boys interested in taking up scouting were advised to undergo "thorough medical examination." They should aspire to be athletic but not imitate musclemen like Eugene Sandow, who had popularized bodybuilding in the 1890s.[61] Overzealousness in sports would harm, rather than boost, healthy growth. "Severe training," wrote Fisher, "should be avoided. All training should be in moderation."[62]

In its attempt to have boys develop vigorous bodies, the BSA preached a mixture of ambition and self-restraint in sports as well as discipline in personal hygiene. A good Scout, Fisher sermonized, should take two soap baths every week (especially after phases of strenuous recreation); eat regularly, preferring simple diets (eating meat not more than once daily); brush his teeth twice a day; have his vision checked; take care of his ears, feet, nose, throat, and fingernails; and get at least nine or ten hours of sleep each night. Boyhood hygiene, as envisioned by the BSA, blended the corporeal with the moral. The handbook prescribed abstinence from alcohol and smoking, even coffee and tea. Scout propagandists declared cleanliness a touchstone of character, the movement's keyword for acceptable masculine behavior. One of the three laws that the BSA added to the British codex (the other two addressed bravery and faith) called on Boy Scouts to keep "clean in body and thought," stand for "clean speech, clean sport, clean habits," and associate "with a clean crowd."[63] Another ardent promoter of Boy Scouting, Theodore Roosevelt, wanted boys to be rough and hard in play but also "clean-minded and clean-lived" in order to "grow into the kind of man" that would make Americans proud.[64] "To be strong," Fisher exhorted the young reader, "one must be pure in thought and clean in habit."[65]

When BSA leaders talked about cleanliness, sexuality was always part of the equation. Many had been taught to abhor the Victorian specters of the pale and trembling masturbator and the insatiable prostitute spreading disease and weakening the body politic. Middle-class moralists waged a war on masturbation, viewing it as a stepping-stone to neurasthenia. For turn-of-the-century elites, neurasthenia, or the "lack of nerve force," was the psychological symptom of a broader cultural malaise in industrialized societies that had turned women into giddy creatures and men into fearful procrastinators.[66] Protestant minister William Byron Forbush, author of the influential *The Boy Problem* (1902), spoke for educators of similar persuasion when he identified "sex-perversions" as the "most common, subtle and dangerous foes that threaten our American life." His suggestion that obscene conversation, "self-abuse," and premature "fornication" among adolescents were best remedied through supervised physical exercise resonated with the vanguards of scouting, an initiative Forbush endorsed wholeheartedly.[67] Sexuality was likened to a raw energy that, if released too early, would sap a boy's vitality. U.S. scouters agreed with Baden-Powell that masturbation "brings with it weakness of head and heart, and, if persisted in, idiocy and lunacy." Boy Scouts should not succumb to low instincts but were expected to conserve their youthful verve for the noble causes that awaited them as adults.

Intertwining personal purity with social morality and racial fitness, the BSA pathologized the combination of youth and sex. Such a diagnosis may seem delusional today, yet masturbation panic, homophobia, and other sexual anxieties mirrored Progressive Era fears of emasculation so clearly that they simply cannot be ignored. As historian Kevin Murphy explained, modern notions of heteronormative sexuality evolved in lockstep with images that portrayed male impotence and homosexuality as a menace to the nation.[68] Defining Boy Scout manliness against the supposed depravity of homosexuals, YMCA educator H. W. Gibson called on scoutmasters to "beware of effeminate men" in their midst, "men who are morbid in sex matters." Vigilant leaders, Gibson went on, "could spot a 'crooked man' by his actions, his glances, and by his choice of favorites."[69] Boston Boy Scout Commissioner Ormond Loomis thought it possible to teach discipline and suppress "the sex impulse" by holding "before the boy an intensely positive ideal of social activity." Scouting's promise of joyful outdoor recreation should accomplish what years of threats and sanctions had failed to do: rescue boys from the clutches of "professional amusement makers" and immoral urbanites.[70] By reimagining adolescence as a restless but ideally asexual life stage, Loomis and his coworkers accused those who licensed underage sex of undermining the foundations of manhood. This social conservatism became an ideological staple of the BSA, furthering the problematic conflation of homosexuality and pedophilia that endured throughout the twentieth century.

Striving to synthesize immaculate boyhood and vigorous manhood, the BSA marketed its masculine ideals as substantially different from other masculinities up for grabs in early twentieth-century America: the ideal of the well-mannered but effete Victorian gentleman, the excessive muscular masculinity embodied by the celebrity bodybuilder Eugene Sandow, the working-class manhood of poor laborers and immigrants, the urban hedonism represented by the young playboy, and the homosexual countercultures in the nation's metropolitan centers.[71] In multiethnic societies, white manhood has traditionally been shaped in opposition to the nonwhite other. Cleanliness, apparently a metaphor for purity and morality, was invoked to set the white male body apart from the dirt and darkness of the uncivilized, even as white men were supposed to demonstrate their superior strength by subjugating inferior races. The Boy Scouts grew out of this logic, yet they also offered the means by which boys and men might be "clean" and "strong," experiencing male power while proclaiming the purity of their intentions.

Contradictions loomed. How would a youth agency that glorified the healthy body respond to the wishes of children hampered by disabilities: the thousands of blind, deaf, or crippled boys in early twentieth-century America who wanted to be Scouts too? Although troops of handicapped Boy Scouts had existed in the shadows since the 1910s, James West, whose personal history of fighting disability made him sympathize with physically impaired children, had to contend with other leaders who were reluctant to grant disabled youths a place in the movement.[72] Also, the rhetoric of cleanliness hardly squared with the exaltation of the rugged outdoors, just as some might have found it inconsistent that the organization worshipped some aspects of primitivism while demonizing premarital sex. To win over actual youth, the BSA had to become synonymous with fun, excitement, and dynamism—in short, with a positive idea of youth. The organization had to position itself as youth's public voice and national symbol.

Official steps in that direction were taken immediately. Under West's management, the organization embarked on a path to self-Americanization. Instead of relying on volunteers, which was the preferred policy of most European Scout organizations, the BSA employed paid staffers and built corporate structures. BSA officials purged the Scout oath and laws from any reference to monarchism or class distinctions. They invented new badges, insignia, and the Eagle Scout, the highest rank attainable in American Boy Scouting. Nationally distinct uniforms for boys and scoutmasters were designed. The American bald eagle was stitched onto the fleur de lis, the international logo of scouting. In 1910, President William Howard Taft agreed to be the first honorary president of the BSA, starting a tradition of chief executives serving in that role that is still in place today. *Boys' Life*, the BSA's monthly youth magazine, began publication in March 1911. In August 1916, the BSA received a congressional charter, an honorary status that brought the Boy Scouts into proximity to the federal government. Meanwhile, white-collar men who were socializing in newly established fraternal clubs—the Rotarians were founded in 1905, the Kiwanis in 1914, the Lions in 1917—pumped money into the Boy Scouts and volunteered as scoutmasters, linking middle-class sociability and modern corporate culture to national service.[73]

Not everybody, though, applauded the BSA's alliance with the state. The most prominent casualty of the organization's Americanism, which intensified in the patriotic climate of World War I, was Ernest Thompson Seton. Seton resigned in November 1915, much to the satisfaction of his longtime rival Daniel Carter Beard, who vilified the British-born Indian lore expert as an un-American royalist. Saddened that the "the study of trees, flowers, and nature" had given way to "wigwagging, drills, and other activities of a military nature," Seton left the organization.[74]

The symbolic victory of Beard's patriotic pioneers over Seton's bucolic Indians offers a clue to the type of Americanness that the BSA sought to nurture in boys. Demographically, the bulk of the new recruits came from native-born white urban or suburban middle-class households.[75] These were the same adolescents who could afford the uniform and easily identify with the fictional characters in Scout literature bored by city life and yearning for adventure and companionship away from their normal routines. Parents, too, seemed to accept that their sons would profit from entering the world of adult-monitored outdoor leisure. But what about the sons of the other, nonwhite or nonnative Americans who lacked the cultural literacy to develop the same kind of emotional attachment to the frontier myth? Could and should black boys, Native American boys, or immigrant boys be Scouts too?

The BSA's founders were split on that question. Representing a national institution, they reflected the country's regional and social divisions on issues of race, ethnicity, and assimilation. White supremacists could draw comfort from the 1913 *Handbook for Scout Masters*, which held that a boy's capacities were determined by "race heredity and local environment."[76] At the same time, BSA leaders exhibited a strong interest in nonwhite masculinities, believing that the naturalism and primitivism of the supposedly uncivilized races could be harnessed to shield young white men from the feminizing effects of modern civilization. If Boy Scout organizers concurred with Stanley Hall that the boy in many ways "resemble[d] the savage" and needed to be treated as such before he moved up the evolutionary ladder, then how could they continue to despise supposedly inferior population groups for alleged barbaric traits that they now saw in their own sons?[77]

Static concepts of ethnic or racial difference were difficult to uphold in an organization that promoted its youth program as bridging the chasms of culture and class. The picture of two Chicago Boy Scouts trying to persuade two Italian American street kids to follow their example testifies that the BSA was willing to admit ethnic newcomers into its brotherhood, even though that image conveyed the hegemony of Anglo-Saxon culture. Native-born white boys showed immigrants what to do, not the other way around. West, for his part, detected in Americanization a unique opportunity to win public approval. If ethnic pluralism was a reality, preventing the disuniting of America would become a major task. Advertising his youth agency as "the great melting pot of boyhood," West publicized numerous cases of how scouting was incorporating foreigners into the national body. In the early 1920s, the BSA cooperated with the Bureau of Naturalization, encouraged new arrivals from overseas to enroll in English and civics classes, and formed honor guards when new citizens were taking the oath of allegiance.[78] Immigrant Scouts played a key role in the BSA's assimilation schemes. BSA authorities hoped they would kindle the flames of patriotism in their parents. They relished stories such as the one of Antonio Balducci, who rose to the rank of Eagle and worked as an ambassador of scouting among Italian-speaking boys on both sides of the Atlantic, despite that his left leg had been amputated when he was four.[79] Another young immigrant who had picked up scouting in Denmark so impressed West that he made him his close confidant. Born Vilhelm H. B. Jensen, he became popular with Scouts worldwide under his Americanized name, William Hillcourt, or his pseudonym "Green Bar Bill," the gifted spinner of campfire yarn.[80]

Local developments did not always match the idealized image of American boys united in productive play across the divides of religion, ethnicity, and race. Racist prejudice, as will be discussed in chapter 4, prevented the equal treatment of Native American and African American youth. West counteracted his open-door rhetoric toward immigrants by giving nativists like Jeremiah Jenks and Henry Pratt Fairchild positions of influence in the BSA national office.[81] Nativism and militant Protestantism reared their ugly heads in statements made by representatives on the local level. Long Island scoutmaster I. S. Southworth found the Catholic Polish and Italian boys in his troop wanting in discipline and physical fortitude. "I cannot run that troop on the patrol system," he complained.[82] Scout official Klaas Oosterhous from Chicago had similar reservations. He considered the regular Scout program "too hard and comprehensive for our Italian boys."[83] Opposition against the BSA's assimilation policies also brewed on the far right. In 1923, the national headquarters had to fend off charges from a resurgent Ku Klux Klan (KKK), which saw its unapologetic Anglo-Saxonist brand of Americanism sullied by the BSA's hospitable attitude toward "Roman Catholics, and Jews."[84]

In ways that were very different, immigrant boys had to deal with occasional resistance from their elders. Ethnic leaders were not amused that the BSA decided in the early 1920s to publish the handbook in English only.[85] The Polish National Council was so maddened by this assertion of Anglo-conformity that it nullified an agreement to merge its youth organization with the BSA.[86] Intergenerational disputes over scouting between immigrant children and their parents were common at the family table. One Sicilian father, seeing in Scout knives a bitter memento of gang warfare back in Italy, forbade his sons to become Boy Scouts.[87] Edward Lee, who grew up during the 1910s in San Francisco's Chinatown, recalled how his mother had wanted to rip up his Boy Scout uniform, which she had associated with violence and cultural intolerance.[88] Despite such barriers, ethnic youngsters continued to spend their free time playing Scout games. Some did so for recreational reasons, others because they viewed it as a shortcut to becoming Americans.

Even though race, whiteness, and religion framed the BSA's view of what constituted proper American boyhood, the organization also foregrounded the improvability of young male bodies and recast youth as a homogenizing social force in a pluralistic society. Boys might graduate from this self-styled "school of democracy" with different grades, but that did not justify turning the open-air classrooms of scouting into racially and religiously exclusive clubs.[89] BSA leaders advocated Anglo-conformity while urging Americans to rethink the boundaries of citizenship. For them, building young bodies and nation building were two sides of the same coin. Both a demographic challenge and an allegory for growth, boyhood came into view as a resource whose use or abuse would decide America's future. Time would tell whether the abilities of individual boys depended on hereditary or social factors.

The Girl Problem

When in doubt, ask "Uncle Dan." In 1922, *Boys' Life* launched a monthly section that invited boys to write to Daniel Carter Beard and seek his advice on issues related to scouting. Most of the questions addressed to Beard, whose public appearances in buckskin clothing had made him a sort of mascot of the BSA, had to do with technicalities such as the fastest way to pitch camp, how to get in touch with fellow Scouts, or how and when to salute the Stars and Stripes. But one inquiry that landed on Beard's desk in March 1933 from scout Joseph Maguire made the national scout commissioner cringe. Young Joe wanted to get Uncle Dan's approval for holding a party in his troop cabin at which both boys and girls could mingle. The response was unambiguous. "Scouting is a he-man's game, a stag affair in which girls do not participate," Beard chided the youngster. "You may meet the girls at school affairs, church entertainments, and social parties . . . for these are not Scout functions. Don't *mix 'em up!*"[90]

Fears of promiscuous gender mixing were by no means Beard's predicament alone. Though painting American youth as classless, transethnic, and nondenominational, the BSA's founders were adamant about the strict separation of the sexes. Scouting was to be a program run by men for boys, a brotherhood that cut across political, geographical, and generational lines. With its preference for male exclusivity, the BSA was in good company. Fraternal organizations mushroomed in the decades before World War I.[91] Offering sanctuaries from the dislocations of industrialization, these associations were also surging precisely at the time when women were stepping more forcefully out of the home and into the public sphere. Other than the women's suffrage movement, perhaps the most visible manifestation of this new female activism was the Woman's Christian Temperance Union (WCTU). Organized in chapters throughout the United States and much of the English-speaking world, its Protestant members battled alcoholism, combated prostitution, assailed sexual violence, sent missionaries abroad, and called for a flawless Christian lifestyle. The WCTU's claim to moral citizenship raised eyebrows among its male contemporaries, especially since the organization's crusade was about ridding the world of "male vice."[92] Should there not be a more prominent role for women in battling social issues if men had proved inept at solving them? What would men lose if they gave in to such demands? As men were pondering such questions with growing anxiety, women marched on, in the shoes of either the college-educated "new woman," the outspoken social reformer, or the self-sufficient working girl.[93]

Female education vibrated with fresh ideas, and woman pedagogues tried to convince their male counterparts that the future of the girl was essential to national development. YMCA superintendent Luther Gulick agreed. Together with his wife Charlotte, Gulick founded the Camp Fire Girls in 1910, which started in Vermont and fused scouting's emphasis on outdoor exercise with feminized traditions of nature study, horticulture, and child rearing. Boy Scout officials acquiesced in Camp Fire's pseudo-Indian philosophy because the movement's Native American acronym Wo-He-Lo, short for "Work, Health and Love," breathed the spirit of domesticity. Girls would make up their own Indian names, run around in ceremonial dresses and ritualistic beads, and playfully learn how to cook and care for their younger sisters. If boys needed a break from the hustle and bustle of modern life to live out their savage instincts, camping in pristine nature, the Gulicks insisted, might also reconnect girls to a purer maternalism uncontaminated by modern vice.[94]

It would take the BSA much longer to form genial bonds with another girl organization that strove to make the Camp Fire Girls irrelevant. The Girl Scouts of America (GSA) were a thorn in the side of Progressive Era boy workers— they did not share Camp Fire's skepticism that girls could not do what boys could. Like their male relatives, the Girl Scouts were the product of transatlantic exchange. Soon after the Boy Scouts had made headlines on both continents, girls developed an interest in the movement as well. And they made their voices heard. During a Boy Scout rally at London's Crystal Palace in September 1909, Baden-Powell was reportedly flabbergasted when he spotted a number of girls dressed in Scout uniform. The notion that troops might consist of children of both sexes was incomprehensible to him. The gender chaos such scenes portended facilitated the rise of a parallel all-female Scout organization, the British Girl Guides, which was formed in 1910 by Baden-Powell's sister Agnes and later headed by his wife Olave.[95]

Such kinship ties did not exist when Juliette Gordon Low returned from England in 1912 and began implementing a similar concept for American girls. What made her adaptation of the Girl Guides so polarizing was the name that she chose for the organization she started three years later: "Girl Scouts." To BSA leaders, this meant more than just a breach of the conventions of female respectability. In appropriating the term "Scout" and claiming khaki as the color for her girls, Low was treading on male territory, figuratively as well as practically. The Girl Scout ideal of womanhood moved beyond the gendered spaces circumscribed by the middle-class ideology of separate spheres. Rather than abiding by the Victorian model of the good mother and housewife who was supposed to turn the home into a haven of tranquility for her enterprising husband, Low's Girl Scouts gave members a far more comprehensive training. Girls wore uniforms, took civics lessons, kept themselves fit, and were to learn, as stated in one of the early GSA handbooks, "in the happiest way how to combine patriotism, outdoor activities of every kind, skill in every branch of domestic science and high standards of community service."[96] The GSA's cultivation of a female brand of patriotism bore fruit during World War I when Girl Scouts, not unlike their boy counterparts, volunteered in hospitals, grew Victory gardens, sold war bonds to strengthen the home front, and began their now-famous tradition of selling cookies. Considering the significant growth that the GSA experienced from 1917 to 1920, it is safe to conclude that the organization's association of young womanhood with national service worked in its favor.[97]

The BSA reacted instantly to what it perceived to be an assault on the ancient bond of manhood and citizenship. Positive reports about the Girl Scouts in the national press made the BSA fear that the public would start questioning the movement's masculine brand, and thus the rationale for strict gender segregation. West issued several thinly veiled threats until the late 1920s that he would litigate Girl Scout leaders if they refused to accept for their organization the British appellation "Guide" or merge it with the Camp Fire Girls.[98] Out of deference to first lady Lou Henry Hoover, who was a strong GSA advocate, the BSA chief executive toned down the rhetoric. Still, West agreed in sentiment with Camp Fire founder Luther Gulick, who told his allies, "We hate manly women, and womanly men."[99] In 1918 the BSA Executive Board published a policy guideline on how members were to treat the Girl Scouts.

The pamphlet was cordial in tone but unapologetic in insisting that the GSA was merely aping a program designed for boys. It specifically opposed the idea that Boy and Girl Scouts would go on joint hikes because of "the extreme difficulties of supervision, the accentuation in the minds of boys of sex questions . . . and the great possibility for embarrassment."[100] Iowa scoutmaster E. G. Stowell vented a similar sentiment in March 1925, reporting that many of his boys felt that the growth of girl organizations would "effeminize the Boy Scout movement."[101] Some BSA leaders seemed in constant worry that masculinizing girls would have a feminizing effect on boys. Others warned that overlaps between the two organizations would increase the risk of premature sexual encounters with potentially devastating consequences for the boys' development. The situation on the ground, however, was far less dramatic. Boy and Girl Scout troops often consisted of children who knew each other from church or school and sometimes belonged to the same family. Partly for this reason, the BSA's campaign against the Girl Scouts gradually wound down until it became a nonfactor in the 1930s.

But even as the Wests and Beards of the movement grudgingly acknowledged that modern coeducational trends could not be wished away, they worked hard to keep their agency a female-free zone. Women were excluded from any position of authority—the only role made available to them after the establishment of Cub Scouting for younger boys in the 1930s was that of den mother. BSA leaders emphasized the "fundamental differences" that set women apart from men.[102] Scout officials portrayed women as the weaker sex, not only in terms of physical strength but also with regard to willpower. It almost appeared as if the BSA tried to turn the tables on female reformers with allegations that women, not men, were sexually loose and morally corrupted, and that regenerative young manhood was the antidote to mounting social vice.

Rather than dealing with actual women, BSA ideologues preferred introducing boys to fictional ones. The ladies that populated Boy Scout literature were more dolls than human beings, desexualized damsels in distress whose only purpose was to serve as training objects for male gallantry. The Fifth Scout Law, "A Scout is courteous," instructed Scouts to be polite to "women, children, old people, and the weak and helpless."[103] Chivalrous behavior, as defined by the 1911 *Handbook for Boys*, meant assisting the supposedly frail and fragile sex at all times. Protecting women from jostling crowds, helping old ladies cross the street, and offering one's seat in a streetcar to girls, women, or the elderly constituted worthy examples of the daily good turn.[104] Scoutmasters were told to inculcate in boys a desire to prove their manhood by teaching them to display the same "devotion and esteem for women" that had been expected of medieval knights.[105] Adult organizers generated rituals to impose traditional gender roles on the rising generation. As early as 1911, the BSA created the National Court of Honor to review cases in which Boy Scouts were said to have risked their lives to save others. Rescuing a drowning girl or pulling a baby out of a burning house was an act of bravery that earned young lifesavers the gold honor medal, the highest award in American Boy Scouting.[106] Not a few boys lost their lives in this type of medal hunt, a pursuit that perpetuated the view that girls and women were inherently vulnerable and dependent on male protection.

It is difficult to assess the extent to which the misogynism of the BSA leadership trickled down into the consciousness of rank-and-file Scouts, but anecdotal evidence suggests that the boys' interactions with girls were far less prudish than the ones depicted in official Scout publications. Heterosexual leisure became the new normal for early twentieth-century teenagers, and Boy Scouts did not grow up isolated from other mixed-sex youth activities occurring around them in camps, clubs, and movie theaters.[107] When Iowa boy scout Duane Paul wanted to make two girls "honor members" of his patrol because he had a crush on the girls, the boys were definitely not out of touch with mainstream youth culture.[108] Infatuation with girls was one of the main reasons why older Scouts dropped out, as one BSA report from the early 1930s lamented.[109] However, peer behavior in an all-male environment could also reinforce gender stereotypes and sexist conduct. Killing time on their trip across the Atlantic, Albert Snoke entertained the jamboree troop by talking one of the Scouts on board, Bill Weber, into cross-dressing as a girl. Weber's exaggerated performance "created quite an uproar," and "the fellows just howled," no doubt in a manner that bolstered their claims to manhood.[110]

Naturalizing gender differences was one of the most effective strategies that men developed in response to women advancing into male-dominated spheres. Yet few youth organizations clung more fervently to the ideal of homosociality than the Boy Scouts of America, even by international standards. It almost seemed as if boys and men were regarded as an endangered species in need of protection. The more the BSA found its cocoon of hegemonic masculinity breached and exposed as a convenient illusion by a society that offered attractive alternatives to young people, the harder it pushed back, demonstrating how fragile constructions of masculinity could be. As domestic gender troubles made proving manhood increasingly difficult, the global arena came into view as one of the last sanctuaries of male authority, one that was well suited to creating American men for an American century. Perhaps in the wide, open spaces of empire there was a place where the chaos of modernity could be recoded, where a younger and purer manhood, unburdened by the frictions of race, class, religion, and gender at home, beckoned.

A New Birth of Empire

In 1912, Robert Baden-Powell toured the globe. His trip, which took the self-anointed father of the Boy Scouts to colonial Africa, the Americas, and East Asia, was an exercise in imperial self-affirmation. At every stop, Baden-Powell shook hands with boys wearing the Scout uniform, which gave literal flesh to his vision of revitalizing panimperial white manhood. While Baden-Powell was asserting a distinctively British role in the rejuvenation of empire, he acknowledged that the Americans had begun to do their part as well. Baden-Powell made this point when he was visiting the Philippines, which had become a de facto colony of the United States after the Spanish-American War of 1898. His travelogue does not mention that the Filipinos had been sucked into America's imperial orbit with the same force and intimidation with which the British had squashed the South African Boers in a protracted guerilla war. Instead, Baden-Powell's gaze was fixed on a "more important product," the first local Boy Scout troops. With relish, he recounted the story of "two patrols of the Manila Scouts" who had displayed exceptional bravery during a recent firestorm, "helping frightened natives into places of safety" and performing "cheerfully and efficiently all the tasks given to them by the firemen and Scoutmaster."[111]

The BSA's extraterritorial presence in places like Manila underscored a fundamental geopolitical reality: the United States had joined other world powers in the race for global influence. Few contemporary Americans, however, would have accepted this reality without some pangs. "Empire" did not glide easily over their lips. If they used that term in relation to their nation at all, they would emphasize differences from, rather than commonalities with, European antecedents. Just as the nineteenth-century proponents of manifest destiny forged the myth of settlers destined by divine will and republican virtue to take control of an entire continent, their Progressive Era descendants maintained that they were exporting liberty and morality, not oppression. This rhetorical trickery mirrored a postrevolutionary mentality that made white Americans believe that their forebears' struggle for independence had immunized them against colonialism. A postcolonial nation, they thought, would not repeat the imperial follies of its former masters. Reflecting on republicanism and its world-historic significance, Americans boasted that their country was superior, even exceptional. Still, after victory in the Spanish-American War of 1898 and the annexation of Puerto Rico, Guam, Hawaii, and the Philippines, the question came back with a vengeance: Was there an American way of empire? If yes, what made it unique?

U.S. imperialists at the turn of the century did not deny their international ambitions, but they routinely couched hard imperial power in the language of Anglo-Saxon civilization. The globe-trotting evangelical missionaries portrayed by Ian Tyrrell imagined a benign Christian empire in which American and British Protestant reformers extended their networks of salvation to every corner of the planet.[112] However, religion seemed only partially appropriate to a national vision of empire that sought to distance itself from European models. It was youth that proponents of a robust American role in world affairs evoked with particular fanfare. National politicians gloried in allegories that depicted the United States as a potent young man longing to break out of the spheres of domesticity and domestic politics. Always adamant in his advocacy of a belligerent masculinity, Theodore Roosevelt asked, "Is America a weakling, to shrink from the world-work of the great world powers?" His answer, of course, was "No. The young giant of the West stands on a continent and clasps the crest of an ocean in either hand. Our nation, glorious in youth and strength, looks into the future with eager and fearless eyes and rejoices, as a strong man to run the race."[113] Republican senator Albert Beveridge joined in the cultural valorization of youth. Juxtaposing American youthfulness with the old age and fatigue of other nations, Beveridge basked in the image of the United States as a young giant bursting with power, energy, and optimism. "No other people have our American unwearied spirit of youth," Beveridge wrote in 1906. Elucidating America's economic, institutional, geographical, and demographic advantages, he added, "Young man, if to be a Roman then was greater than to be a king, what is it to be an American now? Think of it! To be an American at the beginning of the twentieth century!"[114]

If Beveridge's hymns to American youth rang romantic, Stanley Hall's sounded straightforwardly biological. For Hall, it was an inevitable upshot of the young nation's collective DNA that it stood on the threshold of seizing greater political power. Europeans and Asians had high hopes for their offspring too, but could their children draw from the same multiracial heritage and the pool of racial gifts that came with it? Hall's answer was no. In his scientific universe, America's male adolescents were a source of peril and promise. Centuries of ethnic and racial crossbreeding, Hall explicated, had generated white boys with "mongrel blood," which carried "an increased danger of both stunting and collapse." But he also believed that, if properly reared and carefully supervised, American youth could take advantage of their racial hybridity. They could bundle and internalize the best traits individual races had to offer, evolve more thoroughly, and achieve "a higher and more complete unity in the 'cosmic super-man' of the future."[115] There was one limitation: evolutionary perfection depended on whiteness. Only white "mongrels" were held to possess the capacity to outgrow the primitive stages of racial recapitulation. Hall's "super-man" paradigm, as well as his neglect of ethnic mixing in other parts of the world, dovetailed nicely with the predictions of American imperialists that their country was destined for a grand global future. All that was needed was a broad-based national movement that paired organizational rigor with youthful exuberance.[116]

The BSA stepped into the breach. Early Scout leaders turned Hall's belief that the nation's boys carried in them the seeds of future excellence into a powerful narrative documenting the parallel processes of maturation of American boyhood and nationhood. The BSA's founding texts derived the manly code of scouting from a heroic national past. Celebratory accounts of nineteenth-century continental empire encouraged twentieth-century American boys to see themselves as future citizens of a world-class nation. Obscuring white aggression, the *Handbook for Boys* cast the history of U.S. annexations as a moral crusade. In 1848, Americans defeated "the barbaric and military despotism of the Mexican government." They transformed Texas, which, as the handbook explained, was "overrun by outlaws and . . . a most undesirable neighbor," into blooming settlements. In the Spanish-American War of 1898, the United States liberated Cuba from the "inhuman treatment practiced by the Spanish soldiery." Even as Americans acquired an oceanic empire, the handbook told its young readers that "there is no country less warlike than ours."[117] In this sanitized history, America's colonial ventures were presented not as bloody conquests but as an exercise in modern knighthood.

Rather than resort to empire as a mode of self-characterization, BSA authors invented a tradition more commensurate to their version of U.S. history. They found one in chivalry, constructing a lineage of honorable white manhood from the medieval knight to the leaders of present-day America. Wary of republican sensibilities, the handbook identified the pioneer as a modern incarnation of Anglo-Saxon conventions of courage and valor. Echoing Frederick Jackson Turner's frontier thesis, YMCA executive and boy scout author John L. Alexander argued that a democratic American nobility had been forged at the meeting points of savagery and civilization in the West. "Our pioneers," wrote Alexander, "hated dishonesty and were truthful and brave. They were polite to women and old people, ever ready to rescue a companion when in danger, and equally ready to risk their lives for a stranger." They resorted to violence only "to protect . . . wives and children from the raids of the savages."[118] As "heir[s] of ancient chivalry and of the pioneers," Boy Scouts were expected to follow in their ancestors' footsteps and carry their legacy into the twentieth century.[119] Reminding Boy Scouts of their national heritage after the United States had entered World War I, one author penned in *Boys' Life*: "There was the Revolutionary War, after which a Republic was established here which since has come to be an ideal for oppressed men the world over. There was the Civil War, and millions who had been slaves were made free. We sent our men to Cuba, to fight and to die that a people cruelly treated by a foreign master might be independent. We took upon us the danger and responsibility of driving an oppressor from the Philippines, in the far Pacific, and remain there only to help the little brown men learn . . . to govern themselves as free men. . . . We are [now] writing a *new* page of history, and in it *you* will have a part. We shall have new heroes. You can be one."[120]

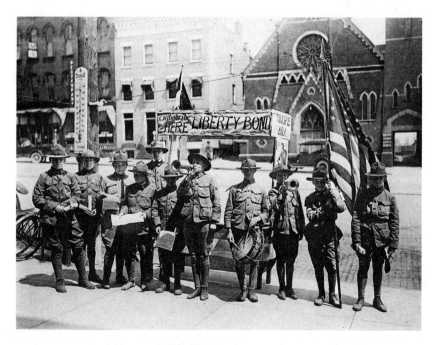

Figure 1.2. New York Boy Scouts sell Liberty Bonds during the Second Liberty Loan Drive, October 1917. Home-front activities during both world wars heightened the BSA's national and international visibility. (Courtesy of the National Archives, College Park, Maryland)

World War I provided a testing ground for whether it was possible to socialize boys into young citizens who understood that U.S. citizenship had global implications. To that end, the BSA promised to mobilize its members without militarizing them. Careful to locate the Scouts' contributions to the war effort in the civilian sphere, adult leaders recruited boys to promote War Savings Stamps and Liberty Bond sales campaigns, act as dispatch bearers for the federal government, and report disloyal behavior in their communities. Other troop activities included gathering charcoal and nutshells to make gas masks and planting Liberty gardens accompanied by the slogan "Every Scout to feed a soldier."[121] Working for America's victory, the BSA scored a huge public relations victory. Uncle Sam's little cheerleaders, recognized by Woodrow Wilson as having "rendered notable service to the Nation," became synonymous with an unadulterated patriotism.[122] More importantly, the spectacle of uniformed boys doing their share in the defense of their country nonviolently concealed the brutality of the war behind a ruse of noble intentions while projecting wickedness onto America's enemies.

International child rescue became the foreign corollary of the BSA's domestic war work. When the United States was still neutral, small numbers of Scouts began taking part in collection drives aimed at helping children in European countries occupied by the Central Powers. Various charities such as the Belgian Children's Fund, the Serbian Relief Committee, Near East Relief, and the American Committee for Devastated France advocated their respective causes in Boy Scout magazines.[123] Although the BSA's investment in wartime child saving was local and limited, the image of one's own youth aiding suffering children in other parts of the world buttressed the idea that moral reasons had driven the United States to intervene in global affairs. Whether this humanitarian image made the war more acceptable for adults or served as a compensatory fantasy for boys too young to join the army, it justified the spread of American power at the same time that it disguised the acts of violence that accompanied it.

In trying to define a proper role for boys in war, youth workers were walking a fine line. Perhaps this explains why BSA officials distanced themselves so vehemently from Hearst's Scout organization when they learned that it had allegedly allowed its boys to bear arms. "We do not put the idea of killing into the minds of Boy Scouts . . . Uncle Sam does not want boy soldiers," the BSA leadership publicized in April 1917.[124] But the truth was that not all boys in the movement were content with performing nonmilitary tasks. Boy Scouts from Memphis, Tennessee, drilled with real rifles until they changed to wooden poles to mollify concerned parents. "That kind of put a damper on it," one of

the boys remembered. "We didn't like it because they called us wooden soldiers."[125] Rather than marching in lockstep with adult expectations, many boys
called to defend American democracy against German barbarism treated the
war as a fast track to the privileges of manhood.

Fiction complemented real-life efforts to paper over the contradiction between boys seeking adventure in faraway places and men killing and dying for
Uncle Sam. Anticipating a market for sales, publishers specializing in cheap
juvenile fiction flooded stores with Boy Scout adventures. Though not every
Boy Scout novel or short story received the BSA's stamp of approval, most
tales amplified the organization's euphemistic language of empire.[126] Two stories deserve to be singled out. George Harvey Ralphson's novel *Boy Scouts in
the Philippines* (1911) revolves around a group of American Boy Scouts dispatched
to the Philippines to unearth a plot against the U.S. government. With ingenuity and pluck, the novel's boy heroes patrol the islands in anticipation of a
looming insurrection. They interrogate deferential natives, fight Filipino rebels,
and expose corrupt colonial officials, thereby bringing to a halt a conspiracy
involving local chieftains, Chinese smugglers, and a shady American businessman. Transplanting the imagined boundary between civilization and barbarism
from the American West to Southeast Asia, the novel depicts U.S. Boy Scouts as
agents of a muscular young empire. Its diction is openly racist: the boys, who
represent opportunity and order, use the derogatory terms "Japs" and "Chinks"
for the Pacific rivals of the United States. Filipino insurgents are portrayed as
shiftless and insidious. However, the appearance of a Filipino Boy Scout who
helps the young Americans bring their mission to a successful conclusion also
suggests the organization's potential for turning colonial boys into future native elites loyal to the United States.[127]

The second story moves the spotlight from the colonial frontier to the interwar frontier of international relations. Published in *Boys' Life* as a serial novel
from October 1924 to March 1925, *The Three Young Citizens* follows the Boy
Scout characters Freckles, Goggles, and Knuckles on a trip across the Atlantic.
The five hundred dollars Goggles possesses makes him a millionaire in inflation-
ravaged Europe. He buys a castle and becomes the Duke of Lichtenstein, ap-
pointing Freckles his minister of war and Knuckles his master of horse. Before
long the Scouts find themselves in the center of a political intrigue instigated by
Austrian aristocrats who want to restore Habsburgian rule in Hungary. Goggles,
Freckles, and Knuckles manage to frustrate the machinations of the pro-
Habsburg faction by luring their leaders into a trap and taking them prisoner.
Eventually the international crisis is averted and the peace is kept—not with
complex diplomatic maneuvers but with the help of youthful wit and faithful

adherence to the Scout laws. The story's mild sarcasm about the efficacy of adult international relations becomes manifest in the cameo role of Lord Robert Cecil, the British coarchitect of the League of Nations, who listlessly watches the three American Boy Scouts prevent another European war.[128] Both stories, *Boy Scouts in the Philippines* and *The Three Young Citizens*, offer a glimpse into the kind of imperial and internationalist attitudes that BSA authors strove to inculcate in the first two decades of the twentieth century. It is hard to say whether this type of juvenile fiction had any lasting impact on the young people consuming it. Yet Boy Scout literature repackaged abstractions like national loyalty and global responsibility in narrative forms that young readers could understand and appreciate.

To that end, the BSA sought the blessings of one famous American in particular. Theodore Roosevelt straddled the worlds of boyhood and hard power. Few Progressive Era American children grew up unfamiliar with the saga of Roosevelt's metamorphosis from an asthmatic boy to the hardy outdoorsman, gallant Rough Rider, and indomitable twenty-sixth president of the United States. His call to pursue "the strenuous life" was associated with a resolute masculinity: the ability to fight fearlessly and, if necessary, ruthlessly for what is right.[129] The paragon of early twentieth-century imperial manhood, Roosevelt embraced his role as the BSA's patron saint. He accepted the title of honorary vice president (only sitting presidents served as honorary presidents) and became the first and only man designated as "Chief Scout Citizen."[130]

Roosevelt's popularity boosted the BSA's early publicity campaigns. He showered lavish praise on the organization, addressed Boy Scout troops, and contributed to the handbook section on patriotism. "I believe heartily in the work you are doing," Roosevelt assured the BSA National Council. "You seek to supply the necessary stimulus to alert and strong manhood."[131] In December 1913, *Boys' Life* printed Roosevelt's "Appeal to the American Boy," which derived the ideal of the brave young citizen from Roosevelt's imperialist exploits during the Spanish-American War: "What was true on a very small scale for my regiment is true on a very big scale of American citizenship as a whole. . . . I have no use for timid boys, for the 'sissy' type of boy. I want to see a boy able to hold his own and ashamed to flinch."[132] In Roosevelt's lexicon of manhood, boys had to choose between two types: the "mollycoddle" (a shorthand for the weak, procrastinating man of ideas) or the "red-blood" (a vigorous and fearless man of action). Endorsing regenerative violence, Roosevelt wanted boys to aspire to the latter, to "stand stoutly" against "enemies from both without and from within."[133] There, in a nutshell, was the triad of courage, chivalry, and camaraderie that American boys should live by in order to develop into Hall's "super-men" of the twentieth century.

Akin to Baden-Powell's desire to establish a new familiarity between men and boys, Roosevelt embodied a boyish type of imperial manhood. As Roosevelt rose up to occupy the highest office in the nation, contemporaries were marveling at how he got away with detesting overblown decorum and drawing strength from the raucous company of youthful men. Roosevelt's public persona melded the brashness and bravado associated with boy-man-hood into the new hallmarks of American power. Caricaturists depicted the president's presumed boyish nature, showing Roosevelt sitting on a rocking horse, commanding toy armies, and using the Caribbean as the playground for his fleet.[134] Expressing the urge of a young nation eager to test its muscles, Roosevelt reminded observers of a leader more juvenile than judicious. This characterization by no means lessened the appeal of Roosevelt's boyishness, which did not signal immaturity or weakness but a healthy disregard for artificial restraint. Roosevelt himself attached great importance to being identified as the person

Figure 1.3. George J. Fisher and a Boy Scout honor Theodore Roosevelt, 1950. Such pilgrimages to the grave of the twenty-sixth president exemplified Roosevelt's lasting popularity as the patron saint of the BSA. (Courtesy of the Library of Congress, Prints and Photographs Division)

who confronted the ordeals of manhood with the heart of a boy. "I had to go. It was my last chance to be a boy" was his answer to a reporter who had asked the fifty-four-year-old in 1913 why he had decided to go on an arduous expedition to Amazonia.[135]

Roosevelt's promotion of the American way of scouting knew no national boundaries, and his ambassadorship marked a countercurrent to Baden-Powell's efforts to establish himself as the movement's global patriarch. During his trip to South America, the elder statesman garnered accolades for his services to boyhood wherever he went. Argentinean Boy Scouts paraded for Roosevelt in Buenos Aires and distributed souvenir buttons with his portrait.[136] After his death in 1919, Roosevelt's sons Theodore Jr. and Kermit carried on their father's patronage of the Boy Scouts. Kermit Roosevelt was awarded the title "Honorary Scout" and wrote articles for *Boys' Life*. Theodore Roosevelt Jr. joined the BSA National Council and worked to heighten the organization's appeal to colonial youth during his stints as governor of Puerto Rico and the Philippines in the late 1920s and early 1930s.

Creating nothing short of a Roosevelt personality cult, BSA members venerated Roosevelt in a series of public rituals that fused patriotism, youth, and imperial manhood. "Our boys, and indeed the whole world, have sustained a great loss," cabled the National Council when learning of Roosevelt's death.[137] Church pews were packed with Boy Scouts paying homage to the chief scout citizen. Shortly after his funeral, scoutmasters and Boy Scouts across the United States planted "memorial trees" to honor Roosevelt.[138] The most spectacular events conducted by the young hero worshippers were the annual excursions to Roosevelt's grave in Oyster Bay on Long Island. Led by Daniel Carter Beard until his death in 1941, these "Roosevelt pilgrimages" attracted several thousand Scouts and their adult leaders from the New York area and beyond. What started as a small outing in October 1920 mushroomed into meticulously choreographed, all-male processions featuring Scout officials dressed in buckskin, members of the Explorers' and Campfire Clubs of America, the Range Riders of the West, several other fraternal societies, Indian chieftains, and archery groups as well as Boy Scouts exhibiting the Stars and Stripes. Airplanes dropped rose petals on the grave as Scout contingents passed by for a salute. To the sound of drums and bugles they placed wreaths at the gate of the family plot where Roosevelt lay interred.[139]

The Roosevelt pilgrimages reveal how the BSA utilized dramatic representations to convey to the young key ideas about manhood, nation, and America's role in the world. Beard regarded the performances as powerful communicative acts, believing that spectacle and ritual made boys much more susceptible to adopting a particular masculine and national identity that was both muscular and innocuous. He wanted the ceremonies to be "impressive, reverential, and awe-inspiring" and BSA uniforms to "adhere to early American customs and costumes," from the cowboy hat and "the American designed knife, down to the shoes and stockings." Pageants, Beard insisted, should emphasize "national folk-lore" because its "historic, romantic, and picturesque qualities" were uniquely capable of "pulling our citizens together in one . . . national body of Americans."[140] Beard was certain that solemnity and theatricality would cast the Roosevelt pilgrimages as meaningful recreation, thereby enhancing their ideological value.

The national scout commissioner staged the commemorative exercises at Roosevelt's grave as evocative rites of passage: "Uncle Dan" symbolically passed the torch of imperial manhood from the saintlike patriarch Theodore Roosevelt to the imagined leaders of tomorrow. At the same time, the Roosevelt pilgrimages reflected broader changes in the cultural semantics of youth. According to Beard, Roosevelt's doctrine of strenuous manhood was continually relevant because of its youthfulness. Beard announced that it was "the radiant boyhood of our late President and the inspired boyish traits of his manhood" that underlay his persistent appeal.[141] Here youth signified less a neatly defined age group than a distinct way of life divorced of age. Any man could claim the mantle of youth as long as his actions spoke of naturalness, idealism, and vigor. Roosevelt's style of masculinity cut across lines of class, age, faith, and generation. In the words of journalist William Allen White, he had "the gaiety and optimism that belong to youth, and youth is not a mere physical adolescence."[142] Dressed in short pants and masking their old age with ritualized play, men like Beard in the United States and Baden-Powell in England transformed themselves into "boy men" keen on forming intimate bonds with actual boys. Although their fixation on young bodies bristled with pedophilic connotations, the Scout leaders' attempts to distract from their biological frailty revealed above all the extent to which old age had become synonymous with weakness and impotence.

Imagining the nation as a father-son compact, Beard's graveside eulogies held up Roosevelt as a moral compass to the rising generation. Roosevelt's gospel of Americanism was one of rejuvenation and expansion. "The highest form of success," Beard declared in 1936, quoting Roosevelt, "comes not to the man who desires easy peace but to the man who does not shrink from danger, from hardship or from bitter toil, and who out of these wins the splendid ultimate triumph."[143] Strenuous heterosexual masculinity not only embodied youth; it preserved it. Beard invoked "the sacredness of youth" to construct a boyish manhood and present it as an antidote to supposedly inferior modern masculinities: the idle homebody and the disobedient rowdy; the greedy materialist and the pleasure-seeking narcissist; "the pallid pimp" and the "enervate of the pen."[144] It is hard to miss the blatant repugnance to a culture valuing intellectualism and experience that lies at the core of Beard's quasi-religious veneration of boyhood. In romanticizing the spontaneity of youth in opposition to the supposed inaction of old age, Scout leaders contributed to an ageist zeitgeist that also inspired fascists and communists. All the while, the analogies between national growth and boyhood development were glaringly evident. Just as the youthful republic had matured into a metaphorical young adult who looked ahead to a bright future, U.S. Boy Scouts were asked to shake off childish whims, channel their unspent enthusiasm into patriotic service, and manfully bear the responsibilities of a dynamic global player. "Stand boldly before the world, as an advocate of American manhood and all that it implies" was Beard's message to the Scouts of America.[145]

Albert Snoke and his friends, who returned victorious from the World Scout Jamboree in Denmark, had done just that. In the eyes of their supervisors, they had gained "the respect of other countries for American Scouting." Having pitted their young manhood against that of other advanced nations, they offered reassurance to a country whose attitudes about its place in international affairs were in a state of flux. This was no small feat at a time when young people had started to flex their cultural and political muscle. All over the world, youth became shorthand for a fast-paced modernity marked by unbridled consumption and liberalized sexual behavior. The Boy Scouts, however, introduced youth as actors of a different type—not as vanguards of cultural emancipation but as agents of imperial regeneration. If youth pointed to a distant future, boy-man homosociality promised an immediate return on investment. Adults trying to forge a lasting pact between fathers and sons sought to make headway on two adjacent fields: reconstituting male authority and raising "physically fit" and "morally straight" young men prepared to shoulder the burdens of empire. Would the boys do their part?

Chapter 2

From Africa to Antarctica

Expeditions to the Global Frontier

It is easy to imagine the smile that Max Mangum's letter from far-flung Tahiti must have put on James West's face. A Mormon and former Boy Scout living in the South Pacific, Mangum wrote about a curious encounter with a group of sailors who had landed in Papeete Harbor in November 1928 to take on coal. The few American missionaries who had settled on the island knew the vessels' names by heart. Mail from the outside world had announced the arrival of the *Eleanor Bolling* and the *City of New York*. On board were the members of a U.S.-led international expedition bound for the Antarctic under the command of Navy Admiral Richard E. Byrd. Mangum's delight at the sight of the mariners, however, was dampened by their conduct. Some men "acted very disgraceful and drank very heavy while in port." Four of them, Mangum reported, were "arrested and taken to jail." The preacher's tone lightened up when he turned to one of the younger seafarers. Eagle scout Paul Allen Siple was a fellow to Mangum's liking. With his nineteen years, Siple struck the missionary as a "perfect example of manhood." Mangum was impressed that the youth "never once touched alcohol" and turned down "fellows who offered him tobacco." Instead, Siple spent his time ashore attending church and exploring the island in the company of Mangum's fellow Mormons, behaving like "a gentleman in every way."[1] The six-foot-tall Boy Scout from Erie, Pennsylvania, Mangum concluded, was not shrinking from physical hardship or succumbing to the temptations of vice. For the moment, West could rest assured that everything was going according to plan.

As Siple was approaching the South Pole, three other Eagle Scouts put their finishing touches on a book based on a trip they had made to British East Africa that same year. Robert Dick Douglas, Douglas Oliver, and David Martin Jr., better known under their Boy Scout names Dick, Doug, and Dave, had spent the summer on safari with the American wildlife photographers Martin and Osa Johnson. Like Siple, Dick, Doug, and Dave had been selected for their overseas adventure in a nationwide competition. Both voyages garnered national and international attention. Instant media sensations, the four Boy Scouts crossed oceans, endured severe weather, hunted wild animals, and held their own in contests with indigenous peoples. Antarctica and Africa were well-chosen destinations. Located at opposite climatic extremes, the two continents conjured up images of an exacting and exhilarating wilderness—untamed, primitive hinterlands where only the fittest could survive. Commercially, the expeditions paid off. The Scouts returned as young celebrities, and the two books they authored, *Three Boy Scouts in Africa* (1928) and *A Boy Scout with Byrd* (1931), became immediate best sellers.[2]

Africa and Antarctica were the climax in a series of offshore adventure tours that the BSA made available to its young members during the interwar years. The organization placed high hopes in sponsoring such trips. Designed to generate revenue, they also reignited public support for the BSA at a time of slackening membership growth. During a period when Americans were becoming more mobile, more secular, and more consumerist, the BSA constructed global frontiers as initiation rites that prescribed culturally sanctioned corridors to imperial manhood. This man-making scheme awarded social prestige to those who proved their mettle in a harsh colonial environment, far away from the feminized spheres of home and hearth. Adult organizers tapped into these borderlands to mold young imperial masculinities that would gain national and international recognition. Inspired by nineteenth-century precedents, they perceived Africa and Antarctica less as geographical locations than as meeting points of civilization and savagery where boys could get in touch with the purest form of masculinity, uncorrupted by the emasculating pleasures of urban modernity. As media productions, these trips fused fantasies of conquest with a middle-class morality as well as notions of productive leisure with the reenactment of a moderate dose of frontier violence.

However, for those journeying to the edges of the mapped world, the passages to imperial manhood were not as clearly charted as the official narratives implied. For the Scouts, these quasi-colonial enterprises were fraught with ambivalence and uncertainty. Though imbued with a sense of privilege, the youths never simply functioned as mouthpieces of adult ideas. They moved through liminal spaces, threshold zones of disorientation and potential chaos where childhood norms had lost their validity and the rules of adulthood were not yet fully applicable. Liminality, as defined by cultural anthropologist Victor Turner, has both temporal and spatial dimensions. Crossing over to another life stage entailed the subject's separation from the familiar surroundings of family, home, and community. Stripped of society's safeguards and confronting the unknown to attain a higher stage of development, Siple, Martin, Oliver, and Douglas were temporarily caught in a state "betwixt and between" with many possible outcomes, which Turner identified as essential to any rite of passage.[3] Carrying the banner of young America to the imagined outer rims of civilization, Siple and his fellow travelers did not simply act as poster boys for the BSA's expansionist designs. They had to learn how to navigate the conflicting spheres of public persona and private self.

Placing the boys at the center of these coming-of-age stories once again raises the question of the latitude young people had in an organization like the Boy Scouts. One impulse would be to center on instances where the youths went off script or challenged adult authority, yet historians armed with a narrow understanding of agency, preoccupied with subversion or resistance, will not be able to explain the many ways in which the Scouts contributed to these journeys.[4] This chapter details how scouting was propelled by a symbiotic relationship between old and young. The expeditions reveal that the Scouts played their part in a collaborative intergenerational effort to stabilize existing gender norms and social hierarchies in a rapidly modernizing society. Though the organizers worried whether the Boy Scouts would stay the course, they had their hands full reining in an overzealous desire on the part of their protégés to accomplish the missions laid out for them. Siple, Douglas, Martin, and Oliver were willing executioners who overshot their mark on occasion. Ultimately, their youthful appropriations of manhood and empire worked well within the broader enterprise to mobilize new recruits for the BSA and dissipate adult fears about wayward youth. Authorship over the meaning of these expeditions resided in many groups: from the boys, who traveled abroad and wrote the book manuscripts, to the adult leaders, editors, and the public at large.

Drawing on material from all these spheres, I develop the chapter's main themes in six steps. I start by illustrating how the expeditions originated against the backdrop of an evolving modern youth culture and diversifying gender roles precipitated by the booming entertainment industry of the 1920s. I then turn to the BSA's attempt to distill the ideal American boy in highly competitive selection processes for the journeys to Africa and Antarctica. I follow that part with a section that shows how and why the BSA sought to benefit from the celebrity status of the two expedition leaders, Martin Johnson and Richard Byrd, who embodied a type of imperial manhood that was related to the prewar Rooseveltian model but was also marketed as jauntier and less belligerent. In the next two parts I delve deeper into the Scouts' personal experiences, demonstrating the extent to which their aspirations to manhood took shape not only in encounters with the primitive but by learning to distance themselves from the masculinities of working-class and colonized men. I end the chapter with an analysis of the star cult building around the Scouts, and how public admiration congealed ideals of boyhood and manhood that presented boyish wanderlust as a remedy for the delinquent tendencies of young age.

Young Masculinities and the Media

The story of these adolescent expeditions has multiple origins. With the deeds of explorers such as David Livingstone, Roald Amundsen, and Robert Falcon Scott seeping into juvenile literature, the final decades of the age of colonial discovery acquired a mythical status for boys growing up in the early twentieth century. Scout organizations the world over wedded themselves to a heroic frontier masculinity. Blazing a trail that other youths wanted to follow, British scout James Marr sailed southward in 1921 as part of the Shackleton expedition to survey the Antarctic Islands. Six years later, two Mexican Scouts hiked from Mexico City to New York City, eliciting nods of appreciation in the U.S. press and defying old racist stereotypes that cast Mexicans as lazy and effeminate. Reporters showered equal praise in 1937 on two Venezuelan Scouts who walked eight hundred miles from Caracas to Washington, DC, to attend an international Scout gathering.[5]

George Palmer Putnam, heir to the influential New York publishing house G. P. Putnam's Sons, did not want American boyhood to fall behind in this international race for supreme young manhood. A titan of the interwar book industry, Putnam asserted his upper-class masculinity not only by flaunting his business exploits but also by cultivating a reputation as a gallant swashbuckler. Putnam first tasted danger as a field artillery lieutenant in World War I before financing his own expeditions to Greenland and Baffin Island to satisfy his hunger for extreme outdoor experience. Though advertised as scientific explorations, these trips, which were backed by the American Geographical Society, followed the pattern of masculine adventures based on the Rooseveltian vision of "the strenuous life."[6] Putnam knew how to turn his public image into cash and recognition. His love of aviation earned him the friendship of Charles Lindbergh, whose autobiography "*We*" he published in 1927 with profitable success after Lindbergh's first transatlantic flight.[7] In the same year, Putnam and Lindbergh got to share another badge of masculinity: both were named honorary Scouts. The BSA had created this network of elite men from the fields of business, science, and discovery to increase its visibility.[8]

With the recruitment of Putnam, the BSA gained additional leverage to market its model of daring border-crossing manhood. Putnam's contacts with adventure celebrities in North America and Europe as well as his promotional talents solidified his image as a romantic and resourceful frontiersman. His son David, who had accompanied him on his expeditions to the Arctic Circle, had already written modestly successful travel books for young readers when Putnam sensed another opportunity. Why not broach to some of his globe-trotting partners the idea of organizing voyages to distant shores with Boy Scouts in a leading role, and have them write books about it? The explorer couple, Martin and Osa Johnson, quickly warmed to the idea. Navy Admiral Richard Byrd, whose flight over the North Pole had been spectacular enough to guarantee him funding from private donors for a trip to Antarctica, also needed little convincing. The BSA sounded its approval too. Recognizing the growing consuming power of white middle-class youth, Putnam was convinced that all parties involved would reap their fair share of publicity and profit.[9]

More was at stake, though, than commercial considerations. Excitement for the Boy Scouts had waned since World War I. The BSA continued to attract young enrollees, but the patriotic atmosphere of the late 1910s and early 1920s that had catapulted the organization to national fame had not lasted. The low point came in 1928 when the BSA was registering more dropouts than recruits.[10] Worries that the Boy Scouts were losing their grip on the nation's youth were not unwarranted. Young people growing up in the postwar years struck adult observers as fundamentally different from previous generations of youth. Adolescents from all social strata suddenly appeared less deferential and more independent. Some contemporaries even saw youth in open rebellion against parental authority. Books such as Denver juvenile judge Benjamin Lindsey's *The Revolt of Modern Youth* (1925), which called for a more lenient approach to adolescent sexuality, hit a nerve because Lindsey sympathized with youth's cultural emancipation.[11] Rejecting the Prohibition-era mores of their elders, the female "flapper" and her boyfriends epitomized a new transnational cohort of college-aged (mostly white middle-class) women and men who embraced an openly hedonistic lifestyle. The electrification of society reduced the grind of household work in families that could afford modern appliances, which increased women's free time in particular. The flapper stood for makeup, long parties, ecstatic jazz music, sensual dancing, smoking, drinking, and a liberal sexuality with women in a proactive role. Although most representations of the period's "flaming youth" showed people in their early twenties, their fashion and language influenced teenage behavior.[12]

While economic growth and the widespread availability of new technologies such as the telephone and the automobile expedited the rise of a modern youth culture, the dissemination of what it meant to be young was predominantly a product of the modern entertainment industry. Businesses saw in youth, in Cynthia Felando's words, "both a commodity to be sold and a demographic market to be sold to."[13] Hollywood movies, radio shows, popular fiction, and advertisements featuring youthful protagonists who defied Victorian values projected alternative gender roles that reached millions of consumers. Mass media and the creation of competing ideals of manhood were closely connected. Facilitating what economic theorists Douglas B. Holt and Craig J. Thompson termed "compensatory consumption," films and magazines brought into circulation a multiplicity of male and female archetypes that teenagers could follow, and on which they could build their identities.[14] Popular representations of movie stars, musicians, artists, and gangsters shaped the tastes of a younger generation fatigued by the memory of war. Their glamorous unconventionality posed a challenge to the sober sense of duty ascribed to the generals, statesmen, and business leaders idolized by the Boy Scouts. Writing for the liberal magazine *Forum*, cultural critic Floyd Tillery rubbed salt into that wound. The managerial classes that had taken control of the BSA, Tillery charged, failed to appreciate youth's true longings. All they did was raise "Little Babbits," spread "selfishness and infantilism," and dwarf "real manhood and full maturity."[15]

With a conspicuous diversity of masculine role models up for grabs, the BSA worried about its prospects in the realm of boy-work. Concerns over the consumer-driven fads of white middle-class youth began to supersede the prewar focus on juvenile delinquency among working-class and immigrant boys. Expanding leisure opportunities exacerbated what Scout executives referred to as the "older boy problem."[16] Boys who had reached puberty increasingly quit scouting for different pursuits. High school sports had become a strong competitor vying for youth's attention, and the growing numbers of younger boys in the organization made the older ones feel immature. Since Siple and the three Safari Scouts were between fifteen and nineteen years old at the time of their selection, it is safe to assume that the BSA saw the expeditions as an opportunity to improve its standing with older boys.

To regain lost ground, Scout leaders labeled rival masculinities deviant and effeminate. Launching a discursive counterattack, organizers spoke of "questionable amusements," "trashy literature," and "demoralizing influences" that eroded respectable citizenship.[17] One sociological study published by the BSA claimed that music and movies full of "rotten relations and coarse comedy" threatened to debase American youth.[18] Given the African American influence on jazz, the racial subtext was clear: youth mingling in dancehalls and nightclubs would lead to unwanted encounters between whites and people of color. "With twenty-seven million automobiles in use, with dance halls, with jazz, with all these distractions enticing the youth of America, too many of them are drawn into the whirlpool," West grumbled.[19] For the chief scout executive, the representatives of the new leisure classes were no apostles of liberation but agents of immorality. West's invention of the term "peace-time slacker" was a shrewd rhetorical ploy moving those speaking, acting, and dressing in new ways into the proximity of wartime cowards and draft dodgers.[20] Leaving adolescents and their search for authenticity in the hands of the entertainment industry, Scout officials warned, would result in a sissified generation of amusement lovers incapable of protecting the nation. "We must find *a moral substitute for war*," urged an alarmed George Fisher in February 1928, "something with a thrill in it, something that responds to and satisfies the biologic urges of youth, or he will find expression in illegal ways. We must meet the need for adventure with rich, emotional experience."[21]

Fisher's call for "a moral substitute for war" reflected nostalgia for a nation disciplined and uplifted by a common cause, where joining a brotherhood of fighting men was seen as the high mark of masculinity. Postwar disarmament, however, brought new challenges. President Harding's call for a "return to normalcy" was shrugged off by a younger generation where few longed to return to a historical trajectory that had resulted in war. BSA officials did not seek another armed conflict, but they also feared the emasculating potential of peace. Against the image of the adolescent boy as a renegade and amusement seeker, conservative educators pitted the image of the male youth as "participating citizen," who traded dubious recreation for the opportunity to learn civic responsibility and national service.[22]

In the years after the war, the BSA propagated an exciting yet conformist idea of boy citizenship in response to a more diversified youth culture. Innovations in mass communication became integral to this task, and stories transported through radio and film worked against the impression that scouting was monotonous and unrewarding. Hollywood-style motion pictures such as *The Littlest Scout* (1919) and *Drum Taps* (1933) showed Boy Scouts cheerfully bringing spies and crooks to justice and earning the recognition of a grateful community. The basic plot line was that social respectability came through civic duty and service, not through narcissistic entertainment. Another practice of masculine self-improvement conveyed in Scout-friendly advertisements was knowledge of modern technology. Boy Scouts were frequently portrayed as mechanically versatile, instructing clueless fathers about new radio models or developments in the automobile industry.[23] Boys should devote their spare time to electronic tinkering instead of making out with girls. Fearful of cultural modernization, the BSA nonetheless tapped into the entertainment industry and used modern twentieth-century technology to revamp its program.

The mass media became central to equating young imperial masculinities with legitimate fun and productive leisure. Putnam's publicity stunts had worked well with adults, so why should they not give BSA officials the upper hand in the struggle for the hearts and minds of America's boys. "When Doug, Dick, and Dave sailed for Africa," Putnam's son David wrote in his preface to the book about the Boy Scouts on safari, "I certainly wanted to go. Any American boy would."[24] The BSA had always sought to present citizenship not as a legal-political abstraction but as a thrilling journey from boyhood to manhood. For the national leadership, the trips to Africa and Antarctica achieved just that. The value of the Scout motto "Be Prepared," one article in *Boys' Life* stated, "was never so happily exemplified" as in the current "exploration and travel opportunities being offered to Scouts."[25] Lighting the path to imperial manhood, these journeys promised to take U.S. Boy Scouts almost anywhere, if need be to the end of the world.

Super Scouts and a Stowaway

Bureaucratic planning may jar with the idea of outdoor romance, but James West took no chances when it came to the question of which type of boy he wanted to see on these expeditions. With promotional articles about Africa and Antarctica, *Boys' Life* sought to whet the appetites of young readers for overseas adventure. Fliers that encouraged Boy Scouts to submit an application were sent across the country.[26] To ensure regional diversity, West called on the assistance of the 650 local Scout councils representing over twenty-eight thousand troops on the U.S. mainland and in the colonies. Their job was to sift through thousands of applications and, after thorough investigation, recommend the best candidates for further scrutiny by the National Council. A group of finalists—six for Antarctica, seven for Africa—spent several days at

the BSA headquarters in New York. The boys were subjected to rigorous physical examination and interrogated by West and other Scout leaders. They met
with several national celebrities and supporters of scouting such as Putnam,
Byrd, and Theodore Roosevelt Jr. Recalling the atmosphere of surveillance,
Robert Dick Douglas wrote in hindsight that "each person on the committee
was watching our demeanor and our reactions on all these activities."[27]

Selections were made on the basis of a rigid ranking and rating system that
reinforced the BSA's notion of what constituted the ideal American boy. Youths
identified as bookworms, whippersnappers using frivolous language, or what
one search committee member referred to as a "stupid—'big-muscle' boy" were
eliminated early in the process.[28] The organizers sought excellence in the areas of fitness, health, camping, and nature study. Eligibility was limited to boys
with a minimum age of fifteen (seventeen for Antarctica). Applicants needed
to be First Class or Eagle Scouts, possess an above-average amount of merit
badges, have good grades in school, be avid churchgoers, and present a physi-
cian's certificate of an examination as detailed as that required of candidates
for the U.S. Army or Navy. A slouching pose, crooked feet, or bad teeth could
kill a boy's dream in an instant. Evaluators read bodily imperfections as character flaws. Local civic and spiritual leaders should testify to the applicants'
"courage, resourcefulness, leadership ability, adaptability, quality of endurance,
initiative, industry," and what the organizers phrased "experience and action
under stress."[29]

Reminiscent of Benjamin Franklin's eighteenth-century catalog of virtues,
the BSA's eligibility list spelled out a rugged, early twentieth-century, middle-
class version of Franklin's ethos of white Protestant manhood. This cultural
bias was relevant not only for how these criteria were interpreted but for who
was regarded as capable of meeting them. The thirteen Scouts who advanced
to the final elimination rounds in New York presented a picture of ethnic uni-
formity. As the finalists from Oregon, North Carolina, Minnesota, Washington, Texas, Pennsylvania, and Alabama were hauled before the cameras and
presented to a curious public, one unspoken verdict lighted up in the flurry
of popping flashbulbs: America's future leaders were to be young, male, preferably Protestant, and, above all, white.[30]

Paul Siple embodied those tenets with a vengeance. His public persona served
his own interests as well as those of the organization. Siple's fifty-nine merit
badges predestined him to be the iconic Super Scout, the youthful paragon
that the BSA had been hoping to recruit for the Antarctica venture. The
Eagle Scout from Pennsylvania fit that role perfectly. Siple attached to his application testimonials from eminent Erie citizens that attested to his physical and

moral qualification. Business executive George W. Hunter hailed Siple as "an outstanding figure in Scouting . . . clean in body and mind." Methodist minister Walter H. Smith called him a "real leader" among Erie's youth who "possesse[d] a character that is second to none."[31] During the final selection, Siple outstripped his five competitors in almost every aspect. Commission chairman Malcolm C. Douglas found Siple's behavior indicative of a "strong physique" and "good personality"—the signature of a young man "willing to work and to take orders."[32] Siple sounded all the right chords in the vetting process. Where some of his competitors irritated the commission with eccentric or insubordinate behavior (e.g., snappy language or arrogant posing), Siple pushed himself to the fore by emphasizing his proficiency in sea scouting, his interest in the natural sciences, and his religiously motivated aversion to alcohol and tobacco.[33] His performance struck evaluators as ambitious but not brash, rational but not irreverent, self-reliant but not disobedient. He was slender and fit but not massively muscular; in short, he was a prototype of the flawless boyman that the BSA cherished. Vowing that he was prepared to face the hardships that lay ahead, Siple was awarded the position.[34]

Before the real Paul Siple embarked on his polar adventure in New York harbor on August 25, 1928, idealized representations of Paul Siple had already begun floating in the media. These images had to bridge an apparent contradiction: How could Siple walk in the limelight like no other Boy Scout before him and still be proclaimed a "typical American youth"?[35] Measuring six foot and one inch and weighing over 160 pounds, Siple was not exactly boyish in stature. West and his allies in the press crafted a narrative that traced Siple's rise to fame back to his small-town roots and adherence to traditional middle-class family values. They described Admiral Byrd's youngest aide as gentle, soft-spoken, modest, loyal to his elders, and undisposed toward grandstanding. Siple morphed into America's Everyboy, the public face of a youth organization eager to defuse suspicions of elitism. "Not every boy may have an opportunity to take part in an event of world importance," West explained, "but every boy can . . . develop such a character that he will be prepared when his opportunities come."[36] Rather than figure as inimitably talented, Siple personified patriotic goodness, Protestant morality, and self-improvement through obedience and hard work. He became, in a symbolic sense, both youth and antiyouth, a counterimage to adolescents in early twentieth-century America who distrusted adult authority and experimented in matters of style, leisure, sexuality, and politics. Boys, George Fisher declared, would find true romance not in premature love but in "new worlds to conquer" and "new trails to embark upon . . . providing new adventure, new claims to sturdy manhood."[37]

Acting as an ambassador of young Scout manhood, Siple was expected to re-affirm scouting as the institution offering adult-guided recreation and upward mobility to male youth.

But even as Siple garnered advance praise from adults, his selection was not uncontested among his peers. Several boys, some of them far below the min-imum age, went out of their way to prove that they deserved to be picked, trying to get a spot on Byrd's team in ways that were not endorsed by the organization. Florida scout Rudolph Patzert rented a small room in Manhat-tan, with a chair as his only piece of furniture, and worked long hours during the summer to keep alive his dream of meeting Admiral Byrd and convincing him to let him join his crew.[38] Nineteen-year-old eagle scout Bill Witt did not take no for an answer either. Eager to be a member of the expedition, Witt, who boasted sixty-five merit badges (six more than Siple), hitchhiked all the way from Oklahoma to New York to press his application with Byrd per-sonally.[39] Another aspiring youth, West Virginia scout Fred Wiseman, had friends in high places cheerlead for him in the local press.[40] Although these attempts did not alter the course of events, they indicate that some Boy Scouts felt extremely confident in their ability to influence and even defy decisions made by their superiors.

Another act of defiance that came to a head on board the *City of New York* almost slipped under the public radar but reveals how youth, manhood, and race operated on these expeditions. Shortly after the ship had pulled out of New York harbor, the crew spotted an unexpected stowaway: Robert White Lanier, a black youth who, equipped with a dozen pencils, a diary, and a cam-era, had been hiding in the ship's forecastle for three days without food and water. Pressed for an explanation, Lanier said he wanted to become the first African American to reach the South Pole. Siple described his black counter-part in a racially condescending tone as a "cheery fellow" and "poor coon" who failed to grasp the gravity of his transgression. Handing the half-starved stowaway a watermelon to eat, Siple made fun of Lanier, remarking that "he was in his glory . . . he sure proved his nationality." Amusement turned into derision when Lanier made a startling statement. The African American youth claimed he was a fellow Scout, prompting a roar of laughter. Whiteness cir-cumscribed Siple's conception of Scout brotherhood. "He was a happy kid," Siple noted sardonically, "but he wasn't much happier than I was, for his job as assigned by the Captain later was, as we expected, that of a mess boy. That relieved me."[41] Siple's laughter and subsequent sigh of relief—he was dismissed from this unpleasant duty and reassigned to less menial tasks—can be read as a tacit expression of imperial manhood. By participating in the black youth's degradation, by emasculating and infantilizing him with the epithet "kid," Siple made clear that the role of the child on this journey was not his to fill. He sought initiation into a young imperial masculinity in the company of people he considered his peers: hardened white sailors, scientists, and officers. There was nothing to be gained from fraternizing with somebody whose skin color precluded him from any position of importance. Lanier's self-identification as a Boy Scout was ridiculed. Erasing any association of scouting with blackness, Siple's book mentions only a "hapless negro."[42]

Beyond Roosevelt

Even as the Scouts' travels to distant continents symbolized a glorious national future, their journeys harkened back to the imagined origins of human history. Europeans had long projected primitivism onto Africa and, to a lesser extent, Antarctica. The "dark continent" held a special place in the white imperialist imagination. Centuries of slavery and colonization had been justified with portrayals of Africa as a place arrested in a precivilized stage, populated by barbaric tribes, murky jungles, and savage beasts. Yet by the early twentieth century, ideas of Africa as a continent stuck in time also carried less gloomy connotations. Its vibrant fauna and pristine wilderness came into view as sharp contrasts to the industrialized centers and metropolitan decadence of Europe and North America, inviting comparisons to an exotic Garden of Eden that held valuable lessons for whites trying to put their societies on a path toward national regeneration.[43]

When contemporary Americans thought about prominent personalities who had ventured to such pristine hinterlands, Theodore Roosevelt often came to mind. The ex-president had sprinkled prewar images of "darkest" Africa with first inklings of "brightest" Africa. During his 1909 safari, Roosevelt roamed through what is today Kenya, Uganda, and the Congo to collect specimens for the Smithsonian Institution—a euphemism for hunting and killing more than five hundred animals, from rhinoceroses and zebras to lions and elephants. Roosevelt presented his travels as one through space and time, and his romanticized descriptions of the savannah reflected the thrill of a man who gloried in traversing a land he freely associated with his Stone Age forebears' existential struggles. His Africa was a prehistoric environment governed by interspecies violence, where a white man could demonstrate his superior civilized manhood and bask in the emotions of an intensely archaic masculinity. Seeing in "the great beasts that now live in East Africa" the same menace that his "earliest paleolithic ancestors" in Europe had stared down, Roosevelt cast his big-game hunting trip as a battle for survival that had reawakened his warrior instincts and reassured him that, although culturally far advanced, he still possessed the masculine prowess of his racial forefathers.[44] The evolutionary significance of the ex-president's African adventure was underlined by the presence of his nineteen-year-old son Kermit, who subjected himself to the same menacing confrontations with wild animals.[45] Kermit's hunting trophies constituted the final link in a transgenerational chain of male power that destined Roosevelt and his offspring to rule.

Roosevelt's long shadow hovered over Douglas, Oliver, Martin, and Siple as they were preparing for their errands into the wilderness. The involvement of Roosevelt's oldest son, Theodore Jr., in nominating the Safari Scouts suggests that their quests were modeled after the frontier exploits of the twenty-sixth U.S. president. Writing for *Boys' Life*, Theodore Roosevelt Jr. gushed that the boys would "follow in the trail of Stanley, Bacon, and other undaunted souls," his father included, "who opened up for us darkest Africa."[46] Visits to the Roosevelt residence in Oyster Bay, where Dick, Doug, and Dave marveled at the family patriarch's safari souvenirs, indicated that BSA officials intended to put the boys in that lineage.[47] A symbolic gesture of equal proportions occurred at a luncheon in honor of Paul Siple, whose pending Antarctic journey took on Rooseveltian qualities when Theodore Jr. autographed the Eagle Scout's Bible, adorning it with a quotation from 1 Corinthians 16:9: "for a great door and effectual is opened unto me."[48] Were Americans prepared to see boys reenact TR's performances of nature conquest and superior marksmanship?

Not quite. In fact, declaring Progressive Era hypermasculinity the undisputed touchstone for young manhood in the 1920s misses significant ways in which the BSA adapted its approach to molding future leaders to a changing society. A new appreciation for professional expertise and managerial proficiency, along with an emphasis on public relations skills, curbed the muscular Christianity of earlier decades. The Boy Scout promotion tours to foreign lands of the late 1920s transcended Rooseveltian anxieties about masculine enfeeblement. Their defining feature was a cultural script suited for the postwar boom years that reconciled the conservative desire to maintain white male supremacy with a general orientation toward corporate capitalism, media innovations, and the rising significance of youth in popular culture. Transplanting the frontier qualities of bravery and self-reliance into the milieus of mass leisure and democratic consumption, this script had its youthful protagonists combine showmanship with bourgeois morality and radiate physical courage, technological finesse, and a boyish wanderlust. As a consequence, the violent realities of empire receded behind the veil of a tightly orchestrated coming-of-age drama that made the passage from boyhood to manhood entertaining, easily consumable, and consistent with the period's white middle-class sensibilities.

Few doubted whether Richard Byrd and Martin Johnson were qualified to act as mentors in scouting's open-air classrooms on the global frontier. Their affable masculine heroics set them apart from Theodore Roosevelt's bloody hunting exploits. Although they preserved core characteristics of an imagined preindustrial manly ethos, which foregrounded fighting instincts and the will to survive, Byrd and Johnson represented a playful, theatrical type of celebrity adventurer explicitly attuned to America's capitalist values and burgeoning entertainment industry. Less stern pioneers than entrepreneurs active in what Byrd astutely called "the hero business," they appeared likable, benign, and youthful.[49] They knew how to shine in front of and behind the camera, demonstrated a mastery over machines, and exuded a boyish resourcefulness and optimism appreciated by the moneyed classes. Moreover, they possessed the media competence that was essential to the making of modern masculinities. If heroism was a social performance dependent on public recognition, the careers of men such as Byrd, Johnson, and Lindbergh confirmed that the popularity resulting from stardom was little more than a successful market transaction.

By the time Dick, Doug, and Dave came out on top in the race for the three spots on the safari, Martin and Osa Johnson had already established themselves as white America's self-anointed Africa experts. Widely hailed for his wildlife movies that catered to the popular tastes of the twenties, Martin Johnson invented for himself the role of the naturalist whose preferred tool for trekking through the Serengeti's animal kingdom was the camera, not the rifle. In the Johnsons' cinematic narratives that captivated millions of viewers of different ages, Africa was no longer presented as a savage continent but rebranded into "one of the most healthful spots on the globe," with landscapes of magnificent beauty that made for "fascinating study."[50] Johnson broke with the Rooseveltian practice of big-game hunting in pledging that he would capture a vanishing paradise on reel. Liberal educators and preservationists balked at the idea that learning how to face danger should mean sending Boy Scouts on a killing spree in lion country. Dick Douglas's parents shared their misgivings with reporters that their son might be caught "fooling around" with lethal carnivores.[51] This coalition of progressive childhood advocates, wildlife enthusiasts, and nervous parents caught the Roosevelts and Putnams off guard, who believed that the prospect of American teenagers battling ferocious animals would generate valuable publicity. In contrast, the Johnsons projected a picturesque, almost tranquil Africa—the perfect playground for adolescent curiosity. Stating that he never took "much joy in killing," Johnson conjured up the panorama of a tamed wilderness in which violence against animals was the exception rather than the rule.[52] James West echoed this description. By declaring the Scout "a friend of animals" and instructing the three teenagers "not to hurt or kill any living creature needlessly," he distanced the BSA from slaughtering sportsmanship.[53] In the majestic plains of the Serengeti, far removed from modernity's raucous noise and the echoes of colonial violence, the boys were supposed to put their Scout skills to the ultimate test without wallowing in cruelty.

Osa Johnson, Martin's wife and professional partner, gave sharper contours to the domestication of hypermasculinity. Her presence added a maternal element to the safari, reminding the audience that the fifteen-year-old Scouts under the Johnsons' supervision were not yet men, and thus still in need of protection and care. Attending to bourgeois gender conventions, Osa fulfilled her "womanly" duties, as Martin observed. She saw to it that Dick, Doug, and Dave received adequate food and shelter after the boys had arrived in Nairobi.[54] At the same time, Osa's twin roles as surrogate mother and adventurous woman raised questions about relations between the sexes more generally and in the traditionally masculine domain of tracking and exploring in particular. Her feminine influence seemed acceptable, though, as long as it stayed within the gendered boundaries drawn by the ideology of separate spheres and remained subordinate to the more meaningful relationship that was supposed to evolve between the boys and her husband. Pictures showing her decorating the couple's tent home while Martin was out pursuing dangerous animals worked against the "unnatural" impression of a white woman living in the wilderness.[55] For the same reason, Osa's name did not make it into the title of the official BSA-endorsed travel account. The book merely states that Douglas, Martin, and Oliver had gone on safari "with Martin Johnson."

Richard Byrd administered his rise to stardom without a strong female partner. Yet the navy admiral, too, sought to make his masculine pursuits compatible with the peacetime sentiments of the postwar era. Byrd's metamorphosis from an elite soldier to a promoter of scientific exploration began not long after World War I, which he had spent away from combat as the commander of two navy air bases in Nova Scotia, Canada. A leg injury had forced Byrd to retire from active duty. His pioneering achievements in a decade obsessed with "firsts" resembled those of Charles Lindbergh. Mixing his flashy outward appearance (Byrd loved to pose in his white admiral's uniform) with testimonies of his exceptional piloting abilities, the officer became a darling of the press.

Commercial sponsors enabled Byrd to accomplish headline-making stunts. His 1926 expedition to the Arctic Circle, which peaked in an airplane mission that, as Byrd insisted, made him the first man to fly over the North Pole, was followed a year later by the first multiengine crossing of the Atlantic.[56] Riding a wave of public admiration, Byrd managed to raise funds for another expedition. He wanted to penetrate the unmapped parts of the Antarctic with a team of geographers and geologists and establish a permanent American base there. The imperialist undertones in Byrd's polar jump resonated from the pronouncement that the United States would join other nations in claiming Antarctic territory for the purpose of scientific study.[57]

Byrd's professed interest in research was somewhat spurious. Whereas Johnson exemplified a restrained vision of frontier boy-man-hood, Byrd contributed to the remasculinization of the sciences. "Why go at all?" he asked. "The human answer is simple. Men do these things because they are men; because in the unknown lies a ceaseless challenge to a man's curiosity."[58] Asked about his motivation to take a Boy Scout with him, Byrd answered: "Because health, loyalty, youth, and ambition mean more to exploration than science and training."[59] Byrd showed little interest in the rigorous research coming out of laboratories or lecture halls. He shored up the validity of a cultural discourse that conceptualized science as a valiant act requiring boyish curiosity and male toughness. Byrd's ideal was that of the scientist-explorer who gladly traded the comforts of university life for the raw experience of making new discoveries in the globe's most tempestuous regions. Pale and flat-chested academics had no business in what one Ohio newspaper referred to as a "red-blooded romance."[60] The downside to Byrd's prioritization of loyalty and grit was that he had difficulty recruiting more than a handful of trained meteorologists and geophysicists.[61] The bulk of the crew consisted of technicians, radio operators, veteran sailors from the United States, Canada, Ireland, England, and Norway, and cameramen working for Paramount Studios. This anti-intellectual attitude dovetailed neatly with the utilitarian ethos of capitalism. One Ohio newspaper referred to Byrd's polyglot team as "a band of hardy adventurers" who got things done instead of getting bogged down in endless deliberation.[62] Putting the natural sciences in the service of constructing robust masculine identities certainly met the BSA's approval. So did Byrd's adventurism, which rubbed against the ideal of probing scholarship.

Richard Byrd and Martin Johnson struck the BSA as exemplary men because they seemed capable of pulling together the period's contradictory strands. With one foot, they stood firmly in the glitzy new world of big business, mass consumption, and the media; with the other, they remained anchored in the value system of Theodore Roosevelt's generation, in which social Darwinist angst had stoked expansionist desires. A society in transition, Boy Scout organizers held, needed a reformed yet stable imperial masculinity. That masculinity, they believed, was best inculcated through the spectacle of picture-perfect sons following on the heels of their fatherly tutors.

Playing a Man's Part

A howling blizzard was raging outside as members of the Byrd expedition team, who had reached their icy destination four months ago, huddled around the loudspeakers in the mess hall, the social sanctuary of the hastily erected polar base the men had christened "Little America." It was April 1929, and the adventurers had begun to brace themselves for the Antarctic winter. The crackling voices and music transmitted by radio stations back in the United States were of poor quality; yet they were the only communication connecting Byrd and his crew to the outside world. The main attraction of that day's broadcast was Paul Siple. Paul's parents had gone on air to send their son a message. Mr. Siple spoke first. He exhorted his son to continue "to do his duty to God and . . . country" and prove to his "companions and the world that Scouting lays the foundation for real manhood." Then came Mrs. Siple, all warmth and affection. She gently kissed into the microphone, signaling to Paul how much she missed him.[63] With their gendered performances of patriarchal authority and maternal sentimentality, Paul's parents reflected the period's middle-class parental norms. Little did they know that their radio message caused an embarrassing scene eleven thousand miles away. Tears welled up in Siple's eyes, threatening to reduce him to the image of a homesick child—a mama's boy posture that was utterly at odds with the intrepid stance Siple was supposed to exhibit. Was a Boy Scout allowed to cry? What did it mean for a young man in Siple's position to go off script, to be overwhelmed by emotions?

No public record of Siple's crying exists, only a brief diary entry.[64] Obviously, this was exactly the kind of behavior that those who looked at these expeditions as demonstrations of the BSA's model of masculinity would have frowned on. Failure to enact its core precepts—toughness, courage, achievement, obedience, and emotional self-control—was a serious concern, not just for the adult organizers but for the youths as well. When we listen to their voices beyond the official soundtrack, we encounter Boy Scouts who are just as disoriented as they are determined, experiencing a reality where learning how to "play a man's part," to use Siple's own phrase, could cause developmental stress.[65] What emerges is a story of uncertainty and inner turmoil that strayed significantly from the polished media narrative. The intimate expressions that survived in diaries, personal letters, and memoirs suggest that the adolescents did not pass the tests of manhood effortlessly but struggled to do right by themselves and their elders.

This is not to say that the four Eagle Scouts did not burst with ambition. One of the trials on these staged quests consisted of learning how to balance deadly violence with civilizational restraint. Poised between big-game hunting and animal studies, Dick, Doug, and Dave's safari had a double identity as zoology excursion and colonial survival training. Despite protest from parents and preservationists, the Boy Scouts not only took pictures of wild animals but killed a limited number for food and trophies. The boys showed few scruples in demonstrating their marksmanship on living beings. Accentuating the thrill of taking down a gazelle or a wart hog, their book treats animals as incitements for the boys' self-preservationist instincts.[66] The prominence of firearms sheds light on the extent to which the BSA was steeped in the nation's gun culture. Proficiency in rifle shooting had been part of the organization's merit badge program since 1916, and *Boys' Life* opened its columns to gun companies looking to sell their products to young consumers. Slogans such as "Every boy should learn to shoot" and "Real men grow up from boys who know how to handle a rifle" propagated the idea that marksmanship was masculine education at its best.[67] Engaging in this practice in British East Africa, Dick, Doug, and Dave furthered the notion espoused by such advertisements that hunting animals in moderation was no blood sport but a fun exercise beneficial to the physical and psychological toughening of young American males.

The episode that inspired the boldest headlines was that each teenager got to shoot a lion. Emplotment amplified the climactic nature of the lion hunt: its central location in the narrative makes it the culmination of prior events as well as the threshold to a new stage of maturation. The pivotal moment when Douglas Oliver killed a lion came to life in short, apodictic sentences, creating the atmosphere of a life-changing confrontation with unbridled primitivism: "At last [the lion] was ready to charge. For a mark to shoot at, there was his head. It was a shot pretty hard to miss. Yet Doug was so excited that he missed his first shot, the bullet going high. In the second, the time spent in reloading, Doug must have felt as if the weight of the whole world was on his back. He aimed again for the angry lion's head and shot. This time the old fellow disappeared into the grass. . . . It was a scary moment." Trepidation gave way to celebration when the lion was found dead. In camp, the Johnsons' native servants performed an indigenous initiatory rite on Doug to mark his passage to

Figure 2.1. Robert Dick Douglas, Douglas Oliver, and David Martin pose with two dead lions in the Serengeti, July or August 1928. With them are Osa Johnson and a native guide. (Courtesy of the Martin and Osa Johnson Safari Museum, Chanute, Kansas)

manhood. They carried the triumphant Scout on their shoulders and held a war dance in his honor. After Doug's "prize head" was cut off, salted, and preserved for the trip home, the boys enjoyed the coconut pie that Osa had baked for the occasion. By defeating, consuming, and overcoming primitivism, the Boy Scouts, according to Hall's recapitulation theory, were advancing to a higher rung on the ladder of civilization.[68]

Framed as Darwinist spectacles with a happy ending, the lion hunts possessed significant symbolic power. In vanquishing the "King of Beasts," the Boy Scouts rid themselves of childish weakness and looked into a majestic future. "Out there it's every man for himself," David Martin boasted; "with a high-powered rifle and a supply of steel bullets, I felt as safe as if I was holidaying at home."[69] The Scouts' performance of masculine fitness turned them into leading representatives of their organization. It reified a cultural hierarchy of youth unfavorable toward nonwhite, non-scouting, and female adolescents, whom the BSA portrayed as physically soft and morally inferior. Praising the Scouts' unflinching courage in the face of danger—the boys reportedly survived several lion attacks while spending one night behind iron bars in the rear of a truck—the organization presented such acts of juvenile bravery as a pipeline to leadership. Martin Johnson outlined a glorious future for the youngsters under his tutelage. For him, Dick, Doug, and Dave were perfect ambassadors of "competent young manhood" who left "a fine impression of the real American boy." Johnson added that he had never been "more proud" of his country than when seeing the Scouts act out their survival skills in a foreign wilderness.[70]

In the absence of their parents, the youths crisscrossing the African savannah developed a close relationship with their mentors. The Johnsons, one of the youths remembered, "practically adopted" them as their own children.[71] For self-confident Osa, this meant retreating into the traditional gender role of the housewife-mother occupied with domestic chores such as washing clothes and cooking dinner after an arduous day in the outdoors. One photograph printed in the Scouts' book shows Osa listening attentively to David Martin as he teaches her how to shoot a gun, obscuring the fact that Osa was quite adept at handling a rifle.[72] At once a surrogate father and older brother, Martin Johnson was to not only guarantee the boys' safety and attest to their development but also ensure that the initiation drama stayed within defined parameters. This was no easy undertaking since the trigger-happy behavior exhibited by Dick, Doug, and Dave stood in an uneasy relationship with the ideals of efficiency and propriety central to respectable self-making in America's postwar business and media environments. At one point, Johnson reprimanded Dick Douglas for giving free rein to his "savage" instincts. The Eagle Scout had brought his bow and arrows along, eager to hunt down a lion in pseudo-Indian fashion. Dick's shot only resulted in a flesh wound, and the howls of the wounded animal so upset Johnson that he prohibited arrow shooting for the rest of the safari.[73]

Johnson's intervention was part of an effort to minimize the use of violence and propagate a boyish middle-class masculinity in which multiple facets blended together: the professional and the primitive, the urbane and the rough, the playful and the restrained. Although the Johnsons played along with the dominant view that lions were brutal creatures undeserving of mercy, their primary commitment was to training youth in a form of wildlife management where violence was hedged in by a larger administrative rationality. Natural resource conservation and ecological diversity, which had become an ideological staple for the BSA, replaced big-game hunting in providing the justification for killing supposedly ruthless carnivores.[74] If left unchecked, Johnson warned, these big cats with their "murderous propensities" would spend their "whole lifetime killing innocent wild game and once in a while assassinating a human being."[75] There was little awareness that humans had been projecting human traits onto animals for centuries, and that human intrusiveness had caused greater harm to the environment than carnivore instincts. Instead, shooting a limited number of lions for the sake of population control while avoiding excessive carnage was justified as the right thing to do.

It is impossible to say whether the boys internalized their mentor's teachings. The swagger the boys displayed back in the United States suggests a more complicated story. Talking to a journalist, Douglas Oliver bragged that he had felt "pretty grown up" putting a bullet into the lion's head. At the same time, Johnson's rhetoric had rubbed off to some extent. All admitted later how Osa and Martin Johnson's compassionate posture toward animals had impressed them.[76] Whites who were massacring game for money were heavily criticized. At the end of the book, as the boys leave the Serengeti, the narrator sadly notes: "All morning we saw no game. It isn't very plentiful here because it has all been shot out."[77] This conservationist streak surfaces throughout the book, which Putnam's people likely edited to ensure that its protagonists were cast as chivalric defenders of helpless mammals threatened by ravenous beasts and greedy hunters. "We certainly had no pity for [the lion] because of its cruelty. But at the same time, we had no dislike," stated the narrator as the safari was coming to a close, indicating that the lion hunt had evolved from a boyish test of courage to a middle-class morality tale.[78] In the same vein, Johnson quoted Dick Douglas saying after the last shot had been fired: "Well, that's over with. Now we can photograph in peace."[79]

Emphasizing how the Scouts learned to exercise restraint and good manners while simultaneously conquering their fear, Johnson's sanitized representation of the safari makes the intertextual alliance between his published recollections and the boys' initiation narrative complete. These stories worked in tandem to promote continuity in good masculine practice from one generation to the next. Upward mobility in the dawning corporatist age, they insinuated, did not come through brute force but through controlled aggression, respect for authority, and adaptability to different social and geographical environments. This educational performance lay at the heart of the U.S. Boy Scouts' trip to the veldts of East Africa, one that was capable of accommodating young people's desire for border-crossing adventure along with the BSA's portrayal of young males as fearless and energetic yet dependent on adult oversight.

A similar intergenerational compact undergirded Paul Siple's quest for imperial manhood. Richard Byrd was to the nineteen-year-old Eagle Scout what Martin Johnson was to Dick, Doug, and Dave. Reminiscent of the narrative pattern of the heroic monomyth, Paul embarked on the road of trials with an authoritative father figure whose approval he needed to complete the initiation. Siple consented to his role as the willing apprentice. Finding in Byrd the characteristics of an "ideal Scout" and leader of men, he followed the admiral with unconditional loyalty.[80] Then again, Siple's relationship with Byrd was subject to a particular set of challenges. Siple was four years older than the Scouts dispatched to Africa, raising expectations as to what he should be able to accomplish. The expedition to Antarctica was riskier than the African safari, as it lasted nearly two years. It also lacked the familial intimacy of the Johnson safari because Siple had to position himself within a more diverse group of men and masculinities. Siple's diary and correspondence open a larger window on the struggles that grew out of his project of self-making and allow for a more detailed investigation of the constellations of age, gender, and male privilege through which he moved.

Press releases acclaimed the Eagle Scout's cheerful endurance as he battled his way through the ice. The major newspaper in Erie, Pennsylvania, carried reports of how Siple survived a killer whale attack and participated in a rescue operation to save a team member who got lost in a blizzard.[81] Private exchanges, on the other hand, paint a much more ambivalent picture of Siple's journey to young manhood. They reveal how worried his superiors were that the expedition could fail at any moment. Although Siple was conscious of the staged character of his rite of passage, adults repeatedly urged him to stay on mission. Scoutmaster H. R. Spencer from Erie wrote Siple and advised him to avoid frivolous behavior by exercising and keeping his "physical shape 100%."[82] BSA executive Malcolm Douglas, who warned that "life at sea brings out the weak points in a man's character," likened the expedition to a monumental test of will that would spur the youth's masculinization.[83] James West reminded the Eagle Scout unequivocally that the eyes of the whole world rested on him, and that his failure would be judged "as the failure of the Boy Scout Movement."[84] Constituting a form of long-distance surveillance, these admonitions illustrate the organizers' fears that Siple might become embroiled in situations that would disrupt the equation of scouting with impeccable young manhood.

Those fears had a base in reality. While adult leaders publicly hailed Siple's conduct, his Protestant middle-class morality was oddly misplaced in the rough and rowdy realm of seafaring. Siple resented the smoking, drinking, and cursing that characterized mariner masculinity. He cringed at the obscenities in a "seaman's vocabulary" and was disappointed to see the ship's captain lose his temper in a squabble with the first mate.[85] Alcohol flowed freely, much to the chagrin of the prohibitionist Eagle Scout. Siple more than once expressed disgust at the conduct around him. Commenting on a drinking spree on board the *City of New York*, Siple noted drily that the men were "not such a bad lot" when sober. During a shore leave in Panama, he anticipated, "those fellows will likely all come back drunk. They did."[86] Some mariners indulged in prostitution, another seafarer practice that the Eagle Scout abhorred. Siple disliked the idea of having sex with the same sternness with which he refused alcohol. His abstinence may have earned him the respect of the BSA authorities but did little to endear him to the bulk of the men. Many reacted with mild sarcasm. When one sailor predicted how the expedition team would look twenty-five years later, he mocked Siple, saying, "Just the same old Paul, unmarred by the years in his clean speech and habits."[87] A journalist accompanying the expedition described Siple as isolated, almost lonely. "He worked hard, kept his mouth shut, listened without comment to the ribaldry that went on about him, and never took part in it."[88] Locating their manhood in hard work, a coarse sociolect, the consumption of liquor, and a boisterous sexuality, rank-and-file members of the crew interpreted Siple's refusal to participate in their male rituals as a sign of childishness, not maturity.

How did Siple cope with the misrecognition he experienced? His responses varied, veering from vilification to denunciation. Wagging the finger at the plebeian culture of ordinary sailors was central to Siple's construction of a masculine hierarchy where discipline and self-restraint were presented as pathways to authority and prestige. The inability to control bodily urges signaled primitivism and the inability to lead. However, the class arrogance and religious bias that informed Siple's definition of the gentleman adventurer also betrayed a great deal of insecurity. When he did not spout off about the demeanor of others, he ingratiated himself with his superiors. Gaining his elders' recognition was a constant concern for the youth, who read every nod in his direction as a sign that he was acquiring masculine capital. After hearing the first mate say that he never saw him idle, Siple confided to his diary: "I swelled up inside at that. Boy! When I know they realize I am doing my best I'll put every ounce of energy in I have." Each word of praise remedied his self-diagnosed "inferiority complex," which likely was a result of other expedition members questioning his manhood.[89] Since Byrd's judgment mattered most, Siple reached out at every opportunity for distinction granted by the admiral. Byrd told the Eagle Scout to take care of the sled dogs and appointed him the expedition's zoologist, whose main assignment was to hunt, dissect, and study penguins, which earned him the unflattering nickname "Penguin Paul."[90] No matter how much Siple begged the admiral to let him go on reconnaissance missions with the other men, Byrd withheld his permission. The commander likely feared the negative press if something happened to his young orderly. Still, Siple

Figure 2.2. Paul Siple in winter explorer gear. This promotional photo was taken in 1933 prior to Siple's second trip to Antarctica. (Courtesy of the National Archives, College Park, Maryland)

reported back to BSA headquarters, "I feel that even as I entered as a boy, I have gained already a bit higher place," glossing over the teasing he endured and the humiliation he felt when his ambitions were not satisfied.[91]

Where ingratiation failed, denunciation set in. The conflict between mariner and Scout manhood came to a head in February 1930. The altercation was triggered by one of the countless drinking bouts with which participants battled the boredom of holding out long stretches in the cold and cramped quarters of Little America. Tensions were hard to defuse in a band of adventurers that were "quite a heterogeneous group," as one veteran put it, with some men openly resenting one another.[92] Siple and his fellow abstainers had complained that the nightly parties deprived them of sleep, but the parties did not stop. In a confidential letter addressed to Byrd, the youth accused the revelers of jeopardizing the entire expedition.[93] In pointing out alleged misdemeanor, Siple acted not only as a Scout but as a member of the Loyal Legion, a secret fraternity Byrd had formed after reaching Antarctica to stifle disobedience and mutinous behavior.[94] Glazed with attributes such as brotherhood, loyalty, and honor, Byrd's moral task force was an easy sell to an Eagle Scout. Siple took the invitation to join as further proof of his privileged status. He did not see the admiral's intelligence service for what it actually was: an instrument to entrench the power of a few men at the expense of their subordinates. The intervention of Siple and the teetotalers had the desired effect. A conference was held, and the "rum ring" was dissolved. Byrd ordered that the remaining alcohol be dumped.[95] Siple, meanwhile, had become complicit in the exercise of an imperial masculinity requiring teamwork and hierarchical subordination, on the one hand, and the suppression of practices that were treated as a threat to the dominant order, on the other.

Neither the dullness of the long polar nights nor the altercations in Little America wound up in Siple's book. This was less a conscious decision made by the author than the result of the censorship policies pursued by top BSA executives. "You would not want anything to get out that would do any hurt to the expedition or to Scouting," Publicity Director Frank N. Robinson exhorted the Eagle Scout after he had blasted his comrades for their loose morals in one of his letters.[96] Robinson and West had no interest in portraying Siple's Antarctic adventure as anything but an uplifting, trouble-free saga of a brotherly band of heroic explorers raising the flag of young America on one of the globe's last unconquered spots. What became available for popular consumption was a bowdlerized account of an ideal Scout who completed the passage to supreme manhood with flying colors and, to quote from Byrd's preface to the book, "went South with us as a Boy Scout—but . . . took his place as a man."[97] In the case of Siple's performance and that of the three Boy Scouts who went to Africa, there was no discussion of gender troubles or unwanted youthful initiative. Only the kind of intergenerational father-son romance that prescribed certain ways of imagining and acting in the world was found acceptable. Subordinate masculinities were either silenced or reduced to stereotyped extras.

Colonial Tutorials

Marketed as tales of white pluck in an unforgiving wilderness, the expeditions also worked as didactic pieces about the place of youth in international and interimperial relations. Adult geopolitical foundations informed the Scouts' national, international, and colonial imaginaries. The world the youths set out to explore and discover anew for their generation was no tabula rasa but a tumultuous arena of great power rivalries, cultural exchange, economic competition, and anticolonial resistance. Moving through this world, Siple, Douglas, Martin, and Oliver did more than imitate the internationalism and imperialism of their elders. They created their own youthful variations of these concepts.

In the tradition of the Western explorer, asserting mastery over nature frequently went hand in hand with the construction of racial difference.[98] By depicting colonial landscapes as alternately primitive or pristine, white travel writers produced knowledge about indigenous peoples that emphasized their cultural distance to Euro-American civilization and thus their essential otherness. Rather than their invisibility, it was their perceived inability to transform nature and master modern technology that marked colonial populations as inferior. The absence of Western institutions in these regions provided the rationale for penetrating and "civilizing" large parts of the globe. The four Boy Scouts were heirs to this ideology, although the colonial gaze they employed spoke less of racial inequality and imperial coercion than of curious youths measuring their manhood in encounters with other races.

A playful approach to questions of empire and racial difference permeates the official narrative of Dick, Doug, and Dave's dealings with Africans. Placed in an anticlimactic fashion between the hunting episodes, the Scouts' interactions with Kenyan and Tanzanian workers hired by the Johnsons offered comic relief. Instead of figuring as autonomous individuals, the natives were referred to as "boys," which limited their space of action to pleasing and entertaining their white bosses.[99] This appellation was no egalitarian gesture but denigrated the black servants, whose adulthood was denied, to a rank below that of the Scouts, even though many of the workers were married and had children. The Scouts frequently made fun of their native companions. They ridiculed Suka, the overseer, dubbing him "black Napoleon" for the way he folded his arms and guarded the tents. They enjoyed the dancing of the sixty-year-old cook, O'Sani, whom they likened to a "monkey on a stick." Racist stereotypes such as joviality and idleness traditionally ascribed to African Americans were freely transposed onto sub-Saharan Africans. When the Scouts fooled around, the natives were portrayed as going along with a great sense of humor, always responding to the boys' pranks with deferential smiles. In a supposedly light moment, Dick, Doug, and Dave "taught" Mogo, one of the young workers, to be a Boy Scout by dressing him up as one. The "good Scout grin," they jokingly noted, "came natural to him." O'Sani was said to be "happy as a baby with a new toy" when the Scouts gave him a rubber poncho.[100] The possibility of mimicry, a strategy employed by the colonized to disrupt imperial authority by aping white behavior, was beyond the narrators' imagination.[101] Lacking the gravity of adult colonial encounters, humor and play gave the American youths leeway in interacting with racial others and drawing their own conclusions about their evolutionary status. Yet these slapstick passages contained little criticism of adult imperialism. In fact, they rehashed for a juvenile audience the popular belief that Africa was inhabited by half-clad, half-witted savages residing in a state of eternal childhood.

The process by which the Boy Scouts positioned themselves vis-à-vis the dominant ideology on race and empire once more reveals the duality of youth: on the one hand, young people were seen as capable of relating to the world with an undiluted gaze. On the other hand, their status was that of liminal citizens, as incomplete persons that needed to evolve into fully grown adults with rights and responsibilities. Dick's, Doug's, and Dave's age may have permitted them to enter into less formal relations with colonized subjects. It also came with the privilege of erring and learning. Initially, the young Americans found it hard to accept the colonial norm of delegating all menial labor to African servants. Their eagerness to show off their outdoor skills and set up their tents in Scout fashion elicited the following rebuke from Martin Johnson: "You are in Africa now. The White Man hunts and travels and explores while the native does the camp work."[102] Eventually, the boys' aspirations to advance to a higher stage of manhood compelled them to embrace the imperial logic of proving one's superiority over supposedly substandard men.

Racialization and infantilization worked together to set the Boy Scouts apart from the natives. In a staged archery contest, Dick Douglas outshot experienced Masai warriors, thereby underscoring that he was prepared to take on the white man's burden. The subtext was that boys so trained were eligible for positions of power and influence, while African men kept lingering in primitive circumstances. Dick took pride in beating the Masai on their turf, disregarding the fact that target shooting was not common practice in tribal East Africa.[103] Adult commentators, too, were gleeful about the Boy Scouts' performance. "There was no native feat of skill," Osa Johnson recalled, "at which the youngsters did not prove more efficient."[104] The story caught the attention of the national press, inspiring the *New York Times* to write such headlines as "Boy Scouts Show Craft in Africa" and "Fifteen-Year-Old Lads Outshoot Natives with the Bow and Arrow."[105] Stanley Hall's prescription for adolescence, which held that young males had to triumph over primitivism to attain civilized manhood, still made for good press in the 1920s.

Far from being the great equalizer, the insertion of youth into colonial constellations perpetuated the notion of unbridgeable racial differences. Assumptions of youthful innocence reinforced the notion that the colonized had forfeited these qualities after mixing with superior races—an assessment that the Scouts themselves echoed. Exploring the U.S. quasi colony of Panama, Siple juxtaposed the productivity of the American occupiers with the destitution of Colón's mixed-race population. Appalled by the crowded city quarters and filthy streets, he wondered how anybody but the lowliest "negroe[s]" could live in such "foul air."[106] Similarly, the Safari Scouts sniffed at the tribal Africans' lack of sanitation, labeling them "ugly, smelly people."[107] Such representations of non-white squalor must be read against the characterizations and self-characterizations of Scout cleanliness that pervade the travel narratives. Martin Johnson had nothing but praise for the manners of the Scouts under his supervision. "Three more polite, clean, and clear thinking boys could not have been sent," he wrote.[108] Later in life, Robert Dick Douglas recounted an instance of cross-imperial learning where one Scottish traveler had taught him the relationship between outer appearance and imperial authority:

> Every evening, when all the rest of us and the other passengers were groaning about the heat, the Scottish gentleman appeared at dinner in a tuxedo. . . . He told us that when he first came to Africa years ago, he learned that the white European must always maintain, however difficult[,] the symbol of his position in life. He told us of other Europeans who had gone to Africa, spending months or years alone among the African natives, and succumbing little by little to the heat, the flies, and the constant appeal of "Why dress up when there is no one here to see you?" Finally, such persons saw no point in shaving, no reason to bathe, and before long, even the natives sensed that such a European had lost all personal pride. . . . Somehow, his comments made a great impression on me.[109]

Ritual ensured power in a hierarchical society—from the ritual of following the dress code of the dominant culture to that of carrying a gun among a people armed with spears. Underperforming on these expectations, David Martin stated in an interview, would embolden the natives to challenge the established order. "White men must show the native that he has a code of honor." If the explorer allows his skills to become rusty, Martin added, "his prestige begins to wane at once."[110] Learning about how to demonstrate imperial competence in the presence of deficient yet furtive colonial subjects reminded the boys of their obligations as future citizens of an aspiring world power.

Of course, cleanliness was no mere physical category. The global frontier imagined by the Scouts and their mentors was above all moral in nature. The youths confronted stark choices about themselves in the borderlands of Africa and Antarctica. It is apt to speak of a rite of passage because crossing frontiers meant a process of self-discovery and self-making as well as initiation into a superior masculine status. The true ordeal consisted of enacting a certain set of norms in the face of overwhelming deviation from these norms. The U.S. Scouts proved worthy of imperial manhood because they stayed "clean" while other sojourners were succumbing to vice. One day, Martin Johnson chased off a group of stylish native girls who had become too familiar with the camp personnel. For him, these East African counterparts of the "modern flapper" were "full of the devil" and a menace to innocent white boyhood.[111] Siple's colonial gaze criminalized and sexualized indigenous cultures in the same way. Locals trafficking in alcohol and sex overshadowed the natural splendor of places such as Panama, Tahiti, and Rapa Nui. In Siple's accounts, disease-carrying and morally depraved islanders willing to sell their wives and daughters for money signaled degeneracy writ large.[112] The Eagle Scout viewed prostitution as a perfidious form of emasculation. Only men strong enough to resist carnal temptations could be entrusted with higher tasks. Siple underscored his asceticism at every turn, flaunting his sexual abstinence as masculine capital. Asked by a reporter whether he had a sweetheart waiting for him at home, Siple replied that he had "the highest regard and admiration for nice girls" but had "never thought much about being in love, being busy with other things."[113] Like the empire builders who valued scouting, Siple articulated a close correlation between a young man's ability to subdue his sexual urges and his ability to help bring the planet's last unconquered spots of wilderness into the orbit of civilization.

Individual development and national destiny were inextricably linked in these expeditions. As emissaries of an uncorrupted adolescence, Siple and the Safari Scouts projected an image of youth that was markedly different from the culturally transgressive youth culture of the 1920s, which contemporaries had begun to associate with the United States. Instead of marveling at teenagers who sought self-realization in frivolous consumption, the world was introduced to model youths who were consorting with famous explorers far away from home. This synthesis of boyhood and manhood demonstrated to other empires the credentials of a young America that stayed pure even as it was becoming more powerful. Europeans surely recognized the colonial vocabulary attached to the polar expedition: it was no coincidence that the explorers named their station Little America, which evoked the drama of nineteenth-century pioneers establishing outposts on the North American frontier. English, French, and German audiences could detect similar parallels in the award-winning movie *With Byrd at the South Pole: The Story of Little America*, which won the Oscar for Best Cinematography in 1930. Moreover, Boy Scouts the world over could read about the frontier exploits of their American peers in national and international Scout magazines.[114]

From this widened perspective, it becomes clear that the BSA's interwar adventure tours and the coming-of-age stories they inspired worked in two directions. Domestically, they were supposed to buttress the cultural containment of a more promiscuous and expressive generation of youth. Internationally, they claimed a rightful place for America's boy-men in the family of empires. The goal was not so much to train the nation's boys in the art of military-style colonial invasion but to make sure that the sons of Europe's elites treated them as equals, that young American manhood was capable of going head to head with the regimented youths of other developed nations. The Boy Scout movement offered the perfect venue for this kind of imperial internationalism.[115] A sphere of cooperation and competition, global scouting facilitated the transnational circulation of imperial knowledge even as it remained organized along national lines. Siple's mailbag burst with notes of admiration from fellow Scouts from the English-speaking world. In November 1928, as the *City of New York* was reprovisioning in Dunedin, New Zealand, the harbor was studded with Boy Scouts waiting to catch a glimpse of Siple. Mindful of his ambassadorial role, Siple used his popularity with foreign youth to present his journey as an expression of international Scout brotherhood.[116] The same sentiment emanated from the BSA-sanctioned account of Dick, Doug, and Dave's stopover in Paris. Treated like foreign dignitaries, the Safari Scouts spent time with French Boy Scouts, shook hands with Marshall Foch, and met the U.S. ambassador to France.[117] Although the off-the-cuff remarks they made when talking to the press lacked the tact of professional diplomats—the teenagers told a reporter that an "American city" would never "tolerate so much dirt" as they saw in France—the attention they attracted exemplified America's growing influence in early twentieth-century Europe.[118] In this advance, youth itself was in the vanguard.

Homecomings

In most rites of passage, the moment of return is no quiet occasion. It marks the young hero's reincorporation into the community after he has proved himself worthy of their admiration. The purpose of such initiation rites is twofold: to solidify the improved social status of the postliminal subject and to grant him the power to renew society at the same time.[119] The way in which the Scouts' homecoming was orchestrated could have been taken directly out of anthropologist Arnold van Gennep's playbook. Before Dick, Doug, and Dave reunited with their parents, they ran into a swarm of cameras and newspapermen. Publicity connoisseurs George Putnam and James West arranged meetings with the press and kept the boys on a tight schedule, demanding that they hand in a first draft of the book before school started. A series of speaking engagements at schools and civic clubs of the Rotary type ensued, sealing the Safari Scouts' role as poster boys of an organization dedicated to regenerating imperial manhood.[120] Selling more than 125,000 copies in its first year of publication, *Three Boy Scouts in Africa* received flattering reviews. One young reader liked the book because "it showed vigor and a youthful point" and was "one of the very few books written from a Boy Scout's attitude."[121]

Americans gave Siple an even more rousing welcome. After being showered with confetti in a Broadway motorcade in honor of Byrd, Siple returned to his starstruck hometown of Erie, Pennsylvania. Siple's parents, West, and a delegation of the nation's finest Eagle Scouts escorted him. Fifteen thousand people attended the homecoming ceremony in a football stadium, where Siple presented a flag flown over the South Pole to the mayor. Not since the end of World War I had Erie's citizens thronged the streets in such numbers.[122] Enthusiasm for Siple was not confined to northern Pennsylvania. Vice President Charles Curtis and members of the U.S. Senate paid homage in writing. A grueling itinerary took the celebrity Scout, who was awarded the Congressional Medal of Honor, to big cities and small towns all across the country. Community leaders basked in Siple's fame, hailing his service as an inspiration to the nation's youth. Many hoped that his popularity would help the Boy Scouts survive financially in a time of economic gloom. Businesses, too, tried to cash in on the Siple craze, using his name to advertise their products.[123] Youths of various ages streamed to Siple's lectures about his Antarctic adventures, claiming Siple as a hero of their own. Boys who had grown up in the 1920s, one close friend of Siple recollected, "could never forget Paul Siple, the Boy Scout with Byrd. They had in youth loved the thought that a youngster, about their own age," had mastered the craft of exploring more quickly than most adults.[124]

The idolization of Siple exemplifies how hegemonic ideas about youth and gender were manufactured and upheld. Obviously, very few of the boys who saw in Siple and the Safari Scouts exemplars of young manhood had the ability or resources to reenact their feats. Yet the unobtainability of certain rewards did not make these feats less attractive. In fact, mass consent and compliance based on the hope of receiving at least some of the benefits of belonging to the dominant group are vital components in the construction of hegemonic gender norms. Boy Scouts and scoutmasters across the United States gained a sense of social importance from identifying with Siple. Daniel Carter Beard called him a hero of the Lindbergh type, and West bragged that Siple's story was inspiring boys the world over.[125] Nobody expressed this imaginary kinship better than Long Island scoutmaster August Horowitz, who assured Siple that "one million Scouts" had been making the trip with him.[126] At the behest of local troop leaders, the young polar explorer visited summer camps and gave motivational speeches to Boy Scouts and potential recruits about how scouting made better citizens. Scouts responded reverently to the young explorer. They packed halls and flocked to campfires to catch a glimpse of their idol. Press photos show Siple presenting awards to awestruck Eagle Scouts.[127] A Boy Scout newsletter out of Atlanta captures the enthusiasm Siple stirred among his peers: "Paul Siple's visit to the Region has been a tremendous success. At Greensboro, Winston-Salem, High Point, and Cherokee Councils united in a Camp Rally attended by hundreds of Scouts and friends. At Raleigh and Durham Paul spoke to Service Clubs, over the radio, was officially received by Governor Gardner of North Carolina, and at Camp Graggy. Over a hundred folks stayed throughout a heavy rainstorm to hear him. . . . At Wilmington Camp Chickagami Paul was royally received by the entire camp and many friends. At Atlanta Paul spent most of the day at Camp Bert Adams and was feted by hundreds of Scouts and friends."[128] A group of Pennsylvania boys needed no extra encouragement: they started a troop and called themselves "Siple Scouts."[129] Though it is impossible to measure the extent to which Siple's popularity translated into new members for the BSA, the cult of personality that developed around Siple constituted a powerful force for social integration while crowding out alternative ideas of boyhood development.

Public spectacle was pivotal to Siple's transformation into a character that exuded unspent masculine energy replete with the innocence of youth. A professionally managed media campaign in which BSA officials were pulling the strings left the Eagle Scout with little room to maneuver. Siple rarely visited camp dedications, attended honor banquets, or delivered radio address without first receiving advice from BSA headquarters.[130] Information control was a top priority for the organization. Public relations strategists wanted the Eagle Scout to address friendly crowds only. Even though the constant traveling and heavy speaking load took a toll on his health and impinged on his college performance, Siple submitted to West's patronage with the same fidelity with which he had followed Byrd to the bottom of the world. The BSA's publicity department monitored the production of *A Boy Scout with Byrd*, and West intervened to ensure that ambiguous sentences were deleted.[131] In the end, the book received favorable reviews and was translated into seven languages.[132] What the reviewers did not know was that Siple's narrative, marketed as an all-male venture, had been guided by a female hand: Carol Siple Kettering had proofread and polished the manuscript while her brother rushed from one event to the next.[133] Although Siple, all pretentions to modesty notwithstanding, enjoyed the limelight and the privileges that came with it, the gullibility he exhibited toward BSA authorities contradicted the organization's claim that it was teaching male youth to be self-reliant.

This symbiotic connection between the four Boy Scouts and their organization persisted amid the woes of the Great Depression and beyond. In the summers of 1929 and 1930, before economic predicaments forced the BSA to pull out of the expedition business, Robert Dick Douglas, Douglas Oliver, and David Martin went on a few more adventures. While Dick hunted grizzlies in Alaska and Doug backpacked along the U.S.-Mexican border, Dave was cruising the Caribbean with the noted German navy officer Felix Count von Luckner—a cross-generational partnership that was all the more remarkable because it united a World War I veteran from a former enemy country with a U.S. Boy Scout under the banner of imperial manhood.[134] During the war, Martin's good standing with the BSA secured him a post in the Office of War Information. Paul Siple, too, continued to embody Scout manhood in the nation and beyond. His prominence earned him an invitation to serve as West's aide at the 1937 jamboree in Washington, DC, where he received ovations from U.S. and foreign Scouts alike.[135] He returned to Antarctica twice before the United States entered World War II—trips that paved the way for his future career as the country's paramount polar expert. Best known for establishing a permanent American presence in the South Pole and representing U.S. interests in the international Antarctic Treaty of 1959, Siple lent his scientific knowledge to designing clothing for soldiers engaged in winter combat.[136] As they climbed up the professional ladder (Siple and Oliver in science, Douglas in law, and Martin in public service), the former Scouts maintained close ties to the organization that had put them in the spotlight, reaping the rewards—material and immaterial—of having performed in their teens the spectacle of a youthful imperial masculinity.

Bearing the imprint of the period's innovations in the sciences, technology, mass media, and consumer culture, the Scout expeditions to Antarctica and Africa in the late 1920s warrant attention not merely for the spotlight they put on the ambitions and struggles of small groups of boys and men, but for the broader cultural work they performed. When disputes over the meaning of boyhood, manhood, and empire in a society fractured along the lines of class, gender, race, and age intensified, the Boy Scouts of America held up a picture of intergenerational conformity over how to make young men. The cultivation of good citizenship and the construction of young masculinities through a strict regime of adolescent development was no local affair. Creating a band of representative youths and casting them as heirs to a hardy manhood in imperial borderlands soothed domestic anxieties and glazed expansionist ventures with references to boyish play and developmental adventure. Of course, the behavior of many youngsters continued to cut across such patterns of identification as they entered the adult world with values that were quite different from those epitomized by Siple and the Safari Scouts. Nonetheless, the BSA's passages to an imagined global frontier rooted the organization more firmly in the nation's consciousness as a movement with a unique competence in fostering collaborative relationships between men and boys.

Chapter 3

A Junior League of Nations

Campfire Diplomacy at the World Jamborees

Flush from the victory in World War I, many Americans found internationalism a dirty word. The mere mention of the term was enough to drive Daniel Carter Beard up the wall. Talk about giving up sovereignty in exchange for vague notions of world peace, Beard seethed in April 1920, was nothing but "insidious foreign propaganda" designed to corrode the country's "national cohesion and spirit." Beard's Americanism, like that of the majority of his compatriots who had seen the doughboys march off to the trenches, was markedly anti-European. Why trust a continent, they asked, that had started a heinous war, bred communist revolutions, and now seemed bent on dragging the United States into a system of global governance? Conservative criticism of the League of Nations was unmistakably gendered. Anti-League Senator William Borah opposed U.S. entry into that body, which he denounced as "a distinct effort to sterilize nationalism." Submitting to the internationalist faction, Beard warned, would sap national virility and move the country away from George Washington to an opaque Wilsonian world order.[1]

Curiously, the same men who equated the rise of internationalist sentiment with effeminacy were quite content with seeing their sons join a league of a different sort. This "Junior League of Nations," or "League of Youth" as contemporaries dubbed it, had no treaty-making powers.[2] Statesmen had no say in it. Rather, these metaphors describe the postwar creation of a transnational fraternity of boys and men who had found a common bond in scouting. The Boy Scouts' Junior League emerged from carefully choreographed peace festivals in the form of multinational summer camps that became known as the world jamborees. What started in 1920 as an indoor pageant of Boy Scouts of various nationalities expanded into mass open-air rallies held almost every four years until World War II. Although the Scout organizations of the British Empire were a dominant force at the outset, Boy Scouts from continental Europe, Latin America, China, Japan, and the United States turned these gatherings into a global spectacle. Apart from a multitude of smaller national and continental jamborees that convened with varying frequency, the interwar years witnessed five major international Scout festivals: 1920 in London; 1924 in Ermelunden, Denmark; 1929 at Arrowe Park, England; 1933 in Gödöllö, Hungary; and 1937 in the Netherlands at Vogelenzang. At their pre-Depression peak in August 1929, the world jamborees attracted up to fifty thousand participants and countless visitors from over seventy countries.[3]

Unlike the League of Nations, its youthful equivalent was immensely popular in the United States. Although the BSA sent only a tiny fraction of its boys to the world jamborees, many more wanted to go. The federal government provided logistical assistance. Local service clubs sponsored entire troops. The young delegates, most of them decorated Eagle Scouts, were hailed by presidents, mayors, church leaders, and business executives. Their smiling faces appeared on film, and their names and pictures filled newspapers across the country. On their return, the boys spoke at Lions, Kiwanis, Chambers of Commerce, and Rotary meetings. How can the public support for these cross-border youth festivals during a period in U.S. history when many Americans supposedly grew wary of taking part in faraway events be explained? The jamborees may have lacked the gravity of official diplomacy, yet the campfire diplomacy practiced during these two-week encampments articulated lofty aspirations for peace and international understanding. This begs the question what it was that made the jamborees less suspect in the eyes of nationalists like Beard, and worth pursuing in the eyes of their proponents.

This chapter investigates the BSA's presence at the world jamborees between the wars. It dissects the perceptions, exchanges, and experiences of the young U.S. Scouts and their adult leaders who journeyed to these sites, and examines public responses to these crossings. It illuminates the transnational networking of U.S. scoutmasters; probes the jamborees' gendered peace messages; analyzes performances of youth, masculinity, and nationhood on a global stage; and follows individual Scouts on their voyages across the Atlantic. In doing so, the chapter pays special attention to concepts of the "national," "international," and "global" that were forged in scouting's imagined community of world youth, both by the organizers and by the boys themselves.

U.S. involvement in transnational scouting after 1918, I argue, spoke not only to the changing nature of international relations but also to the changing meaning of youth. A more mobile, more diverse, and well-organized cohort of young people traversed borders to interact with their distant peers in growing numbers and shorter intervals. These transnational exchanges were encouraged by various parties since many had come to believe that youth represented a uniquely idealistic life stage. Youth were found to be politically and culturally impressionable but were also perceived as less encumbered by the past and less likely to succumb to the antipathies of their elders. The horrific casualties wrought by World War I, nationalist resentments, and economic volatility eroded public confidence in government, leading people to suggest that young people may be better equipped to solve the world's problems.[4]

Although these youth encounters were endorsed by the state, the Boy Scouts and their leaders presented their campfire diplomacy in favorable contrast to official foreign policy. Touted as a less cynical and more authentic alternative to professional diplomacy, transnational scouting fed on prolonged cooperation across the double breach of nation and generation. Organizers of different backgrounds saw in youth potent vessels of reform. The characteristics they associated with male youth—vigor, malleability, purity, to name a few—became powerful discursive tools for the rehabilitation of old elites, who sought to relieve themselves of the burden of responsibility for war and mass destruction. Initiating boys into the duties of postwar citizenship, the world jamborees also offered a reverse rite of passage for men looking to propel themselves back into the carefree realm of boyhood.

Historians of scouting tend to separate the movement's early history into a prewar imperial phase and a postwar internationalist phase, but for most Anglophone organizers, embracing internationalism was about transforming empires, not dissolving them.[5] Young people contributed to the revitalization of imperial networks by making their time, bodies, and enthusiasm available to them. Working with adults, Boy Scouts projected youthful national and imperial identities and a fraternal masculinity cast in the reciprocal language of brotherhood. This chapter tells the story of American boys at the world jamborees as a tale of two intersecting spaces: one in which adult organizers extracted political and cultural capital from bonding with youth, and one in which young people carved out their own realms of experience.[6]

Examining how U.S. Boy Scouts engaged in cross-generational and cross-cultural interactions at the world jamborees requires situating these interactions in the broader context of interwar internationalism. After the machine guns fell silent in 1918, the webs of migration, commerce, and cultural exchange that had made the world a smaller place thickened again. Aided by innovations in transportation and communication, nonstate actors surged in unprecedented waves onto the global stage. Tourism and sporting events, world fairs and exhibitions, and conferences devoted to issues such as city planning, fair wages, public health, education, international law, women's rights, and pacifism conveyed a growing sense of interconnectedness and interdependency. U.S. citizens, too, traveled abroad more often, but they also lived overseas as businessmen, missionaries, teachers, artists, and diplomats.[7] Although the circulation of people and capital was most intense in the North Atlantic, there was hardly a region of the globe that did not experience an increase in cross-border transactions. Ever more cognizant that governments had no monopoly on foreign relations, ordinary citizens were establishing relationships with a wider world on their own account.

One segment of society, however, often goes unnoticed in the panoply of early twentieth-century internationalism. Individually or as part of adult-led organizations, youth became far less limited to local forms of socializing. Writing letters to foreign pen pals, partaking in student exchanges, and backpacking across continents, young people seized opportunities to experience globality in exciting new ways. Youth were on the move, and those frustrated with those who had pushed the world to the brink of destruction saw in young people transgressing the frontiers of distance and tradition the possibility for a better future. Starting in the early 1920s, commentators on both sides of the Atlantic envisioned a less parochial and more self-actualizing youth as the last hope for a morally bankrupt civilization. Writing for the *Atlantic Monthly*, journalist John F. Carter Jr. remarked: "The older generation had certainly pretty well ruined this world before passing it on [to] us. They give us this Thing, knocked to pieces . . . and then they are surprised that we don't accept it with the same attitude of pretty decorous enthusiasm with which they received it."[8] Statements of generational difference hummed with political implications. James M. Barrie, the Scotsman who authored *Peter Pan*, encapsulated the distrust of age best when he told a group of college freshmen in 1922 to beware of old men like himself: "What is wanted is something run by yourselves. You have more in common with the Youth of other Lands than Youth and Age can ever have with each other."[9] What was needed, one Harvard student declared, was "a League of Youth, whereby all the enthusiasm of young men can be concentrated on the cause of rejuvenating the world."[10]

Youth, however, was no monolithic bloc in the bustling interwar years. Carter's and Barrie's conception of youth as white, middle class, college aged, and male had to vie for hegemony with other formations that were not wedded to a specific place either. Harlem Renaissance invocations of the "New Negro" resonated with race pride and laid the foundation for a youthful black transnationalism.[11] Leftist youth movements, spurred by the era's revolutionary socialism, knit border-crossing ties of their own while filling their ranks with working-class children in defiance of traditional racial and gender sensibilities.[12] Youth was also present in discussions about the "Modern Girl," whose autonomous and flashy lifestyle posed a challenge to patriarchy across the globe.[13] Semantic contestations over what youth was and to whom it belonged added a particular urgency to an old truism: owning youth, demographically and symbolically, meant owning the future.

Brothers and Rivals

Robert Baden-Powell was no stranger to navigating the shifting horizons of youth and globalization. In less than a decade since the publication of *Scouting for Boys*, the Boy Scouts had spread to all four corners of the planet. It was not until 1920, however, that Baden-Powell's efforts to institutionalize global scouting beyond the British imperial sphere bore tangible fruit. Out of the first world jamboree sprang the two other major bodies of global Boy Scouting: the ISC, which set worldwide standards for the movement, and the BSIB. Although countries from all five continents were represented in these institutions, the model of globality they projected was undeniably Eurocentric, if not Anglocentric. Baden-Powell, who had been proclaimed "Chief Scout of the World" at the 1920 Olympia rally in London, put his associate Hubert Martin at the head of the nascent BSIB. The stated purpose of the bureau, which was headquartered in London, was to study the scouting methods of different countries, advise foreign youth workers interested in following the Baden-Powell method of scouting, and review requests from national organizations seeking membership in the world Scout family. Martin also directed the bureau's official periodical, *Jamboree*, a quarterly magazine that appeared in English and French with news from the different national organizations affiliated with the bureau.[14]

Appeals to brotherhood in times of political uncertainty were nothing new under the sun. Speaking the language of cross-border fraternalism, Baden-Powell tried to regain from the rubble of war a sense of imperial purpose. Although the world jamborees radiated the spirit of internationalism, they echoed the longings for white unity that had characterized the British Scout exhibitions of the prewar period.[15] Yet despite the rhetoric of Anglo-American kinship, the initial response of U.S. scouters to the British overtures was rather lukewarm. They had every reason to be cautious. Baden-Powell's "internationalist turn" was less about making the world safe for scouting than about saving the British Empire in a volatile postwar world.[16] Meanwhile, U.S. scouters were awash in a sea of nationalism. Mobilizing America's children in World War I had lent credence to the idea that a youthful America had come to the rescue of an aging and weak Europe, a continent that Beard described as "sick nigh unto death." Now, according to Beard, was not the time to bow to "alien influences" and succumb to the "shrewd intrigues" of foreign powers.[17]

The national scout commissioner might have succeeded in putting his organization on an isolationist course, but a younger, more affluent, and cosmopolitan BSA official turned the tide. Mortimer Schiff saw no conflict between patriotic duty and global engagement. The son of the Jewish German immigrant and financier Jacob Schiff, Mortimer came to the Boy Scouts as a respected Wall Street banker. With his fortune and philanthropic inclinations, Schiff quickly rose to the positions of vice president and president of the BSA, which made him the organization's first non-Protestant top executive.[18] Rather than demonstrating a commitment to ethnic and religious diversity, Schiff's selection as president was indicative of the cultural valorization of a new masculine role model: the internationally respected businessman. At a time when the captains of finance and industry patted each other's backs for making the United States the world's commercial hub, the buckskin romanticism of people like Beard appeared hopelessly outdated. Schiff's business ties to Europe, as well as his diplomatic comportment—he was fluent in English, French, and German—attracted wealthy donors, deflected the rugged provincialism urban elites attributed to the BSA, and promised to enhance the organization's prestige abroad.

As the BSA's ambassador-in-chief, Schiff put his weight behind several diplomatic initiatives. Thanks to Schiff's funding, three hundred handpicked American Boy Scouts led by a small delegation of Scout executives were able to travel to London in 1920. Together with West, Schiff represented the United States at the first ISC, which convened after the bustle of the jamboree.[19] He remained a permanent member of that body until his death in 1931. Back home, Schiff promoted a series of international good turns as chair of the newly founded Committee on Foreign Relations (CFR). Partnering with the American Committee for Devastated France, the CFR opened summer camps in the country's war-torn regions to revive French scouting. Money, uniforms, and Scout literature donated by troops in the United States were shipped to French boys, who reciprocated with gestures of gratitude and friendship.[20] Under Schiff's leadership, the BSA acquired a truly global reach: the recipients of its aid and training initiatives ranged from Armenian children brutalized by war and genocide to Japanese youths recovering from a deadly earthquake.[21] To strengthen the BSA's influence in the western hemisphere, Schiff made several goodwill trips to Latin American countries to support their fledgling Scout organizations.[22] World scouting profited from Schiff's business expertise and talents as a networker. After a generous donation from an American benefactor put the nascent International Scout Bureau on its feet, Schiff made headlines in 1929 for supporting the British Scout Association (BRS) with a check for over ten thousand pounds.[23] When Schiff died from a heart attack two years later, Walter W. Head, another representative of corporate America, filled his shoes.

The politics of philanthropic empire that Schiff and Head were practicing was consistent with the liberal capitalism that the United States had begun to export in the form of civic clubs. Lions and Rotary clubs were instrumental in globalizing a charitable brand of marketplace manhood, creating associational links that stretched from U.S. shopkeepers and bankers to European industrialists and East Asian princes. Boys raised to admire soldiers and generals should now eschew the "extremist politics" that, according to Rotary founder Paul Harris, had led the world into the abyss of war. Harris was convinced that only young men trained in applying the virtues of a socially conscious entrepreneurialism to global politics were capable of building a more peaceful and prosperous future. Turning male youth into "ambassadors of goodwill" became a priority for men who shared Harris's vision.[24] Rotary clubs across the United States sponsored student exchanges and helped cover the travel expenses of jamboree Scouts. Strong ideological and personal ties bound Rotary and the Boy Scouts together. Head, who was active in both fraternities, attributed the success of scouting as a great "character building organization" to the fact that it was run like "a great business organization."[25] International understanding, Schiff believed, would sprout more effectively from the "new masters of industry" trained in the nonpartisan ethics of business.[26]

Scout officials on the other side of the Atlantic viewed the proliferation of this new type of businessman-citizen with a mixture of admiration and abhorrence. British and American organizers interpreted their connections in light of their countries' presumed special relationship. Networks of cooperation and advice connected men from both countries. U.S. scouters studied the literature of their British colleagues and attended their events, and vice versa. American efficiency in youth organizing rarely went unsung by foreign Scout executives who traveled the United States in the 1920s and 1930s. Four years after the war, the BSA already had nearly half a million members on the books, more than double the number of Scouts enrolled in England. Returning from a tour of U.S. Scout camps, Hubert Martin marveled at the BSA's ability to tap a mass market and create a national brand. Canadian scouter John A. Stiles told British headquarters that virtually every American scoutmaster he had met worked "in an atmosphere of perpetual . . . growth."[27] BSA administrators took foreign interest in them as proof that their organization had become a global model. "The desire to look forward to us as the great leaders of Scouting was absolutely genuine, even among the British," boasted railroad tycoon and BSA President Colin H. Livingston after traveling to London in 1920.[28]

But how genuine was that desire really? The possibility of American-style corporate leadership creeping into European Scout associations raised eyebrows. No friend of the professionalization of boy work, French scouter Jacques Guérin-Desjardins, who spoke at an international scouting conference in Switzerland in 1926, threw in West's face that scouting "not only *should be*, but *is* a game."[29] The English concurred. Lord Hampton, after his trip to the United States in 1931, criticized the competitive spirit in American youth work. Boys, he reprimanded, should have fun first and chase badges second.[30] British scouters who visited camps run by the BSA saw no Edwardian gentlemen rearing boys in the spirit of playfulness but what Baden-Powell and Martin considered unimaginative "Parlor Scouts," who mistook careerism for citizenship training.[31] Clashes over the proper relationship of outdoor romance and professionalism were no rarity in Anglo-American scouting. In a heated exchange with Schiff, Martin accused the American of being a number cruncher, unable to see that scouting should be a "movement" led by boymen and not an "organization" run like a machine.[32]

Such anti-American reflexes mirrored contemporary concerns about the sprawling nature of U.S. power, a country many thought was behaving like an overconfident teenager: uncouth, smug, and boisterous. Although fears of a communist world revolution solidified Anglo-American scouting, apprehensions about the rising impact of the world's new economic behemoth dampened British enthusiasm for transatlantic cooperation. Canada emerged as a major battleground between U.S. and English organizers. Irritated by "the increasing Americanization of the press and of local customs" in the British dominion, Baden-Powell was stunned to discover in 1923 that Canadian officials had started celebrating their annual "Scouts Day" according to American custom, not English custom.[33] Similarly, British scouters rose up in protest when they learned that the BSA had started advertising *Boys' Life* in England.[34] In private conversation, Baden-Powell took a jab at West's fixation on bureaucratic control. As he saw it, the altruistic "boy-men" in charge of scouting across the British Empire were more faithful to the idea of youth than West's army of "hired men" could ever be.[35] For Baden-Powell, American professionalism represented the artificiality of corporate culture, whereas British volunteerism epitomized true dedication and patriotic service.

West's managerial style also estranged other European Scout leaders, who kept their distance from the BSA chief scout executive. The situation escalated at the ISC meeting following the 1937 world jamboree in the Netherlands, where West got the cold shoulder from several delegates. Baden-Powell, an embittered West reported, had been "in fine form," but the unfriendliness he had experienced at the hands of his paladins, especially Hubert Martin and Lord Hampton, left a few scars. If this old-world snobbery continued, West suggested in a rare fit of anger, perhaps the BSA ought to beg the bodies of global scouting good riddance.[36]

Given the potential for open conflict between the two powerhouses of scouting, granting the BSA a seat at the table of international scouting was as much about maintaining the pretense of world brotherhood as it was about containing American influence. In giving U.S. delegates a hand in the ISC's proceedings, the Europeans hoped to bind the BSA to the resolutions formulated at these meetings. Entrusted with drafting the ISC's constitution, Schiff and West took advantage of this mandate. Several resolutions drawn up at the conferences in Paris (1922), Copenhagen (1924), and Kandersteg, Switzerland (1926), bear their handwriting.[37] The provision coming out of the Paris conference that called for the unification of Scout associations in every country mirrored the BSA's early struggles with domestic rivals.[38] U.S. executives also convinced their British colleagues to throw their weight behind a resolution that pledged all members to combating the unauthorized use of badges and insignia for commercial profit.[39] A resolution passed in Copenhagen in support of religious tolerance in world scouting echoed the BSA's stance on confessional diversity.[40] The decision reached in Kandersteg to allow only those youngsters categorized as refugees, but not ethnic minorities, to form their own Scout organizations, which had become a divisive issue in postwar states of Central and Eastern Europe, echoed the assimilationist nationalism embraced by the BSA.[41] For U.S. executives, opposition to ethnic youth organizing at home and supporting the nationalization of scouting abroad were two sides of the same coin. In turn, West and Schiff compromised on a few themes dear to their British partners. They consented to holding future conferences and jamborees in Europe and recognized Baden-Powell as the head of the global Scout movement.[42]

In one area, however, BSA representatives did not budge a single inch: establishing formal ties between scouting's "League of Youth" and the League of Nations. Starting in the early 1920s, the League of Nations sent observers to the world jamborees as part of a public campaign to instill internationalist ideals into childhood education. "Candor, self-control, friendship, and cooperation" were "the watchwords of both the Scouts and the League," declared the British diplomat and League enthusiast Robert Cecil at the London jamboree.[43] The League's support of youth internationalism peaked in 1923 with a resolution urging member states to relax visa restrictions for traveling Boy Scouts and Girl Guides.[44] The national Scout organizations represented in the ISC reacted differently to the League's advances, often reiterating the positions of their respective governments. With his advice to the ISC "not to identify too closely with the League," Schiff snubbed the delegates from Eastern Europe and Latin America, who wanted closer relations with the League because they viewed it as an advocate for the rights of smaller nations. Schiff learned that lesson in Copenhagen, where Japanese League official Inazo Nitobe had to mediate between the foreign commissioner and Latin American youth workers, who were suspicious of Schiff's plan to increase the BSA's influence in their countries.[45] Baden-Powell upheld a cordial relationship with Geneva, yet he was not very keen on cooperating more than informally with the League either. Facing combined Anglo-American opposition, motions such as the one that called for the introduction of a League-backed merit badge for world citizenship were dead on arrival.[46]

As the falling-out over the League of Nations suggests, the constant appeals to international understanding in the forums of global scouting reflected conflicting interests. The transnational networking of Scout executives could easily inflame nationalist sentiments. On top of existing geopolitical rivalries and the clash of different organizational cultures, many of the ISC's provisions—such as the protection of national insignia and the refusal to admit countries with Scout associations divided by region or religion—furthered the nationalization of the various branches of the Boy Scout movement rather than their internationalization. Perhaps the boys were not wedded to the paradigms of their elders and capable of giving a more persuasive performance of world brotherhood.

Performing Peace

In 1936, nineteen-year-old Owen Matthews enjoyed a brief moment in the limelight. He had won a nationwide student essay contest on the question "How can America stay out of war?" An Eagle Scout from Portland, Oregon,

Matthews had been one of the 406 American boys who had represented their country at the 1933 world jamboree in Hungary. Huddling around the campfires of global youth, Matthews had realized what "true brotherly love meant." He had traded souvenirs and sung songs of brotherhood with Scouts from all over the world, "even though their creed or color might be different." He became pen pals with boys from England to Estonia and Syria to South Africa, and had learned to "love these brother Scouts as much as those in America." Emphasizing a common boyhood that eclipsed the frictions of race, religion, and nationality, Matthews called on his government to send more young Americans abroad. Supporting such trips, he wrote, would surely pay off, for "peace gatherings and encampments of youth from all countries [would] do more to further future world peace than adult conferences held in some castle or other building." Endorsing these sentiments, BSA executives reprinted Matthew's essay in *Boys' Life*.[47]

As puerile as Matthew's prescription for international peace may sound, the claim that boys might do a better job of running the world had become a common talking point at the world jamborees. From the start, these festivals developed a rich repertoire of representational practices that ascribed to their juvenile protagonists extraordinary political and cultural competency. Building on prewar definitions of youth as a life stage that was distinct from both the vulnerabilities of childhood and the constraints of adulthood, global scouting advertised the values of boyhood—camaraderie, idealism, authenticity—as a remedy to the gridlock of international politics. "Here is a healing sight in a war-talking world," a newspaper from South Dakota cheered in 1933, "Youth from many nations seeking to win friends by being friends as only youth can."[48] One popular allegory deployed by the organizers juxtaposed upright and jovial Scouts from different nations with a frail old man personifying a tattered world. The healthy young bodies on parade were a welcome distraction from the bodies devastated by industrial warfare. In a cartoon published in 1920 on the occasion of the first world jamboree, a "War-weary World" in a wrinkled dress coat and leaning on an umbrella bends over to a young Scout in a shining uniform and says, "I was nearly losing hope, but the sight of all you boys gives it back to me."[49] Variations of this theme appeared in 1929 and in 1937 in an illustration created during the BSA's first national jamboree in Washington, DC, with a Scout leading a panting world, again in the guise of an old man, up the mountain of brotherhood.[50] Many of these images rested on a shared understanding that youth symbolized a fresh start, a bright new day after the older generation had shrouded the planet in darkness.

Figure 3.1. "The League of Youth." This cartoon, published in the English magazine *Punch* in August 1920, casts boyhood as a revitalizing force in international relations after the cataclysm of World War I.

It was less the imagery, though, than the theatrics of the jamborees that created for participants and observers a miniature world inhabited by a global fellowship of boyhood. Borrowing from the performative inventory of popular international events such as the Olympics and the world's fairs, the organizers staged a series of mass spectacles for a globalized public sphere. Gaudy media events, the jamborees galvanized entire nations. Print journalism, radio broadcasts, and newsreels made these rallies available to millions of people on both sides of the Atlantic. Empty fields gave way to tent cities, and the elaborately decorated camps of the participating Scout nations formed one big sprawling organism. Distances of culture and geography shrank to a manageable size as each jamboree opened with the March of Nations, during which the Scout contingents paraded one by one behind their national flags into the jamboree arena, past kings, queens, and other heads of state. The extravaganzas in the campground continued with a flurry of pageants performed by the individual delegations, which blended national folklore, historical drama, and demonstrations of scoutcraft. At the 1920 and 1924 jamborees, these demonstrations took on the form of quasi-Olympic contests until the ISC scaled back on the competitions to avoid rivalries among the participants.[51] Sundays were set aside for religious exercises. Reflecting the multiconfessional character of the jamboree camps, Protestant ministers, Catholic priests, Jewish rabbis, and Muslim imams preached peace and brotherhood to boys from different nations and empires.[52]

As these recurring scenes indicate, the planners located brotherhood not simply in a practical ecumenism or friendly cross-national encounters but in affectionate interactions between boys and men. At the top of this intergenerational edifice stood Robert Baden-Powell. With near papal authority, Baden-Powell acted as the jamborees' master of ceremonies. His addresses

Figure 3.2. Flag bearers at the March of Nations in Arrowe Park, England, August 1929. These quasi-military processions coexisted uneasily with the world jamborees' message of universal brotherhood. (Courtesy of the Scout Association, UK, Heritage Collection)

urged the boys to develop fraternal feelings for Scouts of all faiths and back-grounds. "Go forth from here as ambassadors of goodwill and friendship" was Baden-Powell's parting message at Arrowe Park.[53] In light of rising tensions in Europe and the Far East, the apostolic tone of the aging chief scout of the world sounded more urgent during the closing ceremony at Vogelenzang, where he likened the global Scout brotherhood to a "great crusade" aiming at the "removal of international disputes."[54] Dramatic gestures amplified Baden-Powell's peace messages. During the final act of the 1929 jamboree, Baden-Powell buried a hatchet, "the hatchet of war," in a casket of gilded wood arrows. The arrows were then symbolically passed on to the four corners of the globe as a sign of peace between the nations, amid the cheers of fifty thousand Scouts who had lined up like the spokes of a gigantic wheel.[55]

Baden-Powell's Christian symbolism fell on sympathetic ears in the BSA, whose leaders celebrated piousness as a pathway to virtuous boyhood. U.S. organizers held that religious upbringing made for good citizenship, and that faith in God was a prerequisite for peace on earth. Practicing a boyified version of civil religion, in which individual faiths were subordinated to a national theology of freedom, BSA leaders saw in domestic formulas of multiconfessional brotherhood a blueprint for overcoming international rivalries. For the Jewish rabbi Philip Bookstaber, the Twelfth Scout Law held out a moral example to Scout organizations in countries afflicted by religious intolerance.[56] Mormon elder Oscar A. Kirkham, whom the BSA put in charge of its jamboree delegations' religious exercises, praised scouting's youth fraternizations as a "world program for friendship, brotherhood, and peace."[57] Though Kirkham's spirituality diverged from the muscular Christianity of the prewar generation, it conveyed the hope that global scouting would revive notions of Protestant manliness and Anglo-Saxon mission. Americans like Kirkham could identify with Baden-Powell's messianic gestures, which rejuvenated the old imperial trope that it was the destiny of English-speaking people to spread civilization.

No mere talking over the heads of the young, the impresario-like performances of the chief scout of the world pivoted on a credible show of interdependency between nations and generations. The thundering acclamations of the Scouts, who responded to Baden-Powell's speeches with shouts of "Yes!" and "Chief! Chief! Chief!," established their complicity, turning the boys into junior partners in the remaking of global relations.[58] It was the chants of youth—orchestrated and spontaneous—that prompted the most emotional reactions. For men who had survived the war, the jamborees were a cathartic experience. Some wept openly at the sight of uniformed boys from five continents who by the thousands had pledged to build a better world.[59] Whereas soldiers had once charged across the fields of destruction, bare-kneed boys now marched to the tunes of international friendship. The buoyancy with which the Boy Scouts banded together, the English journalist Sir Philipp Gibbs mused, heralded a rejuvenated manhood: noble and strong, but also devoted to fair play and brotherly love. "It seemed to me, as I stood there watching," Gibbs reported from Arrowe Park, "that here was the beginning of a new chapter in history. . . . It was youth's rendezvous, with new hopes, a new vision of life, a great promise ahead."[60]

Youth's enthusiasm proved equally contagious with people from the other side of the Atlantic. Inspecting the camp at Vogelenzang, Mormon missionary Richard Roswell Lyman called the jamborees a "good and effective movement," which "cannot do otherwise than advance greatly the cause of peace for the whole world."[61] Eight years earlier, egged on by the international fan mail he had received, the almost eighty-year-old Beard had traveled to England to attend the third world jamboree. His cranky hypernationalism melted away when Schiff put his hand on Beard's shoulder as they were watching columns of Boy Scouts parading by and said to him: "Uncle Dan, you should be the happiest man in the world to be able to look around you and see all your dreams realized." Moments like these, Beard confessed, "made this tired old world of ours wake up and rub its eyes."[62] It seemed as if the idealism of the boys could redeem the most disillusioned senior.

Scout leaders insisted that their form of youth diplomacy was morally superior to adult internationalism. Many promoted the jamborees and their own role in coordinating them as a corrective to the shortcomings of official diplomacy. "Old men have failed in all their recent conferences," Baden-Powell told the press in Hungary. "Now youth must show them the way."[63] A French scouter was so pleased with how the U.S. contingent had comported themselves in Denmark that he told an American colleague that the boys had done more to reduce anti-American sentiments in Europe "than all the delegations of diplomacy since the Great War."[64] Peace, Beard taunted, could not be made by "swivel chairs"—bureaucrats in charge of "Hague conferences or naval disarmament treaties" who were without character and resolve. The redemption of the world, Beard told Baden-Powell, lay in "that sacred thing we call boyhood."[65] BSA executive George J. Fisher played the generational card again in 1937. "While diplomats blunder and men debate," Fisher exclaimed at the first multinational Scout rally on American soil, "here is youth . . . pledged to a high code of living."[66] Given the movement's ties to the ruling elites, however, such assertions had little to do with challenging power structures and everything to do with restoring patriarchal authority in an age of global-ideological reorientation. As the leader of boys, men could feel young again and elude associations of aging with a decline in masculine authority.

The jamboree planners had high expectations. Their faith in the transformative power of youth applied to individuals and societies alike. Nations that dipped their toes into this "sea of youth," a phrase West used to describe the ceremonies at Gödöllö, would not emerge unchanged.[67] Water is an apt metaphor for the hopes for rebirth from the depths of war that the organizers grafted onto the jamborees—a journey of renewal that entailed a return to the pristine environments of uncorrupted nature. Just as the Boy Scouts were taught to value personal hygiene, camping together in harmony under open skies was seen as a way to purify the bodies of nations and empires. Scout leaders ascribed a metaphysical meaning to these acts of cleansing. In the mind of Pennsylvania scoutmaster Earle K. Herbert, the heavy rain that turned the tent city near Birkenhead into a mudfest washed away old hostilities.[68] Each shower, sermon, and peace song sung at the campfire functioned as a ritual of rejuvenation. "Old ghosts and demons" were "exorcised by this marvelous pageant of young manhood," one observer jubilated.[69] In the floods of youth, histories were whitewashed and new futures invented. The world jamborees' creation of "minor utopias" clearly served adult interests.[70] Bonding with youth aided the reconstruction of masculinities ravaged by war, exculpating the same elites whose policies had made mass destruction possible in the first place.

This reciprocity between the old and the young was also evident in how the world was imagined in global scouting. Although different physical environments shaped each jamboree camp, their layout reflected the hierarchies of global scouting after 1918. Despite the organizers' emphasis on freedom of movement, the tent cities produced their own spatial politics with distinct notions of center and periphery. While three European countries other than England hosted a world jamboree before the war, global scouting retained a strong Anglo-Saxon flavor. Official speeches were delivered in English, and jamboree tunes such as the adaptation of Robert Burns's "Auld Lang Syne," which developed into a Scout song of global reach, were sung in English. Camp topographies mirrored the planners' Anglophile ideas about globalization. Baden-Powell's headquarters usually stood at the center, surrounded by the delegations from the British Empire, the United States, and continental Europe. The outer camps' districts were populated by the smaller, nonwhite, and non-Christian contingents from countries such as Egypt, Syria, Siam, and Japan. Starting in the mid-1920s, campgrounds included radio stations, snack stands, and gift shops, superimposing modern Western cultures of communication and consumption on scouting's back-to-nature nostalgia.[71] Without causing

much of a stir, the spatial configuration of the jamborees replicated a historical narrative of civilization and peace that spread outward from the English-
speaking nations to the planet's most distant corners.

The organizers took pride in their ability to reduce vast distances to the
size of a global village where the Scouts, as one American participant rejoiced,
could travel "around the world in one day."[72] However, their walking tours
led through a theme park of nationalities that had little to do with existing
geopolitical realities. There was no mention of disgruntled Indian youth who
had found an outlet for protest in the nationalist Swadeshi movement. Nor
were there any allusions to the policies of strict racial segregation that kept
native blacks out of white-led Scout organizations in British colonial Africa.
Instead, the grievances of colonialism were drowned out by Boy Scout pageants in which red fezzes, white veils, turbans, and Union Jacks mingled
together in the spirit of universal brotherhood. Imperial and nationalist conflict was banned from the campground, although jamboree organizers were
unable to prevent minor hostilities. It was only after the farewell ceremony at
Vogelenzang that Baden-Powell learned that Polish Scouts had attacked members of the Lithuanian delegation for displaying a map of their country that
included territories under Polish dominion.[73]

The Boy Scout narrative of brotherhood had a clear Western bias, downplay-
ing the wartime suffering of former enemies or current ideological opponents,
in particular of Soviet Russia. Since the movement's anti-Bolshevism prevented
any meaningful recognition of Soviet youth, the few Russian Scouts in exile
who were present at the jamborees could hardly be considered ambassadors of
their country. Germany was another case in point. Although German Pfadfinder
were allowed to pitch their tents at the 1924 and 1929 jamborees, the ISC refused to admit them as equals. To justify Germany's status as a country on probation, the ISC stressed that the country's Scout organizations were fragmented
by region and religion. Rejected as an agent of British imperialism, scouting
remained a fragile association in Germany's heterogeneous youth movement.
Memories of the war were still fresh when a meeting of German scouters
resolved in May 1920 that they would never become part of an international
movement as long as "foreign soldiers were treading on German soil."[74]
Germany's Scout associations, the British ISC official John S. Wilson begrudged,
had "a complete misunderstanding" of the movement's "real purpose."[75] The
BSIB denounced German youth organizing as factious and militaristic. On the
contrary, nations such as France, where Scout activities were also divided along
confessional lines, were given the benefit of the doubt. Belying declarations of
global unity, the different treatment of German Scouts by allied Scout execu-

tives showed the limitations of campfire diplomacy in terms of healing the wounds of international strife.

The absence of large parts of the world's youth made it difficult to imagine that regimented boyhood could transcend loyalties of nation and religion and bring about reconciliation. Few had forgotten the Boy Scouts' home-front fervor in wartime, and few failed to see in the marching and soldier-like drills of the boys at the jamborees remnants of a warlike patriotism. Nationalist images, the sounds of anthems, flags, and uniforms overshadowed the internationalist rituals of the movement. For some, the organizers' peace rhetoric may have sounded more credible had they reached out to other youth groups, including females. "Only young men had come," bemoaned a German socialist who had visited the Hungarian jamboree in 1933. To him, the fact that "girls were missing" made the "teeming crowd" a "one-sided affair."[76]

Divorcing masculinity from war called for quite an imaginative leap, in part because of a gendered understanding of international relations that cast peacemaking as a feminine project. Starting with the feminist pacifists of the Victorian and Progressive Eras, women had been in the vanguard of numerous movements advocating disarmament and nonviolence. Linguistically excluded from the trope of brotherhood, female organizations such as the Women's International League for Peace and Freedom, founded in the United States in 1915, entered the postwar global arena carrying the standard of sisterhood. Their promise was that the womanly qualities of feeling, caring, and empathizing would constitute a more solid bulwark against the resurgence of militarism.[77]

The Girl Scouts erected their interwar platform of peace and friendship on a similar foundation. Like their male counterparts, the GSA and the British Guides created several avenues of transnational cooperation. Assemblies such as the Guide International and Imperial Council, which developed into the World Association of Girl Guides and Girl Scouts (WAGGGS) in 1928, inspired meetings between women leaders from around the world. At the same time, girls could attend world camps and travel to places such as Our Chalet in Adelboden, Switzerland, the first world center opened by the WAGGGS, in 1932, to promote intercultural exchange. Touting civic service, professional self-realization, and world-mindedness, the Girl Scouts encouraged its young members to break down the walls that had kept their sex confined to hearth and home.[78] A healthy infusion of female domesticity, Eleanor Roosevelt told a world gathering of Girl Scouts and Girl Guides near New York in August 1937, could do wonders for the dangerously masculinized world of foreign policy. "Peace abroad depends on peace at home," the First Lady stated, thus fusing spheres many believed should be separate.[79] Girl Scouts and their Guide sisters in Europe and the British Empire thought of themselves as the better ambassadors. Kindly feelings, they believed, flowed naturally from their smiles, songs, dances, flower gifts, and folk costumes around the campfire— far more naturally, it seemed, than from the uniformed Boy Scouts and their martial iconography. Considering the violent subtext of many jamboree symbols (golden arrows in England, hunting legends in Hungary), the Boy Scouts struggled to reconcile their semimilitaristic appearance with a vision of regenerative youth capable of whitewashing their societies' violent pasts.

Paramount to the nuisance of being labeled militaristic, however, was the fear of losing the aura of masculinity. Demonstrations like one pacifist procession in Chicago in 1922 in which Boy Scouts carried a banner reading "Humanity above Nationalism" gave BSA leaders serious headaches.[80] What if international understanding weakened the bond between manhood and national service instead of preserving it? What if young people jumped to wrong conclusions about their role as peacemakers? Robert Baden-Powell argued passionately against returning to the militant nationalisms of earlier times but wondered how boys could be trained for peace without "emasculating [the] nation."[81] Echoing Baden-Powell's concerns, U.S. Scout officials avoided describing their overseas activities with any term that might have branded them unmanly or unpatriotic. One such term was "pacifism," which many equated with effeminacy or outright treason, but American organizers also disliked "internationalism" because of its proximity to revolutionary socialism. "We are not pacifists or internationalists," Mortimer Schiff clarified in 1930, voicing the concern that the BSA's youth diplomacy might be conflated with subversive left-wing agitation or, worse, effeminate peace work.[82] A world without war, Scout leaders suggested, could not be forged by old, fainthearted diplomats or at Girl Scout meetings. Only a tough, uncorrupted young manhood fostering mutual respect and understanding could accomplish that.

Staging Empire

Jamboree organizers who wanted boys to grow into citizens who would feel and think globally had to strike a delicate balance. Trying to reconcile world awareness with love of country meant walking a tightrope between masculinizing peace and reinforcing the masculinity of the nation. This led to some verbal gymnastics on the part of leading Scout officials. Baden-Powell coined the term "world patriotism" to articulate his vision of extending the fraternal ties of nationhood to an international community of youth.[83] Mortimer Schiff's use of the expressions "world fellowship" and "peaceful citizenship" indicated a desire to harness the unspent energy of boyhood for the stabilization of a liberal world order.[84] Although such rhetorical contortions barely resonated beyond the printed page, they epitomized an unfolding conversation in the Boy Scout movement about who and what exactly constituted citizens and nations in an international context. The jamborees offered a unique venue to settle such questions, a global stage that invited playful cross-generational performances of youth, masculinity, nationality, and empire in a postwar world.

How, then, did the BSA represent its country abroad? The drawings of Lajos Marton, a Hungarian scouter who attended the 1924 world jamboree in Denmark, open a fascinating window to how "America" was constructed in the global arenas of scouting. Armed with pencils and crayons, Marton was drawn to the joyful hubbub emanating from the camp of the U.S. delegation. Two scenes that he chose to capture on paper merit special scrutiny. The first depicts a group of bare-chested Eagle Scouts dressed as Plains Indians, with painted faces and elaborate headdresses, preparing to perform a traditional Native American war dance. The second scene shows a crowd of visitors, men and women, ordering refreshments at a tent selling "American Ice-Cream."[85] These two images hint at the ambiguities of the young masculinity that the BSA staged abroad. U.S. Boy Scouts lodged American masculinity in two different, apparently contradictory practices: the ability to master the demands of modern capitalism while drawing strength and character from a mythical frontier past.

Although white Americans had appropriated Native American traditions since colonial times, there is something perplexing about these "redface" performances on European soil. Indians and Boy Scouts were hardly natural allies. Seton and Beard had famously clashed over the place of Native Americans in the organization. Should white boys really identify with a vanishing race, the same tribesmen that their ancestors had vanquished in a brutal struggle for land and manifest destiny? Settling on Indians as ambassadorial figures was a curious choice, to say the least. One would guess that the victims of continental expansion had little to offer to a rising generation that was supposed to sustain the empire their fathers had built. Was there no greater sense of kinship connecting the nation's youth to the brave and vigorous white pioneer, who loomed large in popular memory? Some believed there was, but "playing Indian," as the historian Philip Deloria reminded us, constituted more than a sideshow in the larger American drama of gender, race, and empire.[86] Progressive Era educators influenced by Hall's recapitulation theory held that "going native" was a beneficial experience in the development of white youth.

Children, they thought, would learn what it meant to be an American man or woman through temporary encounters with savagery, by re-creating and acting out the primitive-life worlds of fantasy Indians. Such supervised immersions into an imagined tribal culture were not cultural sensitivity seminars in which Boy Scouts or Camp Fire Girls learned to appreciate difference. Their main purpose was to retrieve from an idealized wilderness the fortitude and subsistence skills that seemed unavailable in the modern world but were considered crucial to preparing young people for the strains of carving out a livelihood in fast-paced capitalist societies.

Transnational developments aided the construction of a distinctively American national identity on the backs of Indians. At the same time that turn-of-the-century educators were rediscovering the "Red Man" for pedagogic purposes, Native Americans had begun to exercise a firmer grip on the public imagination on both sides of the Atlantic. With the increasing mobility of mass culture, Indianness as a form of popular entertainment traversed boundaries faster and with greater impact. Europeans cultivated their own "Indianthusiasm." A mostly literary fascination with the figure of the noble savage helped readers come to terms with questions of authenticity, heredity, and belonging in their own societies, although these questions could have vastly different meanings in different contexts. When Buffalo Bill toured the Old World between the 1880s and the 1900s with his celebrated Wild West Show—which started as a reenactment of the Battle of Little Big Horn before expanding into a colorful imperial pageant featuring not just cowboys and Indians but Arab horsemen, Filipino fighters, Cuban insurgents, and Zulu warriors—he performed in front of audiences already favorably disposed toward a romanticized vision of the frontier. Whether in U.S. cultural exports or German dime novels, perceptions of a youthful and vigorous America drew in varying degrees on a heroic settler masculinity, narratives of white conquest, and stereotypes of Native American ferocity and honor.[87]

Few American scouters straddled Buffalo Bill's showmanship with Native American lore better than Ralph Hubbard. Growing up in an arts-and-crafts community near the Seneca Indian Reservation in New York State, Hubbard became infatuated with Native Americans early in life. This infatuation deepened after his parents took him to a Buffalo Bill event. While traveling west to study different tribal cultures, Hubbard joined the nascent Boy Scouts. His knowledge of Indian rituals and dance impressed BSA administrators, who found this self-studied, native-born expert in Native American culture much more acceptable than the foreign-born dropout Seton. Hubbard authored the section "American Indian Craft" for the 1928 edition of the *Handbook for Boys*, instructing boys how to make tepees, tom-toms, and moccasins.[88] Hubbard jumped to international renown with the Indian ceremonies he choreographed for the world jamborees. Taking the stage as Indian warriors, chieftains, medicine men, and cowboys on foot and horseback, Hubbard and his boy actors received standing ovations in London, Ermelunden, Arrowe Park, Gödöllö, and Vogelenzang. Attracting large crowds wherever they went, the BSA's amateur Indians entertained passengers on transatlantic steamers, put in encores for European dignitaries, and went on extended post-jamboree tours. Shortly after the Olympia indoor spectacle in 1920, they performed for King Albert of Belgium and at the Summer Olympics in Antwerp. Over the next two decades, the Boy Scout Indians danced in front of other heads of state including King Christian X of Denmark, the Hungarian regent Miklós Horthy, and the Dutch queen Wilhelmina. Beloved by his students, Hubbard was invited to their jamboree reunions in later years.[89]

Hubbard's Native American theatrics reflected the growing significance of folklore celebrations, which were regarded as true expressions of national character. Jamboree Scouts singing songs from their homelands and staging regional dances resembled the costumed troupes at the world's fairs that were putting their countries' peasant traditions on display. Some scholars have described these performances as amplifiers of reactionary or antimodern sentiments. Rather than enunciate a nostalgic yearning for rustic simplicity, however, folklore helped naturalize nations and races and anchored them firmly in the postwar international order.[90] Histories were invented and countries were reified in global scouting's carnival of nations. Conducted for public amusement, folklorist demonstrations narrated a people's rise from humble beginnings to modern greatness. Boy Scouts from Greece wore *fustanellas,* boys from Poland twirled to Polka music, boys from Japan dramatized samurai tales, boys from France posed as Gallic warlords, boys from the United States played cowboys and Indians, and boys from colonial dominions such as India exhibited Bengali dances. They all fashioned for themselves a national heritage that oscillated between trying to preserve traditions of martial manhood and presenting boys as the standard-bearers of international cooperation.

As much as scouting's ethnonational exhibitions visualized authentic pasts for present-day orientation, they also revealed the extent to which authenticity was a social construct. Authenticity had to be carefully crafted, enacted, and sold. Hubbard's preparations for the 1920 jamboree included shipping to England "original Indian feather headdresses, beaded jackets, and leather breeches" he had bought from western tribes.[91] Still, his Boy Scout Indians were utterly artificial, with a potpourri of different indigenous customs inscribed on their bodies for maximum effect. Four years later, with Denmark on the horizon, Hubbard organized tryouts in upstate New York to ensure that his jamboree team of Indian dancers would comprise the most talented Scouts.[92] In a stroke of marketing genius, Hubbard disclosed that his ancestry was partly Native American. Claims that "Indian blood" coursed through his veins dove-tailed neatly with a romantic gaze popular in Europe that ascribed to Indian-ness moral purity rather than racial inferiority.[93] Baden-Powell, himself an avid consumer of North American frontier mythology, sought to add credibility to his organization's imperial pageantry by emphasizing its affinity to the BSA's Native American performances. After overseeing an Indian display at the Olym-pia festival that traced British scouting back to the discovery of Virginia by seventeenth-century English explorer John Smith, he yielded the final scene to Hubbard's redface actors. Surrounded by an honor guard of British and U.S. Scouts, the adolescents in Native American garb dazzled the spectators with equestrian feats and tribal dances before a 325-foot painted canvas depicting a pass in the Rocky Mountains.[94]

Gaining recognition abroad created openings for renegotiating Indianness at home. Jubilant about his triumphant trip to Denmark, an emboldened Hub-bard urged an assembly of BSA executives in September 1924 to fully em-brace Native American culture, "else it will be too late to save this only thing truly American. We have drawn almost all our art from Europe, except this."[95] Hubbard's words echoed those of the Dakota leader and Boy Scout supporter Charles A. Eastman, who had confidently labeled his people the "first" or "original Americans."[96] Though enlisting Indianness to bolster nationalism was a clever move in a society looking to distinguish itself from Europe and link the origins of America to the themes of adventure, moral purity, and inno-cence, it raised eyebrows as well. As the Beard-Seton feud had indicated, the BSA also represented a white countercurrent that found nothing to admire about North America's indigenous people, except maybe their reputation for healthy outdoor living. A defeated and dying race, they objected, could hardly inspire national manhood. If heroes were needed to retain the frontier toughness that had made this country great, boys should learn from the likes of Daniel Boone or Davy Crocket, for pioneers "who braved the dangers of unexplored forests and the hardships of an unsettled country" would furnish American youth "with still better ideals."[97] Still, Indians demonstrated a remarkable staying power in the organization, because the transnational popularity of Indianness helped give the BSA a positive global image.[98]

Unable to resolve the dualism of pioneers versus Native Americans, U.S. jamboree delegates dramatized both. The main pageant performed by American

Boy Scouts at the Birkenhead gathering in 1929 put Indians and settlers on an almost equal footing, honoring their parts in a white chronicle of expansion and progress. To function as an allegory of national growth, the show included many characters—medicine men, buffalo hunters, and red warriors; spirit dancers and Spanish conquistadors; Puritans and pioneers; gold rush adventurers and cowboys—mingling joyfully and with little feigned hostility. In the concluding scene, "Uncle" Dan Beard entered the arena, clothed in a splendid buckskin costume and summoning all the characters on stage for one final grand display, which received thunderous applause.[99]

For some, the central message radiating from this spectacle might have been a popular narrative that displayed the contributions of individual "races" to the nation's development and tied their fate to an unfolding contest between primitivism and civilization. Others might have underscored the pageants' role in visualizing America as the country of youth, a nation enacted not only by adolescents but in figurative adolescence compared with the Old World. In this reading, the frontier emerges as a place of struggle, rebirth, maturation and rejuvenation, making the United States, in the words of a British journalist, the quintessential "land of the young man."[100] But it is a third interpretation that is most compelling in the triple contexts of interwar masculinity, cultural diplomacy, and global scouting. Unlike Buffalo Bill's spectacles, which focused on the "massacre" at Little Big Horn and staged elaborate mock battles between intrepid settlers and bloodthirsty Indians, the BSA pageants conjured up a Wild West tamed by gallant men of different races. Although their script placed the pioneer on a higher civilizational scale than the Indian, the jovial gestures of the performing Scouts submerged the fact that winning the West had meant its genocidal conquest. Consonant with Hubbard's emphasis on peaceful Native American craft, adolescents dressed as cowboys and Indians met in an atmosphere of cordiality and reconciliation, which dovetailed nicely with the jamboree's infantilized internationalism. The North American frontier—in a stunning rewrite—was declared the birthplace of friendship between races and nations.

This historical fantasy gained contours in other campground enterprises as well. A spontaneous mock battle at Arrowe Park between South African boys dressed as Zulu warriors and redface American Scouts that ended with hearty handclasps anchored peace in youthful masculinities and fellow feeling.[101] Another bridge-building initiative was the teaching of Indian sign language at the world jamborees. Among the fifteen hundred U.S. Boy Scouts who made the trip to England in 1929 was a group of young sign language aficionados who offered workshops based on scoutmaster William Tomkins's manual *Universal*

Figure 3.3. U.S. Boy Scouts dressed as Plains Indians perform a Native American dance in Arrowe Park, England, August 1929. The BSA's playful appropriations of Indianness concealed a genocidal history of conquest. (Courtesy of the Scout Association, UK, Heritage Collection)

Indian Sign Language.[102] Hoping that peaceful sign language would replace the militarized Morse code, Tomkins argued that his method of face-to-face interaction could humanize international relations. Presenting Indian sign as America's gift to the world, Tomkins told the Prince of Wales in a cordial tit for tat: "You English gave America her language, we now want to give you the American Indian language in appreciation."[103] Though foreign boys flocked in throngs to Tomkins's open-air classes, most study groups in Indian sign language fizzled out, thus sharing the fate of the few Esperanto classes organized by the Scouts themselves, which barely resonated outside a small group of connoisseurs.

The craze for Wild West things found a lasting expression in material culture. Indian and pioneer traditions were canonized in the tepees, tents, blockhouses, and fort facades that were the hallmarks of every U.S. jamboree camp. At Arrowe Park, Scouts from the Midwest carved an imposing fifty-foot totem out of a telephone pole replete with Native American and Scout motifs. They ornamented it with Indian carvings, the Scout laws, patrol symbols, and a majestic eagle on top. One New York patrol handed out Indian arrowheads to foreign Boy Scouts, while another group showed how to make Indian wampum. Lasso tricks and horse riding were the specialty of a Scout troop from Nebraska. Regional identities became palpable in the designs of individual camps, which BSA leaders held up as a visual affirmation of American grassroots democracy. For Mortimer Schiff, the "endless variety and color" invited comparisons to a vibrant marketplace of different approaches that enriched the nation and, by implication, the entire world. New Yorkers were housed in a complete Adirondack wilderness camp; Indiana Scouts spent the nights in covered prairie wagons; Minnesotans reconstructed Ojibwe Indian wigwams; Texans came equipped with Plains Indian tepees; and Scouts from Massachusetts went native by mimicking the tribes the Pilgrims had encountered in the seventeenth century.[104] In symbolic interactions with foreign luminaries, peace pipes took precedence over guns and tomahawks. The ceremonies in London ended with Baden-Powell accepting the Pipe of Peace and blowing "smoke to the four winds."[105] Thirteen years later in Hungary, U.S. Scouts placed a mighty feather headdress on the head of their host, Count Teleki, and pronounced him Chief-of-many-Campfires.[106] Just as young men had once sought their fortunes by going west, scouting told boys that they could attain manhood by crossing the frontiers of international politics. James West drew this parallel when writing about the gateway to the American camp in Hungary: "Our blockhouses were not built for defense against hostile Indian tribes. They were a promise to the Scouts of the World that, in entering, they would find the same spirit, in scouting, of resourcefulness, perseverance and friendliness that marked the early pioneers. . . . Weren't we settlers, too, in a strange land? Hadn't we come to help in the building of an empire—an empire of youth and brotherhood?"[107]

West's choice of words illustrates the shifting semantics of "empire" in the transnational arena of organized youth. Replacing the old language of conquest with a new language of fraternalism, scouting's "empire of youth" tethered Anglocentric visions of peaceful globalization to the reordering of imperial power relations. If the amenities of civilization had made the appropriation of masculine frontier values more difficult, they had to be salvaged with the help of the visual and material enticements of popular culture—trends that were widely associated with the United States. Empire no longer meant the subjugation of "hostile Indian tribes" but their global commodification. The jamborees, like the world fairs and other international exhibitions, contributed to this redefinition: as venues that taught mesmerized audiences how to understand race, class, gender, religion, and age in different contexts; as places where nations parading their masculinities and empires vied for attention; as events that celebrated boyhood's capacity to reform global relations; and as sites that forged and displayed collective identities—in the case of the United States, that of a youthfully robust and benevolent player on the world stage. Ultimately, it is impossible to grasp the BSA's frontier performances outside contemporary processes of medialization and marketization. The faux Indians and ice cream stands that Lajos Marton depicted thus had much more in common than a first glance might suggest.

Far from replicating nineteenth-century values, the artifacts U.S. Scouts exhibited at the world jamborees located manhood in a panoply of practices ranging from the traditional conquest of nature to the modern control of machines. By the 1920s, many of the scientific improvements that fueled the evolution of a modern consumer culture had seeped into America's favorite pastime: camping. Children bound for the woods in their summer vacations began experiencing the outdoors through the lens of a camera, had access to radios, and took a break from camp life by going to a nearby movie theater. American campers learned to enjoy higher standards including electricity, sanitary installations, medical services, and good transportation.[108] BSA officials displaying these innovations abroad celebrated them as a testament to their nation's ingenuity. Claiming that his organization's camping methods were the envy of the civilized world, West boasted that the U.S. delegation who had traveled to the Netherlands in July 1937 "was judged to have the cleanest camp . . . in a country noted for well-kept cities and spotless homes."[109] Exhibition tents advertised BSA craftsmanship and displayed merchandise, handbooks, merit badges, and copies of *Boys' Life* as well as pamphlets on camp hygiene and safety regulations. American Boy Scouts were expected to act as ambassadors of progress, not tourists. Their rubber ponchos were all the rage in rainy Denmark, and the quartermaster stoves and affordable pocket cameras that U.S. boys carried through Europe five years later were the subject of jamboree chatter.[110] Would world integration and peace not flow naturally from an "empire of youth" capable of establishing a healthy equilibrium between nature and modern consumption?

What worked nationally, however, was easily lost in translation. Anecdotal evidence suggests that foreign Scouts did not always fall for a masculinity that combined a rugged frontier mentality with technological proficiency. BSA performances of Indianness sometimes led to unwanted responses. U.S. Scouts dressed as Native Americans were caught by surprise in 1933 when Hungarian children interrupted one of their dramatizations with an improvised Indian yell.[111] Misunderstandings abounded in Denmark as well. Albert Snoke complained in hindsight that the European judges had given his troop's performance a low score because it had not included real Indians. After a follow-up presentation, Snoke and the other redface actors were harassed by Danish spectators who did not believe that the Scouts were fake Indians "until they invaded the dressing room to find white skin under the loins."[112] Ironically, the globalization of playing Indian had become so successful that Boy Scouts from other nations felt confident enough to criticize American youths for misrepresenting Native American traditions, including their reputation for preserving an authentic form of outdoor existence.

In exchanges over the degree to which new technologies should become part of a Boy Scout's education, American pretensions to possessing superior frontier toughness backfired. Quite a few brother Scouts from abroad felt provoked by BSA representatives emphasizing their organization's technological acumen, which reflected the growing economic disparity between the United States and large parts of the world. Unimpressed by the material temptations from the other side of the Atlantic, British jamboree participants scoffed at the U.S. delegation for taking "feminine precautions," seeing in their spring ground mattresses, generous food rations, and dry ice refrigerators signs of an "American plutocracy."[113] American Scouts who spent the wet nights at Arrowe Park were not amused when they learned that their camp had earned the derogatory title "Millionaires' Row."[114] Canadian Scouts alluded to this theme in a comical sketch in which they depicted Uncle Sam as a fat businessman, no doubt to the chagrin of their southern neighbors. Eight years later in Vogelenzang, the Americans were again accused of unmasculine behavior. The Dutch, who slept on the ground, could not fathom that all the U.S. boys had to do was lie down on army cots already prepared for them.[115] The Hungarian Victor Herrmann, who appraised the BSA as a model organization, left the camp of the American Scouts dumbfounded. In America, he wrote, "the boy comes into the ready made camp and shows the visitor his equipment and tells him the prizes," while the Hungarian boy works hard "and is proud of the perspiration he invested."[116]

Had American youth, with their penchant for modern gadgetry, become unfaithful to the simple pleasure of retreating into nature? Had they turned into the overcivilized softies the Boy Scouts' founders so despised? Charges of femininity were the strongest criticism coming from foreigners who had ambiguous feelings about new global markets in which U.S.-style salesmanship reigned supreme. However, by 1933, the trappings of popular consumerism had eclipsed the specter of America's market empire. With their decision to erect a shopping center on the Gödöllő campground where jamboree participants could buy goods from different parts of the world, the Hungarians pretty much ended the debate whether consuming and camping, playing Indian and eating ice cream, were compatible. For an Associated Press reporter, the camp at Vogelenzang was "run like a town, with 64 shops on a specially constructed market square. Banks, fire stations and hospitals, doctors and priests of all denominations are there, and telephone and radio facilities have been installed."[117]

The BSA's exhibitions at the world jamborees hardly propagated an unfiltered version of the "strenuous life." Couched in broader historical transformations, they turned the intertwined processes of man- and nation-making into a spectacle for mass consumption. And yet, the BSA's performances of gender, youth, and nation were not as joyful and inclusive as the dramatizations themselves suggested. The "Little Americas" constructed for the world to enjoy were not socially accurate representations of a multicultural nation. The staged interactions of cowboys and Indians projected white fantasies and glossed over differences instead of engaging with them. Foreign youths learned little about past wrongs, nor did they learn that indigenous cultures were being plundered for the benefit of white Americans at a time when Native Americans had few means to resist. As chapter 4 shows, some Indians used the BSA's interest in their history to make headway in the struggle for civil rights. But Native American involvement did not prevent the richly diverse legacy of North American indigenous life from being sliced up and repackaged into easily digestible pieces of entertainment. Local color and regional diversity became the embodiment of American democracy, not gender or racial equality. People of color, on the contrary, served only as props in the performance of a young, sturdy, and technologically advanced nation that had evolved from regional to global significance.

Adolescent Ambassadors

Boys, of course, experienced the scouting world differently than the movement's adult representatives. Reevaluating the world jamborees through the eyes of adolescent Americans wearing the BSA uniform illustrates how much actual youth invested in these events, that they experienced their trips in myriad ways, and that the significance they ascribed to them depended on where they stood in time and space. The purpose of this reassessment is once again to document young people's agency as Boy Scouts. It emphasizes their ability to explore grand concepts like peace, patriotism, and international understanding on their own; to appropriate them when they served their needs; and to reconsider their meaning when the excitement of overseas travel drew their attention to other things.

Telling the story of the BSA's participation in the venues of global scouting from the boys' point of view highlights important continuities and fluctuations in that history. The world jamborees did not grow steadily and evenly during the interwar years. The high point came in 1929 with more than fifteen hundred American boys in attendance. That number, however, dropped to a little over four hundred delegates in 1933. With the economy in the stranglehold of the Great Depression, fewer parents could afford to send their children overseas. Moreover, the modes of selection, travel routes, destinations, contacts with foreigners, and jamboree and post-jamboree activities changed conspicuously in that period. While the delegations bound for London and Ermelunden experienced military-style leadership, locally organized troops that picked their own Boy Scouts and scoutmasters made up the bulk of the U.S. contingents at Arrowe Park, Gödöllö, and Vogelenzang. After 1924, the delegations also became a bit more diverse—regionally, denominationally, and ethnically. Such differing formations had an impact on how the Scouts related to one another and how they acted out their role as adolescent ambassadors. The allegiances of a young jamboree Scout were highly contingent and in flux. They could expand and contract from the smallest social units (parents, friends, the troop) to large collectivities (organization, nation, the entire "world"), and they could do so independent of adult will.

The BSA selected its young delegates to the world jamborees, who had to be at least thirteen years of age, with the utmost care. Background checks involved medical exams, inquiries into school performances and religious practices, and identifying signs of delinquent behavior. The goal was to incorporate male youth into the nascent arsenal of U.S. cultural diplomacy, to pick stately boys who would represent the goodwill of a victor nation. Boys were expected "to act as American gentlemen, not as rowdy street urchins, wise-cracking and clowning before visitors or on parade," one training manual for jamboree troops stated.[118] The dangers of selecting the wrong boys became evident during the 1933 Roosevelt pilgrimage when, as Daniel Carter Beard grumbled, a Scout recited a patriotic poem "in such a boyish manner" that the boys in the audience "audibly snickered."[119] BSA executives must have felt sorry for Baden-Powell during an awkward moment that almost derailed the farewell ceremony at Arrowe Park. A foreign Boy Scout, apparently a non-English speaker, shared the stage with Baden-Powell and stood "preternaturally unmoved" as the chief scout delivered his closing speech, which ended with the distribution of the golden arrows.[120] Failure to comply with adult prescriptions, the organizers feared, might embarrass the organization and jeopardize its international standing.

Most Boy Scouts had no such intentions. Private recollections, diary entries, and correspondence printed in local newspapers indicate that the youths took their ambassadorial roles very seriously. Gaudy receptions and visits from statesmen and diplomats made them feel like young dignitaries. When the BSA jamboree contingent of 1924 entered Copenhagen, the streets were filled with people smiling and clapping.[121] After the contests had ended, the youths were treated royally in the homes of wealthy Danish hosts. "We all felt [like] Lindberghs," sixteen-year-old Virgil Williams from Illinois exclaimed in Blackburn, England, where his troop was serenaded by a brass band and cheered by seven thousand people.[122] In Hungary and the Netherlands, entire villages turned out to give the young delegates a rousing welcome.

The jamboree Scouts were not simply playing League of Nations; they believed they were making the idea of the League come alive. Amplifying generational distinctions, the boys used their moment in the spotlight to articulate pointed critiques of adult international relations. Citing his young age as an asset rather than an impediment, Texas scout Gibson Sherrard wrote home from Arrowe Park: "It is remarkable how we get along over here . . . we seem to understand [each other] for we seem to all have the same impulses and ideas—anyway, we are just boys. . . . If the older people would have just such a meeting of all nations in a spirit of friendship," Gibson augured, "I don't believe there would be any wars."[123] Safari scout Douglas Oliver, who visited Arrowe Park as a special delegate, sounded a similar theme. "Barriers of language were pushed aside as well as religion and color," Doug observed. "Everyone greeted everyone else with a firm Scout grip and joyful smile."[124] Reflecting on his participation in the world jamboree in Vogelenzang, Idaho scout Aubrey Andelin attributed to boyhood the moral clarity, efficiency, and honesty he found lacking among world leaders. "The friendships made here," Andelin concluded, "will help greatly in furthering world peace and good will."[125] If people were looking for a place where conditions were truly equal for all, Kansas scout William "Bill" Embry Smith opined, let them come to a jamboree: there all were "dressed alike"; there were "no rich and no poor," but all were "living together as brothers live in the same house." All were "desirous of learning to know each other. We were all boys and possessed the instinct to band together, not just with our companions but with all fellow campers."[126]

In all these cases, U.S. Boy Scouts tapped into the notion that youth were unburdened by the prejudices of their elders, and thus uniquely qualified to envision different national and global futures. No longer a mere antecedent to manhood, boyhood acquired a value of its own, and the positive valences of young age led Scouts to assert that they were able to solve international problems in ways older people could not.

Historians may be tempted to read such statements as evidence of juvenile pretentiousness, yet the trajectories of scouting and antiauthoritarianism rarely intersected. The boys' vaguely critical remarks about adult foreign affairs did not target specific groups or individuals, nor did the remarks extend to their leaders. If anything, the jamborees strengthened intergenerational ties in the Boy Scout movement. Nobody personified the faith in youth as a global force for good better than Robert Baden-Powell. The Scouts' admiration for their "Chief" seemed boundless, and not a few U.S. boys traveled great distances to see him, as if making a pilgrimage. One young American named Oscar Hobbs was so determined to meet his idol that he traveled to England as a stowaway because he could not afford the trip. Discovered and put in custody, Hobbs was sent home by English authorities.[127] Cheers, smiles, and clicking cameras welcomed the British chief scout when he visited the American camps.[128] Eagle scout Bill Kemp was at Vogelenzang when Baden-Powell gave his last farewell address. Seeing him at the bonfire with a Jacob's staff and urging "his boys" to work for peace between nations, Kemp recalled, at age eighty-one, was the "the most vivid memory" of his life.[129] Rather than classing him with the political establishment, the Scouts treated Baden-Powell like one of them, a boyish avatar committed to regenerating the world for and with youth.

The binary view of dysfunctional adult politics and youth's instinctive world consciousness was reinforced by a set of intercultural practices that American Scouts developed with their foreign peers. "Swapping" turned into a popular jamboree pastime—so popular that Iowa scout Jimmie Ricklefs penned that people "should not be surprised if we come home wearing Scotch kilts. . . . Everyone is trading their things for the uniforms of other boys."[130] Initiated by the Scouts, trading badges and bartering for souvenirs were held up as a way to win friends and build international trust. Adult organizers were slow to embrace this custom. For them, a Scout returning from a souvenir hunt wearing Dutch clogs, African beads, and an Egyptian fez sent out conflicting signals. They saw a fine line separating boyish curiosity from unbridled cross-cultural mingling, fearing a breakdown of discipline and the blurring of too many borders. By the end of a jamboree, Daniel Carter Beard quipped, American boys would have traded their uniforms away for kilts, turbans, and wooden clogs.[131] James West initially discouraged such casual behavior and warned the young delegates never to forget whom they were representing.[132] But West eventually declared swapping a diplomatic technique that went beyond selfish consumption. "The same Scouts, who, at the start, had been interested in getting the better part of the deal, realized eventually that the 'Change' was one of the best ways of making a lasting friendship," West conceded in 1933. "They became comrades and a 'Change' between them became gifts exchanged as tokens of friendship."[133]

At second glance, however, the pursuit for souvenirs did not always nurture friendships. Fraternal intentions vaporized instantly once foreign Boy Scouts recognized in their affluent peers from across the pond fat cats ripe for a fleecing. Writing to his parents in August 1929, one young American delegate noted indignantly that he had been cheated by the French.[134] A couple of Scottish boys, in turn, regarded the generously supplied U.S. Scouts at Arrowe Park not as brothers but as "the plutocrats of the camp," always willing to back up offers with money. "These lads would have given anything to get a kilt. I had over a dozen offers for my kilt, ranging up to 7 pounds," reported one Rover Scout from Arbroath.[135] Another young Scot described how he fooled the barter-happy Yankees into a lopsided trade: "A young gentleman from a certain northern city conceived the idea of a little private trade with his American friends. Fashioning a bit of firewood after the similitude of a skean dhu, he put it in his stocking and strolled nonchalantly down the American lines. He was soon in the center of an eager group. 'Say boy,' cried one, 'what's that in your stocking?' 'Oh, that's just a haggis pricker,' was the reply. 'We always wear them when we go visiting.' Trade was at once proposed, and the implement eventually changed hands for the sum of two shillings, and a brisk business in haggis prickers soon sprang up."[136] On rare occasions, swapping acquaintances evolved into comradeships. After exchanging badges with Kenneth Hopkins, Kansas Boy Scout Walter Ong wanted to know more about the English boy. They promised to stay in touch and write each other. Their correspondence ranged over five decades, and Hopkins's early letters to Ong show a teenager curious about scouting in the two countries, summer camps, life after school, and the difficulties of growing up in the shadow of the Great Depression.[137]

A manifestation of youth transnationalism, penpalships had become an instrument for Boy Scouts serious about engaging in long-distance communication. The BSA began fostering transnational correspondence as early as 1916 with the founding of its own pen pal agency, the World Brotherhood of Boys. Advertised in every issue of *Boys' Life* and maintained "with the primary object of promoting friendships between boys in different parts of the world," this correspondence club served as a virtual world jamboree to youths unable to attend a real one.[138] Filled with appeals from foreign Scouts wishing to correspond with their American peers, its monthly columns also contained requests from American boys seeking pen pals in Europe, Asia, Australia, and Latin America. Boy Scouts sent letters across borders for various reasons. Some had a genuine interest in other countries; others enjoyed the exchange of gifts, stamps, souvenirs, and Scout papers; still others wanted to sharpen their skills in a foreign language. This was one way to obtain the BSA's merit badge for Interpreting, which aimed at instructing Scouts "to carry on a simple conversation" in a foreign language.[139]

Despite such initiatives, however, language barriers at the jamborees proved difficult to surmount. Interactions with Scouts who did not speak English were often superficial or fraught with misunderstanding. When American boys communicated with their French, Danish, German, Dutch, Polish, and Hungarian counterparts in a jumble of sounds, gestures, and facial expressions, which adults christened "Jamborese," the outcome was humorous at best.[140] One Scout recounted a singing gig with a group of Germans at the 1929 gathering: "Though not all the chaps could speak English, they made a gallant stab at it, chiming in valiantly with the rest. The result was screamingly funny. We literally rolled on the ground at the funniness of it."[141] Language difficulties in Hungary and the Netherlands stopped youths in their tracks as well. A simple "hello" was all that was passed in the Gödöllö campground between a U.S. Scout and a young Syrian named Abu Said. "Abu simply grinned," the American Scout remembered. "He couldn't understand a word of English."[142] An American cartoon from 1937 captured the frustration many boys must have felt when trying to sort through a flurry of foreign tongues. "Gosh . . . ! I don't see any world brotherhood if you can't understand 'em," cried Scout "Jambo," the cartoon's main character.[143]

The Babel-like confusion U.S. Boy Scouts experienced at international Scout events could sap enthusiasm for world friendship. In addition, it betrayed the youngsters' naive presumption that English could somehow be the linguistic seam to hold together a fragmented world. Any hopes that Indian sign might facilitate deeper cross-cultural understanding proved elusive as well. William Tomkins's sign language courses were all the rage in the press and drew large crowds, but on the ground the situation was more diffuse. Jimmie Ricklefs performed Indian sign "until [his] hands were tired" and still doubted whether everything he said had been understood.[144] Most Scouts felt that this sort of gesticulating led nowhere. Language cemented distances within global scouting. Contacts between Scouts raised in different linguistic environments rarely reached the quality that defined the relationships of young Americans interacting with their peers from English-speaking nations.

Meaningful contacts across borders were not hampered by just the lack of language skills. Boys also complained about the lack of time and intimacy. Kansas scout Bill Smith encapsulated the conflicting demands of interpersonal friendship and mass spectacle with the following words: "Two weeks are not long enough to make really good friends when you are surrounded by 50,000 possibilities. . . . I rarely saw the same foreign boy twice at the Jamboree."[145] Scouts and visitors asking for autographs became a common nuisance. Annoyed by the endless stream of autograph hunters invading the American camp, an exasperated scoutmaster at Arrowe Park threatened "to rope [the] camp shut in self defense if it is as bad tomorrow."[146] By the fifth day in camp, scout Eugene Vickery had lost any appetite for being in the public eye. The visitors, he bemoaned, were just standing around and watching them eat "as tho[ugh] we were animals in the zoo or something."[147] Tight schedules that rushed the Scouts from one event to the next, as well as a string of troop excursions before, during, and after the jamborees, left little room for anything but fleeting encounters with other nationalities. Walter Ong's travel diary reads like the story of a Grand Tour in overdrive. In less than three weeks, his troop crisscrossed Scotland, camped near Birkenhead, explored London, passed through Belgium, sailed down the Rhine, saw Cologne, hiked in Switzerland, stayed in Paris, and returned to the United States. Ong enjoyed visiting Old Europe's historic sites, but as the Eagle Scout scurried across the continent, the tourist gaze of a privileged young traveler superseded campfire diplomacy's emphasis on face-to-face interactions.[148]

Although youths like Ong wanted to be tourists and diplomats at the same time, the Boy Scouts journeying through Europe in the interwar period had little in common with the teenage backpackers of the post-1945 period. These youthful sojourners, historian Richard Ivan Jobs writes, drew from the experience of border-crossing travel a youthful identity that was truly transnational and challenged adult demarcations of power.[149] The jamboree trips, on the other hand, were conducted tours, and the surveillance of scoutmasters escorting the boys on their itineraries curtailed their ability to make discoveries of their own. Accompanying adults assumed guardianship over the traveling Scouts to comfort parents who were concerned about the safety of their children, but their supervisory practices also reflected worries that crossing geographical borders might lead to the transgression of moral borders. "The discipline was very strict, much more so than today, and some of us bristled under it and turned to mischief," remembered Ozzie Nelson, member of the 1920 troop.[150]

Albert Snoke probably felt the same way before he left Denmark. Scoutmasters told the boys to be their best in Germany, a country they presented as strict and humorless. "We [were] a little too boisterous for them," Snoke explained.[151] When the group arrived in Paris a few days later, a disappointed Snoke found himself confined to a hotel room: the Scouts were not allowed to go out without an officer. Kept on a short leash, they were told "that the 1920 Jamboree bunch got in bad last time, in fact some almost got kidnapped."[152] No kidnapping occurred then or thirteen years later when a group of Scouts from Atlanta passed through the French capital after the rally in Vogelenzang. Their leader, however, left with a few bruises after a physical altercation with local socialists.[153] If these episodes proved disenchanting for the Scouts, historians should read them as cautionary tales. The world experienced by the youths on their guided tours stood in stark contrast to the world they encountered at the jamborees. Whereas the latter spoke of peace and understanding, the former reeked of vice and radicalism. In one context, youth was a regenerative, vigorous, and idealistic force; in another, it changed to an endangered and vulnerable body in need of protection from foreign perils.

All efforts to contain youthful initiative notwithstanding, a few Scouts traveled roads that diverged from the ones the planners had laid out for them. In Brussels, George Reuland plunged into a street festival where people were dancing and consuming alcohol, fully aware that such merrymaking would never have passed as acceptable entertainment back home.[154] When noticed, youthful freewheeling could incite friction, sometimes even among the youths themselves. Parting from the flock in Cologne, some of Ong's comrades snuck out of the hostel to experience the city at night. The outing had a "wet" ending: it peaked in a drinking bout at a nearby tavern. This incident seemed to have eluded the troop's scoutmaster, but scouts Bill Smith and Samuel E. Neel, who were strict prohibitionists, were up in arms about their friends' beer guzzling. Short of demanding their expulsion from the troop, they wrote an angry letter to Kansas City's scout executive.[155] Although their denunciatory note went unanswered, the spat between the boys demonstrates that U.S. Scouts went abroad with different expectations. Where some recognized licentious behavior unworthy of an American Boy Scout, others found enriching experiences unavailable at home.

Just as identities based on age and nationality did not prevent fissures between and within generations, adult oversight could not avert genuine culture shocks. Mild uncertainties could spiral into bewilderment when U.S. Scouts wound up in situations they felt incapable of navigating. The Scouts were not flawless, and some of their pranks were read as culturally insensitive behavior. One French war veteran could hardly contain his anger when he spotted a young American traveler donning a German helmet. He knocked the helmet off the Scout's head, shook him, and let go only after other Scouts intervened.[156] Harold Leland, member of the 1924 jamboree contingent, spoke kindly about his Danish hosts but was frustrated that "it was hard to make them understand why we do not drink or smoke."[157] Friendly feelings quickly turned sour when the adolescents sensed that their ignorance of local customs was being exploited. Local residents did not necessarily view the Boy Scouts from overseas as young ambassadors but as wealthy Americans representing a business opportunity. Complaints that shifty locals were out to rip off visitors were not uncommon. Snoke thought he "got jipped" on the Dutch Isle of Marken and had a spat with a couple of dancers who insisted on being tipped.[158]

Becoming the object of desire proved a greater challenge for the boys if the other person was young and female. Smiles traded on the campground could result in a casual flirt. "Violet Lee was my girl's name," scout Byron Stoothoff scribbled in his diary after he and his friends had secretly dated a couple of English girls.[159] Howard "Denver" More, another self-professed heartbreaker, peacocked around camp with twenty-five locks of hair he had gotten from female admirers.[160] But since American boys had grown up with an understanding of scouting as a bastion of masculinity, encounters with Girl Guides could also cause considerable unease. Religion, not gender, was often the main line of segregation in European Scout organizations. The Polish and Hungarian delegations, for instance, included boys and girls. Bill Smith, Ong's comrade, felt awkward in the company of girls who visited his camp. The Guides were not shy. "They would come into our tents and stand around looking at the mess tents while we were having dinner."[161] Albert Snoke was surprised by how confidently some of the young females he met in Denmark approached him. Seventeen-year-old Paula from Copenhagen prompted a self-conscious reaction. "After I had been introduced and gazed thoroughly that girl about monopolized me," Snoke reported. "Paula was too darn familiar. I guess that is the way with all Danish girls."[162] Contrary to the transnational community of youth the jamborees were supposed to spawn, exchanges such as this one dramatically heightened a sense of otherness. Here was no fellow youth but an uncannily confident Danish girl.

Constructions of difference based on nationality and gender muddied scouting's doctrine of youth's oneness. Boundaries were also hardened, not overcome, in patriotic drills that U.S. Scouts conducted overseas. Troops traveling through Europe in the interwar years added war memorials to their list of must-see attractions. Cast as an act of duty no Boy Scout ought to miss, tours of the French battlefields were followed by visits to the cemetery at Argonne or Belleau Wood, where the American dead of World War I lay interred. This tra-

dition of battlefield tourism, which memorialized male sacrifice for the nation, started with the jamboree delegation of 1920. Their patriotic pilgrimage
was caught on camera by the Denver war correspondent William C. Moore.
Shot not quite two years after the mayhem had stopped, with the trenches still
littered with shell holes and shrapnel, Moore's pictures possess a rare immediacy
and rawness. A wreath-laying ceremony at Belleau Wood celebrated cross-
generational citizenship and established a lineage of military masculinities, symbolically linking the dead bodies of the fallen soldiers to the young ambassadors'
unmaimed bodies. Meetings with Belgian boys whose hands had been cut off
by German soldiers conveyed to the youths that their fathers had been fighting
for a just cause. Moore's camera also captured supposedly lighter moments
when the Boy Scouts were scavenging the trenches for war souvenirs. Yet the
gleeful smiles of the Scouts posing with German helmets they found on the
battlefield revealed the less gleeful logic of militarized nationalism, in which
brotherhood stopped with one's own fighting men and licensed the plundering
of defeated enemies. Serving less as a pathway to postwar reconciliation than an
initiation into the duties of martial manhood, the trip ended on a morbid note.
The Boy Scouts spent their homeward voyage aboard a confiscated German
passenger ship with the coffins of six hundred doughboys who were being
shipped back to the United States.[163]

Although militarism became less pronounced in scouting as personal memories of the war faded, jamboree units continued to flock to sites of American
military valor in Europe. In August 1929, a detachment of Boy Scouts from
Bronxville, New York, undertook an excursion to Shotwick to the grave of
Leonard Marange, a young pilot from their hometown who had flown for the
Royal Air Force during World War I. The boys paid tribute to Marange and
put flowers on his grave.[164] U.S. troops passing through Paris held memorial
services at the Tomb of the Unknown Soldier and visited the battlefields east
of the city. The shattered landscapes of the western front were daunting enough
to make some Scouts question the sanity of war. "Saw shell-holes, machine
guns, artillery, graves, and all that made the War a 'success,' " a distraught Ong
penned in his diary.[165] At the same time, Ong had no second thoughts about
leading his troop's commemorative exercises. In Scotland, Ong spoke at the
tomb of World War I commander Earl Douglas Haig, and his companions
placed a bronze plaque on the grave with the caption, "The Boy Scouts of
Kansas City, U.S.A., honor the memory of Field Marshal Earl Haig, friend of
the Boy Scouts. In peril confident, in duty devoted, in victory considerate."[166]
Not exactly critical of war per se, these boys rather suggested that an Anglo-
American brotherhood hardened in combat was worth preserving.

Young people's behavior on the campground, too, was not as consistently geared toward universal brotherhood. Rather than building a truly transnational fraternity, flags, pageants, camp folklore, and uniforms representing different nations made the Boy Scouts aware that national distinctions mattered and that one's country ought to be the primary locus of belonging. Emotions ran high during the march of nations. "When American flags approached the reviewing stand, 'The Star Spangled Banner' burst forth," remembered one young delegate at Arrowe Park. "That was a thrill! Hearing the national anthem in a foreign land made quivers race up and down our spines."[167] William C. Westmoreland, who later gained notoriety for waging a murderous war of attrition in Vietnam, reflected on the impact of his journey to England in 1929: "It was my first trip overseas, my first exposure to foreigners, and my first venture as an Eagle Scout. I was proud to wear the uniform of my country in a foreign land. I was eager to do it again."[168] Although adolescent expressions of patriotism rarely descended into jingoism, the competitions at Ermelunden bred antagonistic feelings among the participants. Albert Snoke's memories of the tug of war, which the Americans had lost to the Danes, tell a story quite different from the narratives circulated by the organizers. "It is noted in Dr. Fisher's report in *Boys' Life* in November [1924] that we were happy because we had done well against the heavier team and that inasmuch as thousands of the Danish people were present, we were glad to have them satisfied. This may have been true, but I do not quite recall such an altruistic happy feeling on the part of the American Scouts."[169]

Staying close to their own identities, the youths learned to imagine internationalism through the familiar prism of nationalism—not as a utopian plan for the world to unite but as a road map to peace between nations and empires conceived as inherently different. Wrapped in the language of boyish curiosity, swapping commodified and trivialized discourses of civilizational difference. Childish stereotypes about nationalities were reified in transactions that reduced the complexities of history and culture to a friendly exchange of goods. If Scotland became the equivalent of a kilt and the United States the equivalent of a cowboy hat, why bother to dig deeper? In the end, most boys subordinated their fleeting encounters with Scouts from other parts of the world to their loyalties to troop and country. Portland Boy Scout R. Burke Morden was not prone to romanticize the contacts he had with foreign boys at the 1933 jamboree. Unlike his friend Owen Matthews, Morden was "doubtful" whether the "remarkable show" at Gödöllö would "result in the establishment of a world brotherhood or assure lasting peace."[170]

As time went by and peace proved fragile, skepticism mounted. Long after the faces and names of the boys they had met overseas drifted into oblivion, Snoke, Ong, and their fellow Scouts shared memories of common exploits at troop reunions. Amid the munching of crackers and the renewal of friendships, few of the old men looked back at their boyhood voyages as an education in global citizenship. Given its limitations, Scout brotherhood had not, and could not have, prevented another world war. Spencer Gard, Ong's former scoutmaster, even wondered whether "the promiscuous mingling . . . of races and cultures would lead to world peace rather than to war."[171] In his recollections, Snoke recalled in similar fashion how the boys had put country first. "In retrospect," Snoke concluded, "I doubt that we were all the Frank Merriwells that he [George J. Fisher] so glowingly described. . . . There is little question but that, while the boys truly enjoyed their contacts with the Scouts of other nations, the fact that this was a competitive group . . . really was of paramount importance."[172]

Mulling over the significance of the world jamborees, the editor of a Missouri newspaper anticipated that the seven Jefferson City Boy Scouts who had been selected to make the trip to Hungary in 1933 would "return better Americans than when they departed."[173] Shared by planners and participants alike, the editor's expectation reflects the interests and outlooks that informed scouting's world brotherhood of boys after 1918. Although they had the potential to reshape boys' attitudes, the jamborees often hardened existing allegiances to troop, organization, and country. And while the Americans' desire to fraternize with their foreign brother Scouts was usually sincere, supervisionary regimes and the ephemeral nature of their contacts foreclosed any serious attempt to breach adult demarcations of power. Nation building, not cosmopolitan unity, was the principal outcome of these polyglot encampments. Disparities of wealth, culture, and power corroded the idea of a world brotherhood of boys. Gaining only a faint appreciation of global commonalities, U.S. Scouts, whose copious supplies and nationalist swagger tended to alienate their foreign brothers, were more likely to return with a clearer understanding of what made them distinct as Americans. The result was a stunted transnationalism, which policed adolescent border-crossings, discouraged youthful initiative, and tended to scratch surfaces instead of penetrating them. Scouting's boyish campfire diplomacy hardly captured the era's political, economic, and cultural interdependencies. It infantilized them.

Established for the political hygiene of elites, the remasculinization of nations and empires, and the indoctrination of an increasingly self-actualizing youth, the world jamborees of the interwar years were as much about the rebirth of old men as they were about the birth of youth as an instrument of international negotiation. Acknowledging this does not mean that we should discount the young ambassadors, who adjusted their ideas and practices to new global flows, as pawns of their superiors. Tracking U.S. Boy Scouts as they traversed physical and imaginary boundaries should direct our attention to how ideas about youth as emblematic of hopes for a peaceful future opened up spaces of participation for actual youth. Their Junior League of Nations demands that we recognize them as young citizens eager to find their voice in a more integrated and unpredictable world.

Chapter 4

A Brother to All?

Scouting and the Problem of Race

In the summer of 1937, scoutmaster Heihachiro Ono's gaze wandered across the Pacific. Ono had been asked to study the Boy Scouts in the United States and publish his findings in the official bulletin of the Boy Scouts of Japan. That summer, the BSA held its first national jamboree in Washington, DC. With more than twenty-seven thousand American Boy Scouts and a few hundred foreign Boy Scouts in attendance, the young campers who had pitched their tents around the Washington Monument pitted a youthful optimism against the anxieties of a world battered by the Great Depression. Curiously, the jamboree found no mention in Ono's article. A supporter of his country's expansionist policies, Ono scrutinized the BSA for a different reason. Like their British cousins, the Japanese scoutmaster explained, the Americans had learned to "fully utilize" their major boy organization "for the colonial rule of [their] nation," justifying white dominance at home and abroad in reciprocal terms. Recognizing in nonwhite peoples racial inferiors who "tend to give rise to disasters anywhere and anytime," the BSA had been "vigorously . . . pushing forward nationalization" among youths of color to turn them into loyal subjects for the American empire. With their policies of subjugation and assimilation, Ono suggested, U.S. Scout executives offered a template desperately needed by Japanese boy workers facing similar problems in their dealings with indigenous youth in Korea and Manchuria.[1]

The Japanese scoutmaster's observations diverge sharply from the boyish internationalism highlighted in the previous chapter. At the helm of the BSA stood not peace brokers, Ono stated, but imperialists who were governing their colonial subjects with admirable efficiency. I substantiate Ono's assessment by revealing how efforts to discipline young people of color spurred the BSA's emergence as a global player. Born in the era of high imperialism, the Boy Scouts had to grapple with the legitimizing ideology of race that hid the expansive and exploitative behavior of white societies behind the veils of science, religion, and civilization. Posing as wardens of primitive peoples made Scout leaders in Europe and North America willing executioners of their nations' imperial projects, yet the Fourth Scout Law told all Boy Scouts that they were brothers. The familial rhetoric of brotherhood threw the movement into a confrontation with regimes of racial subordination, prompting the BSA to remap the borders of integration and formulate new rationalizations for the social and masculine status of marginalized boys. Ultimately, I demonstrate that the BSA's gradual acceptance of racial diversity has to be understood within the twin contexts of globalization and U.S. imperial expansion.

While scouting was quickly embraced across the American empire, its adoption by nonwhite youth was not a linear process. Long before BSA leaders agreed on a centrally orchestrated plan to recruit boys of color with the founding of the Inter-Racial Service (IRS) in 1926, local initiatives, often spontaneous in nature, extended the brotherhood of scouting beyond the pale of white America. Acting without the approval of national headquarters, military officers started the first troops in the Philippines before World War I, and African American and Asian American youths marched as Boy Scouts as early as 1911. The growth of multiracial scouting was by no means a foregone conclusion. The idea came under attack from white racists, who shuddered at the thought of their sons camping with the children of "savages," as well as from anticolonial activists, who feared that scouting was a ploy devised by white men to steal their offspring and destroy their culture. Still, multiracial scouting promised enough boons to enough people to gain steady ground. Key to this attitude was a broadly shared faith in modern theories of development that interlaced contemporary ideas of race improvement with an evolutionary understanding of youth. Although BSA administrators practiced segregation and ascribed an inferior character to boys of color, conceptions of youth as a universal life stage that eclipsed the social barriers of the grown-up world complicated the notion of biologically fixed differences. This made it difficult to maintain that only white boys possessed the capacity to grow physically and mentally. It is easy to see how the evolutionism inherent in scouting appealed to minorities struggling for civil rights, but developmental ideas could also accommodate those who favored educating youth of color to further imperial control. Elastic enough to serve conflicting agendas, the discourse of development shows how the BSA became a site of interracial coalitions, power contestations, and a catalyst of racialization in the interimperial world of the early twentieth century.

Developmental theory as a tool for managing youth and race relations coincided with the rise of what the German historian Lutz Raphael has termed "the mobilized nation."[2] With the world wars awakening people to the possibility of unlimited destruction, societies witnessing mass carnage, revolutions, and the collapse of old orders began recruiting more segments of their populations in the hope of averting a similar fate. As nation-states and empires began marshaling larger portions of their material and human resources to vanquish their enemies, they also strove to take fuller advantage of their subaltern manpower. Mobilization did not necessarily mean large standing armies, but it promoted the vision of a comprehensive partnership between the state and civil society based on a militarized ethics of national service. In most youth organizations, the hunger for new recruits gradually pushed aside concerns about racial purity. Paramount to a genuinely democratic impulse was the fear of adult organizers that failing to reach out to youth of color would drive them into the hands of anticolonial and antiracist activists committed to disrupting the empire from within. Eventually, the question was not whether African American, Native American, or colonial boys should become Boy Scouts. The question was how to justify their enlistment in the brotherhood of scouting in a society where the hierarchies of race and empire regulated access to masculine citizenship.

The racial ambiguities in a movement proclaiming to be open to boys and men of all races are difficult to capture in a string of locally isolated studies. Such histories exist, but they leave us poorly equipped to understand how the BSA's racial politics traveled across the geographical and political borders, and how it was influenced by the drawing and redrawing of global color lines.[3] Empire internationalized race like few other political forces, forming long-distance solidarities between groups and nationalities on different levels of various color-based hierarchies.[4] Scout executives were hesitant to frame the problem of nonwhite membership nationally. Making direct analogies between foreign and domestic Boy Scouts of color, BSA historian William D. Murray, for example, found that the organization's interracial program was "related indirectly but significantly to world Scouting."[5] At national training conferences in the 1920s and 1930s, debates about how to promote scouting in the colonies and apply the program to African American, Native American, Mexican American, and Asian American youths overlapped frequently.[6]

Racist ideologies and practices in the Boy Scouts moved within as well as between empires. Japan, Great Britain, and even the League of Nations studied the progress of nonwhite scouting in territories under U.S. jurisdiction, appraising it as a model to govern subaltern youths in other parts of the world. Such appraisals ran counter to the claim that maintaining colonial order was primarily a European problem, not an American one. At the same time that the "color question" was being discussed in the global forums of scouting, transnational exchanges between Scouts and scouters of color made them realize that their anticolonial struggles were intertwined. As a black scoutmaster gushed after returning from Arrowe Park in 1929, "We Africans all hope that the Jamboree spirit, that we are all brothers irrespective of race and creed, will continue throughout life, and that this will be a new era for the world."[7]

To excavate the history of race in the BSA as a history of transfer, accommodation, power, and resistance across boundaries, it is necessary to assemble a multitude of actors and perspectives. Moving from African American communities and America's Chinatowns to Native American reservations, from Filipino villages to Puerto Rican barrios, this chapter focuses on the evolution of scouting for domestic and colonial youths of color in the movement's first three decades. I trace the winding and rocky paths of these youths into scouting by showing how white leaders teetered over the question of admitting nonwhite boys, and also discuss subaltern practices of appropriation and resistance. My analysis charts how local constellations fit into the larger global matrix of race relations without ignoring the political and cultural patterns specific to each group. Putting the voices of boys of color alongside those of white Boy Scouts and scoutmasters inevitably entails gleaning the echoes of colonized youth from sources created by white males. Yet even documents that show no palpable traces of subaltern agency give little indication that BSA leaders simply imposed their will on other cultures. Despite the asymmetries of power and age, men and boys of color made the BSA's objectives of developing physical fitness and masculine character their own, turning them, if necessary, against their white mentors.

United but Not Equal

Rosa Lowe was not known to be an irritable person. But in the spring of 1918, she was at the end of her tether. Lowe wrote a couple of angry letters to James West. Her work for the Anti-Tuberculosis Association had made Lowe familiar with the plight of Atlanta's black children, many of whom were growing up in poor health and unable to thrive. As a progressive reformer who believed that scouting could do much to nurture underprivileged children, it broke her heart to see that local executives barred African American boys from joining the movement. How, Lowe asked, was it possible to deny the uniform of a Boy Scout to black boys at the same time that their fathers were wearing Uncle Sam's uniform in the war against Germany? "By excluding the colored boys the nation is perpetuating undemocratic principles though the world is fighting today for Democracy," Lowe fumed. She then peppered her charge with the dazzling statement that West and his coworkers were failing American youth. "The very name of your organization is a misnomer," she penned, "and should be called, 'White Boy Scouts of America.'"[8]

Did the BSA's founders really think of character building as an enterprise for whites only? Judging by their rhetoric, Lowe's outrage seems amiss. Scout administrators spoke of boyhood and manhood in very broad terms. Early handbooks imagined the Boy Scouts as descending from a lineage of honorable fighting men that included Japanese samurais and Native American warriors.[9] Casting the Boy Scouts as an Americanizing force, Scout leaders portrayed the movement as nonsectarian, classless, and open to boys of different origins. The BSA's constitution contained no racially exclusionary provisions, and early Boy Scout rallies in New York City, which included the sons of native-born and immigrant men, duped progressive educators into believing that they were witnessing the molding of a generation of cosmopolitan citizens. The immigrant journalist Jacob Riis proclaimed euphorically that the BSA had "broken down every imaginary barrier of sect and caste" in its service to boyhood.[10] At one point, Mortimer Schiff denied that racial animosities were plaguing the United States at all.[11] When Baden-Powell visited New York in 1912, Britain's top scouter was impressed that among the troops marching in a parade held in his honor was "one composed entirely of Chinese boys," who "drilled well and smartly," and "also one of negro boys."[12] The only admission requirements that were nonnegotiable, it seemed, were age, gender, and adherence to the Scout law.

However, this public presentation of multiracialism conflicted with varied discriminatory practices in the movement. Southern white supremacists issued sharp warnings that they would boycott the Boy Scouts if the organization forced them to admit black youth. Ignoring the ways of Jim Crow, New Orleans editor D. D. Moore told West in 1911, would "shut out the white boy" and reduce the BSA to a sectional affair.[13] A few years later, southern executives threatened to sabotage the organization if the national council allowed

African Americans to join. White Virginians and Georgians proclaimed that they would burn their uniforms in public.[14] To placate its critics, the BSA gave regional councils license to keep undesirable boys at bay.[15] Under the banner of local self-determination, charter applications from African American troops were rejected. Other racial minorities, too, felt the sting of prejudice. Although Native American lore experts taught Boy Scouts how to play Indian, recapitulation theory held that Native American youth would never evolve beyond the stage of tribal primitivism. Long-standing cultural stereotypes that portrayed Hispanic peoples as lazy and shiftless and Asian Americans as physically weak and deceitful hampered the development of scouting in these groups. Race became crucial to the construction of what the historian Benjamin Jordan called the "Anti-Scout," an imaginary antipode to the masculine values of discipline, strength, and self-control.[16]

Visual representations and social performance normalized the linkage of whiteness and masculine citizenship in the BSA. The idealized Scouts depicted in early BSA literature were exclusively white middle-class boys. Not until the late 1920s did the organization start publishing more favorable images of African American boys posing as Scouts, and then only sparingly. If black characters were shown at all, they mainly appeared in a context of racist mockery. Demeaning jokes in which African Americans figured as lazy half-wits with thick rural accents were printed in *Boys' Life* and told by Scout officials to break the ice at executive meetings. Boy Scout troops staging minstrel shows at fundraising events or singing black spirituals around the campfire perpetuated the notion that African Americans were happy simpletons unable to cope with the challenges of modern life. Black people occupied the lowest rung on the BSA's racial ladder, yet other minorities hardly fared better. Even the positive images of Indianness the Boy Scouts projected at home and abroad did not immediately translate into a concerted effort to recruit Native American youth.[17]

Previous studies have acknowledged these racial divides in U.S. scouting, pointing to the early 1920s as an important watershed. One argument these studies make is that the bravery demonstrated by black soldiers in World War I in conjunction with the pressure coming from domestic reformers like Rosa Lowe compelled the BSA to widen the circle of Scout masculinity and allow segregated troops of color.[18] What this interpretation lacks, though, is an awareness of how these changes were the product of the BSA's entanglement with cultural and organizational transformations of global proportions, and how its leaders reacted to various stimuli from abroad. When U.S. boy workers adopted Baden-Powell's model, they were importing a scheme to secure white supremacy in a world riven by racial violence. As citizens of a colonial power, white Americans could easily fathom how the British were wrestling with the dual nature of imperial scouting as a movement that could be deployed to shore up the authority of white settlers in the colonies as well as to discipline inferior races. Initially, Baden-Powell cared most about how scouting could be used to promote white imperial unity, but the determination with which small groups of Bengal Indians and black South Africans started banding together in non-commissioned Scout units made him think about ways to reconcile indigenous activism with the interests of empire. Against the wishes of colonial administrators who feared that scouting might turn young natives into revolutionaries, British scouters after World War I urged colonial administrators to accept a modified version of the program that tied Scout manhood to loyalty to the colonial state in the hope of alleviating the tensions that came with imperial rule.[19] When writing about the "mixed Scout troops" that paraded past him in New York City, Baden-Powell was highlighting a prescription for maintaining imperial order.

U.S. Army Lieutenant Sherman Kiser was thinking along these lines when he entered a Moro village in the southern Philippines in the summer of 1914. Kiser visited the Moros, the Muslim inhabitants of Zamboanga and Mindanao, at the request of Caroline Spencer, a Protestant missionary from New York whose deceased husband Lorillard had lent his enthusiastic support to scouting.[20] Representing the masculine military and feminine reformist incentives for America's colonial enterprise in Southeast Asia, Kiser and Spencer acquainted the natives with their country's newest youth scheme. Kiser's expedition seemed at once daring and intimate. Acting on Spencer's advice that forming Boy Scout units composed of Moro youths might help pacify U.S.-Filipino relations, the army officer found willing partners in the village. His trip was remarkable because it constituted the first experiment in U.S. scouting among a Muslim population, and because both parties had been involved in a vicious race war that had cost thousands of Moro lives and left countless children orphaned. Having gained the approval of the elders, Kiser gave the village boys their first lessons in scouting.[21] Under Kiser's supervision, the young Moros learned to treat wounded animals, administer first aid, destroy insects on coconut trees, clean their village, box, and pledge allegiance to the flag of the United States.[22]

The letters and photographs shared by Kiser masked this counterinsurgency project as a sentimental boy-man drama bridging the divides of race, religion, and memory. At first glance, the reader witnesses a typical colonial encounter: immature islanders are instructed by a benevolent white tutor devoted to bringing out the best in his wards.[23] Two photos convey the compatibility of

Figure 4.1. Moro children lined up before an American-built settlement house in Zamboanga, Southern Philippines, 1914. (Courtesy of the National Scouting Museum, Boy Scouts of America, Irving, Texas)

Figure 4.2. Moro Boy Scouts taking the Scout oath, 1914. These two photos highlight the ideology of racial uplift and show the capacity of scouting to forge affective bonds between the colonizers and the colonized. (Courtesy of the National Scouting Museum, Boy Scouts of America, Irving, Texas)

colonial scouting and racial uplift. The first photo, taken at the initial meeting, shows the village boys in a disheveled posture, facing the camera in ragged outfits or entirely naked. The second photo narrates their transition from savagery to civilization: the camera zooms in on the boys dressed in brand new khaki uniforms, their eyes fixed on the scoutmaster as he administers the Scout oath. Referring to his Scouts as "little brown brothers," Kiser created a form of imperial tutelage that balanced authority and affect.[24]

Here the familiar narrative of colonial paternalism ends, but there is a second, equally powerful story at work. The father-and-son-like transactions between a U.S. Army officer and Moro youths remade the masculinity of the adult civilizer at the same time that they were aimed at masculinizing the boys. Even as Kiser embraced scouting's mobilizing ideology, it is the military man who saw the possibility of moral regeneration in fraternizing with the boys. Corresponding with the shift in U.S. colonial policy in the Philippines from racial violence to American-Filipino collaboration, Kiser's work with the Moros opened up a space that permitted imperialists to shed their warrior masculinity and separate themselves from the bloody reality of conquest. The soldier-turned-scoutmaster evolved into an older brother, redeemed by the "love" and "friendship" he received from his boys. The boys' approval was necessary for this particular performance of masculinity to work, which allowed Kiser to reclaim the boyish innocence lost in war—to turn the page and start afresh. Accentuating scouting's capacity to heal the wounds of racial strife and forge emotional bonds between colonizers and colonized, the farewell scene epitomizes this recalibration of imperial manhood: "As the boat sailed out to sea those honest little Scouts stood waving a last farewell with tears streaming over their faces. I am sure that every American that stood on the pier lost his heart to the Moro Boy Scouts. I realized as I left them that 'never before in their lives had they had the friendship and felt the kindness of any person', and that it had changed them from little savages into little men, with a love for one fellow-man at least."[25]

Kiser's account decoupled scouting from static primitivism and provided a script for applying the movement's developmental promise to nonwhite races. Once imbued with Scout masculinity, the sons of former enemies would stop resisting their white tutors and accept their dependent status. As Kiser stated, the Boy Scouts could "do more toward the civilization of these peoples than anything else I know of, because so much more can be done with the boy's mind."[26] Making claims about childhood that were simultaneously universal and imperialist, colonial scoutmasters backed by missionaries, businessmen, and military personnel hoped to humanize imperial relations and train future native elites loyal to the American nation-state. Their assumption was that cross-racial brotherhood, if properly executed, could stabilize white power rather than subvert it. BSA administrators on the mainland agreed. The authors of the second edition of the *Handbook for Scoutmasters*, published in 1922, recognized that "honest, earnest Scout hearts beat beneath white and yellow and red and black skins." Accompanying this multiracial redefinition of Scout manhood was a reprint of the picture that showed Kiser's Moro Boy Scouts taking the Scout oath.[27]

The second major impulse for the reorganization of the BSA's racial regime came from the internationalization of the Boy Scout movement. Adolescent performances of border-crossing friendship at the world jamborees drove adult organizers to reconsider the relationship of manhood, national loyalty, and transnational responsibilities. Mass displays in which white Scouts held hands with and sang the same songs as boys of color produced potentially poignant critiques of racial discord at home. Color lines were blotted out at the farewell ceremonies at London and Ermelunden when boy representatives from every continent formed a circle and intonated "Auld Lang Syne."[28] Those unable to go abroad could learn about Scouts crossing the color line from reports published in *Boys' Life* or the international Scout magazine *Jamboree*. The idea of raising male youth in the spirit of cooperation based on characterizations of boyhood as classless, transreligious, and transethnic stood in an uneasy relationship with established hierarchies of race and manhood. The BSA's interwar policies toward youths of color, then, were directly related to the transnational forces that redrew the boundaries between nations and generations.

The irony of nonwhite boys attaching themselves to a movement originally designed to revitalize white empires did not escape organizers in Europe and North America. Yet they waited until 1924 to codify a reality they had not quite foreseen. Flush with impressions from the Ermelunden jamboree, where white boys had mingled with participants from Egypt, Siam, and Uganda, the delegates of the third ISC passed a remarkable set of antidiscriminatory resolutions. They insisted that since the Boy Scout movement "recognized no national barrier in the comradeship of scouts," no organization could tolerate denying membership to boys and men "for any reasons of race, creed, or politics."[29] As chairman of the ISC Committee of Resolutions, West bore responsibility for the wording of these declarations, which ran counter to his domestic policy of dodging race issues and caving to the wishes of white supremacists. It is hard to tell if West pushed these developments or bowed to them, but by the early 1920s his antirevolutionary politics had outweighed personal doubts whether nonwhite boys could be Scouts. Alluding to popular racist tracts that predicted the end of white supremacy, West suggested in 1922 that stemming the "rising tide of color" through scouting would help arrest the "influence of lawlessness and irreligion at work among countless millions."[30] This stance dovetailed with the racial practices of foreign Scout leaders. British officials gave their approval to Scout units of color in colonial societies without granting them the same status. For example, Imperial Headquarters' acquiescence in the policy of white South Africans to funnel black youth into a separate "Pathfinder" movement with different uniforms paralleled models of nonwhite recruitment that were being deliberated within the BSA.[31]

To strike a balance between the transnational imperatives of inclusion and the racial sensibilities of white Americans, West relied on the support of Bolton Smith, an investment banker from Kentucky and the vice president of the National Council. BSA administrators regarded Smith as something of an expert in race relations for drawing up what became known as the Louisville Plan. This middle-of-the-road experiment with segregated African American Boy Scouts dated back to the tentative creation of black troops in 1916 in Louisville, Kentucky. Its goal was to avoid the full-scale integration of African Americans by offering them membership on the basis of the same program while keeping them distant from white recreational activities.[32] Smith's approach was both persistent and patronizing. To Rosa Lowe, he replied that demanding that boys of color be treated on an equal footing with white boys would only alienate white citizens as long as Americans were still "willing to stand for lynchings of colored people."[33] Smith had no patience with African Americans agitating for full enfranchisement. Such demands, he asserted, would do their children a disservice since civil rights demonstrations that were not endorsed by white elites were bound to aggravate racial animosities. Smith defended his assimilationist racism with a transatlantic analogy. Unlike his distant relatives in Africa, the "[American] negro" could "make progress" in a country where the whites were in the majority only "in the terms of [white] culture."[34]

Nonetheless, Smith eloquently proclaimed the link between scouting's pet project of furthering international understanding and the need to ameliorate race relations. Addressing his fellow executives in 1926, Smith argued that the meaning of world brotherhood would not be complete until scouting was made available to black boys.[35] Two years later, Smith once again mixed race and internationalism. He pointed out that racial conflicts were "responsible for some of our most acute international problems" and the greatest menace to world peace.[36] Hinting at anticolonial movements that were gaining momentum across Africa as well as the formation of pan-Africanist groups in North America and the West Indies, Smith warned those opposed to including nonwhites that their intransigence would invite disaster in a world in which the "white race represents a distinct minority" and the "other races are reaching out for knowledge and longing for recognition."[37] If charity and compassion were not good guides for enacting cross-racial brotherhood, self-preservation clearly was.

In the thinking of white scouters, boyhood development was a normative lens for understanding colonial education, international relations, and race management as closely intertwined phenomena. Boys of color might not be capable of rising to the same heights of character as their white counterparts, and some educators continued to stress that "heredity" constricted the realm of improvability for nonwhite youth.[38] However, the belief that boys of color shared with all youth the malleability of young age made them seem qualified for basic components of the program. Baden-Powell articulated a common sentiment when he said that "boys all the world over are boys alike," and if one could reach African Scouts "while they are still young and train them in the right way," there was a good chance "that a very large number of them would grow up into . . . white men with black skins."[39] Such assimilationist fantasies of whitening boys of color, as expressed by Baden-Powell and echoed by Bolton Smith, had little to do with making self-governing men and citizens. Instead, they grew out of a defensive posture that saw in scouting for youth of color a means to breed loyal subjects in order to prevent a future race war.

Organizing Nonwhite Youth

Advertised as an instrument to deescalate racial tensions, scouting for boys of color can be understood as an extension of the educational work begun by white teachers and missionaries in the colonial world since the end of the nineteenth century. This restructuring of imperial power resulted from a growing awareness of the limitations of colonial governance. Recognizing that large swaths of territory with resentful populations could not be controlled by small contingents of soldiers and administrators, colonizers gradually embraced a system of "indirect rule" that promised native elites some of the benefits of empire. Picking local allies and tying their fate to the success of the colonial enterprise obscured systemic inequalities within these regimes. Indirect rule, whether practiced in extraterritorial possessions or used to govern racial minorities at home, reaffirmed colonialism's paternalist ideology, a realm of imperial power where benevolent "fathers" were watching over aboriginal "children."[40]

BSA administrators sought recourse in a particular strand of developmental discourse one might call pliable primitivism. It was pliable in the sense that it considered youths from different racial backgrounds capable of evolving to a higher level of physical and mental aptitude through scouting, albeit to varying degrees. It was primitive because it situated the highest type of young manhood in Anglo-Saxon middle-class culture while declaring all other masculinities inferior. This interest in measuring the distance between primitive and civilized must not be confused with idealized representations of noble savagery proliferated by white scouters who reveled in the fantasy that pure energy resided in non-European races. Accentuating both the immaturity and improvability of colonial subjects, pliable primitivism encouraged BSA officials working at different imperial sites to carve out a developmental perspective for minority boys and draw cross-racial and cross-generational comparisons. In privileging children over adults, scouting reflected the belief that nonwhite boys could be raised to become better subjects without upending racial hierarchies.

Two pioneers of this policy were the Scout executives Alfred S. Macfarlane and Ernest E. Voss. Both men journeyed abroad to advance the program in the Philippines and Puerto Rico. Macfarlane arrived in Manila after local Rotarians had established the first Boy Scout council on the island, which the BSA endorsed in December 1923. The twenty-one charter members were a diverse group—more diverse than any other BSA council at the time. American entrepreneurs and missionaries joined forces with Chinese businessmen and Filipino politicians; funds were acquired from the local YMCA, the U.S. Army, the American Legion, and various Christian churches as well as from the Filipino and Chinese Chambers of Commerce.[41] Shouldering the mission to bring scouting to boys of different ethnic and religious backgrounds on America's imperial frontiers, Macfarlane asked for patience. "Remember," he informed West after taking the job, "that in a territory of 114,000 square miles, 7,083 separate and distinct islands; 47 provinces, 9 subprovinces; 9,495,272 Christians and 885,368 non-Christian people, the work of one man is a slow process."[42] Voss, who replaced Macfarlane in 1929, struck a more melodramatic chord. He equated the task of "extending the benefits of . . . physical and mental hygiene, self control and self development" to "primitive youth" at "every outpost where the American flag flies" to that of a "flaming crusade." "Our frontiers are the world," Voss exulted, "we share these benefits of physical and mental hygiene, self-control and self-development with youth the world over."[43]

Striking the manly pose of the heroic civilizer who carried the gospel of scouting to the outer rims of U.S. state power was typical of globe-trotting boy workers like Macfarlane and Voss. It was a conscious mode of self-legitimization that tied the work done by BSA executives in the colonies to the Protestant middle-class tradition of evangelizing the world, which Ian Tyrrell identified as the cornerstone of America's "moral empire."[44] This trope obfuscated the belligerent roots of U.S. overseas expansion and recast the Boy Scouts as a relief agency devoted to aiding suffering children, not as the rearguard of an invading military force. Colonial scouting was a "missionary project," Macfarlane underscored, and would remain one "for many years to come."[45] Mixing Christian conversion narratives with progressive discourses about child saving, U.S. scouters working with boys at America's imperial peripheries fashioned a charitable masculinity that allowed them to portray their foreign interventions as an exercise in global humanitarianism.

Colonial fieldwork was also brandished as a glorious opportunity to rejuvenate and preserve white masculine frontier values in a modernizing world. As literary scholar Bradley Deane has argued, empires needed the romance of boyhood to function as much as they needed anonymous administrators and ruthless politicians. Men like Kiser, Macfarlane, and Voss fed this desire, transforming uncertain processes into infinite adventure and colonial rule into cathartic play. Speaking to a national assembly of scoutmasters in 1936, BSA executive George J. Fisher used corresponding language to pay tribute to the men who had socialized with nonwhite boys on America's domestic and imperial frontiers. "Wheat in Louisville" and his "glorious inter-racial adventure with 34 Troops of Negro boys," "Ernest Schaffer, who personally organized 60 Troops in the Philippines," "Voss himself—with a great empire in the midst of the Pacific . . . Macfarlane, who preceded him, breaking trails there and in Porto [sic] Rico"—for Fisher, these men were the last "romanticists in Scouting." They kept alive the youthful "spirit of adventure" in the age of modern industry and technology, "adventuring into the dark places; probing into isolated areas; challenging the slum areas."[46] Here and elsewhere, Anglo-American imperial manhood bore no traces of struggle, exploitation, and violence. These simply vanished in the realm of politically productive play that promised to generate bonds of companionship between white men and their nonwhite charges.

The perception of men of character coming to the rescue of ailing boys in primitive surroundings conditioned the BSA's interactions with tropical youth. To combat the high child mortality rates in America's imperial territories, character building, physical education, and health instruction became closely linked. Stirred to action by their encounters with sickly children housed in weather-beaten barrios, scouters partnered with local chapters of the YMCA,

Rotary, and the Junior Red Cross to instill in indigenous youth an appreciation for Western standards of hygiene.[47] In 1921, Puerto Rican Boy Scouts assisted local health officials in distributing brochures on good sanitary practices in the wake of a bubonic plague that had swept the island.[48] Organizers worried about the spread of leprosy founded Boy Scout units for boys with leprosy quarantined in remote locations in Hawaii and the Philippines. On his inaugural tour as governor of the islands in 1931, Theodore Roosevelt Jr. made headlines when he visited the leper colony on the island of Culion, shaking the hand of every Filipino Boy Scout he met. Proclaiming that "in the health of the child lies the strength of the nation," Roosevelt encapsulated a basic rationale of why the BSA reached out to indigenous male youth: the future of the empire rested not just on the happiness and health of white boys but on the survival of colonial boys.[49]

As they were claiming responsibility for the welfare of indigenous boys, organizers expressed fatherly feelings for their dependents. James Wilder, who founded the first Boy Scout troop in Hawaii, radiated paternal warmth and pride after native boys had displayed their skills for the queen and the governor at a rally in February 1916. "How they labored!" he exulted. "Bravo, tenderfeet! Climb high, you will, with such a start."[50] Likewise, Voss called on his fellow scouters in the Philippines to approach the boy not as his "administrative superior" but as a "counselor and friend."[51] The most forceful demonstration of colonial fatherhood took shape during public festivities devoted to remasculinizing civic education that became known as Boys' Week. Organized by Rotary clubs since the early 1920s, Boys' Weeks initiated "Be His Pal" campaigns that encouraged foster fatherhood and told actual fathers to form more loving relationships with their sons. For a couple of days every year, usually in early May, Boy Scouts from San Diego and Memphis to San Juan and Manila attended vocational workshops and participated in mock trials and cabinet meetings under adult supervision.[52] In supporting these events, American child workers dealing with colonized youth anchored their mentorship in intimacy and affect, thereby inserting themselves between the boys and their actual parents.

BSA officials sent to the periphery embraced forums such as Boys' Week because they reinforced their agenda of rearing a generation of colonial male youth willing to serve the empire. Scouting, in this context, was transformed from an institution offering a pathway to citizenship to an apprenticeship program for the making of imperial subjects convinced of their advanced masculinity yet obedient to their white masters. "Thoroughly acquainted with American institutions" and "imbued with their ideals," a 1911 BSA job announcement for a field secretary in Puerto Rico suggested, young natives would reciprocate kindness with loyalty.[53] Showing colonial boys how to be good Scouts, Macfarlane promised in 1928, would "breed a better understanding and love, not only of our Flag, but of the American people, that this Flag represents." The calculation was clear: Scouts so "understood" and "loved" would gladly accept their role as bricks in the wall of empire.[54] Social status and racial classification determined the career paths laid out by scouting. Contrary to the sons of indigenous elites, whose units were run like mainland units, colonial boys with little formal education were offered a modified form of scouting that stressed military drill and imperial patriotism in the hope of teaching them to be productive workers or auxiliary soldiers. The boys were urged to speak English at all Scout meetings. Camping was promoted to turn these "children of nature" into modern conservationists. In Puerto Rico and the Philippines, where the clamoring for independence became louder after World War I, boys trained to be loyal to the regime celebrated the birthdays of George Washington and Abraham Lincoln, helped control crowds, and formed welcoming committees for visiting U.S. dignitaries.[55] Although these actions were largely symbolic, representations of native Boy Scouts saluting the Stars and Stripes made them poster boys for the BSA's aim to mobilize indigenous youth for empire.

Still, overseas recruitment left much to be desired. Enrollment numbers grew unevenly and sluggishly on the nation's imperial frontiers. No solid figures exist for Puerto Rico before World War II, but poverty, natural disasters, mismanagement, and language barriers kept troops small and muster rolls short.[56] The growth rates for the Philippine Islands seem more impressive. In 1925, the BSA counted 1,162 Scouts and 48 troops. These figures climbed in 1928 to 4,724 Scouts and 208 troops. In 1935, the Philippine Council listed 12,447 Scouts distributed in 525 troops.[57] Compared with the total proportion of American mainland youth enrolled in the Boy Scouts, however, Filipino recruitment was underwhelming. Scouting remained concentrated in Manila and southern Luzon but barely penetrated the hinterlands, where the colonial infrastructures of school and church were weak. Religion was another major obstacle: natives who had converted to Catholicism under Spanish rule begrudged the BSA's affiliation with Protestant character-building organizations like the YMCA.

Worried that parents were holding back their children, BSA administrators struggled to dispel fears that scouting "was a clever scheme to Americanize Filipino boys."[58] Another problem was that many Scoutmasters were soldiers who were subject to redeployment, which left numerous troops defunct. To keep them intact, the Philippine Council introduced flexible age requirements, lowered test standards, and gradually handed over responsibility to local Scout-masters of Filipino, Chinese, and Japanese descent.[59] Angered by these changes, Governor Leonard Wood called for a policy of strict Americanization and threatened to withdraw his "present cordial support" if the organization "were under aliens."[60] BSA administrators shrugged off such complaints because they needed the active involvement of local elites to embed the Boy Scouts in foreign soil and camouflage the empire they were in the process of redesigning. Willing to collaborate with nonwhite authorities, local Scout leaders admitted the Filipino judge Manuel Camus and the expatriate Chinese businessman John E. Goo to the Philippine Council.[61]

To be sure, the BSA's faith in interracial collaboration did not extend to all segments of colonial society. Pliable primitivism was an elastic imperial ideology. It involved granting a limited amount of political participation to subjects deemed civilized enough to wield some power in the colonial state while lamenting the incapacity for self-government of people whose nonwhite heritage invited comparisons to savagery. Pliable primitivism offered a perfect excuse for setbacks in the BSA's colonial projects. Macfarlane, who felt obligated to explain why progress was so slow in the Philippines, put the blame squarely on his native subordinates. "The Filipino lacks initiative and leadership ability," Macfarlane judged, and "although he usually starts off with a flurry—after he has used up his stock of ideas there is a decline unless we can reach him in time." Fidgety and unreliable, according to Macfarlane, Filipino scoutmasters were regarded as dependent on having "an American directly over them and interested in the welfare of the troop."[62] Difficulties with the Muslim population in the South were ascribed to their barbarity, not to their violent subjugation. "You might lose your head [if you] get out into the Moro country too far by yourself," Macfarlane quipped before an audience of BSA executives.[63] Voss concurred. Even as he praised the Filipinos' enthusiasm, Voss found them "handicapped" by a "racial heritage of centuries of isolation," a "distinctly oriental psychology," and an average IQ 30 percent below that of his white superiors. "We must . . . face the fact that we are dealing with a very primitive people," Macfarlane summarized, people who had been "held back" by savagery and Spanish colonialism.[64] In the perception of these two U.S. executives, the limitations of colonial scouting were a result of native backwardness, not of bad policy.

Although characterizing natives as incompetent was a typical colonial gesture, BSA administrators did more than reproduce hierarchies of race and empire. In infantilizing indigenous adults and labeling them immature while locating the potential for future growth in their children, they asserted that age was just as significant for colonial state building as race. Colonial boys were never subjected to the same kind of reproach as their fathers. During his eight years as the BSA's top representative in Southeast Asia, Voss collected numerous anecdotes to prove that Scout training put "primitive youth" on the track to advanced manhood. Stories that showed Filipino Boy Scouts saving lives, testifying in court, and combating crime reinforced the belief that native self-rule depended on indigenous boys approximating Anglo-Saxon standards of self-government.[65] This led to a startling reversal of roles: boys "improved" through scouting were expected to educate and police their elders. In one story, Filipino boys had signed a petition to remove a native scoutmaster "whose morals and conduct had much to be desired"; in another, Mohammed Sali, a sixteen-year-old Moro Boy Scout "with a magnificent physique, a clear gaze and a warm firm handclasp," was asked what the older people in his village thought about independence. "We tell them," Sali replied in terms that sounded simple but gratifying to American ears, "that if they are good, independence will be good—but if they are bad, independence will be bad."[66] True or fabricated, these narratives offered reassurance against sprawling anticolonial movements that resonated with nonwhite youths all over the world. Held up as emblematic of the maturation process of a colonized people, the Boy Scouts embodied the U.S. policy of transferring sovereignty at an undefined point in the future, thus bolstering a tutelary regime that at once promised citizenship to its subjects and delayed its fulfillment.

Forming collaborative relations between white organizers and nonwhite boys required promoting scouting as a multiracial enterprise. Colonial scouters took pride in their ability to navigate color lines, which they hailed as a model for pacifying race relations across the empire. Regardless of the low membership numbers on America's Asian frontier, Macfarlane insisted that his work with "Americans, Filipinos, Spaniards, Chinese, Japanese," and "Negritos" helped keep the peace in places never fully controlled by the U.S. government.[67] Skeptics were also asked to turn to Hawaii, where white leaders had begun to experiment with mixed troops before World War I. Hawaii's role as a laboratory for racial integration was widely recognized. Boy Scout units composed of youths of "Chinese, Japanese, Hawaiian, and all varieties of white races," marveled the *Christian Science Monitor* in September 1914, were "working just as hard as their brother troops at home."[68] After the war, Honolulu scout executive Samuel Robley reached a national audience with the claim that there had never been the "slightest class or race prejudice" in managing local units, which had caused "considerable wonder on the part of visitors seeing for the first time a Troop of Scouts where the majority of the boys are white, led by an

American-Chinese Scoutmaster, or where a Hawaiian Scoutmaster is efficiently handling a troop of Chinese and Japanese Scouts."[69] The ripple effects of colonial scouting were felt on the mainland as well. At the 1930 annual meeting of the National Council, a group of New Jersey Boy Scouts staged a pageant that depicted African American, Indian, Filipino, Chinese, Eskimo, Puerto Rican, and Mexican youth as part of the American Scout family.[70]

Stanley A. Harris appreciated such multiracial pageantry. Unlike the colonial precedents set by his colleagues, however, Harris's efforts to open the BSA to African American and Native American boys met with little enthusiasm at first. Registered as a scoutmaster since the organization's founding, Harris became the first director of the IRS. The North Carolinian brought two key qualifications to the job. First, Harris had gained valuable experience after joining the BSA's paid national field service in 1917 and coordinating the establishment of all-white councils throughout the South. Second, that assignment had sensitized Harris to black youths' aspirations for self-improvement, which led him to support Bolton Smith's Louisville Plan. Until his retirement in December 1947, Harris stayed at the head of the IRS, helping to organize domestic troops of color, overseeing training courses for African American scoutmasters, visiting Indian reservations, and raising funds for racially segregated campgrounds.[71]

Tact and diplomacy were essential to Smith and Harris's task. They not only had to earn the trust of nonwhites suspicious of white reformers but also needed to persuade white supremacists that they were not radicals bent on dismantling Jim Crow. Caution was necessary given that the IRS nearly failed to materialize. With a renascent KKK and episodic racial violence exploding across the country, many had toyed with the idea of forming a separate organization for blacks that would resemble the South African Pathfinder program.[72] IRS advocates strongly objected to that idea, arguing that African Americans would cite a fringe organization as an example of racial prejudice. The compromise reached reflected the divisions within the leadership: only after hearing the opinions of several "race experts" and deciding to draw as little public attention as possible did the National Council approve of the IRS. Funding for the program did not come from the BSA but from a grant of forty thousand dollars provided by the Laura Spelman Rockefeller Memorial.[73]

As with other charitable institutions founded by wealthy industrialists, the Rockefeller Foundation's policy of harmonizing philanthropy with the social sciences was not limited to the United States but spread to Europe, Latin America, and East Asia.[74] IRS advocates tapped into this internationalist sentiment to convince skeptics. The advances of science, commerce, and international peace, according to Harris, were chipping away at ancient prejudices. To forsake "our duty toward the negro" would go against the "Christian spirit" and one's "sense of justice."[75] Trying to rally support for African American scouting at the 1928 national training conference, Smith likened the IRS to the missionary work done by American evangelicals abroad. "We send missionaries to Africa but here at home each one of us may become a missionary to the African in our midst. . . . No religious man can deny this program to the boys of any race."[76] At the heart of such comparisons lay a shrewd indictment: America's white Christians would continue to suffer from a credibility problem unless they invested the same energy in uplifting domestic nonwhite races that they had devoted to uplifting colonized populations.

Alabama and Georgia, however, were not Hawaii or the Philippines. Scouting for people of a darker hue was virtually unknown in the Deep South, and whites looking to entrench their hold on power wanted to make sure that it stayed that way. In a letter to the Rockefeller Foundation's Leonard Outhwhite, Harris wrote what he was up against. Many Southerners he met "were opposed to any type of organization among Negroes . . . to the Negro having the same uniform and badge as the white boys," and "would like to keep the Negro down where they could . . . treat him, as a brute."[77] Harris knew that he had to tread lightly if he wanted to convince southern councils that blacks possessed a legitimate claim to manhood. When he was scheduled to speak in Richmond to a group of scoutmasters, a friend advised him to leave town immediately after the meeting because he could not guarantee Harris's safety.[78] The initial responses of several BSA officials Harris met on his southern tours ranged from mild suspicion to polite rejection. Where there was lukewarm approval, white Southerners declared that they would not oppose experiments with black boys but would not divert any resources to that aim either. Making concessions to segregationist sensibilities, Harris and his coworkers recommended a set of locally specific rules: even as the program should be the same for African Americans, there was to be "no mixing" and no Scout contests between white and black troops. As symbols of respectable citizenship and a militarized black masculinity that evoked bitter memories of the Civil War and Reconstruction, uniforms were to be withheld from black youths in all places where southern whites might feel offended by the sight of African American Scouts in their midst. Finally, the IRS pledged itself to respecting the right of every council to "determine when they will handle the situation in their own local community"—the BSA's carte blanche to discriminate against minorities.[79]

Selling the IRS to the African American community was no easy task either. Chronic mutual distrust, caused by decades of racial discrimination, hampered cooperation between white BSA officials and African Americans. Smith admitted that prominent blacks were "skeptical and . . . difficult to interest."[80] Believing that a black assistant would have "more influence" with African Americans, the BSA added the first black man, J. A. Beauchamp, to its professional staff.[81] The decision to hire Beauchamp was pragmatic at best. Even the most able black scouter, Smith told the Rockefeller Foundation, could not be expected "to function as effectively as white Scoutmasters."[82] Uncertain about theories of black inferiority, Harris proposed creating an environment for aspiring African American scoutmasters "where we could carefully observe them, study them, guide them."[83] This was the purpose of the first two training courses held in the summers of 1927 and 1928 at Hampton Normal and Agricultural Institute and Tuskegee Institute. In choosing two of the nation's most prestigious black learning facilities, the IRS aligned itself with an African American educational tradition that sought to counter the stereotype of the "lazy negro" with a modern rural black masculinity grounded in the capitalist virtues of physical labor, moral discipline, and sexual self-restraint.[84] Approximately eighty African Americans, most of them schoolteachers from all southern states except Georgia and Mississippi, gained their scoutmaster certificates at these courses. Reports of black men working earnestly and diligently with their mentors made for good publicity, muting white critics and suggesting to blacks that they could commit themselves wholeheartedly to the program.[85]

The annual reports of the IRS attest to the modest success of these initiatives. By 1935, segregated black troops were operating across the South, even as white recalcitrance remained strong in the states with the largest African American populations: South Carolina, Georgia, and Mississippi. Overall growth rates looked promising—promising enough for Harris to broaden the IRS's orbit to include the North and Midwest.[86] Blacks had been organizing Scout troops in New York and Chicago as early as the 1910s, where whites had interfered less. When the IRS began calculating African American enrollment, it counted 4,293 Scouts in 248 troops for 1926. These figures increased to 9,105 Scouts in 621 troops in 1928, to 15,708 Scouts in an estimated 900 troops in 1933, and to 24,269 Scouts in 1,100 troops in 1938.[87] Still, while African Americans constituted about 10 percent of the nation's total population by the end of the 1930s, their membership in the Boy Scouts made up less than 3 percent of all boys in the organization.[88] Structural inequalities, unrelenting discrimination, and the lack of adequate camping facilities impeded further growth. Many African American troops supported by the IRS lapsed as the Great Depression worsened the already dreary economic situation for blacks.[89]

Figure 4.3. Training course for African American scoutmasters at Hampton Normal and Agricultural Institute, Virginia, June 1928. IRS director Stanley A. Harris (second row, center) sought a middle ground between recruiting boys and men of color and heeding the racist norms of Jim Crow America. (Courtesy of Rockefeller Archive Center, Sleepy Hollow, New York)

Undaunted by these impediments, Harris expanded the scope of his service. His field trips had convinced him that other minorities warranted the BSA's attention as well. Special committees added to the IRS came to the aid of local councils in Texas and California to promote scouting among Mexican American, Chinese American, and Japanese American youth.[90] Harris's pet project was to deepen the organization's relationship with Native Americans. The prospects for "Indian work" seemed rather bright. The Snyder Act of 1924 had granted full citizenship to Native Americans residing on U.S. soil. Federal boarding schools, which had been established to "civilize" Indian children, promised a rich harvest for BSA field workers. Harris found a strong ally in Secretary of the Interior Lyman Wilbur, who gave the green light in 1929 for a nationwide campaign to enlist Native American boys.[91] By then, the Bureau of Indian Affairs, which had feared that scouting might militarize Native American boys, no longer opposed the idea. Three years later, the IRS boasted more than 151 Indian troops operating in boarding schools and reservations across the country, which made Native Americans the fastest-growing minority in the BSA.[92]

Harris found his acumen as an organizer matched by the BSA's cultural affinity for Native Americans. While antiblack stereotypes made African Americans seem only partially qualified for scouting, associations of Native Americans with outdoor vigor and natural purity had become an integral part of the BSA's lexicon of masculinity. At the request of the Department of the Interior, the IRS recommended bringing Indian boys into contact with white Scouts to "stimulate interest in Indian life and history."[93] The positive international reception of American performances of Indianness fastened the imaginary bond between Boy Scouts and Native Americans. It was hardly a coincidence that domestic efforts to recruit Native American boys gained momentum in the same year that Tomkins's sign language coaches and Hubbard's redface dancers were exhibiting their talents at Arrowe Park in front of record crowds. At the 1929 world jamboree, BSA organizers pretended that they cared about the contributions of Native Americans: traveling with the American contingent were six Muscogee Scouts, the first nonwhite members to accompany an official BSA delegation to foreign lands.[94] Representations of African Americans on the global stage were much less benign. The "cotton-field songs" sung by white southern Scouts at these festivals tied blackness to slavery and dependency.[95] With condescending humor, James West labeled the sole African American participant in the 1933 world jamboree "the jolliest fellow of the bunch" and the "best 'fried-chicken preparer' on the continent."[96] At the same time that white organizers refuted the presumption that the Native Americans were a dying race, they characterized African Americans as an inferior race.

Europeans' curiosity about multiracial scouting in the United States was not limited to jamboree pageantry. Foreign youth organizers searching for clues for how to reduce ethnic and racial conflict ascribed a special expertise to BSA leaders in this matter. In June 1925, West answered a query from the League of Nations about scouting for boys of color in America. His picture of immigrant and nonwhite troops "functioning in complete harmony with local authorities" was rosy at best but consistent with the BSA's official policy of painting itself as a "melting pot" that made loyal citizens regardless of race.[97] To Hubert Martin and Lord Hampton, who were struggling to address the conflicting needs of white supremacists in the British colonies and native youths who wanted to be Scouts, the BSA's interracial policies offered valuable knowledge. Noting that it was possible for black and white Scouts to coexist, the Englishmen applauded Smith and Harris's plan to make scouting available to southern blacks without antagonizing local whites. Hampton called Smith a "power in the land" and "pioneer of education amongst the negroes," adding that his "experiment" deserved the utmost support.[98] After the IRS was hatched, Martin gave it ample coverage in the international Boy Scout magazine. He praised Bolton Smith's belief in the "great transformative power of right education," stating that he thought less "of what [African American boys] are now than of what, through education and character development, they might become."[99]

This statement raises a central question: What exactly were the contours of Smith's and Harris's visions of development for nonwhite boys? Judged by today's standards, the term "Inter-Racial" as deployed by white organizers was hardly more than a euphemism. IRS officials dissociated their program from any civil rights agitation. Smith held "a considerable measure of segregation . . . advisable" and opposed full equality between the races as a dangerous social fiction that would poison race relations.[100] Rather than leveling the playing field, scouting for boys of color was supposed to offer a positive sense of subaltern masculinity that earned minorities the recognition of the white ruling class and boost their status in their own communities. "Those familiar with the relations of the two races, deplore the lack of contact between the two races, which once exited," Smith asserted in January 1925. Highlighting the need to reestablish interracial contact without going back to slavery or embracing civil rights, Smith argued that aiming for "at least potential equality" was desirable. This was where the Boy Scouts could play a crucial role, which Smith presented as "the most effective method" to promote "contact between the negro and white ideals of civilized conduct."[101]

Smith's vision deserves to be unpacked in greater detail. His idealization of multiracial scouting as a way to restore the familial reciprocities between "benevolent" masters and "childish" slaves was indicative of a crisis of white imperial control that stretched from America's colonial peripheries to the postemancipation South. Just as slaveholder paternalism had envisaged society as bound together by intimate relations of dependency and obedience, Smith put forward a modern, ostensibly less oppressive version of paternalism that recognized black Americans' aspirations but made their realization contingent on their acceptance of a regime of white supervision. Once they entered the fraternity of scouting, African Americans—and by extension Native Americans, Mexican Americans, and Chinese Americans—would become enmeshed in a network of quasi-colonial relationships comparable to the ones BSA organizers had been forging overseas. The IRS and its promise of "potential equality," thus, served as a template for easing racial tensions and disciplining nonwhite races that were regarded as unruly blocs within the empire.

BSA officials were perfectly aware of the subversive energies fomented by the spread of antiracist ideologies. Youth had become a common focal point for anticolonial activists across racial and political boundaries. Rejecting Booker T. Washington's view that economic success should precede civil rights, William E. B. Du Bois advocated the expansion of higher education for African Americans to equip them with the tools to resist discrimination. In the Harlem Renaissance, the contest between the "New Negro" and the black establishment was fought in generational terms, with the younger ones asserting their freedom and dignity in forms of cultural expression. Marcus Garvey's brand of pan-Africanism sought to inculcate in black youths a sense of collective destiny, telling them to identify with ancestral Africa rather than the United States. Simultaneously, Puerto Rican and Filipino students educated in America returned as teachers to their homelands and fueled the independence movements there.[102] The problem white elites were facing, Harris conceded in 1928, was not that America's nonwhite races lacked sufficient knowledge of the world.[103] Clearly, white organizers thought that instilling "moral and civic consciousness" through scouting could counterpoise revolutionary sentiments and make racial minorities accept their position as subordinate subjects. "We do not want to lead. We only want to be shown how to improve ourselves," one black scoutmaster from Tennessee told Smith.[104] These were sentences that white organizers liked to hear.

An incident from World War I illustrates just how alarmed BSA officials were that white neglect would make disenfranchised groups susceptible to foreign influence. In May 1918, an urgent appeal for help landed on James West's desk. William Mather Lewis, head of the National Committee of Patriotic Societies, asked for the BSA's assistance in combating the spread of German propaganda in black communities in the South. Lewis reported that enemy agents had told African Americans that conscription had been introduced to wipe out their race, and that Germany had invaded Belgium to punish the country responsible for the atrocities in the Congo. If this sort of propaganda was not checked, Lewis feared, a fifth column was sure to arise. Beard dreaded the possibility of race riots.[105] Bolton Smith doubted it would come to that, but he estimated that African Americans had become a political force to be reckoned with. Having moved beyond the docility of slaves, "they are beginning to feel their power, and that sullen discontent which is always slumbering within the breasts of those among them who have begun to think and aspire . . . is beginning to show itself." By failing to engage blacks and their desire for social advancement, Smith warned, the nation would deprive itself of the "efficiency of ten million people."[106]

Smith anticipated the direction the IRS would take in later years. Multiracial scouting was embraced by white elites in the 1920s precisely because it harmonized prevailing practices of segregation and hierarchical social organization with the need of imperial nations to stifle dissent and extract manpower from all social segments. A specific constellation of capitalist labor ethics, scientific rationalization, and deference to white rule overrode the emancipatory promise of masculine citizenship. Rather than make self-reliant men, the IRS aimed to recolonize domestic minorities and turn them into productive workers for the empire. This led to an adapted form of scouting for boys of color with a particular stress on the Scout laws of loyalty, thrift, cleanliness, and obedience—laws that could be used to teach youths to comply with white authorities. Harris asserted that the black boy trained in scouting was less prone to drift into crime and "very much improved as a laborer. He is more industrious, more courteous, and generally more efficient."[107] A scoutmaster working with black youths at the Tuskegee Institute noted a "marked change" in their "demeanor," especially "in the matter of politeness and deference to older people."[108] IRS officials believed that delinquency was not exclusively linked to race. But they also believed that black boys could attain a higher character in an environment managed by white reformers.

Economic considerations drove white efforts to boost Native American recruitment as well. The BSA deemed agricultural and vocational work for Indian youth essential to overcoming the supposed idleness of reservation life that prevented Native Americans from acquiring a modern work ethic. Many Indians on reservations, a 1930 IRS study on contemporary Native Americans diagnosed, "must be trained to go out into industry. . . . Scouting could make a great contribution in addition to normal Scout virtues by helping them to adjust themselves in cities or industrial plants."[109] This statement gained more weight when federal officials began shutting down boarding schools in 1933 in an effort to speed up Native American assimilation. The tribal traditions celebrated in Boy Scout pageantry, it seemed, prevented the transformation of Indian youths into skilled plebeians who would add to the nation's economic power. It was this assimilationist racism, with its double emphasis on social discipline and economic modernization, that persuaded the Rockefeller Foundation to keep the IRS alive during the Great Depression.

Although the professional networks of colonial and interracial scouting that were lodged in different environments were only loosely connected, pliable primitivism and assimilationist racism shared important commonalities. Both concepts emerged at a time of rising anticolonial consciousness and international debates over the correlation of national homogeneity and racial difference. Both depended on willing intermediaries from disempowered groups to funnel nonwhite youths into largely segregated troops. And both reflected the wish to create a modern servant class as a necessary corollary to empire. To continue excluding nonwhites from an organization like the Boy Scouts would risk losing an entire generation of minority youth to forces detrimental to U.S. global power. The language of brotherhood normalized these dependencies—not by signifying a web of egalitarian relationships but by casting the work that white BSA leaders invested in developing nonwhite boys as the kind of guidance a younger boy got from his older brother. In the end, the paternalistic desire to nurture subaltern youth through scouting proved to be a double-edged sword. If youth of color could be trained to stabilize regimes of colonial and domestic race making, who was to say that this kind of training would not also give them the tools to resist such schemes?

Appropriation and Resistance

The historian John Hope Franklin remembered well the day he became a Boy Scout. Franklin had just turned twelve when scouting came to the African American community of Tulsa, Oklahoma, in 1927. Admitted into one of the city's first black troops, Franklin beamed with enthusiasm. He reveled in the troop meetings and summer camps that kindled in him a love for the outdoors. Franklin recalled that he wanted to be "the best Boy Scout [he] could possibly be" and believed in the Scout motto to do a good turn every day. One day, young John Hope was watching the traffic at a busy intersection in downtown Tulsa. His eyes fell on an elderly white lady who was trying to cross the street. Realizing that she was blind, Franklin rushed over to assist her. Niceties were exchanged until the woman asked about the color of his skin. When Franklin said he was black, the woman's mood darkened abruptly. She told Franklin to get his "filthy hands" off her. Stung by her reaction, Franklin left the woman standing in the middle of the street. Franklin had learned a sobering lesson: being a Scout did not shield young males like him from the racist notion of African American men as sexual predators.[110]

Franklin's experiences as a young Scout in Oklahoma capture the dreams and disillusionment, the agony and aspirations of countless boys of color who became Scouts in the early twentieth century. It is hard to fathom that white boys would have suffered the same kind of racial hostility without leaving the organization in droves. Despite the constraints placed on minority youths who wanted to excel in scouting, their attitude toward the movement remained surprisingly positive. This begs the question why boys and men of color demanded a place in an organization whose white leaders found them lacking in character. Disempowered groups disagreed among themselves whether their youths should be organized within or outside the frameworks of white society. For those approving of the Boy Scouts, the answer may sound ironic: by inducting their youths into an organization founded to teach Anglo-Saxon middle-class boys proper manhood, nonwhite advocates of scouting sought to masculinize themselves, discredit racist stereotypes, and prove that they were able to chart their own destinies.

Defying white expectations that nonwhite youths lacked the capacity to comprehend scouting, minority groups began organizing troops of their own before World War I. Supported by black churches, fraternities, and YMCA chapters, African American Boy Scouts paraded the streets of their communities in New York, Pennsylvania, Kansas, North Carolina, and Texas soon after the program took root on U.S. soil.[111] In 1912, the BSA accepted the application of an African American educator who had been drilling black youths in Evanston, Illinois, along the lines espoused by the national leadership.[112] Much of this early activism was due to the initiative shown by the boys themselves. A group of Chinese American adolescents growing up in San Francisco did not wait for their elders' permission. They banded together and started playing Scout games after finding a copy of the handbook in the courtyard of a Methodist church. They contacted BSA headquarters, which sent a representative to guide them through the application process. In 1914, the boys put on their uniforms as members of Troop 3, the first Asian American Boy Scout unit on the West Coast.[113] Although many of these nonwhite troops lacked the resources to survive the first years, the youngsters drew from their participation a sense of cohesion and pride.

There are good reasons why the allure of a movement that promised its followers fitness and fellowship was gaining traction with America's marginalized communities. At a time when physical culture was seen as a pathway to citizenship, perceptions of what constituted the fit and disciplined male body, and who was capable of acquiring one, became a key factor in determining the civic worth of boys of different origins. Ethnic commentary on the Boy Scouts reflected this stance. While older Chinese Americans resented the movement's military iconography, the younger ones tended to welcome the Boy Scouts as an opportunity to rectify the image of Asians as "sick men."[114] Influential African American men, trying to cast off the caricature of the oversexed, animalistic black male body, promoted the Boy Scouts on similar grounds. "The Boy Scout Movement is one that should receive the heartiest kind of support. . . . All sorts of clean, healthy, elevating sports are encouraged, especially those that can be indulged in out of doors" the African American–owned *Chicago Defender* editorialized in 1924, asking parents to "permit their children to grow up" with the "helpful influence of some such organization."[115]

Troubled by the equation of black male youth with delinquency and the high mortality rates for African American children, black reformers supportive of scouting hoped that adult-led drill and purposeful recreation might put their boys on the track to respectable manhood. Bettering health conditions through supervised physical training, according to black educators, would add to the vitality of their race and instill pride in their youth. Some hoped that excelling at outdoor activities such as hiking and swimming would give African American Boy Scouts a sense of accomplishment in a social environment hostile to the molding of vigorous black masculinities. A photograph taken in the early 1930s at a segregated Scout camp near Jacksonville, Florida, indicates just how much African American Scouts wanted to be recognized as able young men. It shows black Scouts standing erect and proudly posing their bodies after earning their lifesaving merit badges.[116] Health, hygiene, and athleticism were also precious ideals for the Filipino advocates of scouting. For scoutmaster Lorenzo Alcantara, Scout training contributed to the toughening of native boyhood. Hiking, camping, athletic contests, crowd control, and other physical activities, Alcantara asserted, were laying the foundation for a "strong efficient citizenry." To ensure their survival in a world of empires, it behooved the Filipinos to not "waste a single man" but to make "every boy an asset to the nation."[117]

Perhaps the most forceful example of nonwhite youths' masculine potential was the induction of black, Filipino, and Puerto Rican Boy Scouts into the BSA's pantheon of boy heroes. The BSA's fascination with everyday heroism reflected anxieties about modern society's instant gratifications and promise of risk-free pleasure, but also spoke of courage, honor, and bravery in Anglo-Saxonist terms.[118] This racially exclusive logic began to crumble when the first youths of color were awarded the gold honor medal, the highest distinction the BSA gave to Scouts who had risked their lives to save others. Boys of different backgrounds were admitted into the organization's National Court of Honor—boys such as the Puerto Rican William Chabert, who rushed through a shower of falling stones to rescue his unconscious companion; the Filipino Theodorico Casipit, who swam after a drowning girl after her boat had capsized; and the African American Sherman Potter, who towed to safety a friend who had fallen through a frozen lake.[119] By the late 1920s, BSA officials who made these incidents public had come to recognize the valiant deeds of minority Scouts alongside those of white boys. They did so in part because life-saving constituted a politically unsuspicious version of heroic masculinity. The very attainability of this kind of masculinity, however, also suggested to racial minorities that participation in scouting might earn them the respect of the dominant group and eventually more rights.

Some nonwhite educators were hopeful that the BSA could be enlisted to champion minority rights and racial tolerance. After the IRS had concluded a training course for black scoutmasters at the Tuskegee Institute, academic director John C. Wright declared that he knew of no movement better "cal-culated to develop the boys of the Negro race of America into the kind of men necessary to bring about a better and more sympathetic understanding between the two great racial groups in America."[120] Writing from a different social and historical location, the Sioux intellectual Charles Eastman, who taught Indian lore to scoutmasters in the 1910s, demanded greater autonomy for tribal Indians by portraying them as healthy, clean, and vigorous outdoorsmen. Na-tive boys, Eastman claimed, were model Boy Scouts. Trained to "resist pain and hardship," the Indian "begins his career with a building of a sound and efficient body"—one that would make any muscular Christian proud.[121] If an Indian boy excelled in the movement, the Blackfoot leader Red Fox James insisted, that youth had "a right to be classed with the great Scouts that have been of so much service to their country."[122] Advocating cross-cultural un-derstanding, these cross-cultural brokers urged the BSA leadership to recog-nize their peoples' contributions to the nation and help them advance.

To be sure, this policy of cautious collaboration also had detractors. When their expectations were not met, civil rights activists did not spare criticism. The National Association for the Advancement of Colored People (NAACP) rou-tinely chided the Boy Scouts for failing to act on its rhetoric of inclusiveness. The two organizations first locked horns in 1919. The National Council had ordered a black veteran-turned-scoutmaster in North Carolina to disband his troop because several white scouters in the area had cringed at the sight of black boys marching in military dress. The NAACP protested sharply, calling on the BSA to acknowledge the wartime heroism of African American sol-diers and value their role in teaching black youth to be patriotic.[123] Seven years later, the NAACP again clashed with the BSA after learning that two black boys from Ogden, Utah, had been ousted from a local Scout troop. A father of two white Boy Scouts had objected to their presence.[124]

Feigned neutrality was no longer an option for the BSA in the next big confrontation between the two organizations. In June 1937, West received complaints from civil rights workers regarding the unfair treatment of Fred Ames, a young black Scout from Rhode Island who had been looking forward to participating in the national jamboree in Washington, DC. Ames had been talked out of traveling to the jamboree by local Scout executives. They told the boy that if they let him go, they would be unable to "protect him" from the slurs that would surely come from white Scouts from Georgia and Virginia, whose camps were located next to that of Rhode Island. NAACP Assistant Secretary Roy Wilkins found this reasoning spurious and inconsistent with the BSA's alleged commitment to racial integration. "It strikes us that to tell a young colored American boy that he cannot attend a national celebration in the capital of his country because of his color is the height—or depth—of humiliation and hurt," Wilkins told West. How the BSA could train its young in "real American citizenship with the tolerance and fair play that that demand[ed]" while catering to "the lowest and meanest form of pettiness and prejudice" was a mystery to Wilkins.[125] When the NAACP threatened to make this a huge issue in the press, West scrambled to repair the damage. At his request, Ames made the trip to Washington and was promised a cordial welcome by the chief executive himself.[126]

Robert S. Abbott, the founder of the *Chicago Defender*, struck an equally combative tone. While Abbott praised local Boy Scouts as the exemplars of young black manhood, his editorials, in which he accused the BSA of condoning racial injustice, had become more militant by the mid-1920s. Instead of telling women not to smoke, the Boy Scouts could "throw open their ranks to all American boys without regard to color, creed, or class"; they could "carry placards condemning lynchings"; or they could "organize a campaign against peonage . . . that has grown out of southern prison camps."[127] As a northern journalist, Abbott had more leeway to denounce racism than most southern blacks. On his trip to Europe in 1929, Abbott created a stir with a cable he sent to the Boy Scouts assembled in Arrowe Park. He called on the representatives of global scouting to use their "influence in abolishing color segregation . . . by seeing that all boys in the southern and other states be permitted to join the same brigades as is done in the North." More far-reaching still, he requested that the world movement exclude boys from the regions of the United States where the "atrocious practice of lynching and burning alive of human beings" was still in place.[128] How, Abbott asked, was it possible for BSA spokesmen to boast that their organization would help make the world safe for democracy when scouting was not safe for people of color in the United States? And why could BSA executives not draw inspiration from the demonstrations of cross-racial brotherhood of their French and Brazilian colleagues, who were putting white and black youths in the same troops?[129]

Evidently, Scout terms such as "manhood" and "citizenship" carried vastly different implications for different groups. For African American activists, developing youth of color through scouting was not about submitting to white ideas of patriotism; it was about forging positive racial identities. Boys should be taught to cherish their culture and stand up for civil rights. Ignoring the National Council's directive to steer clear of politics, black Scouts in Harlem and Chicago demonstrated against lynching. During the Silent Parade on July 28, 1917, in New York City, when more than eight thousand African Americans led by about eight hundred children clad entirely in white stood up against antiblack violence, Boy Scouts distributed leaflets to honor the victims of recent race riots. "We march because we deem it a crime to be silent in the face of such barbaric acts. . . . We march because we are thoroughly opposed to Jim Crow cars, Segregation, Discrimination, Disenfranchisement, Lynching, and the host of evils that are forced upon us," the leaflets said.[130] Seven years later, African American Scouts were seen escorting the black nationalist Marcus Garvey to a public rally in Manhattan.[131]

Chicago's black Scouts, too, meshed leisure and pan-African politics. Citing a British missionary, the *Chicago Defender* claimed that "the training of native youths in the kraals of South Africa furnished the inspiration for the Boy Scouts movement."[132] At the annual Bud Billiken parades, which Abbott launched in 1929 to spotlight the city's poor and underprivileged children, African American Boy Scouts marched as embodiments of a hopeful future for the race. In addition to celebrating black leaders such as Frederick Douglass and Booker T. Washington, Boy Scouts helped control the traffic, guarded women and babies at nearby picnic areas, and monitored crowds at concerts featuring young African American musicians.[133] Although there is no direct line connecting the ethnic youth organizing of the interwar years to the student sit-ins of the 1960s, crusaders against racial inequality hoped to extract from scouting the methods to build a tough and disciplined young cadre of civil rights activists.

Native Americans tried to take advantage of the Boy Scouts as well, yet the strategies they employed to boost their social standing were different from those used by African Americans. While Native American troops were largely segregated and confined to reservations, adult Indians sought to capitalize on the growing popularity of Indian lore in American outdoor culture. Some Native Americans successfully applied for posts as wildlife educators and camp counselors, through which they came into contact with white children. Though their power to disrupt negative stereotypes was limited, Indian camp personnel working with Scouts and other youths turned their cultural heritage into a marketable commodity in an effort to increase their physical and social mobility.[134] Apparently, most Native American leaders saw no conflict between selling Indian ceremonialism and preserving tribal identities. Several tribes consented to "adopting" white Boy Scouts and scouters and giving them Indian names—a transaction that pleased white expectations and raised the tribes' public profile.[135] A Native American educator who started an all-Indian troop at New York's Tonawanda Reservation held that cooperation was the best way to resist assimilation. "The traditional virtues of the red man are no longer taught to the Indian youth of today. . . . The Indian is losing his virtues with astonishing rapidity. A few of us who realize this situation have banded together to revive the ancient creed of the Redman which is likewise the creed of the Boy Scouts."[136] In the end, many Native Americans played along with the public's desire for easily consumable performances of Indianness because they believed it would give them leverage with whites and allow them to reclaim authority over their children.

Subversion through collaboration is also an apt formula to describe the motivation of Filipino leaders who interacted with the BSA prior to their country's independence. Two indigenous organizers—the lawyer and senator Manuel Camus and the country's first West Point graduate, Vincente P. Lim—worked behind the scenes to transform scouting from an imperial institution to a facilitator of anticolonial struggle. Both mastered the art of colonial mimicry. An active freemason, YMCA member, and vice president of the Philippine Council, Camus enjoyed good relations with U.S. colonial officials. On his advice, the National Council permitted native boys to wear the pocket strip "Philippine Boy Scouts" to make the movement more attractive to Filipino youth.[137] BSA administrators prized Camus's "sincerity" and found him a "good right hand," but behind the facade of the loyal intercultural mediator stood an ardent nationalist. By the early 1930s, Camus had managed to induct enough indigenous men into the Philippine Council to gain a solid majority.[138] One of Camus's trusted partners was Major Lim, who had attended several U.S. army colleges in the aftermath of World War I. He became the Philippine Council's acting president in 1932. Together, Lim and Camus represented the civilian and military forces that coalesced to gradually wrest control over the Philippine Boy Scouts from the American occupiers.

The first serious clash between the official U.S. colonial policy of Americanization and Camus and Lim's attempt to utilize scouting for the Filipinization of youth occurred in 1932. In October, E. S. Martin, the BSA's national director of publications, received a package from Manila with disturbing content. Lim and Camus had sent him a copy of a proposed "Filipino Supplement" to the BSA handbook, asking permission to publish it. Written by Emanuel A. Baja, a Filipino officer, the supplement launched a direct attack on teaching indigenous boys the principles of American patriotism. It conveyed an affirmative sense of Filipino history and national identity, telling Filipino Boy Scouts to take pride in their country. The Filipino's Creed reinterpreted Spanish and U.S. colonization as periods of national martyrdom. Good citizenship meant honoring "thousands of Filipino patriots [who] died for their country" and the "principles of democracy" born out of war and insurrection. A rhetoric of blood and sacrifice framed notions of Filipino Scout masculinity: "It is the duty of the citizen to love and defend the flag. . . . He who avoids it forfeits the blessing of his country and all the rights to citizenship."[139] The supplement ended with a revolutionary gesture, asking Filipino Scouts to treat the Filipino flag with the same affection that American Scouts showed to the Stars and Stripes. Never should the Filipino flag fly lower than the American one, nor should both flags be displayed on the same flagpole. When Martin forwarded the supplement to the War Department, the answer was unambiguous. If allowed to go into print, the supplement would become a dangerous vehicle of "independence propaganda."[140]

Even as the War Department's veto delayed the production of a Filipinized version of the Boy Scout handbook for three years, Filipinos continued to assert that scouting had taught them the self-reliant manhood that formed the basis of free nations. This claim to maturity found an international echo with the trips of Filipino delegations to the Hungarian jamboree in 1933 and to the United States in 1935.[141] Seeing those Scouts master the challenges of transoceanic travel made it difficult for BSA administrators to sustain the notion that their distant brothers were unprepared to form their own organization. A coalition of U.S. and Filipino organizers who lobbied policymakers in Washington, New York, and Manila eventually paved the way for the establishment of the Boy Scouts of the Philippines (BSP) on January 1, 1938. American-educated Filipino leaders such as Jorge B. Vargas expedited this process by portraying local citizenship training through scouting and sports as an outgrowth of the imperial civilizing mission.[142]

But even as pledges of friendship were exchanged at the inauguration, the frictions between colonizers and colonized had left scars. Theodore Roosevelt Jr., whose governorship of the islands had ended in 1933, did not conceal his disdain for the people who wanted scouting in the Philippines to become purely indigenous. "With such militancy and incompetence at the helm, I wouldn't be surprised to see the movement there go to waste in but a few years," Roosevelt seethed in December 1937.[143] He could not have been more wrong. Riding a wave of nationalism, Boy Scout membership in the Philippines grew from 15,178 in 1935 to 36,201 in 1941 and continued to soar in the decade following World War II.[144]

Roosevelt's remark indicates just how inept white organizers were at recognizing the power nonwhite groups had to alter the direction of scouting. Subaltern appropriations of a robust masculinity ran counter to a colonial discourse that infantilized nonwhite peoples and denied them agency. Boys and men of color joined the Boy Scouts to escape imperialism's degradation of colonized populations. The prospects of quasi-military training proved enticing. In an anecdote recounted by Henry F. Phelan, a field worker for the BSA in the Sulu Archipelago in the late 1920s, a young Moro thought that being a Boy Scout would entitle him to carry a gun.[145] Under the national defense plan of President Manuel Quezon, the BSP placed a greater emphasis on military education to adapt to the mobilization policies of the new Commonwealth government, which decreed in 1937 that every Filipino schoolboy over six years of age undergo preparatory military training.[146] In the United States, African American activists were confident that scouting would teach black youth how to stand their ground. Appalled by the history of racially motivated violence against his people, Du Bois urged African Americans to invest in "defensive military training." This meant, among other things, to "increase the number of colored boy scouts and girl guides" in black communities across the country.[147]

Although adult ideas about youth mobilization delineate the attitudes of the broad range of minority leaders toward the BSA, they tell us little about the extent to which constructions of race, masculinity, and citizenship entered the minds of young people. Boys, too, grappled with the ambiguities of brotherhood, including the question whether the Fourth Scout Law entailed fraternizing with racial others. Not unlike their elders, many white Scouts showed signs of apathy or outright hostility. Opposition to scouting across color lines was strongest in the South, where parents actively involved their children in the preservation of the racial status quo. White youths were taught the Confederate version of slavery and the Civil War, consumed images of black inferiority, and witnessed lynchings. Ironically, the very racist socialization the IRS wanted children to unlearn buttressed its rationale for segregation. To forcefully integrate white and black Boy Scouts, Harris claimed, would only subject the latter to "roughhousing" and jeopardize the project of multiracial scouting altogether.[148]

Yet there is evidence that youths did not simply emulate the discriminatory practices of their elders. When the IRS was making its first strides, several white Scouts performed good turns in support of fledgling African American units. In North Carolina and Georgia, white boys taught black boys Scout skills and helped them start troops. Donations typically consisted of old handbooks and uniforms. In March 1925, a delegation of white Eagle Scouts made a surprise appearance at a ceremony of the black court of honor in Louisville, Kentucky, which had convened to celebrate the first local black Scouts who had advanced to Eagle rank. The white youths congratulated the black Scouts on their achievement and wished them well for the future.[149] When American Boy Scouts were sent on goodwill tours to Cuba and Puerto Rico, they provided aid, engaged in sporting contests, and exchanged tokens of friendship with their Hispanic brother Scouts. Just as some Boy Scouts enacted a liberal-capitalist ethos of voluntary service by participating in relief programs for needy children overseas, others felt that underprivileged groups at home, including Scouts of color, were deserving of the same kindness.[150]

Occasionally, white boys went further still, crossing the color line in ways that potentially dumbfounded adults. A Miami scout executive found himself challenged by five white Scouts who were wondering "why Scouting wasn't developed for negro boys." In 1934, a group of young Mississippians tested the patience of the state's Scout executives, who had decided that African American Scouts should not wear uniforms. The white youths purchased a handful anyway and made sure the black Scouts got them.[151] In the protected spaces of an international jamboree, some boys imagined a world without Jim Crow. "There was not any racial or religious discrimination at our service," North Carolina scout Charles S. Bartlett wrote on his way to the 1947 world jamboree at Moisson, France. "Why can't it be that way everywhere? There are not many places on earth where a white boy and a colored boy can look at the same songbook together and sing out in praise of God. It is a wonderful sight—more like a dream."[152] A group of Los Angeles Scouts took a stand against racism shortly before the Americans entered World War II. Scoutmaster and BSA historian Keith Monroe remembered the incident. After admitting Massaji Takahashi, a young Japanese American, to the troop, Monroe found himself in the middle of a storm. Community leaders questioned his Americanism; parents threatened to pull their children from the troop. The Scouts then took matters into their own hands. They decided by vote to keep Massaji in and told the boys who refused to accept the vote to leave. At the risk of exposing themselves to accusations of unpatriotic conduct, the same Scouts formed a bodyguard to protect the Nisei boy after the Japanese attack on

Pearl Harbor. These few instances underline that Scouts were capable of forging peer-based solidarities that existed in opposition to adult loyalties of race and nation.[153]

Forming troops under the menace of racial violence, Scouts of color welcomed any direct support from whites. In the Midwest, men and boys from both communities put themselves in harm's way to defend black Scouts against a renascent KKK. Cecil Reed, who grew up to be a successful businessman and civil rights activist, was one of the few African American boys who got to visit an integrated summer camp in the 1920s. The camp idyll near Cedar Rapids, Iowa, was interrupted one night when the boys spotted a cross burning in the valley below. Hooded men had gathered to intimidate the youths, but the Scout executives drew their guns, charged the Klan members, and chased them away. The next morning, Reed recalled, the Scouts mounted their horses. In a show of strength and unity, "white and black Scouts rode through town together . . . no doubt to the discomfort of those Klansmen."[154] Such demonstrations of interracial solidarity, however, remained local in scope and did not influence BSA policy at the top, where officials paid lip service to egalitarian ideals rather than enforcing them throughout the organization.

Domestic and colonial youths of color were aware of this discrepancy. At the outset, many nonwhite boys who joined the Boy Scouts were likely to detect in the movement a corridor leading to social recognition and juvenile self-fulfillment. They wore their insignia proudly—so proudly that an African American scoutmaster claimed in 1941 that a black Scout could wear his uniform "longer than any one else without soiling." For the twelve-year-old African American Franklin Sayre, Boy Scout membership was a ticket to full citizenship: "I am a Boy Scout, so I guess I am a red-blooded, 100 per cent American boy."[155] But the racism these youths experienced chipped away at their enthusiasm, alienating those who sensed that the BSA was merely interested in perpetuating their second-class masculine status. Asked to stand fully costumed before hundreds of flashbulbs, the six Muscogee Scouts at the 1929 world jamboree realized that their primary function was to serve as objects of white desire. To fend off pushy onlookers, they stayed in character, saying "Me no understand, no English."[156] Luis Goenago, a Colombian Scout who had visited the Panama Canal Zone, never made it to a world jamboree, but the arrogant treatment he received at the hands of local American Scouts precipitated a fiery response. "What penalty will deserve a group of Boy Scouts who never has had attention with fourth Scout law?" Goenago wrote to Daniel Carter Beard in broken English. For the Colombian youth, shunning people because of the color of their skin was unworthy of a Scout.[157]

Others expressed their disapproval by staying out of the organization or joining other youth groups. Filipinos who regarded scouting as a foreign import
filled the ranks of the Young Philippines, a nationalist youth organization that
gained prominence in the 1930s. Fed up with the hackneyed portrayals of
Indians in BSA pageantry, the white science teacher and Mohawk activist
Ray Fadden, who had been an Eagle Scout in his teens, started a youth group
to represent Native traditions more accurately.[158] In the case of African Americans, the alternatives available to them often carried leftist credentials. After
being shut out from a new campground outside Philadelphia, several black Scout
troops rescinded their charters and entered a local organization allegedly free
from racial discrimination.[159] A communist youth organizer from Chicago rejoiced in June 1924 that "twenty little Negro Boy Scouts" had switched sides
and joined the city's Young Workers League. Virginia scout James E. Jackson
pivoted to the left after he was publicly humiliated at an Eagle Scout ceremony in 1931. Instead of pinning the medal to Jackson's chest, the governor
of Virginia flung it at the perplexed young man without even looking at him,
embarrassing Jackson in front of his parents. Jackson became a member of the
Young Communist League soon after.[160]

The cacophony surrounding the Fourth Scout Law exposes the contingent
meaning of race in a movement that distilled from the biological fact of youth
certainties about human development at the same time that it refused to erase
conventions of gender and culture. This contradictory constellation turned
brotherhood into a tool of simultaneous exclusion and inclusion. Scouts were to
treat one another as brothers, not necessarily as aspiring men. In the hands of
white organizers, this tool was put in the service of stabilizing empires seen as
imperiled by racial violence, a lack of subaltern manpower, and the spread of
revolutionary ideologies. A spokesman of the Mississippi Department of Education summed up the motivation of white organizers to reach out to boys of color
as follows: "We have got to save these boys for ourselves and for our democracy,
or else Communism and other 'isms' will get them."[161] Nonwhite activists, on
the other hand, exploited the malleability of scouting, harnessing its masculinizing ideology to their constituents' desire for social and political recognition.
They turned the brotherhood of scouting into a rallying cry for self-mobilization,
an antiracist instrument to challenge dominant white masculinities and prepare
their youths for a life of struggle on behalf of their communities.

In teaching white boys to be benevolent toward "lesser" races, scouting projected an inclusive model of boyhood while reiterating the supremacy of "civilization" over "savagery." Racial hierarchies were easier to uphold once they
had been obscured by the universal language of youth. For nonwhite boys who

donned the BSA uniform between the wars, membership could be at once frustrating and fulfilling. Neither African American, Native American, Asian American nor colonial boys were granted the same resources to advance in scouting as whites. Belonging to a segregated organization sharpened a boy's awareness of his place along the color line, but it also sensitized youths of color to possibilities for community beyond the BSA's grasp—possibilities that emerged in the form of rival organizations on the left and right. When historians examine how organized youth movements impacted the socialization of nonwhite youth, they need to avoid making gross generalizations or drawing false analogies. Antiblack racism did not mirror anti-Indian or anti-Asian racism. Still, connecting these histories reinforces a point Robin Bernstein has made about the discursive formation of childhood in American culture—that the idea of innocence, all declarations to the contrary, was "raced white."[162]

Chapter 5

Youth Marches

Depression, Dictators, and War

People may think that the economic and political turbulence of the Depression era took a heavy toll on the BSA. But this was not the case. Although jobless scoutmasters looking for work left troops leaderless and dwindling budgets led to cutbacks in professional staff and spending, the BSA attracted a steady stream of new recruits in the period leading into World War II. Cub Scouting, which was introduced in 1931, brought younger boys and women as den mothers into the movement. Parents unable to afford costly recreational activities sent their children to summer camps run by the Boy and Girl Scouts, the YMCA, and similar agencies. Overall, the BSA grew about 50 percent from 1 million members, young and old, in 1933 to over 1.5 million in 1941 and ended the war just shy of the 2 million mark. This numerical growth coincided with a process of ideological consolidation. The Boy Scouts hardened their all-American brand by serving Uncle Sam in the fight against hunger and poverty following the stock market crash of 1929. The BSA held its first national jamboree, in Washington, DC, in 1937, surrounded by the symbols of U.S. state power. And the organization enlisted in America's home-front army to help defeat the Axis Powers after the Japanese attack on Pearl Harbor. In a time of contraction and confusion, the Boy Scouts were expanding.[1]

How is this mounting demand in scouting best explained? The interpretation offered in this chapter navigates a middle route between the national and the global. There is nothing exceptional about the path taken by the BSA. Youth organizations grew in importance during the crisis years of the 1930s and 1940s in large parts of the world, not just in North America. As young people flocked to adult-led youth movements in record numbers, their value as political actors rose to new heights. Contemporary Americans were aware of this. Studies conducted by the federal government and private citizens acquainted readers with youths from all continents working, camping, playing, singing, and parading to stunningly similar rhythms.[2] Mass spectacles, pledges, uniforms, big rallies, and what historian Mary Nolan called the "masculinist vision of taming nature" united young people into large collective bodies and created a common language of service and sacrifice for the public good that facilitated transnational exchange and imitation.[3] Whatever their ideological orientation, all parties believed that youth ensured the biological survival of their families, ethnic groups, and entire nations. More than any other demographic, young people were said to possess the potential to rededicate societies to a common purpose.

Because of this shared outlook, youth became an embattled resource domestically as well as internationally. As the French socialist Léon Blum remarked in 1934, "We live at a time when everyone assumes the right to speak in the name of youth, when everyone, at the same time, wants to grab hold of youth, when everyone is fighting over youth."[4] Scout officials could never be sure that this universal interest in the young would work in their favor. Communist and fascist regimes introduced state-run youth organizations modeled after the Scout program yet at the same time hostile to it. Just as the Boy Scouts had formed networks of cooperation across national boundaries, the movement's communist and fascist rivals in Germany, Italy, and the Soviet Union were eager to see their programs copied on distant shores.[5] With the communist Young Pioneers of America (YPA) and the German American Jungenschaft, the boy division of the pro-Nazi German-American Bund (GAB), two rival organizations with strong transnational ties of their own sprouted on North American soil. In terms of global ambition, little separated the gospel of the "New Man" chanted by young communists and fascists from the anthem of brotherhood intoned by the Boy Scouts. In view of these intersecting developments, the history of youth organizations cannot be approached as a series of insulated cases. To situate the Depression-era history of the BSA in a broader global landscape of youth politics encompassing civil societies and states means to write a history of organized youth shaped by the simultaneous forces of ideological divergence and structural convergence.

Such a story of entanglements, confrontations, and demarcations requires paying close attention to how different groups of people spoke, moved, and acted in the contested borderlands of youth. There is the level of the organizers, the men who set the BSA's policies and crafted its ideology. Like many self-declared youth experts working in journalism, at universities, and for a growing federal government, Scout officials joined the chorus of concerned adults calling for ratcheting up the supervision of a young generation imperiled by material deprivation and political radicalization. Vulnerability and corruptibility replaced idealism and innocence as the key themes in BSA representations of boyhood. Only by entrusting the nation's future men to their care, BSA spokesmen argued, could parents rest assured that their sons, to paraphrase one New Dealer, would remain "the trustees of posterity" and not end up as "a lost generation."[6] Juxtaposing the image of Boy Scouts as peaceful soldiers of reform against that of violent European-style youth movements yielded several benefits. It rendered leftist critiques of scouting as an authoritarian and militarist institution less effective. It established a binary opposition between youths pledging allegiance to a nonradical, democratic America and those serving foreign dictators. Finally, it rejuvenated and remasculinized the idea of democracy itself, refuting claims that liberal democracies were feeble, effeminate, and unable to take care of their own.

Nonetheless, ideology and actual practice did not always march in lockstep—not in the BSA leadership, not among the scoutmasters, and not among the boys. Contrary to the totalitarian discourse that lumps together communism and fascism as equally un-American ideologies, the BSA's attitudes toward youth groups to its left and right followed uneven historical trajectories. Until the late 1930s, Scout organizers in the United States and Great Britain were willing to turn a blind eye to fascist youth organizations, viewing them as potential allies in the fight against communism. This perception flipped once World War II welded the United States and the Soviet Union into an alliance of necessity. U.S. Boy Scouts traveling to Europe before the war had several amicable meetings with young Nazis, swapping their merit badges for swastika armbands and Hitler Youth daggers. While informal encounters between youths and youth leaders taught to worship conflicting ideologies could reinforce adversarial attitudes, they also produced accounts full of confusion, ambivalence, and curiosity. These bottom-up perspectives are integral to arriving at a multilayered understanding of how the BSA dealt with rival groups in a time of depression, interimperial conflict, and war. Specifically, they show that time, space, and age were crucial variables in these encounters.

If history were a morality tale, it would be easy to say that the BSA would come out of a comparison with its fascist and communist adversaries rather well. There were, of course, marked differences. The official youth bodies of Nazi Germany and Soviet Russia were run by the state, whereas the BSA remained independent of government control. But making such judgments in retrospect would miss a larger point. Historical scholarship has begun to de-essentialize the ways in which democratic and nondemocratic regimes have reacted to the multiple crises prior to World War II by telling complex stories of transnational comparison, contrast, and transfer.[7] Default narratives of the Great Depression sound the cadences of isolation and global retreat, yet the United States remained a colonial power and continued to subdue nonwhite groups. I demonstrate that notions of patriotic boyhood and national service in the long 1930s can be understood only in the broader context of practices of youth mobilization that redefined intergenerational relations across the globe. To tease out the contributions of the actors involved, the following analysis percolates downward from the mobilizers to the mobilized, from the adults on the top to the youths on the ground, all of whom left their own imprints on the politically fractured field of organized youth. It is with this changing field that the story of the BSA during the long 1930s begins.

Nurturing Nazis, Raising Reds

When Depression-era Americans ventured out into the world to study the conditions under which children were growing up, their mood darkened abruptly. Not much of the sunny internationalist optimism of the 1920s, which had celebrated young people as the heralds of world peace, was left. Instead, the forecasts made by youth experts of various persuasions projected clouds of conflict and war. Consider the example of Daniel A. Poling, evangelical youth leader and head of the International Christian Endeavor Movement. Poling's trip to the 1935 summit of his organization in Budapest, Hungary, turned the American minister into a prophet of doom. Poling stared into the faces of grinding poverty, listened to the speeches of political firebrands, and witnessed youths mesmerized by the drumbeats of authoritarian regimes. At every stop, Poling wrote, he had met militarized adolescents riding the waves of "supernationalism." Youth was on the march, marching "at the call of personalities," marching "inevitably, against other youth," marching "for war and not for peace." From Hitler Youths pledging loyalty to the Fuehrer and Italian Balilla marching with wooden guns to Russian Pioneers and Komsomol parading on the Red Square for the glory of the revolution, Poling saw young people headed toward chaos and destruction. "To meet on some frontier," warned the minister, the young "only need to continue marching as they march now. When they meet again the world goes mad."[8]

Poling's ominous forecast reflected a seminal shift in how adults thought about juvenile waywardness: away from the delinquency talk of the postwar boom years toward invocations of an unholy trinity of material deprivation, moral disorientation, and political radicalization. Conservative commentators agreed that traveling the road from childhood to adulthood had become more hazardous for the Depression generation than for preceding cohorts, and that negative domestic and foreign influences had narrowed the path to respectable citizenship. The image of the destitute child suffering from malnutrition and family breakups came to symbolize an ailing planet, and fears of young people declaring war on the status quo undermined faith in the solidity of the international order.[9] Youth's unpredictable behavior, according to a 1937 report by the U.S. government, had become a "world problem."[10] Much of the alarm centered on foreign dictators, who were allegedly sending out their pied pipers to win over disenchanted youths—a form of infiltration that, in Poling's estimate, constituted "an invading enemy more dangerous than any physical foe that could advance upon us from a foreign shore."[11] Journalist Maxine Davis rejected the isolationist notion that distance offered protection from external ills. "What of our own young people?" Davis asked with a sense of trepidation. "They too have been living through the same dark days that caused their foreign brothers to see Mussolini and Hitler and Lenin appear as leaders bathed in light. Can we depend upon them now to live and work and carry on in our own beliefs in democracy, individual liberty, and freedom? Or will they, cynical, dissatisfied, revolt against the established order and lead us into strange and dangerous ways?"[12]

As paranoid as these statements may sound, they need to be read against the increased activities of communist and fascist youth groups in the United States. For reasons of comparability with scouting, the YPA and the youth division of the GAB deserve special scrutiny. Both formations were the product of larger transnational chain reactions that originated with the new governments in the Soviet Union, Italy, and Germany. Communist revolutionaries had been experimenting with novel techniques to mobilize youth since the early 1920s. Under the tutelage of Lenin's wife, Nadezhda Krupskaya, the Komsomol, the Bolshevist organization for youths and young adults aged 14–28, founded a new group for children starting at the age of ten that they initially baptized the Spartak Young Pioneers. Adopted by radical leftists around the world, particularly in Germany, France, and later in China, the Pioneer model also found subscribers in North America. In 1926, U.S. communists took the Young Workers League nascent junior section and changed its name to the YPA.[13] Formally, the YPA was the children's wing of the Communist Party of the United States. Local branches concentrated around schools, urban districts, and industrial centers and were usually headed by older youths enrolled in the Young Communist League (YCL), the English-speaking offshoot of the Komsomol. The YPA was strongest in big coastal cities such as New York and San Francisco, drawing most of its support from Jewish immigrant radicals from Eastern Europe, but it was virtually nonexistent in small-town and rural America. When the organization disbanded in 1934, the junior section of the communist International Workers' Order (IWO) stepped into the breach and carried on the YPA's work.[14]

The fascist regime changes in Europe triggered a second wave of illiberal youth mobilization that spilled over the Atlantic. Mussolini's rise to power animated smaller groups of Italian Americans to don black shirts in support of the new Italian state.[15] However, no ethnic fascist subsidiary attracted greater attention than the GAB, which advocated a rapprochement of New Deal America with Hitler's Germany. Youth moved to the foreground of the Bund's Nazification designs. Inspired by the two major Nazi youth groups, the Hitler Youth and the League of German Girls, Bundists founded the Jungenschaft and the Mädchenschaft for boys and girls, respectively, aged 10–18. Mixing leisure and political education, the Bund's youth division sought to indoctrinate children of German American parentage with the key components of Nazi ideology: anti-Semitism, anticommunism, German cultural superiority, racial purity, and the prioritization of physical exercise and military drill. Three summer camps—Camp Hindenburg in Wisconsin, Camp Nordland in New Jersey, and Camp Siegfried on Long Island—constituted the main laboratories for raising German American youth in the spirit of National Socialism. GAB camp routines involved instruction in racial hygiene, hunting, and shooting; saluting the Swastika alongside the Stars and Stripes; and singing Hitler Youth songs around the campfire. Membership was formally limited to U.S. citizens, but the primary constituents were children of Teutonic stock. Although the Bund alienated most German Americans and failed to get the official endorsement of the Nazi government, its work persisted in broad daylight until the federal government outlawed the organization after the U.S. entry into World War II.[16]

Structural analogies between the BSA, on the one hand, and the YPA and the Bund's youth divisions, on the other, abounded. All three depicted the building of solid intergenerational partnerships as crucial to solving problems regarding juvenile health and crime, gender relations, and loyalty to the state. All three feared that autonomous, self-governing youth would tilt to either careless cynicism or cultural relativism. All three invested in transnational

networks that encouraged children and youths to understand their connections to like-minded peers abroad as vital to the creation of new worlds. And all
three courted young volunteers by stressing communal experience found in
outdoor activities, public marches, and group-specific paraphernalia. From
the red scarf and the Pioneer Pledge "Always Prepared" to activities such as
hiking, camping, and recitals of the Ten Socialist Commandments, the Pioneers seemed, in the words of the British philosopher Bertrand Russell, to be
little more than "a copy of the Boy Scouts."[17] The YPA, one of its leaders
found, was a "worker's Scout movement" untainted by the jingoism of the
original.[18] Baden-Powell, on the other hand, noted after meeting with Mussolini in 1933 that the fascist Balilla was "formed on the lines of the Scout
movement."[19]

The parallels uniting youth organizations across the ideological spectrum
were hard to miss, yet contemporaries did not dwell on them too much. Collective identities, growing as they most often do out of interactions with significant others, thrive on magnifying differences and inventing enemies. Among
the fault lines the Pioneers drew to distinguish themselves, stressing opposition
to the Boy Scouts was paramount. Children who joined the YPA were told to
see the Boy Scouts—and to a lesser extent the Girl Scouts and the Camp Fire
Girls—as guilty of the twin evils of capitalism and militarism. Heeding Krupskaya's charge that bourgeoisie educators were training children to be "the ser-
vile slaves of capitalism," the YPA adopted as its battle cry "The Boy Scouts is
an Organization for Capitalist Wars! Smash the Boy Scouts! Join the Young
Pioneers!"[20] Adult party members writing for YPA publications located the
roots of the BSA's alliance with the military-capitalist complex in World War I.
If the Boy Scouts stood for peace, one author claimed, why was it that the
"Scouts of the U.S. Imperialist Government . . . sold over $400,000,000 worth
of 'Liberty Bonds' to carry on the war against their foreign 'brothers' "?[21] Such
statements were not confined to the printed page. At a May Day Rally in New
York in 1927, fifteen-year-old Irving Lifschitz slammed the Scouts as a "direct
organ of the capitalist class," whose martial fanfare and promise of adventure
"poison[ed] the minds of the children."[22] Condemning the Boy Scouts as the
natural enemies of not just working-class youths but youths everywhere became a centerpiece of the YPA's recruitment strategy.

Rank-and-file Pioneers chanted these anti-Scout slogans with relish, and it
may be tempting to see in these children little more than young simpletons
echoing the party line. Such an interpretation, however, downplays the significance of political agency in the YPA's ideal of a revolutionary childhood.[23]
Harry Eisman, a Russian-born youth organizer who had been orphaned at

seven, gave palpable expression to this ideal. On July 20, 1929, the fourteen-year-old Eisman and his comrades made an unannounced appearance at New York harbor to give a group of Scouts departing for the world jamboree in England a special send-off. As parents were saying goodbye to their sons, the seventy communists, twenty young adults and fifty teenagers, unfurled red banners and shouted slogans such as "Down with capitalism!" and "The Boy Scouts are being prepared for war!" A full-fledged brawl ensued, with the Pioneer boys and girls and their adult leaders on one side, and furious parents and policemen on the other. Eisman, who was in the thick of the fray, was arrested and charged with making a disturbance and attacking a patrolman's horse. In custody, Eisman refused to back down, lambasting the BSA for being "a training school for militarism" that turned boys into "cannon fodder" for the next war planned by the "capitalist bosses."[24] For the authorities, this was no silly prank. After his involvement in another altercation with a group of Scouts, Eisman was sentenced to five years in a reformatory. The story of Eisman's "martyrdom" at the hands of U.S. capitalists spread in the international communist press. In 1930, Eisman received an offer to live in the Soviet Union, which he accepted.[25] Activist children like Eisman and Lifschitz embodied the goodness and newness of communism as opposed to the old order that the Boy Scouts represented. Whereas Boy and Girl Scouts were characterized as "tools in the hands of the bosses" or benighted "slaves" led astray by the forces of reaction, the Pioneers held out the promise of a self-directed and fulfilling childhood.[26]

Crafting a fascist politics of childhood, German American Bundists distanced themselves from the BSA too. Symbolic of a revival of an indomitable and unapologetically nationalist German America after the dark days of World War I, children occupied a special place in the Bund leaders' chauvinist scripts. For Fritz Kuhn, who stood at the helm of the Bund, children were the "life line" and the "only possibility of a final union" between ethnic Germans overseas and the New Germany of Adolf Hitler.[27] A sense of urgency resounded from the proclamations of Theodore Dinkelacker, the Bund's chief youth officer. "We must make every conceivable effort to obtain a tight grip on all German American youngsters," he told Bund members at a meeting in 1937. In Dinkelacker's eyes, the cultivation of a German ethnicity in New Deal America and loyalty to the tenets of the Third Reich were identical duties. If the Jungenschaft and the Mädchenschaft served their purposes, the boys and girls emerging from these divisions "would carry forward our Nazi ideals" and would "ultimately bring victory to the glorious German ideals here."[28] The Bundists' glorification of fascist youth mobilization as implemented by their heroes in

Germany also manifested itself in the realm of material culture. In emulation of the Hitler Youth, Jungenschaft boys wore quasi-military uniforms, sported swastika buttons and Germanic runes on cross straps, and flaunted knifes bearing the inscription "Blut und Ehre" (blood and honor). Young female Bundists, one the other hand, imitated the looks, style, and recreational activities of the League of German Girls.[29]

In the Bund's Weltanschauung, scouting figured as an agent of a voracious Anglo-Saxon Americanism, threatening to devour the German element by luring the descendants of German immigrants away from their cultural heritage. German American youths had to be protected, GAB spokesmen insisted—not from the military-capitalist complex that the communists lashed out against but from the caustic waters of the melting pot, which Bundists condemned as a Jewish plot to further the "mongrelization" of the Aryan race.[30] Anglo-American youth groups were portrayed as tools in the hands of a Jewish-Bolshevist conspiracy and found totally inadequate for inculcating in Germanic youths a sense of duty to race and nation. Bund leaders told their boys to stay away from the Boy Scouts, which they found too soft, too racially degenerate, and too internationalist. Steely manhood and true love for the fatherland, Wisconsin Bundist Karl Möller stated, could not reside in an "international organization" whose "leader and founder, Lord Baden-Powell, [was] an alien."[31] Equations of scouting with feebleness trickled down into the consciousness of ordinary Jungenschaft members. Erich Barischoff had nothing but disdain for the Boy Scouts. "They're sissies," he exclaimed in the presence of federal investigators in 1942. "They don't know what hardships are like. They take little walks while we travel hundreds of miles. There is no comparison between the American Boy Scouts and the *Jungenschaft*. The Americans are babies alongside of us."[32]

Considering fascist attitudes about gender and sexuality, it is safe to speculate that hypermasculine performances were as much about boasting superior physical prowess as about asserting sexual maturity. While scoutmasters sought to keep boys in a preadolescent, asexual state, GAB camp supervisors encouraged a modest degree of eroticism between male and female teenagers. Although Bund youth workers abided by traditional gender norms by preparing girls to be housekeepers and mothers and preparing boys to be providers and soldiers, Jungenschaft and Mädchenschaft groups took possession of adjacent campgrounds and pitched their tents close enough for intimate encounters to occur. Allowing ethnic German youths to explore their bodily instincts in the adult-administered environment of a summer camp had little to do with adolescent self-realization. This was the GAB's adaptation of the Nazis' procre-

Figure 5.1. Young German American Bundists at Camp Nordland, New Jersey, undated. Modeled after the Hitler Youth, the GAB's youth divisions proclaimed loyalty to the ideals of National Socialism while adopting elements from scouting. (Courtesy of the National Archives, College Park, Maryland)

ation policy, which aimed at harnessing the fertility of young men and women with Aryan credentials to the breeding of racially pure Nordic children. Reproductive racism and the politicization of adolescent sexuality went hand in hand in the GAB.[33]

The YPA's politics of gender and race offered a different kind of counterpoint to scouting. The red scarf was worn by children of both sexes, and there was no separate organization for girls. Communist educators practiced co-educational camping, but their rejection of bourgeois family norms did not involve a full-fledged acceptance of young people acting out their sexual urges. Comrades all, boys and girls were first and foremost expected to agitate for the emancipation of the working class, regardless of gender.[34] Girls took the lead in several YPA initiatives such as distributing anti-Scout leaflets in schools or speaking at May Day parades, defying perceptions about their fragility and providing an example of activist girlhood unrestrained by the confines of domesticity. Conservative adults found it hard to cope with the revolutionary energy of girls and their appropriation of a masculine language of revolt that resided in communist political culture. Dumbfounded that female Pioneers were entering physical confrontations with state authorities "as lustily" as boys, the police guarding the BSA jamboree delegation headed to Arrowe Park, the *New York Times* commented, found themselves "at a disad-vantage."[35] Should these girls be treated like their male comrades? Or would a slap on the wrist do the job? Clearly, the gendered convention of an insecure and tender girlhood was seriously disrupted by the possibilities of girl activism afforded by the Young Pioneers.

Communist youth mobilizers reckoned that giving young people key posi-tions in their movement would appeal to working-class boys who had never been too fond of the Scouts. In addition to rejecting the Boy Scouts' politics, plebeian youths questioned the Scouts' masculinity. From the very beginning, middle-class organizers had struggled to make inroads into the communities of the urban poor, where the overzealous young Scout doing a good turn every day had become the object of ridicule. Opinions differed on the question of whether boys should wear army-style uniforms, which underprivileged groups read as a symbol of the power of the state to conscript young men against their will. A study commissioned by the BSA in the 1930s attributed the difficulty to recruit boys from "less-chance areas" to the fact that working-class children "did not like to wear the uniform," and that "boys in these areas call Scouts 'sissies.' "[36] Children whose parents had been active in labor unions might have also overheard their elders deride young guardsmen acting as strikebreakers as "tin soldiers" or "Boy Scouts."[37] Evidently, working-class perceptions of scout-ing as an effeminate, even childish activity, unrelated to the everyday challenges of growing up poor, lasted for more than a generation.

Another barrier the YPA fought to break down was the one separating white from black children, which pitted young communists not only against the GAB's National Socialist racism but also against the BSA's policies on race. With its antisegregationist imagery, YPA periodicals contrasted vividly with the pre-ponderance of white boys depicted in *Boys' Life*. Representations of happily integrated young communists came in the form of a triplet consisting of a white boy, a white girl, and a black boy holding hands or performing the Pioneer salute.[38] African American youths, children were told, were particularly deserv-ing of white solidarity because they not only were victims of racist violence but also bore the brunt of the class struggle in the United States. Admitting black boys and girls to communist summer camps, where they performed Af-rican American songs and sketches for white children, reinforced the party line, which denounced racism as a vicious plot contrived by the wealthy to drive a wedge between proletarians of a different skin color.[39]

The YPA's antiracist propaganda was partly grounded in reality. Pioneer mag-azines gleefully reported on African American boys deserting the Boy Scouts and finding true brotherhood in their ranks. A black Scout named Leslie Boyd, who had been sent by his scoutmaster to spy on a YPA camp in upstate New York, wrote back that he had joined the Pioneers because in "the Pioneer camp, we were all the same, white children and Negro children."[40] Another black defector, fourteen-year-old Shelley Strickland from Philadelphia, became the darling of the communist press on both sides of the Atlantic. One of seven YPA delegates who made the trip to the first International Pioneer Rally in Moscow in 1929, Strickland shared his story of growing up in a country where black boys could not ride the same buses or attend the same camps as white boys with youths from all over the world. Race differences did not exist for the Pioneers, Strickland lectured, whereas the Boy Scouts, "who prize[d] 'humanity' so highly," looked upon black children "as human beings of a lower class." Soviet organizers were so impressed that they published a biographical sketch of Strickland, claiming that he had swayed more than three hundred African American boys to drop the Scout neckerchief for the Pioneer scarf.[41] This figure was likely an exaggeration, but the international publicity given to Strickland stood in sharp contrast to the absence of black youths in the BSA's public relations campaigns.

The networks of age and political kinship that connected the lives of young American communists and fascists to transnational ideological formations made their actions less parochial and more meaningful to those involved. YPA leaders sought to foster in young members an appreciation for the global nature of the anticapitalist struggle, publishing stories about brother and sister Pioneers taking the fight to the bosses in other countries and sending youths like Strickland to international communist youth gatherings in Europe. Likewise, Bund educators sponsored trips to Germany that led to exchanges between Hitler Youths and young Bundists. During the 1936 Olympics in Berlin, Bund leaders told their wards to imagine themselves as part of a collective body of Germandom that stretched from the Nazi homeland to distant German-speaking settler communities.[42]

These transnational connections mattered fundamentally to how U.S. authorities perceived the YPA and the Bund's youth division. Without these networks, American elites would likely have discounted both forms of illiberal youth mobilization as fringe phenomena. Neither the YPA and IWO juniors, which registered almost twenty thousand members by the late 1930s, nor the GAB, with its approximately six thousand to eight thousand members at the onset of World War II, came close to matching the enrollment numbers of the BSA.[43] It was their contacts to fascist and communist movements overseas that allowed U.S. officials to paint the GAB and YPA as menacing outposts of foreign empires bent on subverting the nation's youth.

When several influential U.S. congressmen in the late 1920s and 1930s started identifying major threats to the nation, monitoring the activities of communist and fascist youth organizations stood high on their list. In 1929, a committee of the House of Representatives dedicated to exposing communist infiltrators blacklisted the YPA as an institution directed by the Kremlin and dedicated to teaching children "hatred of God, our form of government, and the American flag."[44] Subsequent committees headed by the congressmen Samuel Dickstein, John William McCormack, and Martin Dies Jr. reached a similar verdict for domestic Nazi youths, asserting that they received their marching orders from Berlin.[45] These charges hardly deterred illiberal youth organizers, but the power of the state to license some forms of youth transnationalism while declaring others incompatible with dominant ideals of childhood precipitated a response. To shed the stigma of "un-Americanness," fascist and communist youth groups resorted to a form of strategic Americanization. The YPA and its successor organization, the IWO juniors, highlighted all-American sports and leisure activities in their youth programs. The Pioneers, one pamphlet advertised, had "hikes, and baseball teams, and football teams, and basketball teams, and summer camps . . . and all the other things that all boys and girls like to do."[46] YPA chapters were instructed to conduct their meetings in English and portray the Young Pioneers as descendants of nineteenth-century North American settlers going west in search of a better life.[47] In the 1930s, IWO youths adopted the slogan "Communism is the Americanism of the Twentieth Century." Agitating for the emancipation of the working class, they argued, was fiercely patriotic.[48]

GAB leader Fritz Kuhn sought to bolster his movement's American credentials by saying that he took no orders from foreign governments.[49] Perhaps his biggest publicity stunt was a rally on George Washington's birthday in February 1939 at New York's Madison Square Garden that drew up to twenty thousand spectators. Surrounded on stage by Nazi and American flags and preceded by the blare and brass of a Bundist drum and bugle corps that consisted largely of children, Kuhn put the organization's anti-Semitism and antiblack racism squarely in the country's white supremacist tradition. Was it not American to fight communism, have the Stars and Stripes displayed at every Bund camp, and "unite with all Americans defending the Aryan culture," as the GAB's constitution demanded? After all, did not America's antimiscegenation laws and Nazism's concern about the purity of blood spring from the same well?[50] While such references did not appease the Bund's critics, they show that the ability of Depression-era American youth organizations to grow and prosper depended largely on their ability to align their transnational ambitions with the national interest as defined by political elites.

The question, then, was whether it lay in the national interest to build up an infrastructure of organized youth loyal to the state and unsusceptible to communist and fascist youth mobilization. Franklin Delano Roosevelt and his advisers were equally troubled and fascinated by European efforts to make youth the vanguards of new regimes.[51] Would the New Deal create its own centralized alternative to the German Hitler Youth, the Italian Balilla, and the Soviet Pioneers and Komsomol? Would federal programs devised to educate, employ, and discipline young people, such as the Civilian Conservation Corps (CCC) and the National Youth Administration (NYA), supplement the work done by older youth organizations like the BSA, compete with them, or simply take their place? To cope with the era's uncertainties, BSA administrators redefined their mission. They ended up presenting their organization as uniquely committed to reinvigorating a flagging democracy and ensuring that its youth would not turn into fifth columnists of foreign dictators. Framing youth mobilization in the service of the nation as an epic struggle between democracy and dictatorship, however, came with its own contradictions and duplicities.

Democracy's Young Soldiers

> The turmoil of Europe is front page news, and wherever men gather in New York today, you hear echoes of a confused world. . . . People are wondering what the madness of the Dictators will eventually mean to the lives of 130,000,000 Americans. . . . What will it all mean to the youth of today who will be the citizens of tomorrow?

Thus begins *America's Answer*, a brochure published with the consent of BSA headquarters in early 1938. A great deal of preparation had gone into the brochure's making—its sloganesque language and dramatic imagery showing youths seduced by dictators made it a powerful piece of countersubversive propaganda. *America's Answer* proved that juxtaposing totalitarianism, a newly coined term that described fascism and communism as equally inhuman menaces, with the "American way" had become central to the BSA's identity. The brochure was the work of the Scout executives of the Greater New York region, where Pioneer and GAB youths had been particularly active. It reached a national audience with its gloomy picture of a country infiltrated by the long reach of Hitler's, Stalin's, and Mussolini's youth agents. Radicalism and war, the authors warned, had not stopped at foreign shores. The Young Pioneers and the Bund's youth divisions had established a foothold in the United States, nourishing American children on the same "diet of hate and intolerance" that had plunged youths in other countries "into a world of blood and guns and hate." Part distress call and part rallying cry, the brochure closed with a plea to support "the country's greatest youth movement . . . the Boy Scouts of America." Whereas the children of dictators were taught to worship "guns and cannons" over "home and family," the BSA was making men out of boys who were "dedicating themselves to the rights and responsibilities of American citizenship and to the principles of tolerance and human brotherhood." Allegiance to leaders fairly selected instead of blind obedience, respect for laws instead of lust for war, participation in community affairs instead of mindless drills—this, the authors declared, was "real training for democracy."[52]

That BSA organizers painted their program in glaringly pro-American and anti-totalitarian colors should come as no surprise. Neither should the emphasis on democracy as the essence of a masculine Americanism. By the early twentieth century, democracy carried almost none of the connotations of mob rule and lawlessness so prominent in the Early Republic. In World War I, it had become the banner under which the doughboys were sent to fight and die in the trenches. Presidents from Theodore Roosevelt and Woodrow Wilson to Herbert Hoover and Franklin Roosevelt lauded democracy as exceptionally fitted to America's economic ingenuity and belief in government by popular consent. People across partisan divides made such generalizations about the democratic character of U.S. society. Yet in doing so, they concealed that democracy was an amorphous concept open to reinterpretation. Early twentieth-century ideas about democracy in American society encompassed different, potentially conflicting practices. Voting, religious diversity, middle-class family values, local self-determination, free-market capitalism, and consumerism provided the ideological pillars of an exceptionalist yet erratic "American way."[53] For BSA officials looking to reassert the organization's Americanness in a moment of crisis, this semantic flexibility posed problems and opportunities: notions of self-government could work against youth's acceptance of adult hierarchies at the same time that they allowed organizers to present the BSA as the backbone of a democratic masculinity grounded in national service rather than a materialistic individualism.

The BSA's promise to forge a patriotic boyhood tough enough to resist the totalitarian menace met a demand stimulated by the reprioritization of gender roles in New Deal America. Scholars of masculinity have convincingly argued that the Great Depression disrupted equations of proper American manhood with business success. Under the strain of mass unemployment, older notions of manhood emphasizing economic individualism, social mobility, and personal self-fulfillment were supplemented by a new appreciation for collective action. As the throngs of jobless men waiting in soup lines seemed to give the lie to the patriarchal ideal of men as breadwinners, increased government action sought to resurrect that ideal. However, programs such as the CCC also aimed at normalizing a masculine concept of citizenship that fused antihedonism and loyalty to the state with a warlike ethos of service and shared sacrifice for the nation. A fraternity of citizens, not a loose assortment of self-made men, was what New Dealers envisioned when they spoke of democracy.[54]

The New Deal's construction of what gender historian Philip Abbott termed a "new masculine public space" that privileged work for the common good over the feminized consumerism of the boom years was mirrored in the BSA's actions.[55] Individualist and market-friendly interpretations of Scout virtues such as resourcefulness and self-reliance lost relevance when BSA leaders compared the economic calamity of the early 1930s to the national emergency of 1917 and 1918. Detailing how Scout troops had been collecting and donating food, clothing, and toys for the needy, Frank Robinson stated in 1932 that "this splendid and quiet worthwhile service certainly approximates, if it does not equal, the national service rendered by Scouts during the period of . . . the World War."[56] In the flurry of propaganda, posters, and processions on behalf of numerous federal recovery programs launched by the Roosevelt administration, Boy Scouts on the mainland and in the colonies were drafted for "national good turns" in the same way that their predecessors had been mobilized for war.[57] Home-front analogies quickly came to mind as troops marched in support of the National Recovery Administration, waving the Blue Eagle and pushing "I will co-operate" cards into the hands of housewives.[58] Militarized performances of conformity with the New Deal overrode individual political convictions. Collective action, not agonizing debate, promised to overcome the emasculating effects of economic victimhood and nudge boys and men away from particular group loyalties toward an inclusive ideal of national service. "We can 'SMILE AND DO' and perhaps inspire others to 'DO' and thus further demonstrate not only the value of Scouting, but of the great democracy of which we are a part," West advised his boy-men in the field. "Why not help bury the 'depression complex' wherever we can?"[59]

Highlighting the import of the Boy Scouts for burying the "depression complex" was not merely about restoring the patriarchal gender order. More importantly, BSA leaders joined a broader conversation about how to enlist youth symbolically and practically for building a robust democratic citizenry trained in virtues such as patriotism, deference to authority, and physical and sexual self-restraint—virtues that gained military overtones later in the decade. Not every American was in favor of aligning the lives of the nation's youth with the interests of the state. Right-wing groups such as the American Liberty League feared "a colored shirt fascist army" loyal to "Roosevelt the Dictator" would emerge from centralized ventures to combat youth poverty and unemployment. Carl Minkley, the state secretary of the Wisconsin Socialist Party, warned that mainstream youth politics offered a "breeding spot for militarism or fascism."[60] Overall, however, such criticisms had little effect on the boys and young men who flocked by the thousands to the BSA, the CCC, and other New Deal–friendly endeavors.

Democratic nation building acquired a particular urgency in an era when communist and fascist regimes declared in unison that liberal societies lacked the muscle to bounce back from the crises that enveloped them. Liberal democracies, they insisted, were like feeble and decadent old men digging their own graves.[61] Rejecting this argument and engaging in an ideological contest over what constituted "old" and "young," U.S. scouters cast their movement as appropriately masculine and fashioned for themselves a youthful identity as the defenders of democracy. Scouting's idealistic language of youth that people invoked in the 1920s to avert another world war proved adaptable to the task of rescuing the nation from fascism and communism, an undertaking that the journalist Henry Luce christened the "rejuvenation of the now decayed and outmoded idea of democracy itself."[62] Three events illustrate how this rescue mission was shrouded in the bipolar rhetoric of democracy versus dictatorship: the first national jamboree in Washington, DC, in 1937, the National Rededication Campaign of 1938–39, and the BSA's war work from 1941 to 1945.

Originally planned for 1935 but postponed because of a polio outbreak in the area, the Washington jamboree spotlighted the bodies of healthy, happy, and patriotic boys to reinforce the twin causes of antiradicalism and national regeneration. Camping in plain sight of the Washington Monument and the Lincoln Memorial, more than twenty-seven thousand U.S. Boy Scouts and a few hundred foreign Boy Scouts melded into a juvenile male polity that emphasized fun, shared public labor, and obedience to the Scout law.[63] International friendship was invoked, but the jamboree was principally a celebration of a resurgent Americanism based on a renewed pact between fathers and sons. An ardent supporter of the BSA, FDR played the role of father-in-chief. Though half-paralyzed and lacking the physicality of his cousin Theodore, FDR possessed a disarming smile and exuded a boyish optimism that made him an ideal honorary president of the nation's largest boy organization. Roosevelt's sponsorship of the jamboree grew out of a long personal involvement with scouting that had started in 1922 when he was appointed chair of the Boy Scout Foundation of Greater New York. Some historians detect in Roosevelt's promotion of conservationism within the BSA a precursor to the CCC, but FDR valued scouting for other reasons as well.[64] Scouting's intergenerational bonds, according to Roosevelt, formed the nucleus of American democracy, of boys and men who had learned the essence of "good citizenship" and "good government" by putting the common welfare ahead of individual accomplishment.[65]

On the surface, the queue of boys lining up to salute President Roosevelt as he was motorcading through the tent city evoked eerie parallels to the forty-five thousand Hitler Youths who had shouted out their allegiance to the führer at Nuremberg two years earlier. The organizers, however, were quick to dispel such analogies, claiming that their rally provided a peaceful alternative

Figure 5.2. Franklin Delano Roosevelt pins the Eagle Scout award on a Boy Scout during the national jamboree in Washington, DC, July 1937. In the car with the president are James E. West and Daniel Carter Beard. (Courtesy of the Library of Congress, Prints and Photographs Division)

to militarized youth in dictatorships. "Over the world we hear the tramp of the feet of youth," George Fisher recalled; "in so many places youth exploited, youth regimented, youth mobilized for selfish aims." But not in Washington, according to Fisher, where boys were listening not to "shouting dictators" but to "the still voices and the spirits of Washington and Lincoln that were among them."[66] Paul Siple, who was touring the campground, drew a similar conclusion. "Scouting trains for better citizenship and not for a better soldiery," Siple remarked, and told the movement's critics to go to the Soviet Union to see what youth regimentation really meant. Delegations from the Philippines, Hawaii, Puerto Rico, and European and Latin American countries served as principal witnesses for a young masculinity that was both global and peaceful. Scout training, Siple underlined, would teach boys to see the world as a place for making friends, not wars.[67] Not all saw it that way, though. When asked by the press how he liked the jamboree, Robert Chester, a British Scout who had made the trip to Washington, came up with an answer that must have disgruntled the organizers. In Chester's judgment, there was "too much militarism in American Scouting."[68]

The contradictory impulses of democratization and militarization also surfaced in the National Rededication Campaign, which aimed at sending out a forceful signal of American boyhood standing united against the domestic and foreign enemies of democracy. Held together by a coalition of conservative and liberal youth organizations including the BSA, the Girl Scouts, the Camp Fire Girls, and Jewish and Catholic youth groups, the campaign was launched in September 1938 in response to reports of fascist violence and the activities of the American Youth Congress (AYC), a federation of college students accused of harboring communist sympathies.[69] Scenarios in which the nation was torn asunder by Nazi fanatics and Popular Front demagogues justified a program of intense ideological indoctrination. "The Dictators know the value of youth," warned the Wisconsin Scout Executive Harold J. Homann, and the "subversive youth programs" with which they sought to "organize misguided children and adults" in the United States were "not a passing fancy."[70]

Under the motto "Do Not Sell America 'Short,'" Boy Scouts were asked to sign "Rededication Commitments" in which they pledged themselves to defending the country's founding principles, rehearsed the Scout oath in troop meetings, and memorized the preamble to the Declaration of Independence.[71] Young Scouts publicly rebuked totalitarian youth movements, while BSA National Director of Personnel Harold F. Pote envisaged the Bill of Responsibilities, which called on Boy Scouts to dedicate their young lives to combating "undemocratic" influences.[72] The BSA's invention of an easily consumable, nonradical past also found expression in the third edition of the *Handbook for Boys*. Encouraging boys to consider themselves inheritors of a proud democratic tradition, the handbook's cover illustration shows a young Scout surrounded by the portraits of heroic white men such as Washington, Lincoln, Theodore Roosevelt, and Charles Lindbergh, and adopting their westward gaze.[73]

U.S. scouting's backward glance may seem an odd choice for a movement that claimed to be just as enamored with youth's future potential as its ideological rivals. Catering to youth's wishes for political participation, the men in charge of the BSA nonetheless aimed at producing a cadre of young males loyal to the old order. More than anything, they sought to exploit boyhood's symbolic and biopolitical capital to manufacture consent around the assertion that the nation's founding myths still radiated enough youthfulness to refute dictators who were contending that the United States was run by flabby youths and "doddering old men."[74] In scouting's Rededication ceremonies, the idea that American democracy had the ability to simultaneously embody a rich past, a spirited present, and a virtuous future was inscribed on the chests of thousands of boys. The best thing Boy Scouts could do, Homann surmised, was to add "their golden threads to the unfinished fabric of Democracy."[75] The gendered concept of youth deployed by the organizers united boys and men around the unfading newness of American democracy, an enduring people's experiment that not only lacked the social and religious distinctions of old Europe but also avoided the intergenerational warfare incited by the fascists and communists. On one side were fathers and sons entering into a solemn pact to uphold a transgenerational commitment to preserving their nation's promise of prosperity and justice. On the other side were dictators and their minions who had abrogated their parental responsibilities by throwing children into the blazing furnaces of revolution and war. American Scouts, BSA executive and governor of New York Thomas E. Dewey surmised, would never have to "turn upon their fathers and mothers and betray them to the state" as was expected of children in dictatorships.[76]

The dichotomy of democratic and totalitarian youth was at the core of a series of didactic pieces that BSA educators put together for children. The December 1939 issue of *Boy's Life* featured the short story "Merry Christmas Hans," in which Dave Smith, a 17-year-old Eagle Scout, enters into a discussion over ham radio with Hans Schuler, a disillusioned Hitler Youth. As their talk unfolds, the Scout decides to broadcast the exchange nationwide. Millions of people listen to Dave talking about the freedoms of scouting and Hans talking about oppression in Nazi Germany.[77] The children's book *Youth under Dictators* from 1941 recounts how political indoctrination and military drill impoverish the lives of the German boy Kurt and his Russian counterpart Valya.[78] With the same dichotomy in mind, the 89-year-old Daniel Carter Beard declared his movement the true champion of youth in an increasingly belligerent world: "Dictatorship is not a new thing; like every thought that the totalitarians have, it is very, very old, so old that the grey hair of its head drags on the ground, so old that the fascists trip on the tip of its long grey beard."[79] Ray O. Wyland, the BSA director of education and relationships, struck the same chord at the 1940 annual meeting of the National Council. "Democracy is young," Wyland exclaimed, and "we will put our Eagle Scouts along any goose-stepping black shirts or brown shirts of Italy or Germany."[80] Proclaiming democratic boyhood the epitome of antitotalitarian politics, BSA leaders promoted an expanded role for themselves with the assertion that children and youth everywhere, not just in the United States, needed a positive example of boy-man homosociality.

The war vindicated U.S. scouters who had been flaunting their organization as a redemptive force for boys around the globe. Each German and Japanese conquest, each distress call from foreign Scout associations forced underground and clamoring for help, was read as evidence that the BSA had the world-historical mission to save democracy for future generations. Calling it the "destiny of America" to come to the aid of a "disbelieving world," politician Paul V. McNutt told the nation's Scouts in June 1941 to "'Be Prepared' as never before" to do their part to defeat the Axis war machine.[81] Before the United States entered the war, BSA officials framed a possible intervention for the survival of democratic boyhood in the metaphor of nations being "kidnapped" and "raped" by "monsters" and "mad werewolves."[82] This dramatic imagery was meant to compel both men and boys to take a stand in the conflict, to rally around chivalric principles so deeply entrenched in scouting. Scouts old enough to become soldiers, one recruitment poster suggested, would fight not to conquer but to liberate "once gay cities full of life, laughter, and music, the sound of children at play and people at peace."[83] A knightly paradigm that linked honor to the Scout's ability to join a global operation to rescue children from the claws of dictators legitimized a leadership role for the United States and the Boy Scouts serving under its flag. Mapping out this hierarchical relationship between masculine American Scouts and a distressed free world attacked by depraved tyrants, Beard put the "burden of responsibility of winning the world back to civilization" on the "stalwart shoulders of the Boy Scouts of America."[84]

After December 1941, BSA officials wrestled with the competing urgencies of giving boys a share in defending the nation and upholding the ideal of a sheltered childhood. Soon after the United States declared war on Japan, Boy Scouts began swarming America's towns and cities. Their many drives to collect materials use in arms production—the paper drive, the metal drive, the aluminum drive, the rubber drive, the milkweed drive, and the grease drive—reached iconic status. When the Scouts were not collecting things, they were handing out pamphlets, distributing government posters, planting Victory gardens, working on farms, training in first aid, and practicing air raid drills. The statistics command respect: in 1942, the Boy Scouts put up 1,607,500 posters, gathered at least 50,000,000 pounds of waste paper, and hauled in more than 80 percent of all the aluminum collected throughout the nation—10,500,000 lbs.[85] At the same time, the violent theme of initiating boys into the masculine sphere of soldiering was hedged in by a modern discourse of youth and childhood that presented underage people as vulnerable and worthy of protection. War service opportunities, an internal BSA memo instructed, should be assigned "according to age and ability," and "strenuous and responsible jobs" (including first aid and rescue work) should be restricted to "Scouts 15 and older." Scoutmasters should "watch out for the welfare of the Scouts" and see that the boys are not overtaxed with chores unbefitting their age.[86] Though driven by practical considerations, such policies made the American way of youth mobilization look morally superior to those of its enemies. It made scouting seem more affectionate, less hierarchical, and more concerned with keeping boys safe from the ugly realities of war.

Like their predecessors in World War I, BSA organizers took advantage of their country's distance from combat to promote the illusion of war as a boyish adventure. Scouts should be prepared for the responsibilities of military manhood without facing unnecessary danger. Illustrations of happy Scouts cheerfully participating in every scrap drive decoupled war from suffering and turned it into something akin to a sporting event.[87] Most Americans seemed to agree that war games were conducive to the socialization of boys in wartime, be it as an outlet for stress or a healthy form of hero worship. Picturing war play as an instinctive boyish urge that was most productive under adult supervision, as Scout leaders did in tandem with government officials, retained a sense of adult authority and public morality in a society in which absent fathers and loosening family ties evoked the specter of juvenile delinquency. "At this time of unrest," West asserted in January 1942 in a pamphlet circulated nationally, "youth in particular needs the stabilizing influence of the Scout Oath and Law."[88] Equating age- and gender-appropriate war games and home-front service with good citizenship, Scout leaders likened delinquency to unpatriotic (or worse, treasonous) behavior.

However, BSA officials also admitted that wartime scouting was as much about keeping boys away from mischief and violence as it was about preparing them for military service. Adjusting to the exigencies of war, West conceded that the "Boy Scout program . . . does give the basic training for a good citizen or a good soldier."[89] After the outbreak of hostilities in Europe, the BSA put in place the Emergency Service Corps to allow First-Class Scouts fifteen and older to participate in civil defense exercises. In 1942, the organization opened an honor roll for former Scouts in the armed forces and began cooperating with the government-sponsored High School Victory Corps, which trained students for war services. "Pre-Ranger Training" was introduced to teach Scouts map reading, aquatics, rifle shooting, and stalking the enemy.[90] Boasting that the U.S. officer corps was disproportionately composed of former Scouts, BSA headquarters coined the slogan "One Fourth of America's Armed Forces . . . Scout Trained" and reprinted endorsements of army men who praised scouting as "the most complete, all-around, pre-induction training that can be given at that age level."[91]

Achieving combat readiness was not the only concern. Writing from the Pacific theater, Caroll H. Sawyer, a former Scout who joined the U.S. armed forces, hoped that the war would not only toughen young men but also broaden their horizon. Sawyer did not deny the viciousness of the war, but it was a price he was willing to pay if it brought about a future America with citizens "strong in body, schooled in personal sacrifice for a noble cause, and intimately conscious of more than the people who live next door." Sawyer was thrilled at the thought that for the next several decades tens of thousands of former Boy Scouts would be "ex-soldier[s] who ha[d] been to the far corners of the world, learning fraternity, respect, and common interest for *all* the peoples of the world."[92] Sawyer's vision was consistent with the belief that U.S. scouting encouraged young males serving their country to assume a new internationalist outlook while protecting underage youths from premature military involvement. Claims like this were of enormous propaganda value. They played into the perception that the United States was fighting the good war—for humanity and the right of children everywhere to enjoy the safeguards of an American-style democracy.

This idealistic posture raised questions not only about the future scope of U.S. democratic influence but about its content as well. Seeking to produce an uplifting spectacle of patriotic boyhood in times of depression and war, the BSA leadership never championed conformity as an end in itself. At the heart

of their propaganda campaign lay the intention to present their boys as ambassadors of tolerance and diversity. In the BSA's inclusive ethos, boys were
uniquely equipped to overcome the ancient barriers of class, religion, and race.
The Twelfth Scout Law, with its provision "to respect the convictions of others
in matters of custom and religion," was to outshine the totalitarian oppression of faith groups. In January 1939, West used the violent persecution of
Jews in Germany as an opportunity to remind America's Boy Scouts that their
nation had a providential role to play as long as its religious freedoms prevented it from sliding back into the "dark ages" of intolerance. Declaring
tolerance "the very keystone of democracy," West, perhaps unwittingly, recalibrated the meaning of religion in scouting. Religion was inherently masculine
if exercised by boys and men who were protecting "the right to worship God
in accordance with the dictates of [one's] own conscience."[93] Contrary to the
1910s and 1920s, when reverence had been yoked to an assimilationist Americanism, the term was now invoked to celebrate religious diversity as the basis
of a peaceful social order.

Stressing the universal character of democratic boyhood, BSA organizers
in the late 1930s and early 1940s felt comfortable extending the message of
tolerance to the arena of race relations. "Shoulder to shoulder in the Scout
uniform you will find sons of the poor and the rich . . . Catholics and Jews
and Protestants . . . boys of every race . . . linked by common interests and by
common ideals," *America's Answer* propagated. Accompanying this statement
was a group picture of six Scouts—four white, one Hispanic, and one black—
smiling into the camera with their arms wrapped around the shoulders of the
boys next to them.[94] Racial inclusiveness was also the theme of a wartime pageant titled "Americans All—United under One Flag," performed by Scout
troops across the country in April 1942. One image depicted a group of white,
Native American, Mexican American, and African American Scouts saluting
the Stars and Stripes.[95] The comparison with earlier definitions of democracy
is striking. In 1927, West had used the term to condone racial segregation,
maintaining that scouting in the United States, "being strictly a democracy,"
would not interfere with the right of local councils to admit or reject "negro
boys" as they saw fit.[96] By the eve of World War II, BSA administrators had
changed their language. Democracy no longer meant the right to exclude but
the duty to include.

Democracy, interracial friendship, and antitotalitarianism converged in an
exemplary manner in a play performed by a group of Illinois boys and their
scoutmasters in February 1938. Titled "The State of the Youth of the World
Today" and written in the aftermath of the world jamboree in Vogelenzang,

the play linked the BSA's crusade against dictatorial youth to calls for racial reform at home. The main character in the play is a Boy Scout named Fred Olsen, who travels to an international youth camp in the Netherlands. After the jamboree, he journeys onward and meets a member of the Italian Balilla, a German Hitler Youth, and a Soviet Young Pioneer. Drawn into discussions by his new acquaintances, Fred is taken aback by the aggressive and hateful rhetoric of Europe's fascist and communist youths. The play ends with Fred returning to the United States, extolling the greatness of the nation's founding fathers, and calling on a new generation of Scouts to become men and citizens devoted to the intertwined causes of interracial understanding and international peace. The closing scene features a white Scout and a black Scout holding hands in front of the Lincoln Memorial and watching Abraham Lincoln rise up and recite the famous line from the Gettysburg Address "that this nation, under God, shall have a new birth of freedom."[97] A more dramatic appeal to U.S. Boy Scouts to help transcend the racial divisions of the past in a time of global-ideological conflict was hard to find.

Given the diversity of the BSA's membership, such expressions of racial pluralism should not be dismissed as mere platitudes or the rhetorical posturing of a few leaders. Yet historians aware of the contradictions between ideology and practice should be skeptical about the substance of pledges made by organizations and their members to live democratically. Appreciating diversity in the abstract did not have to involve a dedication to embracing difference, and talking about friendship and brotherhood in the absence of another crucial democratic idiom, equality, could lend itself to stabilizing preexisting hierarchies rather than subvert them. Tolerance, in other words, did not require Scouts to accept all other Scouts as equal.

Moreover, the BSA never became a mandatory national program, and young people emboldened by the New Deal's investment in youth were free to strive for more egalitarian alternatives. Formed in 1934 out of a palpable frustration with the democracy of old men, the student-led AYC claimed to speak for more than four million adolescents and young adults and demanded the provision of federal aid to all destitute youths from sixteen to twenty-five years of age, irrespective of sex and color. The "Declaration of the Rights of American Youth," issued by the AYC in 1936, describes youths as citizens with responsibilities and rights, such as the right to organize and participate in the democratic process.[98] It is telling that the BSA leadership told its members to shun the AYC, an organization that rejected the tutelage of older men and wanted black and white youths to work together for the same goals.[99]

Scout pageants may have waxed lyrically about the possibilities forged through interracial friendships, but none of these antitotalitarian gestures translated into serious efforts to remove the institutional barriers separating white boys from nonwhite boys. Not only were national race policies upheld—segregated dining facilities at the Washington jamboree worked against black-white friendships, and the IRS continued to operate throughout FDR's presidency and beyond.[100] BSA leaders also agreed that certain programs should not be extended to all groups. In 1936, a special commission on interracial activities decided that the BSA's ambitious "10-year plan" to reach one out of every four American boys by the end of the decade should not apply to black boys. IRS workers interpreted the fact that African Americans were hit harder by the Depression than any other population group as a sign that blacks were lacking in masculine resourcefulness. Because of this, they recommended making the policy of white supervision of black scouting in racially segregated areas a national rule.[101] During the war, African American Scouts in the South were denied participation in war bond rallies and had to organize separate parades. When black Boy Scouts started distributing government posters, BSA authorities wanted them to hand out posters with African American themes.[102] When race riots ravaged the black communities of Detroit and Mobile, Alabama, in 1943, Scout leaders failed to speak out. It was this silent endorsement of black oppression that made the African American poet Langston Hughes wonder whether the war would really free the Boy Scouts from the "shameful legacy of segregation and Jim Crowism."[103]

Another glaring contradiction created by wartime conditions was the internment of Japanese American families. Of the estimated 112,000 citizens and noncitizens of Japanese descent who were forced to leave their homes and spent the remainder of the war incarcerated in military detention centers, many had embraced scouting as an institution that would testify to their loyalty to the United States and prove the compatibility of their ethnicity with the reigning ideology of Americanism. Since the early 1920s, Scout officials and federal administrators had praised Japanese Americans as a model minority for exactly that reason.[104] That American-born children of these immigrants had been enthusiastic Scouts, however, did not shield them from racial profiling and imprisonment. On February 19, 1942, President Roosevelt signed Executive Order 9066, condemning Japanese American families to a life in concentration camps. A photograph showing two Japanese American Boy Scouts in Los Angeles posting a notice that unnaturalized Japanese, Italian, and German immigrants had been declared "enemy aliens" by the U.S. government captures

Figure 5.3. Japanese American Scouts during a morning flag-raising ceremony at the Heart Mountain Relocation Center, June 1943. Despite its lofty rhetoric of democracy, wartime scouting was complicit in the incarceration of U.S. citizens of Japanese descent. (Courtesy of the National Archives, College Park, Maryland)

this bitter irony. They were among the Boy Scouts who soon would have to do their daily good turns behind barbed wire.[105]

Loyal to the federal government, BSA officials supported the jarring spectacle of Japanese American scouting in what contemporaries euphemistically referred to as "evacuee" or "relocation" centers. In an agreement with the War Relocation Authority (WRA) signed in June 1942, the BSA pledged to lend its staff and expertise to monitoring Japanese American boys who had become Scouts on their own initiative. With the exception of sports, scouting was one of the few recreational opportunities available to young internees. Joining a troop and participating in Scout games helped boys who spent a considerable time of their childhood away from home maintain their youth in degrading conditions. Asked how he and his family endured at the Heart Mountain Internment Camp in Wyoming, William "Bill" Shishima recalled that forging bonds with fellow Scouts had buoyed his spirits. Scouting "kept us busy," Shishima remembered, and sustained the boys' faith in a better future.[106]

The lack of money and equipment in the camps notwithstanding, the detainees were expected to abide by all the rules and regulations of the Scout program, including the requirements to wear a uniform and pay membership fees.[107] Although the BSA paid lip service to the fraternity of Scouts and lobbied the WRA to permit Japanese American Scouts to go on supervised camping trips, organizers favored a policy of strict segregation. They sought to avoid contact between Japanese and white American Scouts because they feared that "pranks" and "psychological obstacles" would weaken the young internees' morale.[108] Racializing Japanese American Boy Scouts as imperfect Americans, the national leadership asked IRS chief Stanley Harris to inspect the progress of scouting in the detention centers. Harris's recommendation to "emphasize Caucasian leadership" of these troops reflected an ideological disposition to mistrust Japanese Americans because of their race, even as administrators hoped that "Oriental" boys who had been thoroughly Americanized could help U.S. authorities separate loyal from disloyal internees.[109] These hopes were not unfounded: on the eve of the first anniversary of Pearl Harbor, Japanese American Boy Scouts had protected the U.S. flag during a riot at the Manzanar War Relocation Center.[110]

The discrimination Japanese American youths endured during World War II did not approximate the gross inhumanity experienced by Jewish children in Nazi-occupied Europe. But the separateness of these two cases cannot hide the fact that the democratic posturing of the BSA was at odds with the inequalities that structured scouting in African American communities and Japanese American internment camps. To enhance their antitotalitarian credentials, white organizers bound themselves to lofty ideals about tolerance and diversity that they never fully implemented. The main stimulus behind harnessing the political imaginary of boyhood to the rejuvenation of American democracy was the desire to link youth to continuity, not radicalism. If Scout organizers marveled at the mobilizing power of the totalitarian cult of youth, they also emphasized youth's seductibility and grew increasingly wary of boys acting without adult supervision. Nonetheless, picturing fascist and nonfascist youth organizations as fundamentally different was little more than a convenient myth. A sober look at how BSA leaders and youths perceived and interacted with their rivals at different historical junctures will illustrate this.

Adversaries with Affinities

By the time the United States entered World War II, the BSA had wrapped itself in the period's democratic nationalism, claiming a vanguard role in the effort to mobilize the nation's boys around the ideals of inclusion, tolerance, and the passionate defense of the "American way." Moving from a global economic crisis to an international political crisis, adult organizers had adjusted their focus from reinvigorating deprived and depleted youths to making them immune to totalitarian propaganda. As a result of these shifting priorities, the BSA's anticommunist and antifascist campaigns stressed that the relevant differences that existed were between the United States and the world, not so much between Christians and Jews or white and black. Such proclamations, however, entailed deliberate acts of erasure, the purging of evidence that revealed that there never was a fixed equidistance between U.S. scouting and its adversaries on the left and right. A much more intricate and muddled story emerges once the intertwined dynamics of age, gender, ideology, and war are discussed from the boys' point of view. Lurking behind the veil of propaganda were U.S. Boy Scouts fraternizing with Hitler Youths in Europe or identifying with Soviet children fighting German soldiers. Socialized in similar organizational structures and impacted by similar adult-child hierarchies, many of these boys discovered that they had more in common than the official rhetoric made people believe.

Although there were no formal ties binding the Balilla and Hitler Youth to foreign Scout organizations, young Scouts traveling through Europe in the 1930s were pleased to learn that their fascist peers were eager to get in touch with them. This mutual fascination blossomed at the margins of the world jamborees, which small delegations of Balilla and Hitler Youths attended as part of fascism's international charm offensive.[111] Judging by the few sources that shed light on this subject, the Scouts were quite taken with what they saw. The nearly 1,000 Balilla boys who had traveled to Hungary in 1933 were welcomed "in a friendly fashion," as one British official recalled. The gaudy uniforms and parading skills of Mussolini's young black shirts left U.S. scout Irving Klepper "much impressed."[112] This childish curiosity in the feats and flashy uniforms of same-age youths popped up again in the aftermath of the 1937 gathering at Vogelenzang. Looking back at his trip through Nazi Germany, an aged Ken

Wells recalled how his Scout group was nearly drawn into a marching duel with a troop of Hitler Youths. "We stepped aside and, as an act of courtesy, applauded, as they passed," Wells remembered. When the German leader offered to return the favor and invited the Americans to march past the young Nazis "so they could salute" the Scouts, the young Wells "fumbled for an excuse"—not out of ideological misgivings but because he was afraid that his party, untrained in marching, "would have looked ragged and undisciplined" by comparison.[113] The marching contest did not occur, yet here was an American Boy Scout who equated military drill with clean and disciplined manhood, thereby contradicting leaders who asserted that scouting made youths resistant to militarist impulses.

Enjoying such contacts, young Scouts tended to forget that becoming too familiar with youths who had been taught to obey different masters might get them in trouble. Political ideology rarely structured the Boy Scouts' encounters with young Nazis. Intersecting organizational and material cultures as well as shared juvenile interests eased tensions and provided entry points into a carefree realm of youthful exchange. Flags, uniforms, banners, badges, parades, and peer-group dynamics in the Hitler Youth were things to which each Scout could relate, regardless of political orientation. Potential antagonisms dissipated in the gaudy receptions Nazi officials staged for itinerant jamboree Scouts in cities across Germany. Incoming youths from England, South Africa, and the United States happily accepted the flower gifts of members of the Nazi League of German Girls and swapped paraphernalia with Hitler Youths. After passing through Germany by train, one South African scoutmaster noted in 1933 that "there could have been scarcely one [Scout] kit that did not contain Nazi armlets and a swastika."[114] A photograph printed in an Atlanta newspaper in September 1937 depicts a group of Boy Scouts posing with swastika armbands and Hitler Youth daggers, which led the editor to conclude that the Americans had "literally traded the shirts off [the] backs" of the young Germans they had met.[115] A firm handclasp here, a rewarding barter there—the same ingredients that characterized scouting's transnational youth culture could be easily remolded to fit different political environments. Owen Matthews could attest to that. On their way home from Hungary, Matthews's troop spent a couple of days in Berlin, where they had a picture taken that shows them in the company of Hitler Youths and shaking hands with a Nazi stormtrooper.[116]

In looking at these incidents, adult organizers might have felt justified in their concerns about youths' impressionability and their inability to understand how a hostile regime was taking advantage of their curiosity. But young people, organized or independent, insisted that their age-based networks were not beholden to the same rules as adult ones. Few expressed this conviction more forcefully than Darrel Brady, a Mormon Eagle Scout from Minnesota who had been backpacking through continental Europe in the 1930s. Brady became known to a wider audience at the 1939 convention of Rotary International in Cleveland, Ohio, where he gave an impassioned speech about the unifying power residing in youth. Brady had originally gone to Germany as an eighteen-year-old missionary to protest the Nazi ban on scouting, but the kindness and generosity he experienced by ordinary Germans his age or younger softened his militant stance. "If there is a war—remember this," Brady told the convention, "youth didn't start it, and we don't want to fight it." Only the "rotten propaganda" of politicians stood in the way of people recognizing that "the rest of the youth of this world are about the same as we are, and that they are good human beings who would be better friends than enemies." According to Brady, in the simple question of a German boy, who had asked Brady if they could be friends after he had fixed the boy's bike, lay a truth more universal than any of the artificial barriers drawn up by states and their leaders.[117] If Brady's speech exemplified a broader trend, it was that Boy Scouts who had forged international relations of their own were not always easy to convince that they had to surrender their faith in boyhood's peace-building capacities to deteriorating political conditions.

More often than not, however, the dissonances between adult political discourse and youths' boundary crossings left traveling Boy Scouts confused. Take the case of the English scout H. T. Wickham, whose diary provides a vivid glimpse of the clashing sentiments arising from the Scouts' encounters with fascist Germany. En route to Gödöllő in the summer of 1933, Wickham marveled at "hundreds of Nazi flags and banners" greeting them in Cologne and noted a "great joy on the part of the British contingents" as throngs of Hitler Youths, "all with the brown uniform, cap, and swastika armlet," gave the visitors the Nazi salute. Similar spectacles with brass bands and loud cheers from young throats awaited the jamboree delegates in Bingen and Nuremberg. At the Würzburg train station, the diary states, "the strict German discipline failed" and "swapping became fast and furious." That Wickham was well aware of the regime's suppression campaign against the German scouting movement becomes evident in his description of persecuted Catholic Scouts who rushed past the Nazi guards at Würzburg and tossed flowers through the compartment windows. Still, the English Scout's portrayal of Hitler's Germany defied binary characterizations of good Scouts and bad Nazi youths. Unable to reconcile ideology and experience, Wickham wrote: "They [the Hitler Youths] all seemed so friendly and pleased to see us, and we became very friendly with the young Nazis—yet Hitler's policy was supposed to be [an] antagonism to all other countries. What are we to believe?"[118]

The uncertainty articulated by the young Wickham was as much the result of such transactions as it was a product of conflicting signals from the top. Until the violence against Jews and other minorities in the late 1930s solidified negative perceptions of fascism, British and U.S. boy workers had encouraged attitudes toward fascist youth in Italy and Germany that ranged from mildly critical to openly favorable. Baden-Powell is on the record for giving Mussolini a pass on outlawing scouting in Italy in 1927. Recognizing in the duce a "boy-man" like himself, Baden-Powell claimed that the Italian Scouts had been "naturally absorbed" into the Balilla, which had successfully applied the principles of "Scout training to the national education."[119] The initial reactions of U.S. scouters to Mussolini and Hitler sounded equally complaisant. Returning from the Eighth International Scout Conference in Stockholm in August 1935, BSA President Walter Head was asked to describe his impressions of youth developments in Europe. Ignoring the persecution of non-Nazi youth groups in Germany, Head told the press that scouting was still going forward in that country, as it "had been merged in the general youth movement of the Hitler government," which was shaping the nation's youth into "splendid manhood."[120]

BSA Chief Executive James E. West agreed, conceding that Hitler's and Mussolini's young supporters had "made much for years back of the values" that came "from those experiences which overcome softness."[121] Numerous Scout leaders discerned in fascist youth estranged relatives rather than sworn enemies, even as they advised against any form of cooperation between the Boy Scouts and the Hitler Youth. In October 1937, Baden-Powell urged the ISC to reconsider its opposition to the Hitler Youth, suggesting that it do "something friendly" with the Germans.[122] Baden-Powell's proposition, while not universally shared, suggests that Scout officials not only tolerated the Scout-fascist exchanges about which they later felt embarrassed. They also kept their options open to the possibility of incorporating organizations like the Hitler Youth into a global coalition against communism.[123]

The tenuous peace that existed between the BSA and youth groups to its right diverged conspicuously from the warlike rhetoric Scout leaders used to condemn communist youth. Most Scouts learned to see in the atheism and revolutionary internationalism of the Young Pioneers infinitely worse things than in the hypernationalism of the Hitler Youths. After the October Revolution, Beard compared communist agitators to mosquitoes bent on sucking the lifeblood out of the nation. He blamed the "Red Peril" for every evil imaginable under the sun, from the toppling of governments and the erosion of parental authority to underage drinking and sexual debauchery.[124] Declaring social deviance the cultural equivalent of political rebellion was typical of interwar anticommunists of the Beard type. For them, the promiscuous mixing of sexes and races at bars and jazz clubs was akin to the Bolshevists' perceived assault on traditional gender norms. In 1919, West alerted a group of Chicago businessmen that neglected boyhood breeds Bolshevism.[125] Equating Bolshevism with the immoralities of urban street life, West drew a straight line from fighting the German Hun to staring down the Red Radical, both of whom were labeled grave threats to the nation's youth.

Street action cemented the link between Scout citizenship, young imperial manhood, and anticommunism. To divert attention from socialist youth groups marching with labor activists on May Day, the BSA partnered with Rotary International in the early 1920s to turn May 1 into a day to celebrate the patriotic spirit of boyhood. Reminiscent of the home-front spectacles of World War I, these Loyalty Day parades put the spotlight on thousands of uniformed boys filing in military-style columns past grandstands composed of local business and municipal leaders. The boys displayed the Stars and Stripes and held up signs reading "Boys, The Nation's Greatest Asset," "For God and Country," and "The Boys of Today Will Be the Citizens of Tomorrow."[126] Colorful pageants and sporting events attached to these demonstrations dampened their militarist tone, yet the visions of citizenship enunciated at these rallies were profoundly reactionary. Girls were sidelined despite the recent ratification of women's suffrage, and the boys' marching bodies epitomized the durability of a masculine Americanism based on fierce loyalty to the nation's authorities. This involved the license to intervene aggressively, or violently if necessary, against threats to the body politic.[127]

Although interest in the Loyalty Day parades dwindled over the decade, Boy Scouts took their anticommunist message to heart. Targeting "Reds" became a popular way for boys to play the role of the good citizen-soldier, reenact their fathers' wartime service, and retaliate against YPA-led assaults on Scout meetings. Boy Scouts acted as strikebreakers during the West Virginia Coal Wars of 1920–21 and New Jersey's Passaic Strike of 1926, where, according to a communist leaflet, local Scouts "spied on Pioneers, were utilized to break the morale of the strikers, and urged their children to tell their parents to go back to work."[128] Akin to YPA members who went after the Scouts, the latter took considerable delight in disrupting the rallies of their adversaries. "Chief is over in the park at the communist meeting. . . . Don't you know anything about the fun we have been having with the Reds?" wrote a Scout from Erie, Pennsylvania, to Paul Siple in May 1930.[129]

Declaring war on communism offered a welcome opportunity to fasten intergenerational and interimperial bonds. Because the "Red Peril" was framed as a global menace, BSA organizers asserted that it had to be confronted outside the nation as well. Foregrounding child saving as a justification for empire, the Loyalty Day parades reconnected metropole, periphery, and the larger English-speaking world. The movement, a Rotarian planner exulted in 1923, extended "from a far-flung line from Prince Albert in Saskatchewan to Cristobal Colon and from Edinburgh in bonny Scotland to San Diego in California."[130] When it came to combating the revolutionary new man with the patriotic boy-man, Rotary International and international scouting complemented each other. British and U.S. scouters promoted the view that proletarian internationalism was incompatible with Scout brotherhood and a threat to peace. If nothing else came out of the world jamborees, West stated in 1922, they would at least serve as a "powerful bulwark" against "the rising tide of Bolshevism."[131] In 1924, following Hubert Martin's advice, the Anglo-American–dominated BSIB and ISC ruled out any form of cooperation with Soviet youth officials.[132]

Extending the same hospitality to communists that fascist youth delegates were granted in the early 1930s was out of the question. At Arrowe Park, members of the British YCL who had been spotted in the jamboree campground were charged with distributing anti-Scout leaflets, and one was taken into custody.[133] At the same time, Western Scouts organized aid for exiled Russian scouters in France, England, Yugoslavia, and the United States. BSA publications asked readers to sustain these exile associations with small donations and letters of support.[134] Fittingly, *Boys Life* published fictional stories of American Scouts traveling abroad to rescue their beleaguered Russian brothers from Soviet henchmen.[135]

Word War II led to an uneasy truce. Disparaging remarks on communists became inopportune in Scout circles after the United States and Great Britain had stated their intent to cooperate with the Soviet Union to defeat the Axis powers. Remaking foes into brothers-in-arms, BSA propagandists began highlighting cross-partisan virtues such as patriotism and heroic sacrifice, and even presented Soviet child soldiers as role models. Scout magazines kept their young readers abreast of developments in the Pacific and Atlantic theaters, filled their columns with information about modern weaponry and battle tactics, and published stories of boy valor in the fight against the Axis powers. Perhaps the greatest recognition was reserved for the British "Blitz Scouts," who had seen action during the German air raids of 1940 and 1941. Four of them, John Bethell, Roy Davis, Stanley Newton, and Hugh Bright, were sent on a six-week publicity tour through the United States in July 1942. Speaking over the radio and to sellout crowds in stadiums packed with Scouts of both sexes, the Blitz Scouts recounted how they had spotted planes, extinguished flames, and helped with the evacuation of civilians. Young Davis, noted a *New York Times* reporter, even left "a trail of broken Girl Scout hearts."[136] It is impossible to gauge the extent to which American boys identified with their British peers, but it is easy to imagine that their performance enhanced a boyish fascination of war as a rite of passage leading to chivalry, celebrity, and a sexually attractive masculinity.

Depicting Russian youth in the fight against Nazi Germany proved to be a more delicate subject for U.S. propagandists. *Boys' Life* waited until September 1943 to acquaint readers with Konstantin Gregorivich Konstantinov, a seventeen-year-old Cossack youth who had joined the Russian army and was wounded four times in combat. Printed to inspire American boys to keep doing their part, Konstantin's letter started with the following words: "I guess I don't look like a soldier. I weigh 152 pounds, and I'm only five feet four inches tall, but I already killed at least 74 Germans."[137] Another Soviet boy soldier celebrated in the American press as an example of unflinching patriotism was the pioneer Michail "Mischa" Nikolayev. Only fourteen years of age, Mischa made headlines on the other side of the Atlantic for his daring exploits that involved capturing enemy soldiers and stealing their horses.[138] But while the stories of Konstantin and Mischa might have captivated U.S. Boy Scouts longing for similar experiences, they remained less than perfect role models for American educators. Most Americans read the widespread military involvement of Soviet children as mine cleaners or regular combatants not as an emergency measure but as proof of the communist disregard for the safety and welfare of children. Journalist Quentin Reynolds, who introduced Mischa to the readers of *Collier's*, a popular American middle-class magazine, stated accordingly: "The duties of Pioneers are not nearly as pleasant as those of Boy Scouts," and their job was not "one which would appeal to an ordinary American boy."[139]

In trying to comfort American parents that their children were content with being kept off the battlefields until they reached the proper age, people like Reynolds missed a deeper irony. The unsettling truth was that many American boys would have loved to trade places with Mischa, Konstantin, or the Blitz Scouts. The same youthful enthusiasm that adult organizers had hoped to spark for the war proved the most difficult to control. When boys felt that they were not making any meaningful contribution to the war effort, hopes of achieving glory fizzled out quickly. The BSA registered most of its deserters in places where boys became bored with the tasks they were asked to fulfill. The story of fifteen-year-old Theodore Petzold from New York is a case in point. A journalist writing for the *New Yorker* in July 1942 called Petzold a "typical Boy Scout" who was "enthusiastic" about his work. Yet Petzold did not spare his elders from criticism. The government, he complained, "[didn't] always seem to know what it is doing." After collecting three hundred thousand pounds of wastepaper, Petzold's troop was told to stop, with no explanation from officials other than that they had run out of storage room. They "never hear what is being done with the stuff they collected," and seeing the aluminum they gathered piled up in backyards or left around in store windows for months without being processed "gave them moments of disillusionment."[140] Disappointed that their adult superiors were not taking them seriously, Petzold and his friends started having second thoughts about their service. Chasing wastepaper and hunting scrap metal that nobody needed—was that what they had signed up for? It was conceivable, the article concluded, that Petzold's one and a half million fellow Scouts felt the same way.

Youth's desire for heroic action clashed with adult conceptions of childhood, and it obviously did so more frequently than the men in charge of scouting were willing to admit. Even as boy workers placed a variety of potent weapons into Scouts' hands—from economic utility to democratic sacrifice—the boys were not uncritical of these offerings. As one sociological study commissioned by the BSA in 1943 found out, there was little that Boy Scouts hated more than being infantilized by their superiors. Boys of all age groups, according to interviews the researchers conducted with Scouts and scoutmasters across the country, felt that their jobs "weren't big enough" and exhibited a remarkable envy toward the war service opportunities available to older youth and men. "We could learn to watch for airplanes if they would trust us" was a complaint typical of elementary school boys enrolled in the Cub Scouts, whereas Boy Scouts aged twelve and older expressed wishes such as "we could do home defense and learn to be guerillas" and "older Scouts should be used as messengers behind the lines."[141] In light of prewar anxieties that youth would enter the war "demoralized" and "devitalized" as a result of the Great Depression, adults were taken aback by their children's lust for combat.[142] Boys eager to be young warriors were hard to satisfy with tasks such as planting Victory gardens or serving as couriers, which barely distinguished them from the Girl Scouts, who performed many of the same duties. With the possibility of soldiering legally foreclosed to males under eighteen (or seventeen with parental consent), underage boys created fantasy war zones in which they acted out dreams of battlefield heroism and admired the frontline bravery of their peers in England and the Soviet Union.

Just how conscious U.S. Scouts were of their place in a wider world at war became manifest in the enemy images they constructed. Expecting to find naive boys who needed to be instructed about the nature of their adversaries in Germany and Japan, BSA executives discovered the opposite. Growing up in an atmosphere of national crisis and increased ideological polarization, U.S. children found in the friend-foe paradigms of the adult world a preferred coping mechanism for the war. In conversations with their superiors, Boy Scouts accused the Germans of "murder[ing] critics, enemies, and their hostages" and described the Japanese as "brutal torturers" and "sly, wily, and not to be trusted."[143] What concerned adult organizers most was that in their zeal to destroy the enemy the boys had adopted a racialized view of their opponents that made it difficult for them to see Americans of Italian, German, and Japanese descent in a positive light. "The patriotic fervor of wartime tends to create intolerance towards the beliefs and practices of persons who are not in one's group," the BSA's 1943 membership study stated. "Intolerance grows even though democratic nations try to prevent it."[144] This rejection of supposedly disloyal groups was not unique to children, yet its prevalence among the nation's youth contrasted sharply with the BSA's claim that its young volunteers were cheerful and innocent fighters for the democratic values of tolerance and difference.

It remains a matter of speculation how many Boy Scouts would have exchanged the Scout hat for a GI helmet had the age of enlistment been lowered to sixteen or fifteen. To get past recruitment officers, some boys forged documents or simply lied about their age. Class and deprivation were key factors as many of these estimated fifty thousand to two hundred thousand teenage soldiers, some of whom were detected and discharged by the authorities, entered the army to escape poverty.[145] It is hard to imagine that BSA officials were unaware of underage soldiering. They may have found the implications of boys fighting and dying too troubling to deal with and thus probably chose to gloss over the number of boys who were joining the armed forces. At the very least, underage soldiering speaks to the fact that the developmental fault line between boyhood and manhood, and the transition from being protected to becoming a protector, were objects of an intergenerational tug-of-war that played out simultaneously with the Allied war effort.

Exceptionalist accounts of the BSA in the long 1930s rarely go beyond stating that the American way of boy mobilization was morally superior to the youth programs of the so-called enemies of democracy. This view needs to be banished in favor of a more globally informed history that crosses the frontiers of ideology and age. In the years of depression and war, the BSA never formed a hermetically sealed organism unreceptive to outside impulses. It was in contentions with communist and fascist youth that young and old Americans began to understand the democratization of boyhood and the cause of a benevolent America coming to the rescue of a beleaguered world as mutually dependent. Like its opponents, the BSA associated mobilizing the nation's boys with the end of resignation and an energetic move toward a brighter future. Youth, largely imagined as white and male, meant vigorous action, the key to jolting societies out of the apathy of crisis and self-doubt. Even as Scout organizers denounced fascist and communist youth organizers as malevolent seducers, they, too, demanded service and sacrifice from their young in the fight against totalitarianism. World War II posters carrying the deceptively simple slogan "We, too, Have a Job to Do" held out the promise of relevance to millions of boys barred from serving in the military. For boys wanting to make a difference, whether they came from democratic or nondemocratic regimes, such promises proved too tempting to ignore.

Chapter 6

Are You a Crusader?

Raising Cold Warriors

Few paintings represented the suburban sensibilities of Cold War America more lovingly than Norman Rockwell's *Homecoming*. Radiating domestic warmth and familial intimacy, the painting, featured in the annual BSA calendar for 1961, shows a sporty and suntanned young Scout welcomed home by his father. The Scout's duffel and pack, as well as his sunny demeanor, indicate that he has just returned from a long trip. The boy, who has been out in search of adventure, is the central figure in the picture toward which all other figures gravitate. The first to greet the boy is his father, in gray pants and a white shirt, his outstretched arms resting affectionately on the boy's shoulders. Running down the stairs at a conspicuous distance from the father are the other members of the family—the younger brother in Cub Scout uniform, the mother, and what appears to be the Scout's sister (only her legs are visible). An unmistakably masculine aura permeates the picture, wrapping itself around a trouble-free space usually associated with a feminine homeliness. While idealizing the white middle-class nuclear family of the postwar era, the painting anchors this ideal in a special emotional bond between father and son, with the boy, not the man, serving as its prime fount of energy.

Norman Rockwell, whom one scholar called the "premier illustrator of American boyhood," built his career on artwork revolving around young males.[1] Famous for his rustic portrayal of Franklin Roosevelt's "Four Freedoms," Rockwell's rise to prominence in the United States paralleled that of scouting. The popularity of the painter and his main object, the BSA, for which he had been working as an illustrator since 1912, peaked at a time when the confluence of

Cold War nationalism and the arrival of the baby boomers drove the organization's membership to record highs. In the years after World War II, Rockwell's pastoral and humorous depictions of Boy Scouting reached millions of American households. Known for their mixture of patriotism and play, piety and a prankish exuberance, the illustrations elevated the Scout to an iconic symbol of a traditional all-American goodness. Portrayed in the company of proud parents, devoted scoutmasters, former presidents, and foreign Scouts, the boys represent all that is right and virtuous about a nation that lived with the threat of nuclear annihilation. A cheerful conservatism runs through Rockwell's paintings, suggesting that all would be fine if mothers and fathers burdened by the period's domestic pressures and international uncertainties simply retained the chirpy we-can-do-it spirit of their sons.[2]

Taking its cue from Rockwell's boyish visualizations of an all-male utopia, this chapter moves the Boys Scouts to the center of the nation's imperial imaginary after 1945. Americans witnessing the rise of global military alliances, decolonization, and international institutions such as the United Nations (UN) rarely thought of themselves as imperial actors; yet the power of the United States to shape events abroad was undeniable. The significance of scouting for America's emerging Cold War empire was predicated on a series of intersecting developments. Demographically and culturally, the BSA experienced its golden age in the 1950s and 1960s. Children of the baby boom generation were flooding extracurricular institutions aimed at serving youth. So crucial did children seem to the material and moral welfare of postwar society that sociologist William H. Whyte Jr. characterized America during the fifties as a "filiarchy," a world rotating around the needs of the young.[3] Counting about 2 million members at the end of the war, the BSA boasted more than 6.5 million active Scouts and scouters by the early 1970s.[4]

Accompanying this membership surge was a strong ideological commitment to the two main pillars of Cold War culture: anticommunism and civil religion. Adult organizers taught boys that the defense of the "free world"—a key idiom of the period—depended on the vigorous protection of the right to worship God according to one's faith. This rhetoric took on a greater significance for a rejuvenated leadership. With Daniel Carter Beard, Robert Baden-Powell, Ernest Thompson Seton, and James West dead or retired by the end of World War II, a younger cohort of second-tier officials moved to the top of the organization. Although the BSA's new leaders, most notably Chief Scout Executive Arthur A. Schuck and the Danish-born scouter and author William "Green Bar Bill" Hillcourt, had been tutored by the founding fathers of U.S. scouting, they were launching their own initiatives to strengthen the organization's links to traditional gender roles, heteronormative family values, and the global spread of an American-style democracy.

The end of World War II marked a watershed in the intertwined histories of American empire and youth. At the same time that the victory over the Axis powers left the United States as the sole Western superpower, the teenager came to replace the adolescent as the dominant idiom for young people of high-school age. This terminological shift reflected the fact that the young would not easily surrender the economic and social liberties they had gained while their fathers had been away fighting the war. Postwar educators echoed older theories of adolescence in pathologizing the unsupervised teenager who was roaming the streets smoking, drinking, and defying authority. However, as they were crafting Cold War ideologies, public authorities sought a middle ground between extending the state of dependency for nonadults and respecting the agency of teenagers and their capacity to assume an antitotalitarian "democratic" character.[5] Many hoped that scouting would provide that middle ground.

With programs such as the World Friendship Fund (WFF) and the Crusade to Strengthen the Arm of Liberty, which will be discussed in this chapter, the BSA sought to reestablish itself as a fulcrum of masculine orientation for males of different age groups. As in previous decades, the negotiation of civic-imperial duties in a nation reconstituting itself along ideologically charged distinctions between capitalism and communism forged scouting ties between men and boys that were at once hierarchical and symbiotic. In exchange for lighting the path to masculine citizenship, adult organizers found in their dealings with boys relief from the constraints of Cold War manhood. Men in the nuclear age were expected to meet their responsibilities to home and country ungrudgingly, be it as family men who provided for their wives and children, as indomitable statesmen who vowed to "get tough" with "commies," or as "organization men" who subjected themselves to the whims of the marketplace in the hope of climbing the corporate ladder.[6] In the literature of the period, white middle-class men are confronted with a paradox: awash in patriarchal authority, they also found their quests for self-fulfillment curtailed by the deindividuating effects of mass society, which reduced them, in the words of the Democrat Adlai Stevenson, to "wretched slaves of specialization and group thinking."[7] This tension between individualism and conformism found perfect expression in the figure of the commuter, of gray-suited husbands and fathers leaving home for work and disappearing in faceless crowds to balance the dream of suburban domesticity with the demands of urban employment. Underpinning the reigning ideology of anticommunism, the commute became the site where fantasies of unbound mobility were submerged by the desire to tame the dangerous forces of radical dissent and atomic conflict. As a form of "domestic containment," which historian Elaine Tyler May identified as an important corollary to international containment, the daily commute mirrored the tradeoff between security and autonomy that defined Cold War manhood.[8]

Here the Boy Scouts made a crucial intervention. Providing ludic relief for boys and men trapped in the rationalities of the atomic age, scouting promised to remake commuters into crusaders. The crusader was the quintessential boy-man of the early Cold War, reflecting the renaissance of religion in postwar scouting in particular and the convergence of patriotism and Christianity in U.S. public culture in general.[9] Although Americans repeatedly invoked religious imagery to fashion their ideological conflicts as holy wars, the crusader had a high affinity to the knights and pioneers in Boy Scout literature.[10] He connoted liberating adventure over constricting conformity, playful exploration over tedious routines, and moral clarity over secular uncertainties. Exceedingly boyish in nature, the crusader offered redemption in a double sense, coupling the ambition to redeem the world from atheistic communism with the promise to redeem males from the narrowness of family and business life. Akin to the mythic "American Adam," whom R. W. B. Lewis described as "self-reliant and self-propelling, ready to confront whatever awaited him with his unique and inherent resources," the ideal Boy Scout, clean, athletic, and unafraid, pitted his Rockwellian innocence against those doubting the righteousness of the American way.[11]

The crusading boy-men in Scout uniform closed the gap between America's old continental frontier and the new frontiers of a global superpower. It was in the playful yet somber pose of the God-fearing frontiersman that Schuck asked America's scoutmasters in November 1949: "The Scout nations are looking to our great Democracy to save the world through creating and maintaining a Democracy worthy of emulation of all peoples of the world. . . . Are You a Crusader?"[12] In teaming up with boys in an imaginary crusade against evil, men hoped to break out of the limitations of a self-imposed containment culture and embraced the productive illusion of an innocent masculinity, with its own rules, values, and group-specific modes of recognition. More than a footnote of the Cold War, the Boy Scouts filtered America's free-world empire through performances of cross-generational and cross-border fraternalism.[13]

To demonstrate how the crusader became a masculine ideal in postwar scouting, I trace the formation of this ideal in three different arenas. Civil defense programs established by the federal government in the late 1940s and 1950s

Figure 6.1. "Are You a Crusader?" Printed in the November 1949 issue of *Scouting*, this piece of Cold War propaganda depicts the BSA as the first best bulwark against Soviet aggression.

provided a rich field for Boy Scouts and scoutmasters eager to enact their Scout beliefs in the context of the early Cold War. Answering the call to help defend the nation against foreign threats, patriotic youth took the lead in spreading civil defense propaganda among friends and families. Scout preparedness began to stand for the prospect of surviving atomic warfare as Boy Scouts built bomb shelters with their fathers and instructed parents on how to respond to a nuclear strike. The frontiers of scientific discovery demarcated a second arena that crusading boy-men were supposed to enter. From the start of the Explorer Program for Scouts fourteen and older in 1949 to the educational initiatives following the Sputnik crisis of 1957, the BSA touted science as an honorable pursuit for boys dedicated to strengthening America's leadership role. This was achieved by divorcing science from academic scrutiny and linking it to boyish fantasies of exploring and conquering unknown spaces.

The crusader masculinity promoted by the BSA gained additional contours in the arena of foreign relations. In the third and final section I show how U.S.

Boy Scouts, through participating in multinational jamborees or establishing donor relationships with Scouts from other nations, became convinced that it was their mission to mobilize the global Scout community behind an intensely anticommunist version of world brotherhood. Recoding disillusion and anxiety into a storyline of salvation and liberation, the crusader was the BSA's answer to the question of whether its followers could still chart their own destiny when entire societies were staring into the nuclear abyss. This role allowed boys and men to mask the complexities of the grown-up world, regain a sense of youthful optimism about the future, and subdue feelings of impotence in the face of possible total annihilation.

Defenders of the Realm

Imagine an atomic bomb going off in the heart of Manhattan and thousands of New Yorkers erupting in applause. This bizarre scene occurred on May 24, 1952, at the annual Scout-O-Rama at Madison Square Garden—a public display of Scout games, skills, and historical pageantry. The bomb, to be sure, was a dummy dropped by cardboard bombers hovering over the Scouts crowded in the middle of the arena, waiting for their signal to spring into action. The signal came with the flash of the bomb's "explosion," after which the boys demonstrated emergency drills they had learned as part of their civil defense training. More than three thousand Boy Scouts and scoutmasters participated in the mass event "Should Disaster Strike," showing the audience how to evade the bomb's deadly impact, seek shelter inside and outside buildings, and perform first aid, with boys standing in as injured civilians. All this might have left a less positive impression on the spectators than intended, yet the organizers made sure that the afternoon would not end on a gloomy note. After dramatizing the nation's pioneer past, the boys watched Ambassador Warren Austin, the chief U.S. delegate to the UN, decorate six Scouts with Silver and Eagle awards and heard him say that scouting helped "to establish the United States as the great leader of peace in the world."[14]

At a time when fears of a nuclear confrontation with the Soviet Union were rampant, the Scouts' playful approach to questions of war and peace might appear grotesque. Yet few organizations offered greater reassurance to adults doubtful about youth's will to prevail in the early Cold War than the BSA. Play allowed boys and men to process their fears, reducing the specter of atomic warfare into manageable scenarios. Historians have recognized the political and symbolic significance of children for boosting the fighting spirits of nations catapulted into the atomic age.[15] A significant portion of the U.S. government's civil defense propaganda was directed at the young. After the Soviet Union had acquired nuclear capability in 1949, government agencies such as the Federal Civil Defense Administration (FCDA) and the Office of Civil Defense (OCD) blanketed schools with leaflets instructing students on how to protect themselves if the enemy struck, and issued films teaching basic survival tactics to children. The FCDA-produced *Duck and Cover* film, which became an instant classic after its release in 1952, features a Cub Scout diving to safety from his bike after noticing the bright flash of an exploding atomic bomb.[16] To spread their message, state authorities relied on Boy Scouts, whose motto "Be Prepared" came to epitomize aspirations of national preparedness. Civil defense set up the Scouts as exemplary youths and model Cold War citizens. Their participation in defensive atomic drills conflated the image of the imperiled child with the claim that U.S. policies were unsullied by an aggressive imperialism. Refashioning preparedness into a game of good versus evil with boys and men in leading roles, the BSA presented the standoff with communism as a conflict that was survivable and winnable.

From the Korean War to the Cuban Missile Crisis, American Boy Scouts staged several civil defense exercises that adult scouters and government officials considered suitable for teenage boys. Intriguingly, this coalition of scouting and the state bore a greater resemblance to youth mobilization in communist countries than to youth mobilization in other Western nations. English Scouts, for example, were barred from joining the British Civil Defense Corps, which was limited to volunteers eighteen and older.[17] In October 1950, Arthur Schuck met with FCDA administrators to discuss how boys of various age groups could contribute to state and local civil defense operations. The tasks agreed on ranged from first aid, messenger services, and distributing food and clothing to people bombed out of their homes, to searching for lost persons and assisting emergency teams, to setting up and operating evacuee camps.[18] This framework was specified in four civil defense booklets the BSA printed in 1951 and was declared mandatory reading for Scouts across the nation.[19] Although adults exempted younger boys from mentally and physically demanding tasks, they insisted that nuclear preparedness was a warlike civic duty that required the mobilization of the entire population, with virtually no exception. Boys of Cub Scout age, too, were asked to contribute to the safety of the community. The things asked of a younger boy "must fit his capabilities," one of the booklets stated, "but somehow we must challenge him to a feeling of responsibility."[20]

Public action reinforced these prescriptions. Boy Scouts served as message runners and participated in mock atomic attacks in more than one hundred cities, rescuing people, administering first aid, and posing as casualties and evacuees. In 1956, more than eight thousand Explorers stood watch at aircraft observation posts while Scouts walked door to door to hand out civil defense manuals and anticommunist tracts.[21] One year later, nearly three million Boy Scouts delivered the OCD's *Handbook of Emergencies* to an estimated thirty-seven million households. During the Berlin Crisis of 1961, Scouts erected model fallout shelters and assisted the National Guard and the Salvation Army in provisioning public shelters.[22] These performances of preparedness evoked positive memories of home-front service during World War II, nourished the fiction of national security, and provided Americans with an uplifting image of mobilized boyhood. Similar to the mythic frontiersmen who had braved obstacles in the wild with boyish pluck and courage, young males in uniform providing unselfish service were supposed to reassure a frightened populace. "If [children] are prepared to 'live like pioneers,'" stated a civil defense pamphlet for schools in Pennsylvania, "they will be a help, rather than a hindrance, in times of crisis."[23]

Were Americans really willing to expose their young to the gloom and doom of atomic warfare? Pressing boys into a more active home-front role certainly was a prickly affair. For one thing, it seemed to go against the grain of the dominant Cold War discourse of childhood—observed by politicians, educators, and parents—that children of all backgrounds needed the greatest possible protection to mature into productive and self-confident citizens. Evidently, few felt that teaching children to be on constant alert would run counter to that objective. Yet even as the baby boomers' parents held that they were raising free children instead of communist robots, there was a strange silence about the potentially traumatizing effects of turning youths into little cold warriors. Unwilling to take a critical stance toward Cold War preparedness, the BSA covered up the terrifying and emotionally upsetting realities of the day by infantilizing them with allusions to boyish adventure and game-play. It was an uncomplicated world steeped in what Tom Engelhardt referred to as America's postwar "victory culture," in which fantasies of male camaraderie and an eventual triumph over evil glossed over ambiguity and anguish.[24]

Most of the emergency drills promoted by the BSA were conceived around the notion of fun and efficient teamwork between men and boys. Adult organizers propagated that scouting yielded the best results when scoutmasters refrained from bossing around their wards and became their pals.[25] Civil defense, they believed, fostered such trusting relationships. The 1951 guide *Pattern for Survival* suggested a number of games to "provide some fun and worth while [*sic*] purpose" and maintain the Scouts' interest in civil defense by "colorfully dramatiz[ing] a number of emergency situations."[26] In "Lost Persons Search," individual patrols and troops had to locate a lost "youngster," preferably some Scout's younger brother, in prearranged sectors of their communities. "Night Hikes," "Orienteering Expeditions," and "Survival Hikes," during which boys were to refine survival skills from "sand bagging" to "rowing" and "rescuing of persons," appealed to their sense of adventure. "Emergency Scavenger Hunt" was a game in which Scouts had to collect "blankets, clothing, food etc." from friends and neighbors that would be of vital importance in the aftermath of a major disaster. The contributors were to sign their name on a sheet of paper, and the patrol with the longest list of names won.[27] Pairing ludic relief and productive leisure, these mobilization games, ideally supervised by one or more scoutmasters, were supposed to climax "by a camp fire . . . in the evening, with fun and fellowship for all."[28] Brimming with analogies from the spheres of outdoor adventure and sports, BSA literature boyified civil defense and depicted it as playful cooperation involving young and adult males.

Declaring civil defense a form of productive leisure, adult organizers made scouting the centerpiece of a strategy of dual containment: Boy Scouts mobilized to stop the spread of communism would also help to stop the spread of juvenile delinquency. New research on the late 1940s and 1950s has shown the extent to which adolescent waywardness, urban crime, and deviation from middle-class heterosexual norms were invoked as threats to national security equal in scope to the Soviet menace.[29] Although youthful misbehavior had long been identified as a disruptive social force, the Cold War delinquency scare was fueled by concerns that rebellious teenagers would be dangerously susceptible to alien ideologies. In the anticommunist imagination, racial integration, feminism, rock-and-roll music, and teenage sexuality figured as harbingers of a gigantic left-wing conspiracy bent on draining America's fighting spirit. Calling "the boy problem" of his time "an alarming condition confronting America . . . and the world" and attributing the "psychic revolt" of youth against their elders to "a bad home, bad associations or some other destructive forces of environment," BSA Field Commissioner August Kietzman wrote in 1958 that transforming "lawless gangs" into future "wealth producer[s] and citizen[s]" was as momentous a task for his organization as participating in "home defense."[30] After the war, the BSA extended its reach into social areas where crime, unrest, and unorganized youth were strongest. Poor, parentless, and mostly African American children, whom organizers listed as "vulnerables,"

Figure 6.2. Boy Scouts participate in a civil defense exercise in Norfolk, Virginia, June 1954. This photo also shows the rare example of an integrated Scout troop in the postwar South. (Courtesy of the National Archives, College Park, Maryland)

were targeted by Scout executives who reopened the domestic imperial frontiers charted by the pioneers of interracial scouting in the 1920s as they were venturing from the suburbs into the cities.[31] The urgency with which Cold War scouters sought to turn supposed hotbeds of delinquency into "campfires of democracy" reflected the fears of communist infiltration that energized postwar mass mobilization.[32] The best way to mobilize boys, Scout organizers believed, was to persuade them that they had the chance to partake in a stirring crusade against evil.

BSA officials advocated the making of little cold warriors in terms of a moral crusade. The theme of Scouts as knights in shining armor evoked dazzling images of youthful adventure while tapping into a rich discursive tradition of righteous warfare. Scoutmasters overseeing the civil defense drills of their charges emulated World War generals John J. Pershing and Dwight D. Eisenhower, who tried to convince soldiers of the sanctity of their cause by drawing parallels to the medieval crusades. The boys, too, felt the allure of a fantasy world in which kings, castles, dungeons, and dragons recast the disciplinary regime of Cold War vigilance as a gallant quest to deliver mankind from the three monsters that threatened to devour it—"Hate," "Communism," and "Atheism."[33] Chivalric pageantry and allegory took center stage during the three-year Crusade to Strengthen the Arm of Liberty, which was launched in February 1949 with a ceremony in front of the Statue of Liberty in anticipation of the BSA's fortieth anniversary. BSA President Amory Houghton articulated the *Deus vult* for a new generation of boy-men. Announcing the crusade's goal to generate "more and better Scouting for boys," Houghton urged Scouts and scoutmasters in thinly veiled imperial rhetoric to perceive themselves as heirs to an ever-expanding kingdom of God that brought order and peace. "I see a great re-birth as I go about this country, a rebirth of conviction and willingness . . . to give the effort that is necessary to make the Scout movement advance to greater heights." Whether the future was "to be one of freedom or despotism," according to Houghton, depended chiefly on the extent to which "every boy and every leader . . . receive[d] the thrill of new adventure and the challenge that results from taking part in this nation-wide Crusade." Conflating national and international interests, Houghton wanted the crusade to "furnish a triumphant demonstration of the effectiveness of the nation's leading youth movement, dedicated to maintaining the American way of life, and to sharing these God-given ideals with the peoples of the world.[34]

The crusader enthusiasm emanating from the top was more than matched by the creativity individual troops displayed at the local level. To pledge allegiance to the Strengthen the Arm of Liberty campaign, Scouts stitched the crusade's official emblem, the outline of the Statue of Liberty superimposed on a fleur-de-lis, onto their uniforms.[35] Other Scouts emblazoned the flags of their packs, troops, and senior units with crusade shields and signed "rededication pledges" that were printed in a medieval font.[36] Perhaps the most colorful dramatization of the crusade theme came from the smallest members of the BSA family. In February 1950, Cub Scouts and their cubmasters turned out fully costumed with armor and shields made out of cardboard to perform knighting ceremonies on each other. Forming circles in imitation of King Arthur's Court and the Knights of the Roundtable, the young crusaders pledged themselves to defending their country and protecting the poor and weak. After completing the oath, the Cubs walked under an archway of swords formed by the other boy knights and were initiated to the roundtable by the cubmaster posing as King Arthur, who tapped each boy on the shoulder with his broomstick sword.[37]

Medieval role-play was not the only performance of crusadership deployed to tighten scouting bonds between boys and men. Seeking to build durable intergenerational partnerships in the fight against communism, Kansas City businessman Jack Whitaker planted the seeds of another crusade project. Following Whitaker's lead, more than two hundred communities in thirty-nine states and Hawaii, Guam, Puerto Rico, and the Philippines erected Little Sisters of Liberty—copper replicas of the Statue of Liberty—in public places between 1949 and 1952.[38] The dedication ceremony in Cheyenne, Wyoming, on May 27, 1950, was typical. A large crowd filled the streets as Cheyenne's Boy Scouts, nearly one thousand strong, led a parade up to the state capitol, where an eight-foot, four-inch replica of the Statue of Liberty was waiting to be unveiled. American Legion personnel; junior and senior high school bands; state, county, and city officials; local clergymen; and members of the U.S. armed forces joined the parade, making it a festival for old and young. During the ceremony, eagle scout Don Cluxton, epitomizing boyhood's gift to the nation, mounted the dedication platform and presented the statue to the governor of Wyoming. Governor Arthur G. Crane thanked the "patriotic citizens who voluntarily give their time to guide and direct the Scouts" as well as the "youthful citizens faithfully following the Scout oath" at a time when "liberty is menaced."[39] The platform on which Crane and Cluxton were recognizing their joint duty as males symbolized national resilience and a sense of civic responsibility shared by men and boys. It was not just the boys who were playfully initiated into the worlds of sovereignty and empire. The older men also found solace in the fraternal ties that bound them to their imaginary younger brothers—ties that assured them that they were not alone in their desire to perpetuate a body politic predominantly imagined as Christian, white, and male.

To suggest a flattening of age hierarchies is not to deny that the BSA served as a vehicle for regimenting male youth. Yet even as the creation of an egalitarian space of boy-men relations under the guise of Scout brotherhood was partly illusory, that space could never have thrived had it required the absolute submission of one group (the boys) to the dictates of the other (the men). Teaching Boy Scouts the basics of civil defense was as much about reducing their vulnerability as it was about empowering them to become good citizen-soldiers. Boys who were "Explorers or Boy Scouts today," one BSA booklet predicted, "may be called into the armed forces. Whether or not they come home may well depend on what they learned" in civil defense training.[40] The Korean War, which was raging when these words were typed, added urgency to this argument. Writing for *Boys' Life*, Hillcourt reminded Scouts of the fraternal bonds that connected them to the soldiers fighting overseas. "American men—many of them former Scouts—are fighting for freedom far away. Here at home we're preparing for troubled days ahead by setting up Civil Defense. Are we, as Scouts, in on the great things that need to be done? You bet you[r] life! To the hilt, 100 percent!"[41] Blurring the lines between scouting and soldiering, such statements foregrounded the fundamental sameness of boys and men in uniform. With this band-of-brothers rhetoric, the BSA created an atmosphere where males of various age groups could cultivate emotionally rich and satisfying fraternal feelings only slightly offset by differences in age, rank, and experience.[42]

The fusion of patriotism, Christianity, and masculinity at the core of the U.S. Cold War effort reinforced the belief that boys and men tied together through scouting shared a special destiny. Juxtaposing the morality of democracy with the depravity of communism, BSA leaders rooted exemplary boyhood and manhood in serving a fatherly God and protecting those who worshiped him. In the eyes of their Creator, Arthur Schuck asserted in February 1955, boys and men were essentially the same: "Brotherhood of man follows from a belief in the Fatherhood of God. A nation whose citizens serve God and country endures."[43] According to the 1961 handbook, doing one's duty to God was like a magic chord connecting boys to their country's divine origins and the men who had made it.[44] Perhaps no allegory better conveyed the idea of a holy union between America's Founding Fathers and Cold War sons than Rockwell's painting *Our Heritage*. Commissioned by the BSA in 1950 and reissued several times over the next decade, the painting shows one Cub Scout and one Boy Scout reverently watching an iconic George Washington kneeling and praying for victory at Valley Forge.

It was at the presumed same spot during the second national jamboree in July 1950 that Schuck powerfully invoked the ideal of boy-man communion in the struggle to defeat atheism and communism. The Cold War had just turned hot on the Korean Peninsula when the BSA chief executive stepped in front of the microphone to address the nearly fifty thousand Boy Scouts and scoutmasters who had pitched their tents on the old revolutionary battlefield. Schuck's speech echoed the appeals to Scout brotherhood made earlier at the jamboree by Truman and Eisenhower while peppering them with an extra dose of crusader imperialism. Old and young, Schuck thundered, needed one another more than ever, now that they were summoned to join forces in a crusade "against totalitarian Russia, the anti-God. . . . Remember that each of you is important. You are a crusader—a crusader for freedom, a crusader for democracy, a crusader to strengthen the arm of liberty. Go home with a new vision—with a new dedication—with a new consecration to service to your God, your country and humanity."[45] In the eyes of Philadelphia reporter John M. Mc-Cullough, Schuck's soaring oratory, which was followed by the Scout salute from almost fifty thousand arms and the mass singing of "Auld Lang Syne," had a unifying effect on the generations seldom seen elsewhere: "Rank on rank the Scouts stretched. The melody of the sweetly ancient song of parting, faltering at first, gained strength and volume until it was a moving, majestic chorus. Here and there a youngster who found the moment too much even for his fortitude bit at quivering lips. Cheeks glistened with tears. Near me the muscles of a grizzled Scout leader's throat worked to stifle emotion."[46]

If this scene suggests that scouting was an emotional force that rallied the nation together in times of crisis, Cold War performances of boy-man homosociality gestured that the survival of liberty pivoted on boys and men, not girls and women, making common cause. The BSA's desire to differentiate not only between "freedom" and "totalitarianism" but also between male and female became palpable in the organizers' attempts to retain distinct spheres of action for both sexes. No mention was made that girl organizations such as the Girl Scouts had been practicing defensive mobilization with comparable energy, although their nuclear emergency training was more centered on the home and thus hardly challenged the prevailing gender order.[47] Female service went virtually uncredited in BSA reports. This is all the more astounding given that the operations of local Boy Scout troops began to depend increasingly on female volunteers. Wives and mothers drove their sons to camp, helped them earn merit badges, and oversaw projects when the men had to put in extra hours at work.

Even the den mothers, who were responsible for guiding record numbers of Cub Scouts, were a thorn in the side of some male crusaders. Misogynist scouters mocked ambitious mothers in the movement as "Dominating Delilahs," labeling their influence on boys detrimental to developing healthy male identities.[48] In trying to curb unwanted female agency, BSA organizers joined a wider discussion about the dangers of "momism," a contemporary shorthand for blaming social problems on white mothers bent on mollycoddling their sons.[49] Viewed as both subordinate and menacing, dependent and unreliable, women remained ambiguous citizens, and their subversive energies had to be contained and kept away from the boy-men's sphere of play and power in much the same way that Scouts were expected to contain the spread of communism.

One site where the interlocking projects of marginalizing female roles and consolidating male superiority played out was the domestic sphere itself. As nuclear technology was revolutionizing the duties and dangers of warfare, the home became a Cold War battleground, and women and children were seen as the first casualties of an atomic strike.[50] The BSA's civil defense propaganda echoed the trope of female-child victimhood but also deviated from it in significant ways. Scout-trained boys, not men, were depicted as supremely qualified to ensure their family's survival. Inverting the conventional father-son hierarchy, Scout literature put boys in the position of providing for the safety of their loved ones. A series of photographs printed in the April 1951 issue of *Boys' Life* shows Scouts helping a disoriented father find the way to the hospital in the wake of an emergency, giving first aid instructions to their parents and siblings, and planting Liberty gardens designated to feed "both . . . [the] family and . . . the nation."[51] Advocated as a popular do-it-yourself enterprise that would bring fathers and sons together, the building of fallout shelters in the family backyard was a recurrent theme in BSA publications. Young Scouts building shelters with their fathers were portrayed as equal partners whose idealism drove the project forward. Although adult organizers agreed with Eisenhower that civil defense was lodged in the "moral structure" and "spiritual strength" of the American family, they pointed to the mobilized boy, not the man, as a paragon of U.S. fortitude and leadership.[52] The symbolic linkage of boyhood and national security had the dual effect of sidelining female initiative while reaffirming the masculinity of the traditional values of personal responsibility and civic duty—not by means of paternal dictate but through young people cheerfully appropriating those values.

Obviously, such idealized images had little to do with the everyday history of scouting at the time. These images were ideological constructs that reflected adult desires to make male youth comprehend the perils and obligations created by the Cold War. As propaganda tools, their purpose was to animate boys to join their elders in fighting communist aggression and to sway fathers into believing that they could become better men through fraternizing with their sons. Boys were to learn the duties of citizen-soldiers, yet the tacit presumption was that men would also relearn the masculine virtues of service, patriotism, and sacrifice with forays into the child's world of play and make-believe. When August Kietzman postulated that "the boy can be a better citizen than many a man is today" and that "the fate of the nation and humanity is in [the boy's] hands," he understood that the processes of masculinizing boys and boyifying men were tightly interwoven.[53] For BSA authorities like Kietzman, this was as much an admission of the young postwar generation's rising social and political clout as it was of the fear that boys socialized in environments with no proper adult supervision might be lost to men seeking to perpetuate their hold on power.

It is not surprising, then, that BSA officials were reluctant to discuss whether the actual behavior of young Scouts always matched the intergenerational bonding rituals so central to Cold War scouting. Polls conducted by the U.S. government in the late 1950s and early 1960s indicate that few sons and fathers actually spent their weekends building family shelters or engaging in civil defense drills.[54] Serving as a volunteer air observer, explorer scout John Limehouse confessed in May 1955 that the flashes of excitement barely compensated for the long stretches of boredom when there was nothing to report.[55] To question the utility of the BSA's civil defense program, some Scouts and scoutmasters turned to humor. In February 1961, a joke by Florida scout Mike Monahan was printed in the Think and Grin section of *Boys' Life*. In the joke, Boy Scouts were ordered to play victims in a civil defense drill. When the rescue team finally arrived on the spot where one Scout had been lying "wounded" for hours, they found only a note saying "Have bled to death and gone home."[56] The most piercing satire on the BSA's crusades flew from the pen of the California author and scoutmaster Keith Monroe, who hid behind the pseudonym Rice E. Cochran. Leading a troop of Scouts to Valley Forge in the summer of 1950, Monroe presented a strikingly unceremonious account of the jamboree. "The arena shows were compellingly sedative," Monroe noted, and all the Scouts could do was to "endure the public-address system, through which they were drenched with grandiloquent rhetoric. Neither the President [Truman] nor General Eisenhower nor the other dignitaries used language which conveyed much to juvenile minds. Inasmuch as exposure to radio from infancy has developed in modern boys the ability to ignore the most insistent and vehement disembodied voices, the arena audience soon sought its own amusements. Some studied comic books until the twilight failed. Others threw paper airplanes and spitballs. Most simply whispered and wrestled among themselves. By the time an arena show ended, around eleven, nearly everyone was asleep."[57]

Monroe's Valley Forge observations cast doubts on the ability of adult leaders to communicate effectively across generational lines. At the very least, they illuminate the degree to which contemporary youth culture, exemplified by Monroe's reference to comic books, had crept into postwar scouting, often to the dismay of older men who linked the spread of comics to delinquency. Young minds and bodies may have been malleable but never docile or submissive. To BSA authorities, selling the vision of boys and men forming extrafamilial ties for the purpose of securing male dominance at home and U.S. supremacy abroad may have mattered more than its actual fulfillment. Despite the sometimes awkward distance between ideology and practice, imagining civil defense as a righteous and winnable crusade generated homosocial spaces where Scouts and scouters could detach themselves from nuclear-age anxieties while reconstituting the power structures that ensured white male privilege. After the Sputnik shock of 1957, BSA leaders once again promised that Scout fraternalism could mobilize youth and shield manhood from the emasculating influences of mass consumerism, female domesticity, and workplace monotony as they approached yet another frontier—the conquest of outer space.

Rocket Scouts

As much as civil defense provided an arena in which men could discover their potency and boys their potential, the relationship of scouting and Cold War preparedness remained an uneasy affair. It is hard to imagine how the somber warnings of Bert the Turtle, who explained to children how to "duck and cover," seeped into the language of a movement that kindled visions of penetrating wide open spaces. There were undeniable inconsistencies between the fortress mentality arising out of demands to protect the home against atomic warfare and the wishes of Scouts and scoutmasters to transcend the close confines of the bomb shelters they were supposed to build. If the romance of the outdoors and dreams of adventure in faraway places drew boys to scouting, adult organizers had to blaze complementary trails to satisfy these urges without undermining the Cold War consensus. Thus began a search for new frontiers—this time in the skies—where stories of boys in spaceships and time machines corroborated ideas of U.S. technological, intellectual, and moral superiority.

Fantasies of space travel permeated the BSA literature of the 1950s and 1960s. *Boys' Life* opened its pages to a host of juvenile science fiction authors whose extraterrestrial adventures tapped into a growing market of teenage readers eager to immerse themselves in alien worlds.[58] To incorporate this new genre, the editors had to make concessions: they had to shed their traditional distrust of youth culture and submit to the tastes of their young readers. Perhaps reluctantly, *Boys' Life* began aping comic industry trends with the inclusion of a "Colored Section" in its monthly issues in 1951—a series of cartoons that dramatized biblical themes, Wild West ventures, and quests into outer space. "Space Conquerors," a serial comic strip that ran from 1952 to 1972, is a prominent example of the kind of fantastical intergalactic fiction deemed safe for youthful consumption. In several storylines, intrepid space explorers fly to moons, planets, and faraway solar systems. Projecting a young audacious masculinity, these fictional astronauts navigate foreign stratospheres, encounter new forms of life, extract precious resources from the worlds they visit, make peace with friendly alien races, and battle hostile ones.[59]

As the term "conquerors" suggests, BSA periodicals followed contemporary popular discourse in depicting space travel as an act of endeavor equal to the fortitude exhibited by brave white explorers who had expanded the boundaries of civilization and carried progress into the wilderness. Like the western frontier, space was a dangerous place, and only males with sufficient bravado and skill were regarded as capable of penetrating and taking possession of it. Colonization was the major theme in a range of pseudoscientific speculations in *Boys' Life* about the leading role American boys could assume within one or two decades in traversing the universe for the glory of mankind. Grandiose predictions of U.S. galactic supremacy were embedded in Roy Gallant's semi-fictional two-part essay "Escape from Earth" (1954), which took Scouts on an imaginary journey from the founding fathers of rocket science to an era of interplanetary expansion.[60] Fantastical visions abounded in other places as well. In the August 1956 episode of "Space Conquerors," the founding of the first Boy Scout troop on the moon, "sponsored by the Lunar Colonists Men's Club," was declared a milestone in the grand scheme for "the conquest of space."[61] Robert A. Heinlein's cosmic adventure story "Satellite Scout" (1950) catapulted scouting farther into the unknown: Bill, a California Eagle Scout, and his family are part of an emigration society that land on the icy surface of Ganymede, one of Jupiter's moons, where they start a farming colony. The homestead venture succeeds thanks to the survival skills of Bill and his band of brave Boy Scouts.[62] In relocating the familiar narrative of white settler imperialism into outer space, the stories defied the Cold War stalemate and implied that the times when hardy American boy-men could thrust their will on foreign worlds without fear of retaliation were far from over.

This nostalgic futurism also exposes the BSA's ambivalent attitude toward a new type of masculinity that emerged in the early 1950s—that of the Cold War technocrat. In the organization's literary flights from the precincts of an increasingly suburban modernity, boys were equipped with the most innovative gadgetry. At the same time, science and technology received little appreciation beyond their capacity to adapt the old heroic pioneer model of masculinity to rapidly changing social and cultural conditions. Whiz kids who valued expert knowledge and scientific rationality coexisted uneasily with the charismatic boy explorers who forged ahead boldly into the unknown. Take the case of the "Time Machine," a series of science fiction stories published in *Boys' Life* between 1959 and 1989.[63] In these tales of time-traveling Boy Scouts, the tacit conflict between the pioneer and the technocrat plays out in the relationship between Bob Tucker, the patrol leader, and his companion "Brains" Baines. While Baines's wonkish qualities are needed to operate the time machine, it is Tucker who frequently saves the day with his boyish pluck, innate determination, and sparks of ingenuity. This celebration of good-natured, unfettered boyhood attributed to young space-and-time wanderers like Bill and Tucker resembled the cult of personality built in the 1920s around Paul Siple and the Safari Scouts. The romantic idea that boys possessed a natural curiosity that should not be straitjacketed by academic rigor—and that they would not have to answer for small transgressions committed in good faith—appealed to men worrying about losing their identities in the face of big corporations, scientific networks, and nuclearized superstates. The space-traveling juveniles in *Boys' Life* were more than cute billboards for a technologically advanced America. The boy astronauts reenacted America' expansionist past through the imaginary colonization of space.

Taken together, these stories represented male longings for a moral order in which good and evil, the self and the other, were clearly distinguishable. Boyhood and space exploration, both of which operated beyond the boundaries of adult civilization, became complementary metaphors for past and future worlds. In reaching back to idealized moments of learning and wonder in their own childhood, the authors told Americans not to relinquish the fun-loving zest and playful energy of boys as they pushed toward new frontiers.[64] The joy of discovery, the inquisitiveness of youth, and the desire to surpass the limits set by established customs—all these qualities that seemed to defy the stern rationality required to manage the nuclear arms race of two superpowers came together in the Rocket Scouts celebrated in *Boys' Life*.

Since boys did not have to repeat the errors of their fathers, their imaginary space journeys also involved utopian experiments over how to balance the acceptance of racial diversity with an attitude of zero tolerance toward alien ideologies. As a cautious nod toward the civil rights movement, the "Time Machine" series added Rodney Carver, an African American Scout, to its cast of boy explorers in 1965.[65] Most interstellar encounters showed the youthful crusaders through time and space as ambassadors of universal peace, but the depravity of some alien races left the Rocket Scouts no other choice than resorting to force. The parallel between communism and alien aggression is most pronounced in battles between Scouts and Martians, who are portrayed as technologically sophisticated but willing slaves of a nefarious totalitarian regime. Typically, the red invaders are repelled by boy heroes through a combination of wit and resolve. This is the case in Roland A. Martone's science fiction story

"The Boy Who Saved the World" (1956), in which McCarthyist anxieties about a looming Soviet takeover provide the backdrop for the story about a Martian plot to conquer Earth.[66]

U.S. fears of Soviet world domination reached fever pitch when the first Sputnik satellite was launched into the Earth's orbit in October 1957. For BSA officials, the Soviet coup bore all the characteristics of a productive crisis, allowing them to market scouting as a pathway to making up lost ground in the space race. Sputnik weighed heavily on the minds of American youth organizers—so heavily that the May–June 1958 issue of Scouting devoted three articles to discussing Sputnik's implications for American youth, manhood, and aspirations to global leadership. Boy training and space exploration became entangled in rallying calls to restore U.S. supremacy. "The best thing that has happened to the United States of America in our generation is Russia's Sputnik. It is proving the most effective therapy conceivable for our indifference and negligence, our concentration on comforts and convenience, our devotion to all but our patriotic obligation to this best of all lands," one article explained. The authors downplayed the competing power of the Soviets. As they saw it, Sputnik had exposed the softness and complacency of an advanced consumer culture—social ills that the Boy Scouts were avowedly combating. Beating the communists in space required making the better men, which would happen only if Americans invested more in youth, "the most precious reservoir of the present and the future." The Boy Scouts, the writers claimed, were that investment. They would "take wayward impulses" out of millions of boys and teach them how to "live productively in an age of science."[67] Linking science education, youth preparedness, and anti-delinquency, one author anticipated that every dollar spent "on an organization like the Boy Scouts" rather than on "television sets . . . cosmetics . . . liquor [or] tobacco" would help to make "America . . . secure against anything that could possibly challenge us in the future."[68]

No massive redirection of assets took place, but American Scouts and scouters gladly embraced space as a new frontier and the possibilities it offered for inscribing oneself in traditional narratives of U.S. expansion. In May 1957, fifteen-year-old Dennis Driscoll predicted in Boys' Life that scientists were about to unlock the secrets of manned space travel. "The space comics and stories which you are reading now will come true," Driscoll rejoiced, "just as the books and stories of Buck Rogers, when he lay in bed wondering of the jet age, have come true."[69] The BSA program presented the revamped Explorer program as the perfect training ground for tomorrow's astronauts. Renamed from "Explorer" into "Exploring" in the aftermath of Sputnik, the program adopted as its logo a rocket-shaped arrowhead penetrating a circle.[70] This imagery conjoined technology, masculinity, and potency. An Exploring flier from 1958 titled "Rockets, Rocks, Rhythm" made the most of this theme, mixing elements from rocketry, nature study, and contemporary youth culture. Promising that Exploring gave adolescent males the chance to "learn more about rockets" as well as to "listen to the newest rhythm platter" (if desired in the company of girls), the flier demonstrated how Scout propaganda had evolved from shutting out popular culture to putting it in the service of the BSA's masculinization schemes.[71] Permissive of pizza parlors, parties, and mixed-gender socializing, Exploring became the organization's countersubversive task force: instead of problematizing teenage independence as a source of social unrest, it sought to enlist independent-minded teenagers in America's imperial agenda by making rocketry seem as cool as rock music.

The BSA's relationship with the National Aeronautics and Space Administration (NASA), established in July 1958, served the same purpose. Collaboration promised mutual benefits to both parties: BSA leaders needed NASA to make Exploring more attractive, while NASA officials saw in the BSA a recruitment station for future space cadets. Starting in the late 1950s, Boy Scouts frequented federal space facilities, where they learned about career paths in astronomy and rocketeering. When Scout officials introduced the Space Exploration merit badge in 1965, NASA was instrumental in spelling out the requirements. Scouts were present at Cape Canaveral, where they witnessed spectacular launches and formed honor guards at homecoming celebrations for astronauts.[72] John Glenn, the first American in space, and those who followed him became masculine role models for an entire generation of Scouts.[73] The space race, former scout Brent Troutner remembered, "gave fertile young minds something to idolize and look up to. . . . My true heroes were astronauts—absolutely and unequivocally and totally." Glenn returned the favor, commending the Boy Scout and assuming several honorary positions within the organization.[74]

German rocket scientist Wernher von Braun, who had worked for Nazi Germany before the U.S. government put him in charge of its aerospace research program, also made it into the BSA's pantheon of space heroes. Regardless of his former affiliation with Hitler, von Braun became an honorary member of the organization in April 1963. Braun's induction reveals the compatibility of the cult of audacious youth so central to National Socialism with the frontiers of the space age. Thanking the "finest organization for boys in the world" for welcoming him in their midst, von Braun predicted in the presence of a group of Boy Scouts at NASA's research center at Huntsville, Alabama, that by the end of the decade "former Scouts—brave men, who as boys had *your* training, wore *your* uniform, and won *your* awards—will explore the surface of the moon." Interestingly, von Braun framed the space race not in terms of an ideological competition but as a test of masculine resolve that pitted the optimism of youth against the cynicism of old age. "While some reluctant, doubtful, or stubborn adults have to be dragged screaming across the threshold to space, I have never found any reservation about its exploration among our youth. . . . Your confidence and enthusiasm about the future is contagious," the German American scientist told the Scouts. The ways in which the rhetoric of youthful service and devotion to a higher cause in U.S. scouting resembled fascist youth organizations once again casts a much more complex, if not sinister, interpretation of organized youth in liberal democracies. From the BSA's ranks, von Braun anticipated, would emerge "the men who will direct this country," including the "scientists, engineers and—perhaps—the astronauts" that would fulfill one of mankind's oldest dreams. After all, "12 of our 16 astronauts [were] former Boy Scouts," the former SS officer added.[75]

These figures continued to climb over the next decades. According to the BSA, 180 of the 312 pilots and scientists who became astronauts had been Scouts.[76] The first man to walk on the moon, Neil Armstrong, was an Eagle Scout, and ten of the eleven Americans who came after him had garnered Scout badges in their teens.[77] More than any other masculine profession of the 1960s and 1970s, astronauts straddled the realms of boyhood and empire. For many, Glenn, Armstrong, Edwin "Buzz" Aldrin, and other heroes of the skies embodied the ultimate Boy Scout. At a time of international calamity and domestic unrest, they assumed the mantle of youthful bravado, taking risks, pushing boundaries, and hoisting the Stars and Stripes outside Earth's orbit. Transposing empire into outer space stabilized the Cold War gender order and had the distinct advantage of permitting boys and men to play with rockets without the danger of military escalation. The rationale behind the BSA's promotion of space exploration is hard to miss. For its advocates, it represented another innocent crusade that meshed the causes of scientific discovery, democratic boyhood, and U.S. global leadership.

Friends of the Free World

At the same time that some boys were reaching for the stars, others were reaching across terrestrial boundaries to engage with a wider world. The Cold War frontiers of space and international relations converged in the BSA, where the battle against communism increasingly served as a pretext for those insisting that the Scout virtues of kindness, courtesy, and friendship did not cease at the water's edge. Boys and men answered the call, projecting themselves into the arenas of international relief, campfire diplomacy, and global anticommunism. They donated money, uniforms, and handbooks to foreign Scout organizations through the WFF, forged transnational bonds at national and world jamborees, and declared solidarity with young people rising up against Soviet-style governments. The BSA's cross-border activism linked U.S. Boy Scouts' curiosity about world affairs with the question of whether children the world over would grow up enslaved or free.

The seeds of the BSA's commitment to free-world empire were planted in the final days of World War II. Why the WFF originated when it did is not easy to determine. Apparently, reports about U.S. soldiers organizing boys in war zones into makeshift Scout units provided the initial impetus. "Almost every council in the country can tell . . . stories of world-wide Scout friendships, stories which have come back to them from Scouts and Scouters in the armed forces," noted *Scouting* editor Lorne W. Barclay in January 1945. "Some are working as leaders of British Scout Troops in England, others are helping to organize Scout Troops in Italy, some have gone camping with Scouts in Egypt, India, Australia and New Zealand; many . . . are aiding Scouting in France."[78] These scoutmaster-soldiers linked their activities on behalf of war-shattered boys to the repudiation of totalitarian barbarism and the universalization of the ideal of a happy childhood. Boys "who had been taught ideas and principles so far from ours" were redeemed through scouting, wrote Sergeant James M. Cotter from Italy in September 1945. "How eagerly they accepted the Scout program—a chance to be real boys—to play games and to sing songs and to be able to decide for themselves what they wanted to do."[79] This self-representation of BSA affiliates as agents of liberation and the global emancipation of children formed the ideological nucleus of the WFF.

Foregrounding themes such as "Scouts of the World—Building Together" and "The Good Turn with a Long Reach," the WFF helped transmute U.S. military power into a conquest of children's hearts and minds. Authorized by the National Executive Board on December 14, 1944, the WFF made headlines as the BSA's version of what later became the Marshall Plan.[80] In just a few months, the initiative grew into a major relief operation geared toward rebuilding Scout organizations in war-ravaged countries. Money and material gifts—mostly surplus equipment in the form of handbooks, badges, camping gear, and uniforms—poured in from across America. These donations were then shipped abroad and distributed through the State Department, the World

Scout Bureau (WSB), and the United Nations Relief and Rehabilitation Administration (UNRRA). Originally targeting needy Scouts in Europe, Africa, and East Asia who had suffered under German or Japanese occupation, the WFF evolved into the BSA's pet project for assisting scouting in underdeveloped countries worldwide. Contrary to the sporadic international good turns performed after 1918, the WFF was tightly woven into the BSA's institutional fabric. Since its inception, it has amassed and sent overseas goods worth more than eleven million dollars.[81] As a corollary to the WFF, the BSA introduced the World Brotherhood badge in 1952, which Scouts could earn by becoming pen pals with a foreign Scout, drawing a map of the nations where scouting was permitted, learning about national heroes in at least three other countries, talking to a native speaker in a foreign language for five minutes, and explaining how to identify a fellow Scout in another country.[82]

Although boys rarely grasped the complexities of postwar global realignments, picturing them as clueless pawns in the hands of scheming men would misrepresent their involvement. With remarkable idealism, young Scouts breathed life into the world friendship movement. When the BSA unveiled its Shirts Off Our Back campaign in February 1946, Cub and Boy Scouts were the first to donate old uniforms to further the cause of international understanding. Articles of clothing sent abroad had notes attached to them asking foreign boys to get in touch with their young benefactors.[83] Realizing that support for the WFF was lacking with their parents, the boys of Troop 1 of Mendham, New Jersey, organized a big family picnic where the Scouts raised 155 dollars, one for each boy who had been a member of the troop since its founding.[84]

To boys who wanted to cultivate deeper relationships with foreign youths, international child sponsorship programs held out the option of "adopting" entire groups. Adoption initiatives multiplied as a consequence of the huge number of orphans worldwide caused by the war.[85] The Boy Scouts of Culver City, California, became "foster fathers" to a troop of orphaned and leprosy-stricken Filipino Scouts, supplying them with clothing, medication, and a movie projector "complete with fifty feet of cowboy film."[86] Perhaps the most spectacular BSA adoption project was hatched by the Cub Scouts of Bethesda, Maryland. The plan of these nine- to eleven-year-olds to "adopt" and feed eight destitute European boys for one year earned them an invitation to the State Department in February 1948. Secretary of State George C. Marshall praised the boys' "little Marshall plan," which he thought was "of great international importance in establishing relations of friendship and good will and trust which are so important to our Government, to our people and to the world and to peace."[87]

Figure 6.3. Cub Scouts from Bethesda, Maryland, present their "Junior Marshall Plan" to the secretary of state, George C. Marshall, January 1948. The Cub Scouts' plan to adopt war-stricken children in Western Europe was part of the BSA's world friendship initiatives after World War II. (Courtesy of the George C. Marshall Foundation, Lexington, Virginia)

For politicians like Marshall, the young had become active participants in, and cogent symbols of, a seismic shift in U.S. foreign relations. As historians Tara Zahra and Sara Fieldston have detailed, postwar American and European relief agencies agreed that the work of rescuing children from the deprivations of war was tantamount to the work of rescuing nations and the prospect of a better world.[88] Young Americans' transnational philanthropy authenticated contemporary child-rearing philosophies, which held that democracies needed healthy and emotionally stable children in order to flourish. These engagements reassured U.S. elites that their offspring possessed these qualities at a rate commensurate with their future role as leaders of the free world. "In the short period of my lifetime," Marshall added, drawing a parallel between the rising significance of childhood and growing global stature of his country, "we are now recognized everywhere as being the most powerful Nation in the world."[89] If the Cub Scouts of Bethesda harnessed American power to build bridges of friendship across oceans and continents, as Marshall's statements suggest, one could reasonably hope that youths in other countries would be bound to their benefactors by feelings of gratitude, not envy or suspicion.

Responses from abroad validated the image of a benevolent American empire that harbored no vile intentions toward those it sought to lift from despair. After receiving a package of Scout literature from the WFF, a Lithuanian scoutmaster sent his thanks in broken English, pledging that his "friendship" to his "scouts brothers in America" would "always . . . be so hard and true."[90] Similar messages came in from Scout representatives from different continents. The Boy Scouts of France, according to their Chief Scout, "were deeply touched" by the BSA's efforts "to help their European brothers" as it assured them "once more of your friendly feelings toward us." BSA aid also made it to Hungary, Czechoslovakia, Greece, Italy, the Philippines, and all the way to India, whose recipients said that they felt "much obliged to the Boy Scouts of America for the good turn that [had] been done."[91] BSA organizers gladly reprinted such flattering notes, but some also worried that they might imbue their young ones with a premature sense of superiority. "They didn't ask for charity" was the directive coming from the top, and the stated purpose of the WFF was merely to give foreign Scouts "a helping hand until they could get on their feet again."[92] In order to reconcile foreigners with U.S. global supremacy, American Boy Scouts were told to tread lightly. Only empathy among brothers, not the clemency of victors, could win the allegiance of others.

The WFF, however, went beyond reflecting the belief that children, because they were unencumbered by the animosities of older people, were key players in efforts to mend cross-border ties ruptured by war. It portrayed boys as ideal ambassadors of reconciliation, whose smiles could warm the hearts of former adversaries. The affective power of boys to remake enemies into brothers was on full display at the national and world jamborees of the late 1940s and early 1950s. At the international Scout gathering at Moisson, France, which the organizers advertised as the Jamboree of Peace, a group of French Scouts defied adult regulations and invited seventeen German boys to stay with them. Asked to explain themselves, the Scouts said they were acting "in the name of Scout brotherhood and no more war."[93] Four years later, a group of American boys en route to the world jamboree in Austria surprised the mayor of Naples with a miniature Statue of Liberty as a token of U.S. amity toward Italy.[94] The Boy Scouts of Hawaii, who "adopted" the Boy Scouts of Japan only seven years after Pearl Harbor, demonstrated that friendship had to entail forgiveness.[95] Two years before the United States and Japan reestablished diplomatic relations, Boy Scouts from both countries at Valley Forge clasped hands across the chasms of

Hiroshima and Nagasaki. It was at that occasion—in appreciation of Japan's youth returning to the family of free nations—that the Japanese flag was hoisted on U.S. soil for the first time after the war.[96]

Even as organizers trumpeted the theory that Scouts were by nature generous and given to camaraderie, adult leaders left nothing to chance. BSA delegates to the world jamborees were briefed meticulously prior to their departure lest they misapprehend their roles as de facto diplomats. The send-off packages every boy selected to go to Bad Ischl, Austria, received included a *Jamboree Public Relations* manual with recommendations on how to avoid awkward situations. "The way you wear your uniform—clean, neat, not at all cluttered with souvenirs—will make an impression on people," Scouts were told. "The absence of wolf whistles when a pretty girl goes by will make an impression—or at least not make a wrong one." Boys who abstained from what adults defined as licentious behavior were promised something that few youths could ever claim—a vital position in international affairs. As the manual stressed, "Maybe you don't know how important you are. . . . Yes, you, an Explorer, can help win the peace by helping people from different parts of the world understand each other."[97]

The BSA was not the only American youth organization that asked its members to serve as unofficial ambassadors. In various contexts, children and youth were in the vanguard of a more democratic culture of foreign relations that extended from high policymakers to schools, churches, and individual families. American child sponsorship reached out to destitute and parentless children overseas to brush up the image of the United States abroad. President Eisenhower's People-to-People program connected ordinary Americans with people from allied nations through penpalships, cultural events, and city partnerships. YMCA workers expanded their civics programs with foreign policy simulations such as the "model United Nations," where students slipped into the roles of different states and discussed world affairs in mock General Assemblies.[98] Girl organizations, too, sought to foster in young females a feeling of responsibility for developments beyond home and nation. Much like their boy counterparts, the Camp Fire Girls and Girl Scouts built bridges to their sister Scouts across the oceans, but they also emphasized the salutary influence of girls whose commitment to a global humanitarianism grew out of domestic concerns for family, friendship, and service.[99]

However, the female versions of world friendship barely overlapped with BSA invocations of brotherhood. This hints at the contested semantics of the term "friendship." Boy Scout friendship, by referring to homosocial ties between boys and men, was already a gendered, and thus exclusionary, concept. Grafting this concept onto the realm of international politics while silencing female expressions of the same concept exacerbated gender divisions. With its attempts to balance patriotism and internationalism, the GSA ran into trouble in 1954 when Florida journalist Robert LeFevre protested that the revised Girl Scout handbook spouted "UN and world government propaganda" instead of teaching time-honored American values.[100] The Illinois Department of the American Legion, a staunch ally of the BSA, echoed LeFevre's outrage, recommending its members withdraw their support from the Girl Scouts "until such time" as they stepped back from their "One-World citizenship" rhetoric and purged "un-American influences from [their] handbook and publications."[101] Caving to the pressure, GSA leaders announced that they would edit controversial phrases, even as they dismissed the criticism as ludicrous. World friendship, as this episode suggests, could be understood as either productive or subversive. Males might be able to operate it, but in the hands of females, who were depicted as emotionally more susceptible to a utopian internationalism, the promotion of cross-border relationships seemed, as one journalist put it, "a dangerous idea."[102]

Shunning overtly cosmopolitan language, the BSA avoided this kind of scrutiny by anchoring its devotion to world friendship in a vision of international order based on free and independent—not interdependent—nation-states. World brotherhood, at least in theory, was never about eroding national boundaries. The desire to mend the ailing bodies of foreign boys through the WFF was linked to the desire to heal the bodies of nations devastated by war or infected by communism. Scouters on both sides of the Atlantic believed that renationalizing children was the key to reconstructing nations. They supported scouting in areas inhabited by European war refugees, whom relief organizations had come to label "Displaced Persons" (DPs).[103] Cramped in temporary camps and housing facilities in Allied-occupied central Europe, DPs faced an uncertain future, awaiting repatriation or resettlement. For the American Harry K. Eby, who toured the U.S.-occupied zone in Germany in late 1946 and early 1947 at the request of the BSA and the WSB, building robust Scout programs for refugee children in the midst of confusion and chaos was of utmost importance. Observing the activities of Lithuanian, Latvian, Estonian, Ukrainian, Russian, and Polish troops filled Eby with "admiration for the vitality of peoples who, under great difficulties and handicaps, express such devotion to their youth." UNRRA officials frowned at the unconcealed militarism displayed by nationalistic youth groups from Eastern Europe. Eby acknowledged that revanchism ran counter to the "furthering of International good-will and understanding, not enmity, between the nations."[104] Still, the international Scout community followed Eby's advice and welcomed the DP Scouts as brothers. Perceived as future citizens of a free Europe, DP boys with their own national uniforms and insignia became a common sight at postwar regional and world jamborees.[105]

As the fear of communism increased in the United States, so did the tendency to declare free-world and socialist constructions of friendship diametrically opposed to one another. The common vocabulary uttered at the world jamborees and the major international youth gatherings of the Eastern bloc, the World Youth Festivals, irked Scout organizers in the United States and Western Europe. If both sides portrayed their youths as champions of peace and friendship, one side had to be lying. Numerically, the World Youth Festivals were more than a match for the postwar jamborees. To surpass the limitations of bourgeois male homosociality, socialist organizers opened their gatherings to boys and girls, white and nonwhite youth. In the 1950s and 1960s, the festivals drew roughly twenty thousand to thirty thousand delegates of both sexes, with the largest meeting in Moscow in 1957 counting thirty-four thousand young participants. Demographically, the festivals slowly evolved from strictly socialist rallies to global events that included a broad array of self-proclaimed anti-imperialist youth groups. Soviet-style Komsomol deputies, Latin American revolutionaries, African nationalists, and Western student radicals and civil rights activists flocked to the same meeting grounds.[106] Vying for resources, public attention, and the hearts and minds of young people, the world jamborees and their counterparts on the left illustrate how youth had morphed from a locus of human reconciliation to a major Cold War battleground.

Two events that captured the growing antagonism between these international youth meetings were the Seventh World Jamboree at Bad Ischl and the Third World Youth Festival in East Berlin. Both rallies took place almost simultaneously in August 1951. Adult geopolitics interfaced with transnational youth mobility as thousands of young travelers descended on central Europe to attend their respective gatherings. Not all youths from Western countries were bound for Bad Ischl, and young communists who passed through Southern Germany and Austria on their way to Berlin had to endure considerable harassment from French and U.S. military authorities.[107] The 710 U.S. jamboree delegates were spared this treatment, but not the admonition that their presence near the Iron Curtain would be read as a ringing repudiation of communism. "World brotherhood or world destruction"—for

Schuck, these were the two choices young people were facing at this critical hour.[108] U.S. Scouts traveling through Italy found a special platform to affirm that their pilgrimage to Austria amounted to a crusade against communist infidelity. In the presence of Pope Pius XVII, who welcomed the young Americans at his summer residence outside Rome, they sang "God Bless America" and the Scout hymn "On My Honor."[109] Truman reiterated this point, hoping that the jamboree would be "another living lesson to all nations that boys can work and play, sing and play together as brothers . . . if an evil-minded minority would only let them." With the urgency of conviction, the president made a bold comparison: he likened the methods with which young people were being "mobilized and marched . . . under the hammer and sickle" to how Hitler and Mussolini had regimented youth "in organizations dedicated to the idea of racial hatred and war."[110]

Truman's remarks signify how the BSA's crusade against Soviet-dominated youth was fueled by theories of totalitarianism that did not distinguish between Nazi crimes against children and the supposed communist assault on the family. U.S. organizers highlighted bipolar assumptions about free and enslaved boyhood to justify the BSA's extraterritorial activities. A poster with the caption "Scouting Makes for Freedom," published in July 1956, reflects this outlook. It shows a rising sun in the shape of a fleur-de-lis shining its light on a smiling Boy Scout who has cast off the shackles of Italian fascism, German Nazism, and Soviet communism.[111] Growing up in a free world led by a strong United States was paired with happiness and security, whereas young people's lives in the communist world were paired with misery and darkness. "Brainwashed," "subservient," and "a grave threat to the free world" were terms used by BSA authors to describe the state of youth in socialist regimes.[112] Anticommunist resistance movements in Eastern Europe hardened this binary approach. Putting a pro-American spin on the failed Hungarian Revolution of 1956, one article juxtaposed the image of a "Hungarian orphan" fleeing "from the communist terror" with that of an American Boy Scout living "happy, secure, and free."[113] The BSA was not alone in maintaining that communists made little automatons instead of little citizens. Yet U.S. scouters and their allies insisted with particular verve that their organization was the only association in the world strong enough to defend the ideal of a free childhood.[114]

BSA leaders jumped at every opportunity to outshine even their closest partners. One such opportunity presented itself when the British Boy Scouts experienced a grave crisis in the early 1950s over allegations that young communists had infiltrated them. The rumors gained a wider audience with an interview that nineteen-year-old Paul Garland, the Bristol secretary for the West of England YCL, had given a local newspaper. For Garland, who had risen to the highest ranks of British scouting, the Iron Curtain did not seem to exist. He had been a delegate to the 1951 world jamboree and attended youth gatherings in Eastern Europe. Garland's refusal to disown his Scout past turned the affair into a scandal of the highest order. After the exposure of several more "Red Scouts," the BRS scrambled to repair the damage, but the public outrage had already reached Parliament. While a minority criticized the ousting of left-leaning teenagers from the Boy Scouts as Britain's descent into McCarthyism, the majority countered that it was impossible for a young person to be a Scout and a communist.[115] The debate raged on for months, which some might have interpreted as the sign of a healthy democracy. Arthur Schuck did not. When U.S. senators disclosed in August 1952 that communists had been plotting to infiltrate the BSA, Schuck responded that his organizations had successfully "weeded out" all suspicious men.[116] The message was clear: at a time when others had become soft on communism, the BSA had built a wall around its boys that no red agent could penetrate.

Narratives of boy refugees from Eastern Europe seeking asylum in the United States nourished the myth that the BSA provided a haven for freedom-loving youths the world over. Characteristic of the Boy Scout literature of the time, these stories constructed a simple moral geography, dividing the world into zones of oppression and freedom, with America figuring as the Promised Land. To underscore the world-historic significance of the Crusade to Strengthen the Arm of Liberty, the February 1949 issue of *Boys' Life* led with the story of a migrant boy who had found a new home in the United States. Forced out of his country, now an "alien land" run by a dictatorial government, the boy became a member of the BSA. He did so, the story explains, not out of a sudden, casual whim, but because "he felt a keen obligation to the country that [had] . . . given him the chance to reshape his life in a society free from the oppression of individuals."[117] A variation of this theme appeared eight years later in the wake of the Hungarian uprising. "Escape to Freedom" is the story of two former Hungarian Scouts who risked their lives defying the country's communist regime. It details their odyssey from the days of Nazi-occupied Hungary through their involvement in underground scouting all the way to their flight to the United States. Arriving in America, the youths reportedly "wept shamelessly with joy" at the kindness shown by their hosts. Experiences like these, Schuck noted, demonstrated that "the Boy Scouts of America [had] a greater responsibility for freedom and democracy" in this day and age "than ever before." The "constant threat by the spread of communism," Schuck continued, had to be stymied by "increasing the bonds of world friendship among Scouts everywhere."[118]

Schuck's call fell on fertile ground. For some boys, establishing fraternal relations with foreign Scouts went beyond foraging through basements for old shirts and used handbooks. After returning from Moisson in 1947, Glenn Burr and Charles Burch from Wichita, Kansas, received an urgent letter from their Czechoslovakian jamboree acquaintance, Richard "Dick" Hrdlicka. Forced to go underground by communist authorities, Dick asked for help. Over the next three years, Glenn and Charles mobilized their scouting connections to get Dick a scholarship at a university in Kansas and raise the money to pay for his airfare to the United States.[119]

Transnational mobility, to be sure, was no prerequisite for making friends the world over. U.S. Scouts who never went abroad were just as capable of imagining themselves as belonging to a global fraternity of youth. Curiosity, creativity, and a printing press were all that Jim Sanzare, a fifteen-year-old patrol leader from Philadelphia, needed in 1945 to start *The International Panther*, a magazine dedicated to fostering friendly relations with, and collecting information on, Scouts in other lands. Published at varying intervals, Sanzare's magazine reached a wide audience. By the early 1950s, the *Panther* had become a household name among Scouts on both sides of the Atlantic. Meanwhile, Sanzare declared with the posture of an idealist that he had been paying all publication costs out of his own pocket.[120]

Where, now, are the political and discursive linkages between the boys' benign transnationalism and the empire from which it sprang? Historian Mimi Thi Nguyen has an answer. Rather than see in liberal empire a contradiction in terms, Nguyen identified the promise of liberating countries from benighted forms of government as the "core proposition" of modern American empire. The "gift of freedom," according to Nguyen, came with a debt—the debt of gratitude and the tacit assumption that the liberated were obliged to endure unequal power relations and the empire's prerogative of resorting to violence when it saw fit.[121] Ngyuen's reading of U.S. empire makes it possible to recognize in Scout performances of world friendship not simply a ploy for the ambitions of the Western superpower—a scenario in which confusing the heartfelt wish of boys to help their distant "brothers" with imperial geopolitics would have invited incredulity and outrage. More significantly, it reveals just how much the alleged irreproachability of U.S. foreign policy benefited from the image of good-hearted boys projecting the Scout values of kindness, courtesy, and friendship onto the international arena. The BSA's donor relationships cannot be divorced from the imperial power structures that supported them. Even if the boys were not aware of it, their transactions undergirded the gradations of masculine and national sovereignty within the "free world," in which the liberty of others was depicted as contingent on the willingness of U.S. boys and men to dispense it.

A brief foray into the BSA's visual representations of world brotherhood after 1945 captures these asymmetries. One popular advertisement from the first years of the WFF features an American Boy Scout sitting on top of the globe and pulling a foreign Scout in a ragtag uniform out of the abyss. If the American boy let go, the war-ravaged youth would be irreversibly doomed; thus, what appears to be an act of heroic kindness actually cements a hierarchical relationship in which foreign Scouts assume the role of the dependent brother and U.S. boys act as junior leaders of the free world.[122] American Boy Scouts are also at the center of Rockwell's allegorical depictions of cross-border fraternizations at the world jamborees. In 1963, Rockwell finished one of his most recognizable works, *A Good Sign All over the World*, which portrays a group of Scouts—one American, two Scottish, and what appears to be one African and one Middle Eastern boy—dancing and laughing on top of a mountain. All eyes in the picture, with the exception of the bagpipe player's, are fixed on the American Scout, as if to suggest that the harmony will last until the young American stops dancing.

Rockwell composed his second major jamboree illustration, *Breakthrough for Freedom*, in 1967 at the height of the Vietnam War. Six Scouts, with determined looks on their faces, march past an ensemble of flags toward a common goal in the distance. Both the American boy and the Stars and Stripes dominate the picture's visual hierarchy, while a Vietnamese Scout occupies the center of this international phalanx, flanked by representatives from Syria and Great Britain. With the BSA delegate in the foreground, the destiny of Vietnamese youth, decimated by war, is symbolically linked to the willingness of the free world to back U.S. Cold War policies. Against the dual backdrops of the Vietnam War and the 1967 world jamboree in Idaho—the first on U.S. soil—Rockwell sought to immortalize the imperial aspirations of his country while at the same time hiding them behind the visual ruse of boyhood camaraderie.[123]

The different roles ascribed in Rockwell's image to the Scouts from the United States and South Vietnam—one embodying freedom, the other receiving it—designate race as an organizing principle in BSA constructions of world friendship. It is telling that the organization framed its crusades around wars at the imperial periphery, in particular in Korea and Vietnam, and not around civil rights or decolonization. To cater to white middle-class sensibilities, boys qualified by WFF administrators as worthy of being rescued were cast in

Caucasian features, even if they hailed from parts of the world where whites were in the minority.[124] As the civil rights movement made headlines around the world, BSA propagandists began visualizing nonwhite Scouts more frequently, in part to join a national effort to deflect international criticism of U.S. race relations. However, Scouts of color remained unpopular subjects, much like the African American youths whose presence in the BSA before 1945 was grudgingly tolerated. In the few instances where domestic or foreign Scouts of color became targets of imperial benevolence, the expectation was that subaltern youths would repay white gestures of friendship with unconditional allegiance to their benefactors. To give to others, one author stated in 1947, white boys would not have to travel far; they could simply go out and "find Scouts" in their communities "with other racial and cultural backgrounds."[125] Touting their program as an opportunity for boys to forge long-distance relations, WFF advocates also argued, not without irony, that imperial benevolence should begin at home. Putting African American and Native American Scouts in the same box with destitute foreign youths meant treating them not as fellow Americans but as persons of another country.

This paternalist stance persisted with minor adjustments in the midst of increasing racial tensions in the United States and the global South. BSA officials in favor of a more integrationist approach worked to put the organization on a seemingly more inclusive path. In 1953, IRS Director Weaver M. Marr proposed the slogan "One of every ten Scouts is a Negro Scout" to shore up the National Council's policy of bringing more black boys into the movement.[126] By the end of the decade, white organizers had reached out to a greater number of African American schools and churches. Stories highlighting the accomplishments of black Scouts had become a regular feature of the IRS annual reports. In 1960, responding to the complaint of a Korean American scoutmaster, administrators began using "Asian" instead of the offensive "Oriental" as part of the official terminology of the IRS.[127] The following year witnessed the renaming of the IRS to Urban Relationships Service.[128] In addition, white liberals tried to shed the "white, Anglo-Saxon, middle-class image" of the Boy Scouts by funding inner-city programs such as the "Stuyford experiment," which aimed at recruiting black and brown boys from low-income, crime-ridden neighborhoods in seventeen U.S. cities.[129]

Most of these reforms, however, were symbolic. The BSA's white leadership felt content with casting an image of themselves as advocates of moderate racial progress. Publishing multicultural imagery did not change the fact that there were few integrated troops. Postwar organizers fell short of meeting their recruitment goals for African Americans, Asian Americans, and Hispanic

Americans. The promise of interracial friendship coming from the mouths of BSA leaders rang hollow to most nonwhite youths. Taught to resist segregation, they had little interest in joining an organization whose spokesmen, rather than confronting racial injustice, worried about "the increasing rate of crime" and the "upsurge of violence" in America.[130] One sixteen-year-old white teenager was quicker to grasp the discrepancy between rhetoric and reality than many of his elders. "We keep doing things for [disadvantaged youths] and feeling terribly noble about it," he told *Scouting* magazine in November 1968. "But we would never ask any of our underprivileged, different-colored classmates to be part of our social activities. We don't feel comfortable doing things *with* them yet—only *for* them."[131] A more honest admission that Scout brotherhood upheld social divisions was hard to find.

While white Scouts and scouters were grappling with a changing racial landscape, black chapters of the BSA found a way to maintain their identities as Scouts and identify with antiracist movements at the same time. During the Freedom Rides, black Boy Scouts in Detroit knocked on countless doors in their neighborhood to raise money for civil rights.[132] Internationally, a small group of Scouts led by the African American scoutmaster Homer Meade discovered world friendship at a place most white Scouts would have shunned. In December 1964, Meade and his six Boy Scouts, two white and four black, boarded a plane to Nigeria's capital, Lagos, where more than three thousand Scouts from twenty-four countries were convening for the Nigerian Jubilee Jamboree. At a time when African nations were moving toward independence and African Americans were pushing the civil rights agenda, the Nigerian jamboree opened up an alternative space for transnational youth fraternization, making it possible for U.S. boys to perform with sub-Saharan youths the same brotherly rituals that had come to define the white world of scouting. However, all was not well at the festivities. The jamboree was held during nationwide elections, and rioting in the streets left the Scouts confined to the Lagos National Stadium for twenty-four hours. Still, almost every activity at the encampment filled U.S. delegate Thomas Welch "with an appreciation of . . . world brotherhood . . . in its grandest sense." It even made him envision an alliance between a youthful America rife with democratic opportunity and budding African nation-states seeking to cast off the shackles of European colonialism—a sentiment few white officials echoed at the time.[133]

Just how much Welch's assessment was at odds with the white majority becomes evident when it is placed next to the story of another scoutmaster who had set his sights on Africa. Together with three friends, the Hungarian American scouter Edward Chaszar crossed the Atlantic in early 1960 to visit Tunisia,

Libya, Nigeria, Togo, Ghana, Ivory Coast, Liberia, Senegal, and Morocco. The purpose of his trip was not to fraternize with anticolonial activists but to warn African youths and their leaders of the dangers of communism. As the head of the U.S.-based Hungarian Scout Association in Exile who had been active in organizing relief for expelled Hungarian revolutionaries, Chaszar felt especially qualified to lead this mission. "We came to tell Scouts in Africa what happens to Scouting when communism takes over the government," Chaszar explained. Distributing copies of the booklet *The Crushing of Hungarian Scouting*, Chaszar and his companions cited the Soviet invasion of their native country as the prelude to a possible communist conquest of Africa. White paternalism, anticommunism, and Cold War foreign policy structured the visits of the Hungarian American scouters. As a result, they were incapable of seeing in the growing interest of young Africans in the Soviet Union little more than a disturbing sign of black gullibility. Chaszar's encounter with Africa confirmed his sense of cultural superiority. Rather than trying to understand why young Africans were gravitating toward Moscow, he believed his Euro-American heritage entitled him to teach people of color a lesson about the menace of totalitarianism.[134]

To shed light on the racist, gendered, and U.S.-centric foundations of world friendship is not to deny that individual Scouts cared sincerely about their distant peers. The BSA's world friendship campaigns thrived less on anticommunist ideology than on their simultaneous ability to appeal to young people's desire for meaningful participation in public affairs as well as to satisfy their eagerness to outgrow the confines of family, school, and church. And yet, the same boys who were working to improve the lot of children stuck in less fortunate circumstances were hardly in a position to anticipate the consequences of their actions. The WFF was neither a transnational nexus nor a Cold War weapon, but both. Precisely because childhood and friendship were universal categories, they were perfectly capable of obscuring the divisions of race, gender, and ideology that managed the internal as well as external relations of free-world empire. That America dispatched its Boy Scouts, with their friendly handshakes and infectious smiles, alongside calculating statesmen and combat-ready generals to bestow freedom on others helped solidify a gentle, almost irresistibly benign story of American ascendancy. The WFF's proposition that the happiness of foreign youths depended on material and moral contributions from America's Boy Scouts shored up the discourse of a free world unable to prosper without U.S. guardianship. Boys who thought of themselves as little liberators could gain a sense of maturity prior to reaching manhood. Men, on the other hand, were looking for ways to reconnect to the moral certitude of boyhood, which promised liberation from insecurity and drowned out doubts about their ability to impose order on a restless world.

As popular as the belief might have been that the BSA was sending out its boys to deliver the planet from chaos, it left them poorly equipped to understand the repercussions and limits of U.S. power. The infantilization of friendship made it harder to realize that other nations were not inhabited by young people living for no reason other than to stand in as grateful subjects of a liberal empire that regarded noncompliance with its ways as threatening. Vietnam, which signaled the loss of American innocence to youths the world over, is a case in point. In light of the horrific casualties resulting from the military strategy devised by the eagle scout and General William Westmoreland, the facade of youthful idealism began to crumble, revealing reckless naivety instead.[135] In the attempt "to remake Vietnamese society . . . we are still acting like Boy Scouts, dragging old ladies across streets they do not want to cross," marveled Senator J. William Fulbright in 1966.[136] No stranger to the field of international youth exchange, Fulbright was wondering whether the Boy Scout virtues of honor, duty, and service had become mere fig leafs for the country's headlong interventionism in Indochina. At a time when more boys were conducting their Scout training under the guidance of enlisted men, he was not the only one.

Chapter 7

Innocents Abroad

Scouting across the U.S. Military Empire

In January 1945, the editors of *Scouting* advertised a short play written by Ohio scout executive O. W. Bennet that celebrated the recent victories of America's armed forces. The play starts with two fictional Scouts, a Cub Scout and an older Scout, kneeling before a large map of the world with the United States at its center. The map is empty, with no indication of national borders or geopolitical constellations. The only visible signs are small flags placed at various points showing the locations of U.S. forces fighting in Europe and the Far East. Each time the younger boy asks about the location of a particular country, the world is darkened for dramatic effect, after which the older boy reveals with a flashlight the units deployed to liberate the country. He goes on to tell the Cub how former Scouts serving in that unit are helping foreign youths "get back the best of their old way of life" and "quit being jealous and greedy." Dramatizing the transnational reach of U.S. military power, the play insinuated that scouting did not simply follow the Stars and Stripes. Rather, it suggested that the United States was emerging as a global force for good because of scouting.[1]

This short play encapsulates just how symbiotic the relationship between the BSA and the U.S. military had become by the end of World War II. The personal and ideological bonds between these two institutions grew tighter as the United States was weaving a transnational web of military bases to buttress its global interests. Contemporaries found in the widened geographical foot-print of America's armed forces a visible manifestation of the nation's new superpower status. Recent scholarship on the U.S. military empire has gone beyond analyzing how the bases reflected policies to unilaterally project American power, reading them as "hybrid spaces" that assembled players from the domestic and foreign, military and civilian spheres.[2] These accounts differ significantly from the outposts of freedom narrative hovering over America's massive military buildup in Western Europe and East Asia. Instead, they raise awareness of how the centers of U.S. military concentration—much like the imperial frontiers along which they were located—functioned as contact zones that shaped the relations of servicemen, military families, civilian staff, and local populations. The trajectories of the imperial and the transnational that converged in these "offshore Americas" after 1945 reveal the split personality of the U.S. military empire, which flexed its muscle to reinforce American supremacy abroad while trying to nurture deeper relationships with the societies it claimed to protect.[3]

As a result of America's postwar occupation regimes in East Asia and Western Europe, the BSA established a more durable presence overseas. In addition to familiar images of U.S. boys representing their country at world jamborees, the American Scout troops that mushroomed on foreign soil expanded the BSA's global reach. Organized chiefly by military personnel, these Scout units consisted in large part of the sons of officers and soldiers stationed on America's imperial peripheries. The majority of these Scout troops operated in the three countries that hosted up to 90 percent of the U.S. armed forces that were deployed internationally during the Cold War: West Germany, Japan, and South Korea.[4]

Following on the heels of a sprawling network of bases, weapons, soldiers, and civilian employees, the BSA chapters in these countries grew as the local U.S. military presence increased. As part of the reinforcements sent to South Korea and West Germany in the wake of the Korean War, the BSA brought structure to its fledgling overseas program with the founding of the Transatlantic and Far East Councils in 1953. Over the next years, the membership figures for both councils rose steadily. According to the annual reports submitted by the Tokyo bureau, the number of U.S. citizens and their dependents enrolled in the Far East Council climbed from 2,961 in 1953 to 7,500 in 1958, and to 13,554 in 1965.[5] The statistics coming out of the Heidelberg office of the Transatlantic Council reflected a similar trend: in 1953, 6,154 boys and men wore BSA uniforms in Western Europe; this number scaled to 20,111 in 1958 and to 30,150 in 1965.[6] It was not until the large-scale redeployments during the Vietnam War and the partial demobilization of the early 1970s that troop sizes in overseas scouting and the military as a whole, particularly in Western Europe, began to shrink.[7]

I investigate how the BSA and its allies in the military sought to shape intergenerational relations and transnational engagements among U.S. and foreign boys living within the purview of America's cross-border network of military bases. In doing so, I weigh in on an ongoing scholarly conversation about what Ann Laura Stoler portrayed as the intimate side of empire.[8] Political and military elites agreed that the effectiveness of U.S. foreign policy—first in the postwar occupation of Germany and Japan, then during the Cold War—rested not just on the display of military might but on its moderation through treaties, civil society initiatives, and the affective capacities ascribed to women and children whom policymakers regarded as "unofficial ambassadors." Military families, as Donna Alvah has pointed out, were not only viewed as a civilizing influence on the masculinity of soldiers prone to be caught drinking or engaging with prostitutes. In addition, service wives and children were entrusted with cultivating friendly relations with local residents.[9] Scouting was useful for both tasks. Underscoring the shift in U.S. military strategy from temporary to permanent bases in Western Europe and East Asia, adult-child interactions gave a sense of normalcy to those living in zones filled with memories of the past war and anxieties about the possibility of a future one. Scouting provided the symbols, rites, and objects of a transnational culture of organized youth through which American nation-builders hoped to establish trust with local partners. The belief that the BSA could further the objective of rearing young democracies fed into presumptions of U.S. superiority. Although no attempt was made to coerce foreign youths into an American-led movement, the expectation was that postwar West Germans and Japanese would generate youth organizations modeled after those favored by their tutors.

The juvenile spaces of empire mapped in this chapter shed light on the intertwined developments of the militarization of boyhood and the boyification of the military. Contrary to earlier decades, the strong connection between the BSA and the U.S. military raised few objections in Cold War America. Boy Scouts living in close quarters with soldiers on foreign bases were part of a larger dynamic in postwar scouting that ranged from the militaristic elements in civil defense to the drilling and marching introduced by former army cadets and war veterans acting as scoutmasters.[10] Adherence to military style had a long tradition in scouting, be it through uniforms or the merit badge system, even as accusations that the BSA was a junior branch of the U.S. military had caused alarm at a time when large standing armies were declared a threat to liberty. This antimilitarist stance, however, all but vanished in the wake of the global conflicts with fascism and communism that kept Americans permanently mobilized. With the rise of the national security state, middle-class Americans began to reappraise military elements as necessary tools to building men that were tough and aggressive but also gracious and noble.[11] Out of the symbiosis of scouting and soldiering emerged a new type of boy-man, a citizen in arms prepared to tackle an unprecedented set of global commitments with youthful energy and untainted morality. Radiating generosity and goodwill, scenes of soldiers bonding with Boy Scouts on America's Cold War frontiers cast an idealized image of the U.S. military empire, hiding its violent aspects and the contradictions involved in maintaining it.

Picturing GIs and their dependents as innocents abroad, rather than ugly Americans, added legitimacy to a growing U.S. military infrastructure. This involved emphasizing scouting's capacity to foster relations between boys and men both within and beyond the foreign base system—relations that sought to incorporate local youths into U.S.-centric hierarchies of masculine honor, political tutelage, and military patronage. Before the first American Boy Scouts migrated abroad with their families, BSA leaders were already partnering with international Scout officials and U.S. military authorities to oversee the reconstruction of scouting in West Germany and Japan. As I will show, these contacts helped paint a picture of the occupation in which men acted as brotherly tutors, not conquerors. The goodwill these men invested in dealings with foreign youths preceded the mutual affinity that the organizers hoped would sprout out of interactions between native-born Scouts and their U.S. peers. All this allowed the BSA to normalize its relationship with the military, which, ironically, had troubled contemporaries much more at a time when this relationship was much less pronounced.

Neither Military nor Antimilitary

Charges that scouting indoctrinated children for war had placed a burden on the movement from the start. These accusations were not pulled out of thin air. The martial timbre in Western education around 1900 expressed itself most visibly in the spread of boy brigades and increased enrollment in military schools, and nothing provided Boy Scouts with a greater sense of pride and belonging than their khaki uniforms. Scoutmasters instructing boys how to march, drill, and shoot with rifles offered fodder in plenty for critics. The Boy Scouts, opined the American trade unionist R. A. Dague, were the invention of a "professional mankiller" who, supported by the "monarchs of Europe and the plutocrats of America," baited children with "bright uniforms . . . grand picnics [and] fun and good times" while teaching them "to implicitly obey the orders of their officers."[12] When Baden-Powell stopped in Portland, Oregon, to promote his scheme at a public rally in March 1912, members of the Industrial Workers of the World shouted him down. "If you stay with that bunch," one of the labor activists accosted a dumbfounded Boy Scout, "they will have you shooting at your parents and friends."[13] For its opponents, the BSA represented the paradox of a society that taught its boys military values even as it decried militarism as irreconcilable with democracy.

Five years later, when the United States declared war on Germany, the propinquity of scouting to soldiering was on full display. Marching and regular drill gained traction in Scout troops across the country. Boy Scouts hardly missed a parade, serving as flag bearers on Memorial Day and joining the veterans of the Civil War and the Spanish-American War in commemorating the fallen. Just as widespread were the premilitary exercises conducted by retired army men who had become scoutmasters. Although BSA leaders pushed back at the notion that scouting bred militarism, decrying the latter as a European disease, most youths felt like Rear Admiral Schuyler N. Pyne, who proudly remembered his time as a Boy Scout during World War I. Pyne thought there was nothing wrong about learning "right shoulder arms, left shoulder arms, port arms, and all the things you do with a rifle" when the country was at war.[14]

While opposition to regimented youth was strongest on the far left, the taint of militarism drove a wedge between parents and their sons. Working- and middle-class parents often forbade their little ones to join the Scouts because they regarded them as a junior branch of the army. Immigrant sons clashed with their fathers, to whom the uniform was a bitter reminder of military conscription in their homelands.[15] The Salvation Army and other peace campaigners wagged their finger at any sort of cadet training, and images of Boy Scouts carrying rifles incensed even the most lenient educator.[16] "Be Prepared," the motto Baden-Powell had coined for scouting, Daniel Carter Beard grudgingly admitted, could easily be construed as a "war expression."[17] After the war, scouting continued to evoke the specter of militarism. League of Nations officials found the movement "semi-military," and Hollywood motion pictures showed Boy Scouts delivering frontier justice to lawbreakers.[18] Meanwhile, West battled allegations from left-wing commentators that his organization reared young soldiers.[19]

A partial makeover seemed necessary to protect scouting's good name. In the climate of demobilization after 1918, Boy Scout leaders turned war bodies into peace bodies by shedding some of the movement's martial components. Reacting to foreign criticism that American Scouts looked like soldiers, U.S.

officials added knee socks, shorts, and neckerchiefs to the Scout uniform to soften its military features.[20] In addition, BSA leaders adopted the "International Left Handshake," global scouting's official gesture of universal brotherhood.[21] Foregrounding scouting's nonmilitary features, men such as Mortimer Schiff replaced the aggressive wartime rhetoric with the semantics of peaceful citizenship. U.S. presidents, acting in their capacity as the BSA's honorary presidents, echoed this shift. "It stirs our imagination and kindles our emotions to contemplate the possible implications growing out of this pilgrimage of these young men and boys . . . camping and living together for two weeks in good fellowship and harmony," cabled Franklin Roosevelt to the Scouts departing for Gödöllö, Hungary. "Such gatherings as this are among the most important contributions to world peace that have ever been developed."[22] Rather than teaching youth how to fight, the jamborees should teach boys to engage in friendly transactions around the campfire. Here and elsewhere, the remasculinization of foreign relations after the carnage of war was equated with success in a nonviolent global marketplace of nations.

In responding to criticism from the left, however, the BSA did everything to prevent a backlash from the right. Not pleased that the organization kept wavering on the issue of premilitary training, Theodore Roosevelt warned against feeding boys "the mushy milk and water which is the stock in trade of the apostles of pacifism."[23] In November 1914, amid growing trepidation over the bloodshed in Europe, one of the nation's most decorated officers, Leonard Wood, resigned in protest from the BSA's Executive Board after reading an antiwar article by Andrew Carnegie published in *Boys' Life*, which Wood likened to treason.[24] Eager to mollify the warrior faction, West changed course. He purged the organization's top ranks of suspected peace advocates, allowed Boy Scouts to parade for preparedness, and began reciting the Executive Board's vacuous slogan that the organization was "neither military nor anti-military."[25] Riding a promilitary wave nonetheless, the BSA denounced critics of the U.S. entry into World War I as mollycoddles, recruited war veterans as scoutmasters, and gained the support of the American Legion. In return, the U.S. Army supplied the American jamboree delegations with tents, clothing, and camping equipment, while military leaders stressed that scouting would "help to make good citizens and good soldiers."[26]

Rather than tout their good relations with the armed forces, however, BSA administrators in the interwar years minimized them. Paramount to their dislike of socialism and pacifism was the fear of alienating those parts of the population who had come to see in the absence of military elements in modern child rearing a reliable measure of civilization. Combating the "military bugaboo" remained a priority for a youth organization that wanted to appear child friendly and nonpartisan.[27] Two developments ultimately helped the BSA cast off the stigma of militarism and create more favorable conditions for an open alliance with the military. The rise of communism and fascism offered an opportunity to externalize the evil of throwing children into the furnace of war. People who had criticized military education as antithetical to a democratic childhood now found it integral to protecting their young ones from a far more horrible fate. "The word 'military' had a nasty connotation," explained General Bruce C. Clarke, commander of the U.S. Army in Europe and president of the BSA Transatlantic Council, in 1962, "[and many] suspected that the Boy Scouts was a subtle movement to militarize our youth. But history has proved these fears false. . . . Today, more than ever, we are concerned about national security. As a nation, we are following the Scout motto 'Be Prepared.'"[28]

The second development had to do with the children themselves. If the ways in which boys and girls were cheering at patriotic rallies, playing war games, and avidly following military campaigns in movies and theaters provide a peek into their mentality, we can assume that children generally embraced military culture as a way of practicing for adulthood.[29] Thousands of Eagle Scouts followed in the footsteps of their famed predecessors Paul Siple and William Westmoreland, finding employment in the higher ranks of America's armed forces.[30] Even those who stayed in the civilian world saw in the uniform a pathway to manhood, not a straitjacket of obedience. BSA representatives on foreign soil after 1945 were relying on that distinction as they sought to establish a firm foothold for their organization in Western Europe and East Asia.

Masters and Apprentices

In December 1948, William C. Wessel concluded his European sojourn in high spirits. Twenty-four years after Wessel had led the BSA's world jamboree delegation to Denmark, the fifty-five-year-old national director of Cub Scouting spent three months touring occupied West Germany at the request of the BSIB and the U.S. military government.[31] Few things ran smoothly in a country reeling from the material and psychological aftershocks of war. Millions of German children were ill nourished and ill clad. After talking to Allied officers, German educators, and local youths, Wessel was convinced that postwar Germany offered fertile ground for a robust democratic youth movement to rise from the ashes of the Hitler Youth. He marveled at the spread of countless youth ventures ranging from the revival of Weimar-era groups to new self-directed initiatives. In this flurry of activity, Wessel predicted "a great future" for the Boy Scouts. Filling a vital "need" for youthful "sociability, recreation, and self-development," scouting, with its "magic formula for self-propulsion," deserved "all the support" it could get from the men and women who were striving to remake fascist Germans into free citizens. A cause worthy of anybody who called himself a Scout, the task of reeducating entire nations, in Wessel's reading, meant sacrifice, not self-aggrandizement. It presented an opportunity not for imperial conquest but for harnessing the regenerative power of youth to the redemption of America's former enemies.[32]

At first glance, Wessel's optimism about the shared future of scouting and the moral reconstruction of Axis youth seemed warranted. Under the auspices of the U.S. military government, membership in the Boy Scouts of Japan, whose Western roots had always bothered Japanese nationalists, quickly rose above prewar levels, climbing from 14,410 in 1949 up to almost 75,000 in 1960.[33] Although U.S. policies of nonfraternization lasted longer in Japan than in Germany, creating emotional, social, and racial barriers between occupiers and occupied, BSA officials started advising native youth workers almost immediately after the cessation of hostilities. A joint Japanese-American committee formed in 1947 laid the groundwork for the reorganization of the Boy Scouts of Japan. U.S. soldiers contributed to this development: their casual contacts with Japanese boys, whom they taught baseball, football, and Scout games, posed a counterpoint to antifraternization measures intended to limit encounters between American GIs and Japanese civilians.[34] Fully restored in 1949, the Japanese association was readmitted into the ISC in July 1950. It cultivated particularly strong ties to the BSA, which made an American observer rejoice that scouting had "become an integral part" of Japan's new "democratic way of life."[35]

Top-down patronage and bottom-up initiative also spurred the reconstruction of postwar scouting in the American-occupied parts of Germany. Permitted by the military government, the Boy Scouts were among the few youth ventures sprouting up in Bavaria, Hesse, and Wurttemberg that were encouraged by the Office of Military Government, United States (OMGUS) "with the aim to make possible the successful development of democratic ideas." The American policy of "cultivating ideals of fair play, tolerance, and honesty" through scouting stood in striking contrast to youth work in the British Zone, where occupation authorities banned Pfadfinder units from reorganizing until 1948.[36] As early as September 1945, U.S. military officials urged BSA executives to meet with liberal German educators to work out a plan for the resumption of scouting in Germany.[37] The WFF flanked these efforts by supplying nascent Pfadfinder groups with translations of Anglo-American Scout literature.[38] In 1948, Bavarian youth leaders collaborated with Walter Kunkel, who had followed Wessel as the BSA's chief adviser in West Germany, to lay the groundwork for the first interfaith German Scout federation, the Bund Deutscher Pfadfinder (BDP).[39]

In spite of these promising signs, however, the bridges built between military personnel, boy workers, and youths in the United States and former Axis nations stood on shaky ground. Compared with local sports clubs, youth hostels, and leftist youth groups, Pfadfinder organizations were "slow in developing," according to an OMGUS report from 1948. Finding "satisfactory leaders" proved more difficult than anticipated.[40] Given that all occupying powers assumed that young people were crucial to the transition from fascism to democracy, ridding schools and youth movements of undemocratic influences stood high on their list.[41] Allied reform efforts extended to native men applying for leading positions in Pfadfinder associations. Although official denazification did not target West German scouters, their U.S. counterparts were reluctant to work with them if they found their faith in democracy lacking.[42]

To ingratiate themselves with the Americans, some Germans left no stone unturned to purge their ranks of Hitler sympathizers. In Munich, joint investigations produced incriminating evidence against Richard Etzel, a Pfadfinder leader charged with spreading Nazi propaganda. The politics of denunciation, however, was not confined to political ideology. The same Pathfinder administrators who exposed Etzel were urging U.S. officials to bar another German scoutmaster, whom they accused of being a pedophile, from working with the Americans.[43] Hurt and alienated, banned youth groups rose up in protest, turning the language of democratization against its originators. "I believe we left the Third Reich behind us, then why should one prohibit a youth group whose members languished in prisons and concentration camps?" fulminated a representative of the Weimar-era Bündische Freischar after occupation authorities had refused to accredit them.[44] Mutual distrust caused by war and an unfamiliarity with local conditions narrowed the avenues of cooperation between American and native youth workers.

As in other reeducation settings, BSA officials and their allies evoked national and racial stereotypes to justify their paternalistic approach to reeducation. Gradually "emancipating [themselves] from the thought-patterns of feudalism," a majority of Japanese youth, stated a United Nations Educational, Scientific and Cultural Organization (UNESCO) report from 1951, had "not yet learned to think creatively and objectively, for peace or for international understanding."[45] When American occupiers spoke of the "German problem," they used it as shorthand for the evils of authoritarianism and militarism. Doubtful about the political maturity of a people who had followed a dictator, military educators recommended that translations of BSA handbooks stress scouting's democratic character in a language so simple that Germans could appreciate it.[46] In Japan and Korea, where the imagined bonds of whiteness and Christianity were lacking in relationships with locals, the reeducation discourse betrayed more than a whiff of racism. Take the example of the Korean officer and youth leader Lee Bum Suk, who came under public scrutiny in 1947. Originally planned as a Boy Scout organization, Lee's Korean National Youth fell out of favor with its backers in the U.S. military for allegedly mimicking the Hitler Youth. American concerns that Koreans were susceptible to extremism meshed with an Orientalist discourse that cast nonwhite people as childlike and incapable of self-government. "Because Koreans are so immature politically, because they have no heritage of freedom," one journalist commented on Lee's Boy Scouts, "they can be . . . easily manipulated . . . by organizations which can destroy the decencies and ideals now sprouting so painfully and slowly in Korea's barren political soil."[47]

Such failed schemes did not escape U.S. occupation authorities, whose encouragement of scouting did not automatically result in preferential treatment. Military administrators rejected any separate deal with the Boy Scouts, arguing that privileging any one youth group would violate the "three ds" of reeducation—democratization, demilitarization, decentralization. OMGUS officer Dwight P. Griswold made clear to an army colonel and BSA enthusiast that giving preference to a national youth movement modeled after the BSA would counteract the policy of "building strong 'grass roots' organizations at the local level," which stood "in contrast to the German tendency to develop . . . organizations dominated from a central headquarters."[48] The Boy Scouts were more than welcome, according to Griswold, but only as part of a coalition of locally organized ventures designed to keep youth off the streets and enable them to learn democracy from the bottom up. To curb juvenile delinquency and promote democracy, U.S. policymakers sought to involve a multiplicity of actors, including the Girl Scouts, the YMCA, and Catholic and Protestant youth groups.[49] None of these initiatives, though, reached the scope of the German Youth Activities (GYA), a program launched by American military personnel in 1946 to deepen interactions between U.S. soldiers and German children at youth centers supervised by the army. To break totalitarian patterns of thought and behavior, GYA centers emphasized sports, singing, handicraft, discussion groups, and material aid.[50]

What made U.S. authorities hedge their bets on the coeducational GYA rather than solely on a movement of boys and men in uniform? The meaning attached to uniforms in occupation regimes is central. Early on, the convention of wearing Scout garb clashed with the Allied prohibition of uniforms that made the public display of military-style attire punishable.[51] For German Scouts, the uniform ban proved a bitter pill to swallow, and allegations that many ran around in leftover Hitler Youth uniforms made matters worse.[52] The Pfadfinders' efforts to subvert the ban illustrate how fundamental the right to don their movement's insignia was to their sense of pride and identity. Some protested the regulation by ignoring it, which prompted the military police to apprehend a few of the more recalcitrant Pfadfinder.[53] Others petitioned for exceptions, pleading with the occupiers to permit emblems and badges.[54] Alexander Lion, the self-anointed German Baden-Powell, shrewdly implored American authorities not to confuse the Pfadfinder "dress" with military uniforms. Upholding the ban, Lion maintained, would amount to a huge setback in leading "our German youth the way to true democracy and brotherhood of youth in all countries."[55] Lion could have reinforced his argument by pointing out that the occupiers were applying their own regulation only loosely. In July 1947, the Army newspaper *Stars and Stripes*, which reprinted the military government's policy that no German Scout should be caught wearing a uniform, caused a stir by publishing pictures of U.S. Boy Scouts camping out with a group of German Pfadfinder in their traditional outfit.[56] Struggling to end the confusion, OMGUS rebuffed all requests to drop the ban. Granting the German Pfadfinder all the privileges of an internationally respected Scout association, the military government scoffed as early as August 1946, would seem "premature almost to the point of absurdity" for a movement that was still "on probation."[57]

The language of probation and maturity should ring familiar to any student of Western colonialism. Although Germany and Japan after 1945 were not colonies in the formal sense, U.S. administrators mapped onto these societies the colonial polarity of likening the occupiers to responsible adults and the occupied to immature children. Historian Petra Goedde made a similar point in her study about postwar interactions between U.S. soldiers and German civilians. "By concentrating on youth, Americans were able to create an image of infantile citizens who had to be taught how to use the power of citizenship morally, responsibly, and democratically," Goedde finds. "Youth education could thus serve as a model for the democratization of the rest of the German population."[58] Viewed in this light, denying German Scouts the right to wear uniforms not only reflected demilitarization policies but also hastened the infantilization of a defeated nation, making the uniform even more desirable as a symbol of sovereign manhood. The struggle over the uniform thus mirrored the potency and predicaments of a dependency discourse that sought to improve entire populations by treating them as errant adolescents requiring correction.

Though not explicitly informed by colonial precedents, the subordinate position of German and Japanese Scouts and scoutmasters resembled the childlike status that BSA officials attributed to Scouts of color. Just as the IRS had initiated separate training courses for African American scoutmasters, postwar BSA administrators invited Boy Scout leaders from former Axis nations to "intern" with stateside troops and learn the American way of scouting.[59] One intern was twenty-four-year-old Georg Pruser, who spent the summer of 1952 in Rockford, Illinois, as the guest of BSA executive Harold Homann. Once a glowing Hitler Youth, Pruser played his role as the denazified German to perfection. He told Scout officials that discussions with Homann had strengthened his opposition to "government-sponsored youth movements" and helped him interpret "the constructive balance between individual action and group discipline."[60] Statements like these convinced C. M. Finnell, another veteran scouter, that reeducating foreign youths was worth the effort. Traveling to Japan in 1953, Finnell reported that the BSA's presence in the Far East already bore fruit. He found Japanese leaders "keenly aware" that scouting offered "a natural tool to provide actual practice in the democratic way of life." As one of his counterparts assured him, "We Japanese believe that the United States of America is the only nation in the world strong enough to stand on its own feet. But above all, she is a nation with a heart, willing to help all other democratic nations to band together to bring peace to the world."[61] Such quotes facilitated the task of legitimizing a quasi-colonial relationship that cast U.S. scouters as schoolmasters and the occupied peoples as students willing to learn from their American tutors.

The consolidation of this paternalist attitude, which posited that the United States was responsible for the moral recovery of its former enemies, hinged on spreading narratives that cast indigenous youth movements as flawed. In Anglo-American accounts, the problems in Germany had not begun with the Hitler Youth but with its fractious Scout organizations that had already drifted dangerously toward nationalism and militarism. In a country notorious for teaching young people how to march rather than think, one OMGUS officer warned, scouting was "not automatically endowed with a halo."[62] John Steiner, the director of Wurttemberg's Education and Cultural Relations

Division, argued that scouting was largely considered "militaristic by the German people" because of its nationalist overtones in pre-Nazi Germany.[63]

Anglo-American educators saw in the bickering over Allied regulations a glaring memento of the petty rivalries that had poisoned relations between the disparate Pfadfinder groups of Weimar Germany, which the ISC had never recognized. Before their postwar successors could join the world federation, John S. Wilson declared, they first had "to serve their apprenticeship and, what is more important, to prove to themselves that they are a united Scout body."[64] The patronizing attitude of Western youth workers also shaped discussions about the future of democracy in Japan. The reinstatement of the Japanese Boy Scouts barely altered perceptions of the Japanese as submissive people. A study submitted on behalf of UNESCO in 1951 reveals just how much Orientalist assumptions underwrote the belief that the democratization of Japan's youth required Western oversight and patience. "Blind obedience to power," "lack of international understanding," and "lack of respect to human rights" were identified as "obstacles" that Japan had to overcome before it could join the fraternity of free nations.[65]

However, American doubts over the democratic capabilities of ordinary West Germans and Japanese were more than matched by the misgivings expressed by local actors. To the dismay of Anglo-American scouters, the majority of West German teenagers felt more comfortable banding together in homegrown youth groups organized by churches, trade unions, sports clubs, and political parties than enlisting in associations closely aligned with the occupation forces. That scouting retained an aura of foreignness became evident in exchanges between Allied officers and local youth workers. Already in December 1945, Pfadfinder leaders warned that creating the impression that the new Scout organizations in Germany were being "called to life from the outside" would constitute a "cardinal psychological blunder."[66] Eager to win German support for scouting in the British Zone, Colonel Alan Andrews told his subordinates to avoid references to Baden-Powell in their speeches. The mere mention of Baden-Powell's name, said Andrews, would disgruntle Pfadfinder representatives.[67] At an informational meeting in Bremen in May 1947, boys in the audience dismissed scouting as "a sort of youth education devised by older people" who cared little about what young people wanted.[68]

The criticism that those in charge spoke *about* youth but not *for* youth raises a fundamental question: Was it possible to trust adults who were struggling to dissociate themselves and their organizations from a troubled past with the democratization of youth? Young people who had their own ideas about how

youth organize themselves begged to differ, and even those in the military government who felt that the Pfadfinder groups deserved a boost did not increase
their popularity by recalling that their predecessors had made common cause
with the Nazis. Representatives of competing German youth ventures articulated similar reservations. A youth committee in Heidelberg had not forgotten that local Pfadfinder groups had been among the earliest backers of the
Hitler Youth, while the German Peace Society and the International Women's
League warned about the possibility of a "militant organization" to reemerge.
The secretary of the Stuttgart chapter of the Social Democratic Party echoed
these concerns, labeling the Boy Scouts "the spiritual preschool of militarism."[69]
All this did not bode well for the future of scouting in a nascent democracy.

Ultimately, what kept the Boy Scouts afloat in this sea of dissent was the
belief that they could help stave off far greater hazards in the lives of young
people. A widely shared view among postwar U.S. educators was that unorganized youth growing up in the rubble of war were not just hotbeds of delinquency but also highly susceptible to communist infiltration. A confidential
military report that wound up in the hands of two BSA officials in September 1945 had come to that conclusion. The report asserted that undesirable
"political propaganda" flourished in places where children and teenagers were
congregating without adult supervision. The authors drove home the point
that scouting, if "properly organized and operated, could be an effective counter
agent to Communist propaganda and philosophy." Joining the Scouts, they emphasized, would enable young Germans to foster relations with functioning
democracies unlike the previous generation that had been "robbed of . . . the
careless days of boyhood."[70]

Much of this was wishful thinking. Allied surveillance and scouting's militarist baggage seriously limited the movement's appeal to West German youth.
U.S. occupation authorities found these limitations worrisome in light of the
massive buildup of the socialist Free German Youth (FDJ), which became the
official youth movement of the German Democratic Republic. Should U.S.
policymakers have promoted the Boy Scouts more aggressively, if need be against
the wishes of the local population? George C. King, assistant to the U.S. high
commissioner for Germany, thought so. Contrary to the FDJ, which had enlisted millions of young people in the cause of building a new state by lifting
them "into positions of responsibility," King told his superior John J. McCloy
in June 1951 that the Americans had foolishly "turned their backs on German
youth as being too young or too contaminated." King felt that a "significant
opportunity" for mobilizing the West Germans had been squandered. Because
the German version of scouting "was tainted with Nazism," and because of

"the ridiculous regulations about uniforms and formations," King lamented that U.S. authorities "all but outlawed the very organizations we could have used to [our] best advantage."[71]

America's role in the reorganization of scouting in postwar occupation regimes is riddled with ambiguity. U.S. authorities were eager to wield the Boy Scouts as a tool of democratization, yet they degraded local Scouts, whom they did not view as equals, by stripping them of their badges and uniforms. Boy Scouts the world over took pride in their young manhood, yet those singled out for reeducation were thrown back into a state of childhood. The BSA joined the BRS and the ISC in demanding that the West German Scout groups meld into a unified body, yet they ended up accepting a compromise that allowed these groups to retain their independence under an umbrella organization founded in 1949, the Ring Deutscher Pfadfinder (Council of German Boy Scout Associations).[72] Some Americans hoped that the Japanese and West German Boy Scout organizations would attract enough members to be a match for their socialist rivals, yet these hopes were dashed by Allied policies of decentralization as well as by the objections voiced by local actors, who continued to spot on scouting's emblems the stains of militarism. It was with these contradictions that American Boy Scouts made their first strides in the youthscapes that evolved on the fringes of the U.S. military empire.

Sons and Soldiers

"No American community is complete without Boy Scouts."[73] This is the first sentence of the article "Scouting behind the Iron Curtain with Freedom Outpost's Troop 46," which appeared in the *Berlin Observer*, the official newspaper of the U.S. armed forces stationed in West Berlin. The article relates the activities of sixty-five sons of U.S. soldiers stationed abroad and their scoutmaster, who was an active serviceman. At first glance, little distinguished the camping trips, merit badge tests, flag ceremonies, and court of honor gatherings carried out by Berlin's American Boy Scouts from the routines of stateside troops. However, the members of Troop 46 also got to do things of which their distant brothers could only dream. They organized charity events for West Berlin's orphans, met frequently with local Pfadfinder groups, became proficient in the use of firearms, and camped within sight of the enemy. The author of the article was impressed by the Scouts' ability to run a functioning program in a densely militarized space. Here were boys "growing into good citizens" and acquiring "manhood" while learning to master harsh conditions in a city under siege—from overcoming the "lack of interest[,] supplies" and available space to taking on the challenge of coming of age on the frontlines of the Cold War.[74]

The story of Troop 46 brings into focus the adjacent terrains of "soft" and "hard" power on which the sons of U.S. servicemen registered with the BSA's Transatlantic and Far East Councils treaded. In straddling the spheres of soldiering and philanthropy, these boys strengthened the two pillars on which the self-image of the U.S. military empire after 1945 rested: benevolence and resolve. Historians Donna Alvah and Emily Swafford called attention to how the institution of the military family helped the U.S. military reinvent itself in the early days of the Cold War as a force for democracy, thus legitimizing, according to Swafford, "the anti-democratic fact of a global standing army."[75] The presence of hundreds of thousands of wives and children on military bases outside the United States came to embody America's long-term commitment to remaking the societies it occupied. Yet that presence also reflected the gendered and aged division of labor that this commitment entailed. Women and children were expected to put a benign face on U.S. demonstrations of masculine military might by engaging in supposedly feminine activities such as working with orphans, raising money for the poor, and forging friendly relations with local populations.

Since the Boy Scouts were situated at the intersection of hard and soft power, their example illuminates how military dominance and gestures of goodwill complemented one another in U.S. occupation regimes. The parallel growth of scouting for American girls on foreign soil reveals a similar dynamic, yet the GSA's cooperation with the U.S. military coexisted uneasily with enduring stereotypes of female vulnerability and the Girl Scouts' vision of peace through international sisterhood.[76] The Boy Scouts, by contrast, appeared as the natural companions of soldiers because of their shared gender. BSA troops located in the European and Far East commands put a special emphasis on boy-soldier relations. Servicemen acting as scoutmasters were to mentor the boys in their troops according to the "older brother" method. Officers and soldiers who had been Scouts in their youth could relate to this idea. Lieutenant Harry L. Corkhill and his two assistants, Sergeant Robert J. Hughes and Corporal George Hedge Jr., relived their boyhood days in the early 1950s as leaders of Troop 457 at Kobe base, Japan.[77] Army chaplain Darrell C. Richardson, a district commissioner in the Transatlantic Council who had started as a tenderfoot at the age of twelve, proudly referred to himself as "a man among boys."[78] Initiating boys into the military with its codes, ranks, and command structures, U.S. servicemen who supported the Boy Scouts also found comradeship, youth, and a sense of self-worth in an organization that declared character, not age, the true measure of manhood.

Playing soldier was a method used consistently by military scoutmasters to socialize boys into an imagined band of brothers while softening the roughness and hierarchies that pervaded it. Boys who joined the Scouts at an army camp received hands-on instruction in an array of modern weapons to become confident in their presence. Soldiers taught firearm safety courses, let the boys ride in tanks, and even took them to the skies in fighter jets and transporter planes.[79] "Military adventure training" included weeklong camping trips, blistering hikes in the company of servicemen, and tours of battlefields where American soldiers had bled. The Scouts' equipment, too, was mostly military—combat boots, pup tents, canteens, and 2.5-ton trucks that took the boys to their campout destinations.[80] The boundaries separating scouting from army cadet training all but vanished during Command Day. These vocational simulations were carried out at select military posts in Europe where Explorer Scouts slipped into the role of army generals and "took command" of base operations.[81]

To the extent that military communities were envisioned as extended patriarchal families, the rituals of father-son bonding in overseas scouting could take on elaborate forms. Father-son banquets sponsored by individual troops allowed boys to raise money for costly excursions and merit badge projects.[82] Held to garner the support of servicemen for fledgling Boy Scout units on U.S. army bases, these banquets cast the relationships between the boys and their military fathers as emotionally intimate and close. BSA enthusiasts in the armed forces hardly missed an opportunity to provide uplifting images of young and adult males sharing in a military culture of masculine accomplishment. Reports of Eagle Scout ceremonies in camp newspapers were embellished with photographs of proud army dads congratulating their sons on reaching the BSA's highest rank.[83] This display of affectionate father-son interactions had an important subtext. At a time when parental advice literature discouraged authoritarian child rearing and told fathers to be their sons' pals, flaunting this ideal turned attention away from the aspects of a military existence that put an enormous strain on families: long absences, redeployments, alcohol abuse, illicit sexual relations, and the physical and psychological stress of living on the front lines of the next possible world war.[84] In addition, the healthy boy-men relationships advocated by the BSA promised to put a lid on cases of juvenile misdemeanor such as drinking and shoplifting that were a part of everyday life for American service families.[85] Newer social histories of the Cold War have painted the picture of an "Army in Anguish," of U.S. military communities riven by racial conflict, drug abuse, and low troop morale, particularly during the Vietnam War.[86] In this toxic environment, the performance of a military fatherhood rooted in mutually fulfilling father-son activities could relieve pressure from military families and renew cross-generational faith in the integrity of America's democratic mission.

Recollections of former Scouts indicate that the boys savored the fact that being a Boy Scout abroad had brought them in close company with enlisted men. "We got to do a lot of things with the military," such as "go[ing] on cruises with a Navy crash boat," recalled Tom Tippins, who had become a Sea Scout in Tokyo during the early 1950s.[87] Looking back at his time as a Boy Scout at Ramstein Air Base, Germany, in the late 1970s, Bruce W. Doole appreciated that scouting in a military community had taught him "American values," something he believed "can be overlooked when teenagers are overseas."[88] "Considering that most of the Scouts' fathers were in the military," said Joseph Mait, a member of Troop 80 in South Korea from 1970 to 1972, "the influence of the military was high and our relations were excellent." To underscore his point, Mait added that the only bad scoutmaster he had to deal with abroad was a "civilian."[89] Walter Hamscher, another Troop 80 alumnus, had equally fond memories of his boyhood in Korea. The younger soldiers, Hamscher recounted, "were absolutely hilarious and just great fun to be around, very much like older brothers, and I think they were just there for a break from their own routines, and clearly were enjoying it."[90]

Since few of the younger servicemen who became scoutmasters had leadership experience, the boys often took matters into their own hands. "Our troop was more boy-led than most in those days, because the boys had to take initiative to get anything done," recounted Winston Davis, who joined Nuremberg's Troop 24 in 1957.[91] Seeing their units make headway on foreign soil heightened the teenagers' self-esteem and made them feel superior to other youths who stayed away from the Scouts. "I was not one of the guys who drank, smoked, and hung out at the teen club," said Joseph E. Boling about his participation in Scout activities at Itazuke Air Base, Japan, from 1957 to 1960.[92] In environments with few recreational outlets, the fellowship that boys and men experienced in scouting provided relief from the rigors of soldiering and encouraged boys to aspire to a military masculinity.

Unlike boys organized in stateside units, American youths who joined a Boy Scout troop overseas were more likely to encounter ethnic and racial diversity in their own ranks. Once President Truman issued Executive Order 9981, which formally ended segregation in the U.S. armed forces, in July 1948, military authorities had no legal recourse to exclude the sons of African American servicemen from white Boy Scout troops. One of the first military communities to integrate its Scout program was in West Berlin. Photographs printed in the newspaper of the Berlin command show black and white Boy Scouts speaking the same oath and working together on the same merit badge project. Some white boys welcomed the opportunities for cross-racial socializing. On base and at campouts, Walter Hamscher noted approvingly, "there was always a racial mix of soldiers; for me at that age that was a new and positive experience." Nonetheless, the vast majority of American Boy Scouts and scoutmasters on foreign soil were white, because the overwhelming number of men serving in the military between World War II and the Vietnam War were white. Black soldiers and their families stationed abroad faced continuing discrimination. Meanwhile, the Transatlantic and Far East Councils showed no inclination to get involved in debates over racism that encumbered black-white relations in the military and sullied America's image as the leader of the free world.

Apart from a shared sense of whiteness, boys and servicemen found community in the fantasy of holding out on the frontiers of freedom, a term repeatedly invoked by U.S. officials in the heat of the Cold War. In 1950, General Maxwell D. Taylor, commander of the Allied troops in West Berlin, compared the situation in the divided city to "the early frontier—every half hour we have to put down our plough to pick up our gun, only we don't have the Indians up here."[93] A youth organization steeped in frontier mythology easily identified with this analogy. The Iron and Bamboo Curtains became the new frontier, and BSA members of all ages were quick to liken the troops located in Europe and East Asia to intrepid explorers building outposts within shooting distance of the enemy. "Scouting 19 miles from the shores of Russia—the idea intrigued me," wrote Far East Council executive Edward P. Black, who helped organize a Boy Scout unit on Wakkanai Air Station in northern Japan in September 1964.[94] Camping on foreign soil, Black's colleague J. Edgar Gamble mused, brought the boys in touch with the virtues of their nineteenth-century ancestors since the boys had to confront "many of the same challenges that [their] pioneering forefather[s] had" to overcome.[95]

U.S. scouters and Scouts in Europe related their activities in the familiar pattern of young men venturing out into the unknown, braving ordeals, and returning home triumphantly.[96] American Boy Scouts who traveled to West Berlin after 1961 could earn a special patch for hiking a "freedom trail" that took them along sections of the Berlin Wall and for writing a short essay on what freedom meant to them. Don Atwood, who walked the freedom trail in the late 1970s, found it "very sobering . . . to see first-hand the stark differences between East Berlin and West Berlin."[97] David Teska, formerly enrolled in Frankfurt's Boy Scout Troop 444, referred to his 1981 trip to Berlin in similar fashion, remembering tense encounters with East German border guards and calling the trail "a demonstration of western freedom as opposed to the austere repressive situation that existed in East Berlin."[98] Even if few boys were fully conscious of the political implications of their sojourn, the annals of scouting on the outer rims of the U.S. military empire are littered with references to Cold War binaries. Why else did the Transatlantic Council name its largest summer camp, which opened with great fanfare in 1956 near Marburg, Germany, Camp Freedom?[99]

Camping near the Iron Curtain was rife with political symbolism. Military authorities wanted the Scouts to contribute to the ideological battle against the Soviet Union. Speaking to an assembly of American scoutmasters in Japan in February 1956, General Lyman L. Lemnitzer expected that the boys would embrace their roles as freedom's little sentinels. Scouting, Lemnitzer said, gave youths living so close to the enemy "the background they require[d] to meet and overcome Communist ideology and techniques."[100] Although service children were inundated with Cold War propaganda, there is little indication that fighting communism was a priority for boys who became Scouts on overseas military installations. "We did not consider ourselves symbols of freedom," Joseph Mait explained, even though the boys in his troop were well aware of the tensions on the Korean Peninsula and the global repercussions of the Vietnam War.[101] If communism became a subject of conversations among U.S. Boy Scouts in Europe or East Asia, it rather served as a springboard for someone to tell a joke or conjure up fantastic stories of adventure and survival. A Scout at Ramstein Air Base from 1976 to 1979, Chip Pierce spoke with his friends "about what we would do if suddenly the Soviets crossed the border and we were to become separated from our families—the major idea was how to make it to Switzerland using skills we had learned in Scouting."[102] Few seemed to harbor genuinely hostile feelings toward their Young Pioneer or Komsomol counterparts. In hindsight, Don Atwood regretted that no contacts existed. "There was still a feeling of kindred spirits, and we just wished that the politics of it all could be done away with and forgotten and we could just meet together as Scouts."[103] The political heft assigned to the boys by military leaders, thus, could trigger responses that were far more imaginative and empathetic than official anticommunism would have tolerated.

Certain of youth's impressionability, members of the U.S. armed forces organized troop excursions to sites of past and present conflict to initiate the boys into a military brotherhood that extended deep into history. Dutiful acknowl-

edgments of American heroics during World War II and the Korean War were
a regular occurrence in conversations among Scouts. Boy Scout slang and jokes
were colored with phrases such as "Today, South Fortress, tomorrow the world"
and "It's just a campout, not Operation Overlord." For Scouts stationed abroad,
Bataan, Normandy, Bastogne, and Osan were more than distant names taken
from a history textbook.[104] The battlefield and graveyard tours organized for
American Scouts based in Western Europe and East Asia resembled commemorative pilgrimages, which could have a powerful emotional impact on the boys.
James Kidd, a Boy Scout with Troop 17 out of Mannheim, Germany, could
not forget the day he visited the Luxemburg American Cemetery and Memorial, which was opened in December 1944 to valorize the Americans who
died halting the German Ardennes campaign. "Even being rambunctious teens,
we knew that this place expected . . . no . . . demanded our respect," Kidd recalled. In total silence, the Scouts assembled in proper formation and walked
past the graves of countless soldiers until they reached a solitary marker. "Nobody stood beside me as I stopped just in front of this history-changing sign.
Without fear of repercussion or taunting, I openly wept," Kidd admitted.
Struggling to regain his posture in front of what turned out to be General
George C. Patton's final resting place, Kidd then "rendered the only honor
[he] knew to give . . . a Scout salute."[105]

Such tributes to the fallen aside, the reality of military-base scouting was
not always that idyllic. Although most informants had positive memories of
earning their merit badges under the tutelage of enlisted men, their recollections betray occasional signs of generational discord. Walter Hamscher spoke
openly about the fault lines separating the boys from the soldiers. The military
was "a very stratified society," Hamscher recalled, and the friendships formed
between the sons of officers rarely extended to include the sons of lower-rank
men. Age differences and the disillusioning experience of war could also frac-
ture the myths of brotherhood and goodwill so central to both the U.S. military and the Boy Scouts. The older men on Hamscher's base who had seen
combat "seemed to be all about control, discipline, rules, and order . . . kind
of sad and grim." Hamscher ascribed the men's behavior to how they were
grappling with the Vietnam War. These men, he speculated, were "probably
the most profoundly affected" by the war's domestic and international repercussions. When pushed too hard by their superiors, Hamscher and his friends
fired back with phrases such as "Okay, Uncle Adolf" and "Hey, we're not the
Hitler Youth."[106]

An exchange of jibes usually cleared the air, but clashes between the boys
and soldiers over the conflicting imperatives of boy-man comradeship and the

hierarchical nature of the army could expose deeper rifts. The story of Terry Ballard, a military dependent who lived in the Philippines in 1959 and 1960, illustrates this. No sooner had Ballard relocated to Clark Air Force Base did he become a Boy Scout—a decision he later regretted. A staff sergeant who became Ballard's scoutmaster drilled the boys so hard that "a number of the Scouts passed out from the heat." Another serviceman, Ballard remembered, verbally abused the boys by saying that they lacked toughness, declaring in front of their parents that he "fear[ed] the day when these kids [had] to fight a war." Frustrated by the authoritarian style of leadership, Ballard ended his career in the Boy Scouts after only a few weeks.[107]

Readers may not be surprised that official army accounts made no mention of unhappy boys and disgruntled adults. Yet for all efforts to eradicate traces of intergenerational conflict, there is circumstantial evidence to suggest that not all servicemen viewed the Boy Scouts in a positive light. In the unit of an American technician serving in postwar Italy, nasty remarks about the Boy Scouts, whom battle-hardened veterans called a "bunch of Sunday School kids," were no exception.[108] Whenever they entered the hazardous world of soldiering, BSA advocates had to work against associations of scouting with naivety and softness, which lived on in military expressions such as "This is not a Boy Scout camp" or references to premilitary drilling and parading as "Boy Scout stuff."[109] Lingering notions that the Boy Scouts were not sufficiently masculine might explain why it proved so difficult in some places to recruit adult leaders. Judging by the complaints printed in military newspapers in the late 1940s and 1950s that bases were suffering from a shortage of scoutmasters, few enlisted men seemed keen on volunteering.[110] Neither did service children flock to the Boy or Girl Scouts in droves. Looking back, Winston Davis wondered why "more kids didn't join the Scouts," especially since he thought that "there wasn't all that much to do" on his post near Nuremberg.[111]

Demographic figures substantiate Davis's impression. In 1960, toward the height of the U.S. military presence in Germany, when 327,446 dependents were staying in Europe with their husbands and fathers, the Transatlantic Council counted 16,682 active Boy Scouts in its area of competence (most of whom were operating out of West Germany).[112] Even by the most generous estimate, not more than an average of 10 to 15 percent of the American boy population in West Germany between ages eight and sixteen were enrolled in the Boy Scouts. This is still a noteworthy figure compared with stateside numbers, but far from what one might consider a total institution.

Overall, the relationships of Boy Scouts and soldiers suffered from an apparent contradiction. The same brotherly affections that were supposed to arise out of the close association of young and old males could also endanger the gender status of enlisted men. To defuse this tension, boys and men began identifying additional activities that allowed boys to support U.S. foreign policy in a more age-appropriate fashion. This is where the Boy Scouts crossed over into the less masculine-coded sphere of unofficial ambassadorship, of army wives and service children trying to foster good relations with local populations and shape the image of Americans as friendly protectors.

Big Brother Is Playing with You

In March 1958, Major General B. M. Bryan Jr., deputy chief of the Far East Command in Tokyo, issued a public statement that must have warmed the heart of every BSA official. Bryan ranked the American Boy Scouts stationed in Japan as "ambassadors of goodwill," calling them "our greatest assets" in efforts to convince the host nation of the U.S. Army's noble intentions.[113] While Bryan endorsed a global role for the Boy Scouts, his statement was by no means exceptional. Children became an indispensable component in the foreign policy arsenal of states on both sides of the Iron Curtain.[114] Nations increased their activities in the realm of international child saving but also regarded children and adolescents as quasi diplomats who were called on to embody their country's amiability and compassion in foreign relations. Supporting penpalships, summer camps, student exchanges, and other outlets of youth ambassadorship, populations caught up in a nuclear arms race persuaded themselves that enlisting the creativity of their young ones would help them secure international peace and prosperity for future generations.

Numerous institutions proceeded from this insight, but projecting youthful innocence proved particularly challenging for military occupation regimes that, after an initial punitive phase, did not want to be seen as intimidating and oppressive. In the immediate postwar years, scenes of children receiving chocolate from U.S. soldiers and opening aid packages fed narratives of the occupation that mitigated the harshness of defeat and portrayed the Americans as just victors who persecuted war criminals but spared the blameless. Scouting figured prominently in some of the earliest exchanges between GIs and local boys. At first incidentally and then more frequently, American soldiers moving through Italy and Germany adopted the role of children's protectors and tutors. Lieutenant Vernon A. Gifford, who started a Boy Scout troop in Naples in 1944, stressed the "great . . . need" for scouting in Italy to get "the begging boy of [f] the street."[115] Acting on the assumption that children in the former Axis nations

Figure 7.1. A Japanese woman welcomes Explorer Scouts visiting her country on a goodwill trip sponsored by the U.S. Air Force, March 1956. (Courtesy of the National Scouting Museum, Boy Scouts of America, Irving, Texas)

needed material aid and moral guidance, individual servicemen saw in scouting the means to inculcate democratic values in foreign youths. Teaching the boys Scout games around the campfire, these soldiers believed, would enable them to unlearn totalitarian practices and recognize the liberators' good intentions.[116]

In defeated Japan, involving local youths in U.S.-led Scout activities contributed to efforts pioneered by American state and private actors to reform Japanese education and put the nation on a path toward becoming a Western-style democracy.[117] Although children were not exempted from the army's non-fraternization regulations, scouting provided a forum where native boys and members of the occupation force could meet on cordial terms. With increasing regularity, American servicemen tied knots and performed first aid in front of Japanese youths, assisted them in forming their own troops, visited their meetings, and welcomed them to their installations.[118] When James West passed away in May 1948, Japanese Boy Scouts participated in a memorial ceremony held in Tokyo to honor the late chief scout executive.[119] Because of their perceived malleability, Japanese boys entertained by American military personnel became a testing ground for U.S. schemes of Japanese-American reconciliation. Contacts with local youngsters through scouting represented an ideal opportunity to project American benevolence at a time when antifraternization sentiments were still strong on both sides.

What started as a trickle in the late 1940s broadened into a steady flow of collaborative events in the 1950s and 1960s designed to acquaint American Boy Scouts with their foreign counterparts and win their affection. Base commanders trying to improve relations with civilians found kindred spirits in boys enacting the Fourth Scout Law. Young Americans' interactions with German and Japanese Scouts ranged from niceties exchanged and souvenirs swapped during camping trips to friendship pacts forged between U.S. Scouts and local troops. Occasionally, such pacts resulted in Americans becoming honorary members of foreign Scout groups or took on the form of joint good turns. In Mannheim and West Berlin, American Boy and Girl Scouts joined German Pfadfinder in distributing Easter gifts to needy children.[120] At the German-American friendship weeks—annual fairs that began in 1952 at military sites to shore up popular acceptance of the U.S. presence in West Germany—Scouts from both countries entertained visitors with singing contests, demonstrations of handicraft, and Native American pageantry.[121] These displays usually ended with solemn declarations of friendship that cast the Western alliance as rooted in fraternal bonds that extended from statesmen and generals down to the youngest citizens. Starting in 1952, Scouts from Tokyo and Okinawa made regular visits to nearby U.S. installations, where they traded troop insignia and national flags with American boys.[122] As part of a reforestation project in 1962 near Nauheim, Hesse, Boy Scouts and Pfadfinder planted an "international friendship forest" covering four acres to honor the blossoming partnership between the United States and a democratic West Germany.[123] In West Berlin, members of Troop 46 surprised twenty-four German Scouts with a special treat. They invited them to come along to England, where they attended the Transatlantic Council's jubilee celebration of the BSA's fiftieth anniversary in 1960 as one German-American contingent.[124]

Perhaps the most spectacular enterprises that connected Boy Scouts across the U.S. military empire during the early Cold War were the Pacific and Atlantic Airlifts carried out by the BSA in cooperation with the U.S. Air Force. Remotely inspired by Operation Kinderlift, an initiative that flew disadvantaged youngsters out of West Berlin to American military families in Germany, the airlifts harnessed American air power to the BSA's commitment to turning its young members into ambassadors of generosity and freedom. Advertised as "good-will" tours with the objective to "further international understanding," the program consisted of two legs—the first leg in the summer of 1955 took sixteen American youths to Western Europe in exchange for the same number of young Europeans who were airlifted to the United States. The second leg in 1956 focused on transpacific exchanges involving Scouts from the United States, Japan, Korea, and the Philippines.[125] Echoing the democratic people-to-people idealism of the Eisenhower administration, the airlift's primary aim was to train future leaders. All participants were accomplished Scouts aged sixteen or seventeen, and all had been nominated and carefully vetted by their local councils and national headquarters. These were, in the words of an organizer, the "high type of young men" who might one day become "Mr. Ambassador" or even "Mr. President."[126]

From casual encounters at the campground to the orchestrated exchanges of the airlifts, American Boy Scouts' accounts of their dealings with their foreign peers betrayed a remarkable consistency with the objectives formulated

Figure 7.2. American Boy Scouts stationed in Heidelberg, Germany, deliver food donations to a local children's hospital, January 1952. Child-to-child charity painted a benign picture of the U.S. occupation in West Germany and Japan. (Courtesy of the National Archives, College Park, Maryland)

by the adult leadership. Like many civilian pedagogues, U.S. military educators were convinced that children and teenagers, because of their young age, were more capable than their parents of bridging cultural differences and representing the American way of life in an unthreatening manner. Army leaflets written for military families in the 1950s promoted the idea of children as ideal ambassadors who could reduce tensions between the soldiers and local people, including those that resulted from bar brawls, rape, and other crimes committed by servicemen on and off base. "Loving, well-mannered children can be a tremendous help in showing foreign men and women a better picture of American life," one leaflet declared.[127]

For the Scouts, fraternizing with youths from other nations provided an exciting diversion from growing up in the provincial confines of small-town America or behind the heavily guarded gates of a military camp. Despite occasional gaffes in conversation, which were "quickly laughed off," the interactions with Japanese and French Scouts that James M. Boling recalled transpired "in the sense of brotherhood . . . without friction of any kind." Not even France's withdrawal from NATO in 1963 tarnished the good relations. Local Scouts, Boling added, "welcomed our continued presence."[128] Trading patches and neckerchiefs with British, Canadian, and German Scouts at an international camporee, Don Atwood reminisced, "was a great experience, and we all made some new friends."[129] Asked to summarize their impressions of the Pacific Airlift, the participating Explorer Scouts were just as enthusiastic. Sixteen-year-old Joe Dodson, for one, was certain that learning to get along with Japanese and Filipino youths his age had made him "a better Scout, a better leader, and . . . a better citizen of the United States of America and the world."[130] Such statements might have been shaped by adult expectations that the Scouts were supposed to exhibit exemplary conduct abroad, yet they also illuminate how the boys understood their role in recasting America's international influence as gentle and unassuming, even in times of political disharmony.

However, American boys rarely interacted with foreign Scouts on an equal footing. The donor-recipient relationships that framed many of these encounters positioned the Americans as the materially and morally superior party, even if the boys did not want to appear that way. Early exchanges with children in the occupied nations were generally of a charitable nature. In West Germany and Japan, Boy Scouts involved themselves in donation projects coordinated by American women's clubs, Girl Scouts, and the Red Cross. Collecting spare clothes and donated toys for orphanages, they were praised in the military press for putting a smile on children's faces.[131] Boys of Cub Scout age and older participated in a series of toy drives, such as the Tide of Toys program of Berlin's American Legion chapter in 1951, which conveyed the impression that the U.S. military was genuinely concerned with restoring happiness in the lives of disadvantaged children.[132] This type of child-to-child generosity usually peaked around Christmas, but in societies where this holiday held no special significance, scenes of Scouts and soldiers playing Santa Claus could generate awkward moments. This was the case at a Christmas party arranged for three hundred native children at Showa Air Force Base in 1948. A picture taken at the occasion depicts two Japanese boys timidly approaching an ominous-looking Santa, with the caption, "These two think that Santa is a little frightening since he does not resemble an Occupation American or a Japanese; however, they think he is a nice person because he brought a present."[133] Cultural mistranslations of that sort, however, did not prompt the occupiers to question the utility of Boy and Girl Scout charity for painting a less invasive picture of the U.S. military presence overseas.

In order to understand how much Americans valued the contributions of these young ambassadors to humanizing the U.S. military empire, one needs to recall the degree to which the BSA's sponsorship of postwar Scout groups in Japan and West Germany was overshadowed by triumphalism and mistrust. The idealism of the soldiers who helped rebuild the German Scout movement was applauded by some but triggered reservations among those who were slow to leave the war behind. According to an investigation conducted by U.S. military early in the occupation, the biggest obstacles for joint German-American Scout activities involved "the attitude of American parents to their children playing with German children" and the fear "that contact with German children would indoctrinate American children."[134] Meetings between American and German Boy Scouts in the 1950s could be rather tense, and both sides only slowly warmed up to each other.[135] That BSA observers who were sent to the U.S.-occupied parts of Germany adopted an overly didactic approach did little to improve the situation. Next to worrying about the long-term effects of National Socialist propaganda, Wessel and Kunkel had little patience with the coeducational traditions that came out of the German Youth Movement. Gender-integrated camps constituted "a real problem," Wessel warned, and Scout groups needed to be cordoned off from such tendencies to protect them "against psychic and moral damage."[136] Creating a healthy democracy robust enough to cast off fascist residues and withstand communist aggression, Wessel suggested, was not just a question of political education but one of sexual morality.

Not pleased with the prescriptive behavior of their big brothers from overseas, German Pfadfinder leaders wondered at times where the consulting ended and the surveillance began. An exchange between two officials in the BDP in January 1950 underscores the organizers' unease about having to put up with Allied advisers in their midst. In a letter to Kajus Roller, the BDP's top scouter, Pfadfinder leader Kurt Garke expressed concern that granting outsiders too much influence would turn their organization into "a stomping ground for the internal rivalries of the occupying powers." Open resistance against British, French, and American tutelage, Garke cautioned, would be futile. Then again, Garke could relate to a Pfadfinder unit that had ejected an American adviser from their meetings because they thought he was spying on behalf of the U.S. military government.[137] The BDP's ambition to manage the transition from fascism to democracy on its own terms became even more apparent in September 1949 when its leaders rejected an invitation to participate in an international Scout rally in Bad Kreuznach, Germany. Roller, who thought the invitation came from a dubious source, told all members to shun the rally. He feared that it could generate footage showing "German Pfadfinder . . . once again marching, drumming, and trumpeting in Hitler-Youth-like fashion." The times, Roller wrote, when Pathfinders would act like "squalling militarists" in front of newsreel cameras were over.[138] If the occupiers were serious about demilitarization, Roller grumbled, why would they insist that others emulate their own Scout organizations, which seemed to lack a critical distance from all things military?

In trying to make the occupation seem less militaristic, the proponents of Boy Scout ambassadorship may have achieved the opposite of what they intended. Further complications arose from the fact that the youths representing America in distant lands did not always behave like model teenagers. Hudson "Bill" Phillips, who moved to Stuttgart in 1951 with his father, an army chaplain, had a couple of stories to share that punctuated the innocents-abroad narrative cherished by BSA leaders and military authorities. One embarrassing incident that Phillips recounted involved American Boy Scouts from West Berlin who had been caught throwing cherry bombs out of a train window as they were riding through East Germany. The juvenile prank so exasperated military officials that they reprimanded the boys and had them fill out affidavits of explanation. Phillips also recalled a more serious misdeed that took place at an international Boy Scout meeting in Scotland in 1953. Where previous generations of American boys had put on airs of superiority by showing that they were materially better off than youths born elsewhere, members of the 1953 delegation made a mockery of the national sensibilities of their German peers. The Americans almost caused a brawl by hoisting the Texas state flag above the West German national flag. More often than not, according to Phillips,

American Boy Scouts felt much more comfortable "stick[ing] with other Americans," and "to step out of this peer group was still a very bold move."[139]

Disconcerted by incoming reports of juvenile misbehavior abroad, BSA authorities responded with an information campaign that sought to bind American Boy Scouts traveling or living abroad to certain rules of conduct. Among the prescriptive literature created for this purpose was the pamphlet *Travel Tips for Scouts*. The pamphlet began by telling the young globe-trotter that foreigners tend to "have a distorted image of the U.S.A. . . . You can help correct this, and do a great service to your country, by carefully preparing yourself to be a good ambassador for the B.S.A., and the U.S.A.!" This meant internalizing the belief that the United States stood for peace, national self-determination, and international cooperation, and giving "enlightened assistance" to underdeveloped countries. The second half of the pamphlet used a series of caricatures to impress on the youngsters how not to behave abroad. They should not be the "Breast-Beating Know-It-All," who acts as if he "knows more about the country he's visiting than his hosts do"; the "Impolite Boor," who "doesn't care about the customs of other people"; or the "Gaudy-Plumed Spendthrift," who "tries to cover up his own inferiority with money" and "could write a book on 'How to Lose Friends and Make People Hate Us.'"[140] Clearly, as much as adult organizers believed that children and teenagers were instinctive internationalists, whose presumed genuineness was seen as a diplomatic asset, they also worried that boys who failed to live up to these expectations might tarnish America's image in the world. In general, the organizers' interventions seemed to have little effect, and especially older Scouts resented the wish of their elders to control their every move. "We should have been treated more like men and equals than as little kids," criticized explorer scout Jerry Solberg after returning from East Asia.[141]

The same contradictions between the normative directives of adults and the erratic behavior of youth that lessened the impact of boy-to-boy diplomacy in Europe also surfaced in the Far East. Daniel Cheung, a descendant of Korean immigrants who joined BSA Troop 80 in South Korea while his father was stationed there, was particularly perceptive about what he described as the "cultural ignorance" of his fellow Americans, admitting that their "lack of sensitivity to host country norms and customs" had made him cringe. Cheung remembered well how some of his friends were "fooling around" as they were standing on old tombs, not realizing that these were the graves of revered ancestors. To the dismay of their Korean associates, American Boy Scouts also liked to climb and sit on Buddha statues, which were sacred symbols to the local population.[142] Good relations were further hindered by the inability of sojourning Scouts to deal politely with the divergent realities of American abundance and East Asian scarcity. When visiting Japan or the Philippines, several world jamboree delegates and participants of the Pacific Airlift complained about the food or nagged about the crude accommodations.[143] Even where mischief was absent, these examples indicate that U.S. Boy Scouts' explorations of the Far East were more likely to reproduce than to transcend Orientalist stereotypes that portrayed Asian societies as exotic and backward.

At a time of growing international resentment of American power, the BSA was not spared the kind of criticism leveled at U.S. foreign policy at large. When the student protests in North America and Western Europe over the actions of the U.S. military in Vietnam were gaining momentum, the BSA came under attack from factions of the West German BDP that were openly siding with the New Left. These socialist Pathfinders did not shy away from controversy, and their agitation against what they viewed as an unholy alliance between organized youth and Anglo-American aims for world domination culminated in the tract *Weltpfadfindertum und Imperialismus* (World Scouting and Imperialism), which was published in 1973. Clothed in the neo-Marxist jargon of the student movement, the arguments put forward by the authors aimed at prompting all Pathfinders to sever their ties to the BSA, which they accused of being a "fig leaf" for the "neo-colonial policies" of the United States.[144] The BSA's world friendship initiatives, they contended, were modern-day tools of imperial penetration, disguising the fact that the foreign aid projects conducted by American Boy Scouts served to "perpetuate the economic exploitation" of poorer nations. To prove their point that the BSA bred little imperialists, the authors presented and translated snippets from *Boys' Life* and *Scouting* that consisted of gun advertisements, information on how to obtain the shooting merit badge, documentation of the leadership's affiliation with big business, and reports of BSA emissaries building up Scout units in South Vietnam.[145]

For the West German New Left, nobody better epitomized the linkage between empire, militarism, and the American way of scouting than William Westmoreland. The Eagle Scout emerged as the perfect villain in German anti-BSA publications after the My Lai Massacre of March 1968, which had resulted in the deaths of an estimated 350 Vietnamese civilians. According to his critics, Westmoreland bore culpability for the slaughter of unarmed men, women, and children. Calling the U.S. commander "a symbol of the genocide in Vietnam," a leftist Pfadfinder article established a correlation between Westmoreland's socialization in the Boy Scouts and his alleged war crimes. It was no coincidence, the article stated, that "while a democratic youth movement had been fighting for years to end the war in Vietnam," U.S. scoutmasters were continuing to teach boys "to obey orders without question," thus "raising the kind of soldiers that the veteran Boy Scout Westmoreland would have wanted."[146] The verdict of the article was clear: as long as the BSA inducted men like Westmoreland into its pantheon of heroes, its trails led to imperial violence, not fraternal benevolence.

Although charges of imperialism were part of the standard rhetoric of young people who stood on the left ideologically, the question of whether American Boy Scouts operating in tandem with the U.S. military served as auxiliaries of empire is of crucial importance. The young Scouts and their adult supporters who traversed the vast overseas network of U.S. military bases may have believed that their actions were altruistic and therefore beyond reproach. They may have convinced themselves that enlisting children and adolescents in the task of forging bonds of friendship with their host nations would ban the specter of empire and make the hierarchies of wealth and power more tolerable for those situated in the lower echelons of the Cold War order. However, at the same time that American Scouts performing charitable deeds or fraternizing with foreign boys understood their nation's growing economic and cultural clout as a positive force, a less harmonious story unfolded on the other side. To the European New Left, the sons of American servicemen who were chasing merit badges on foreign soil were the progenies of empire, not its negation. It would take the social unrest of the global sixties for this idea to gain traction in American society and unsettle relations between the BSA and a new generation of youth.

Epilogue

The Woes of Aging

As Americans were celebrating the nation's bicentennial in 1976, the country's largest boy organization was in the middle of a stunning makeover. Sixty-six years after its incorporation, the BSA announced that it was changing its name to Scouting/USA. Scout administrators had thought long and hard about adopting a new logo—so hard that they solicited advice from a marketing firm. Rebranding the BSA as Scouting/USA was not an easy decision for an organization that cared deeply about its traditions, but one the current leadership thought was overdue. In dropping the word "Boy," scouters sought to flaunt their latest modestly inclusive policies toward young females, who were no longer barred from membership in the Explorer program. The name change was also meant to highlight an increased sensitivity toward the concerns of African American males, at whom the label "boy" had been hurled as a racist insult. In their desire to be politically correct, the administrators also replaced "America" with "USA" to acknowledge, as one spokesman said, that they were representing a nation, not an entire continent. These and other amendments, they hoped, would give the organization "modern strength" in a changing world. And strength was what the organization desperately needed.[1]

Never did boyhood seem more elusive to youth organizers than during the riotous late sixties and the crisis-stricken seventies. Within only eight years, the BSA lost roughly one-third of its members. In 1972, the organization boasted 6,524,640 active boys and men on its rolls. That number plummeted to 4,326,082 in 1980. This dramatic downward spiral left the faithful gasping for explanations. Those with a knack for reproductive statistics pointed to the

nation's declining birthrate: by the end of the decade, in part due to a growing availability and acceptance of contraception, the number of births had
dropped significantly since the baby boom years, with women having fewer
than two children on average. Others blamed the BSA's problems on economic calamities. In times of recession, they argued, fewer men had the time
and leisure to bond with boys around the campfire.[2] This explanation, however, has little validity considering that the Boy Scouts had grown steadily
during the Great Depression, at a time when economic prospects had been
much bleaker. The BSA's response to the crisis it faced, including forsaking its
revered name, suggests that its leaders were trying to come to terms with a
broader mix of developments. "America is a disturbed land," declared the
Annual Report for the year 1968. "Young people are deeply involved, whether
it be discontent with our foreign policy, demonstrations and riots in our cities,
or our escalating crime rate."[3] Sucked into the whirlwinds of the era's countercultural movements, an organization that had touted its youthfulness for decades suddenly appeared like an old man, too lethargic to cope with the erosion of traditional notions of gender, citizenship, and America's role in the
world, and too weak to salvage its greatest asset—the regenerative power of
innocence.

The End of Innocence

Before Peter Applebome discovered the pleasures of disappearing into nature
as a father, scouting had not evoked warm feelings in the journalist and writer.
Growing up in suburban New York during the 1960s, Applebome had found
the Boy Scouts as "arcane, musty, old-fashioned, and inscrutable as a Masonic
initiation rite." Like many of their peers, Applebome and his friends had enjoyed playing in the outdoors or wandering off into the woods after school;
yet they refrained from wearing "odd-looking uniforms" and swearing "ab-
struse oaths." If scouting ever crossed the teenagers' minds, it was with an
"instinctive, dismissive sort of disapproval." They found plenty of subject matter
for contempt—the "drab hopelessly uncool uniforms! The borderline fascist
marching! The hilariously goofy grownups in those ridiculous shorts, neckerchiefs, and high socks! And the world around us had the same low-level
disdain."[4] What really turned Applebome off, though, was not scouting's dubious politics. It was the "dorky superfluidity of it. . . . Why join a pack when
we already had one?" In the age of civil rights, Vietnam, and antiauthoritar-
ian protest, the anti-Scout invectives uttered by Applebome were not an isolated

case.[5] What used to be the domain of radicals was increasingly taking hold of the social stratum on which the organization had depended the most—that of white middle-class youth.

In the words of the conservative commentator Heather MacDonald, the "counterculture and the Boy Scouts were a train wreck waiting to happen."[6] The historian Thomas Borstelmann came up with another fitting metaphor in his synthesis of the 1970s—that of a line of thunderstorms rolling across the country, striking their object with a series of jolts.[7] In assessing the impact of these thunderstorms, scholars have offered sweeping but not altogether unconvincing explanations. The work of sociologist Robert Putnam deserves special mention. In his seminal study *Bowling Alone*, Putnam cites the Boy Scouts as one of many cases to demonstrate a decline in "social capital" in post-1960s America, by which he meant the erosion of traditional organizations, a growing distrust of political parties, and the trend toward individualism. Inventions that privatized entertainment, such as the Walkman, the VCR, and the first video games, seemed to corroborate Putnam's thesis. At the same time, Putnam has been roundly criticized for his cultural pessimism as well as for understating the significance of alternative forms of social organizing.[8] Still, civic disengagement was a reality that affected a broad swath of secular and religious institutions. "Relevance" became the new magic word in a society in which unconventional visions of community and quests for personal self-fulfillment were gaining greater acceptance.[9] In the meantime, older models of organizing youth, and with them the pursuit of young imperial manhood, were falling out of favor with the children of a changing nation.

The first jolt that rattled the BSA came leaping out of the racial confrontations of the late 1960s. While the moderate phase of the civil rights movement seemed more in line with the organization's cautious integrationism, the race riots that engulfed American cities after the assassination of Martin Luther King Jr. left the BSA scrambling for a response. The BSA's answer to decaying urban centers and rampant violence was an expansion of what was commonly referred to as inner-city scouting. The goal of this campaign was to funnel minority youths, in particular African Americans, into an urbanized version of scouting that stressed street smarts over wilderness prowess. Instead of learning how to avoid blisters from long hikes through the woods, city boys, guided by scoutmasters from their own communities, camped in vacant lots and learned how to read subway maps, disinfect rat bites, and avoid drugs. The African American photographer John Shearer, an outspoken supporter of inner-city scouting, hailed the program as an expression of the BSA's "new liberalism" since it encouraged "ghetto kids" to "get 'a natural high' from Scouting

rather than to get stoned on drugs." The organization's old motto, "Be Prepared," Shearer found, had "been replaced with a new one: 'Be Relevant.' "[10]

Traditionalists, however, thought the revisions went too far. Some complained that boys could now earn their Eagle badge without ever having to
venture out of the city. Others were taken aback by images of African American Scouts imitating the looks of Black Power activists by donning black be-
rets and combat boots.[11] Moreover, the humble strides the organization made
in black communities did not compensate for the decline in white membership. This prompted organizers to reinstate camping as a mandatory part of
the program. Inner-city scouting survived, yet so did the juxtaposition of white
boys as promising and black boys as problematic.

On a symbolic level, the BSA's retreat into urban spaces replicated America's global retrenchment during and after the Vietnam War. This is not to say
that the organization apologized for its unflinching support of U.S. policies in
Indochina. The BSA's continued embrace of patriotic rituals and military re-
galia put it at odds with an ever-more-vibrant antiwar opposition. The paths
of the Boy Scouts and the young protesters rarely intersected, but when they
did, the former would sneer at the "impractical flower world of the Hippie,"
while the boys with the neckerchiefs would serve as a laughingstock or as a
grim reminder of the moral bankruptcy of the so-called establishment.[12] Either
way, in the judgment of most critics, the Boy Scouts bred infantile flag-wavers,
not well-informed citizens, keeping boys and men in a bubble of immaturity
where they told each other puerile stories about America's inherent goodness
despite overwhelming evidence to the contrary.

But there was also a deeper irony. Some of the most iconic radicals with
ties to the civil rights and student movements had been Scouts in their adolescence. Antiwar organizer Mark Rudd, who later became involved in the militant Weather Underground group, reportedly told a journalist during a sit-in
that in fighting American imperialism he was adhering to the moral principles expressed in the Scout law.[13] Another prominent radical who spoke posi-
tively about his Boy Scout days was Bobby Rush, the Black Power activist and
cofounder of the Illinois chapter of the Black Panthers. Rush said that the
Scout program had taught him "to set goals" and had instilled in him a desire
"to excel."[14] Revealing once again how scouting's official politics did not
necessarily mirror individual experience, the involvement of Scout-trained
youths in countercultural networks shows that the idealism and comradeship
of a Scout troop defies easy left/right classification. Scout camaraderie could
be relived just as decisively through organizing sit-ins and joining radical
movements.

Figure E.1. President Gerald Ford in conversation with BSA delegates in the Oval Office, February 1976. The BSA placed a bigger emphasis on racial and gender inclusiveness in the crisis-ridden 1970s, but its popularity waned nonetheless. (Courtesy of the Gerald R. Ford Presidential Library, Ann Arbor, Michigan)

Far less decisive, and more hesitant, were the attempts made by adult organizers to reconcile old ideals of boy-man homosociality with youth's demands for greater autonomy. This was in part fomented by the sexual revolution as well as the decade-long fight for lowering the legal age for voting from twenty-one to eighteen, which became reality in 1971, when Congress passed the 26th Amendment.[15] For men troubled by these social and political transformations, the promise of finding redeeming companionship with boys was as alluring as ever, although many of the boys were changing before their eyes. Gone were the mandatory shorts and the clean-cut boyish hair. Instead, young Scouts started wearing their hair long, their pants loose, and sported flashy headgear and colorful neckerchiefs. This departure from the cadet-like masculinity of earlier days was accompanied by a new focus on coeducational elements. One of the few growth sectors in a time of contraction was the Explorer program, which became fully available to youths of both sexes in 1969.[16] The BSA also granted women a bigger role in Cub Scouting, even as it refused to recognize female scoutmasters such as Catherine Pollard, who led a troop of teenage boys in Connecticut during the mid-1970s.[17] Hard as it may be to believe, the loudest outcry against the mild push for gender desegregation in the BSA came from the Girl Scouts. GSA officials came out strongly against the new brand Scouting/USA, arguing that the name would only confuse people and convey the false impression that the two organizations had merged.[18] In a sense, this was the Girl Scouts' belated payback for when the BSA had tried to bully the GSA into changing its name in the early 1920s.

Just in time for the Reagan counterrevolution, the conservatives in the BSA regained the upper hand. Much of their anger centered on the Improved Scouting Program, which they viewed as surrendering to the forces of liberalism, multiculturalism, and feminism. Unveiled in 1972, the revised program made the acquisition of camping and tracking skills secondary to fighting drugs, managing family finances, caring for children, conserving urban environments, and bettering neighborhood relations. A new edition of the BSA handbook reflected the desire to adapt scouting to the tastes and needs of the current generation. Simply labeled *Scout Handbook*, the edition not only deleted the word "boy" from the title to lend an appearance of maturity to the program but also explained at great length how scouting could improve the condition of minority youths surrounded by crime, gang violence, and drug dealing.[19] Determined to make the Boy Scouts relevant again, the reformers declared community work and environmental activism the modern-day equivalents of pioneering. For their critics, however, prioritizing social work over hardy outdoor adventure amounted to the betrayal of the original idea and hastened the emasculation of scouting. Many scoutmasters refused to abide by the revisions, with one contending that "the Eagle rank, respected throughout the country as a top-notch achievement for youth, has been cheapened drastically."[20] When the numbers kept dropping, the conservatives in the BSA mounted the barricades. Seventy-nine-year-old "Green Bar Bill" Hillcourt came out of retirement to write the 1979 edition of the handbook, *The Official Boy Scout Handbook*, which retained some of the previous edition's social welfare concerns but pivoted back to the outdoors.[21] Once more, as the cover image of Hillcourt's handbook indicates, the ideal Scout was male, white, and at home in nature.

Echoing Ronald Reagan's sunny optimism, Hillcourt and his allies proclaimed a new day for the Boy Scouts. Indeed, after the membership malaise of the 1970s, enrollment was on the rise again. A resolute patriotism displaced the cautious liberal reforms of the previous decade.[22] My own memories of joining a Cub Scout pack in Hillsboro, Oregon, in the mid-1980s attest to this shift. I was only nine years old, but I can still recall the oaths, prayers, and solemn odes to God and country that pervaded our pack meetings. For a boy who had spent most of his childhood in West Germany, this was another world entirely. To earn my wolf badge, I had to learn how to properly fold the American flag, and I served as the standard-bearer of our pack at one of the monthly Scout gatherings at my elementary school. My career as a Cub Scout ended when my family returned to Germany, but I kept reflecting on my American sojourn during a brief stint with a German Pfadfinder troop, where professions of loyalty to the German state were strikingly absent and coeducational activities much more pronounced.

The countercultural forces that BSA organizers thought they had banished came back with a vengeance in the early 1990s. A series of prominent lawsuits supported by progressive institutions thrust the Boy Scouts into the grinder of the late twentieth-century culture wars. No longer silent about their marginal roles, women began suing the organization for equal privileges. Nonbelievers who had been denied membership in the BSA were slamming its discriminatory policies toward atheists and agnostics. BSA leaders had sought to rid scouting of "godless men" since the early 1920s, yet the growing acceptance of secularism in many other Scout organizations the world over made the BSA even less willing to compromise on religious issues.[23] The most spectacular court cases involved gay boys and men protesting the Boy Scouts' rejection of homosexuality. Worried about the negative publicity that accompanied these legal battles, national leaders aligned themselves in the culture wars with the conservative base—the churches and communities that were rallying around the same heteronormative norms that the BSA officials of the 1990s had internalized when they joined the Scouts in the 1950s and 1960s. In a 5–4 decision announced on June 28, 2000, the Supreme Court upheld the right of the BSA as a private organization to exclude persons whose behavior it found morally objectionable.[24]

It was a Pyrrhic victory. To Scout-trained men in the U.S. armed forces, America's post-9/11 wars in Afghanistan and Iraq presented a welcome opportunity for regenerative imperial adventure, and a chance to resurrect the infantile story of Americans wielding their power for noble causes.[25] These familiar narratives, however, were diminished by the trouble brewing on the domestic front. The BSA, continually pounded by liberal groups for its stance on homosexuality, descended into a phase of angry public feuds and inner rivalries over what had come to be termed the "three Gs—God, girls, and gays."[26] As they did thirty years earlier, membership figures tumbled at a rapid pace, falling below the four million mark in 2012 for youths and adult volunteers combined.

The low point came in June of the same year when the Oregon Supreme Court ordered BSA headquarters, now located in Irving, Texas, to release more than twenty years of documentation that revealed the ugly flip side of boyification: child abuse. For the first time, publicly available proof documented that boy-man homosociality had made the organization attractive to sexual predators. More jarringly, it showed that the BSA had systematically shielded scoutmasters accused of molesting boys for the sake of protecting its brand.[27] To be sure, the wall of secrecy that the organization built around child abuse had been crumbling for a while. The first to punch a hole in it after years of talking with law enforcement officials, child psychologists, perpetrators, and victims was the journalist Patrick Boyle. Chronicling sexual abuse in the BSA from the 1970s to the early 1990s and counting more than one hundred reported cases of abuse each year, Boyle argued that boy molestation was inseparable from the organization's history. Boyle repeated the claims of historians who had speculated that Baden-Powell was a closet homosexual, and that his love for the Boy Scouts grew out of his suppressed sexual desire to be with boys.[28] The question of whether Baden-Powell crossed the line from boyification to boy abuse, however, has little to do with the question of how innocence was manufactured around the possibility of immoral behavior. The Boy Scouts' founders avoided talking about pederasty, but they also took precautions to banish the same. Beginning in 1911, the BSA created the Red Flag List (known today as the Ineligible Volunteer Files) to gather information on men who lacked "the moral, educational, and emotional qualities deemed necessary for leadership."[29] Established to keep radicals, atheists, and sexual predators at bay while hiding cases of child abuse from the public eye, the files remain confidential to this day.

Struggling to regain the lost center, national leaders lifted the decade-long ban on gay boys in May 2013. Two years later, BSA President Bob Gates led the charge in the organization's executive committee to adopt a resolution that allowed homosexuals to be scoutmasters.[30] Progressive advocacy groups such as Scouts for Equality also applauded the decision to open membership to transgender boys, which the organization announced in January 2017.[31] In June of the same year, the BSA distanced itself from President Donald Trump, whose campaign-style speech at the national scout jamboree in Virginia was condemned by many former and current scouts as irreconcilable with the "wholly non-partisan" nature of the organization.[32] It is hard to foresee whether these measures will extend the BSA's life span for another century. A true sea change seemed iminent four months later when the organization's board of directors made headlines with the announcement that it would no longer bar girls from joining its core programs. Trapped between liberals who find the BSA lacking in its commitment to inclusivity and conservatives who slam the organization for caving to political correctness, the Boy Scouts may be headed toward new frontiers altogether. Then again, making predictions is not the stuff of history.

The Grimace behind the Smile

I confess that writing a book that fuses the supposedly light subject of youth and childhood with the weighty theme of empire runs the risk of sowing confusion. With the advance of modern nationalism and decolonization, empire has begun to acquire a negative meaning that it did not always possess. Youth and childhood, by contrast, generally evoke tender feelings. But I hope that I was able to show that this distinction was neither static nor unbridgeable. In portraying themselves as bequeathing a beneficial legacy for humankind, empires claimed to act on behalf of a civilizing mission that depended on the participation of a broad coalition of people, including the young. Demands to protect children and adolescents made up a crucial component of ideologies of imperial self-legitimization that traveled across geographical and political frontiers. Yet the trajectories of youth, childhood, and empire were interwoven in more than just one way. Lurking beneath the desire to revitalize empire by mobilizing the young was the equally significant longing to make benign ideas about youth and childhood applicable to the moral regeneration of aging elites.

Throughout the twentieth century, the BSA's attempt to cultivate collaborative relationships between boys and men in the outdoors, away from urban vice and female influence, spoke to the entangled processes of empire building at home and abroad. Empire always seemed, in the words of Philippa Levine, "a very masculine enterprise," but scouting also sought to turn boys into accomplices of the transnational hierarchies it produced.[33] Simply focusing on how the Boy Scouts primed boys to be men would miss half of the story; for if the organization brought out the best in the boys, they could also become beacons of morality to their fathers.

Founded during the apex of Jim Crowism and Euro-American colonialism, the BSA reflected the era's racist assumption that population groups classified as different "races" required different treatment. Its hesitant steps toward including African American, Native American, and colonial boys, while keeping them segregated, reinforced existing patterns of racial degradation. Barring people from membership based on gender and political ideology shored up the dominant discourse in which the white, preferably Christian, boy functioned as a surrogate for who and what counted as American. Since the BSA amplified popular identifications of girlhood with fragility, girls were pictured as less capable of fulfilling that role. The correlation of boyhood, national identity, and imperial destiny thrived in times of international conflict and postwar reconstruction. American Boy Scouts saluting the flag at a local campfire or a world jamboree came to symbolize a friendly, peace-loving "free world" that was sufficiently robust to defend itself against the godlessness of communism and the belligerence of fascism. This constellation buttressed claims that the BSA was a better sentinel of universalist ideals of childhood than all its adversaries combined, even if defending those ideals meant involving boys in wars that were supposedly fought to protect them.

Even more consequential than how scouting encouraged international contacts that favored U.S. interests were the ways in which it tucked away the violence, fears, and insecurities caused by pursuing these interests under a layer of boyish innocence. I proposed the concept of boyification to capture the mechanisms that allowed the BSA to recast imperial practices as playful masculine adventure and expressions of a wondrous curiosity about the world. To be sure, boyification resonated differently in different social and temporal contexts. There was nothing manly about embracing boyhood for men of color, to whom the word "boy" was an emasculating racist insult. The primary beneficiaries of boyification were white upper- and middle-class men eager to engage the world with clean hands. As the novelist Jennifer Weiner recently wrote, we may chuckle at Americans' lasting infatuation with youthful and seemingly unaging pranksters and go-getters—from the "good ole boys" Bo and Luke Duke from the popular television series *The Dukes of Hazzard*, who were "never meaning no harm," to current cable hosts such as Ryan Seacrest or Chris Hardwick, who made millions with their boyish charm.[34] Yet in idolizing their boy-men, Americans have also furthered a specific variant of white male privilege. A nation with the soul of a good boy may have committed its share of misdeeds but may still be able to shrug them off. Why prosecute someone whose only fault was a frisky overzealousness to do the right thing?

Historians have called attention to the tensions between adult concepts of youth and the way young people's behavior strayed from the roles that adults had conjured up for them. These competing dynamics acquire particular urgency in youth organizations that are intimately wedded to the ideal of harmonious adult-youth interactions. Readers interested in the subversive capabilities of young actors will be most impressed by how boys and men of color drew from scouting the means to challenge their subordinate status. But as legitimate as this interest is, an obsessive focus on subversion mischaracterizes the organization's complex intergenerational dynamics. The agency of young Scouts often corresponded with the intentions of their superiors, and it was the rule rather than the exception that boys complied, sometimes enthusiastically, with the organization's precepts. At all times, boys were able to act in accordance with the aims of their leaders even while they were pursuing their own aims. This was true of Paul Siple's colonial rite of passage on America's Antarctic frontier as much as it was of the home-front service and civil defense exercises mounted by countless Boy Scouts during World War II and the Cold War. The allure of masculinity made many Scouts want to follow in the footsteps of their elders, but the important point is that the BSA's views on race, gender, and America's place in the world would have carried much less weight without actual boys amplifying them.

And yet, it was the words and deeds of youth that were most likely to crack open the mask of innocence, laying bare the various power disparities that skulked below the surface. Adult presumptions about the inoffensiveness of boys who had been trained to be good Scouts made BSA officials believe that their young charges were ideally qualified to put a jovial spin on American empire and conceal the reality of white male privilege behind the veil of world brotherhood. However, as boys were crossing scouting's physical and imaginary frontiers, they were also prone to reproduce these power disparities in close encounters with others. The racist gestures made by the Safari Scouts in their dealings with native Africans may have been casual but could be incredibly blunt. Similarly, U.S. Boy Scouts engaging in campfire diplomacy responded to difference by embracing surprisingly rigid conceptions of national identity, bragging of American superiority in ways that belied the ideal of children as inherently friendly ambassadors. At all times, youth's reactions to unfamiliar worlds proved too unpredictable to control. While adults sought to take advantage of the idealized innocence of childhood, the idiosyncrasies of youth revealed its instability.

Fluctuating between subversion and subservience, the diversity of youthful subjectivities that existed within the BSA had more in common with the rise of a transnational youth culture than scholars tend to acknowledge. Long before the New Left declared young people vital to national and global change, youth organizations had socialized their affiliates into cross-border networks that stood at the crossroads of preserving old worlds and creating new ones. We need to stop treating organized youth as antithetical to modern youth culture and appreciate them as an integral part of it. Students who took to the streets to protest the Vietnam War were convinced that young people had a responsibility, and a duty, to act reasonably and forcefully on behalf of the common good. But so were millions of Boy Scouts who told adults to vote, take care of the environment, lead healthy lives, and love their country in peace and war.

From its early twentieth-century ascent to its post–Vietnam era decline, the BSA was as adept at mapping trails to manhood, citizenship, and leadership as it was at obscuring their destination. This is not to imply a moral equivalency between the Boy Scouts and rival organizations that had grown out of communist or fascist dictatorships. Empires, like nations, come in different shapes and forms, are capable of coercion and integration, and constantly redraw the lines of inclusion and exclusion. Ultimately, *Our Frontier Is the World* is about reconciling the presence of boys in empire with the roles they played in sustaining it. As child rearing became more profoundly enmeshed with efforts to preserve masculine privilege and imperial authority, boyhood functioned as a prism through which assertions about the benign character of American power could be projected outward. To that end, the BSA promoted a vision of boy-man-hood that was oddly resistant to development even as it claimed to make men out of boys. This vision came to reflect an anti-evolutionary understanding of politics, from the paternalistic desire to brand colonized peoples as immature to harnessing the promise of youth to the rejuvenation of men.

At scouting's frontiers, empire's ugly grimace lay hidden behind the endearing smile of a boy. Edmund Vance Cook's poetic image of the smiling Boy Scout, with which this book began, served the larger purpose of cloaking U.S. expansionism in the mantle of boyish innocence. But it has also stood in the way of cultivating the prudence and wisdom in dealing with others that mature leadership entails. Cherishing the authenticity of boyhood should not blind us to the dangers of powerful men governed by the narcissism of adolescence. With a puerile sense of historical depth and responsibility, we impoverish youth and old age alike. The stakes of ignoring the perils of boyification are high.

Appendix

Questionnaire

American Boy Scouts on U.S. Military Bases Overseas after 1945

1) Where were you stationed?
2) What kind of activities did your troop(s) undertake in the countries you lived/visited?
3) Did you come into contact with foreign Scouts? Were these interactions pleasant? Can you recall any awkward moments?
4) How much did being part of a military community influence your scouting experiences? How would you describe your relationships with the soldiers and officers?
5) As a Scout, did you ever think or talk about World War II or the Cold War, particularly about rival youth organizations in the communist world?

Notes

Introduction

1. Gates, "Boy Scout Jamboree, Fort A.P. Hill, Virginia, Wednesday, July 28, 2010."

2. Kimmel, *Manhood in America*, 168. Prominent conservative apologists of the BSA are Zeiger, *Get off My Honor*; and Perry, *On My Honor*.

3. I use "scouting" and "Boy Scouting" synonymously without ignoring the rich tradition of Girl Scouting in the United States. Both organizations are equally entitled to refer to their members as Scouts. For stylistic reasons, I use "United States" and "America" as interchangeable terms.

4. For critiques of the Turnerian model of the frontier as a moving border separating "civilization" and "savagery," see Pratt, *Imperial Eyes*; Adelman and Aron, "From Borderlands to Borders"; and White, *The Middle Ground*.

5. On imperial masculinities as a form of "hegemonic masculinity," see Connell and Messerschmidt, "Hegemonic Masculinity."

6. Kaplan, *The Anarchy of Empire*, 1.

7. Proctor, "Building an Empire of Youth," xxvii. For current global membership figures, see the Scout Association, "World Scouting."

8. BSA, *Handbook for Scoutmasters* (1944), 45–46.

9. On the overlaps and differences between transnational, international, and global history, see Iriye, "The Internationalization of History"; Thelen, "The Nation and Beyond"; Gabbacia, "Is Everywhere Nowhere?"; Bender, *Rethinking American History in a Global Age*; Tyrrell, *Transnational Nation*; and Bayly, Beckert, Connelly, Hofmeyr, Kozol, and Seed, "AHR Conversation: On Transnational History."

10. On the spread of individual organizations, see Rosenberg, *The 4-H Harvest*; Hermann, *"Mit uns zieht die neue Zeit"*; Mulready-Stone, *Mobilizing Shanghai Youth*; and Ponzio, *Shaping the New Man*. On youth as a driving force in modern globalization, see Jobs and Pomfret, *Transnational Histories of Youth in the Twentieth Century*; and the special forum edited by Honeck and Rosenberg, "Transnational Generations."

11. Leading proponents of this interpretation are Maier, *Among Empires*; Münkler, *Imperien*; Bender and Geyer, "Empires: Might and Myopia"; and Immerman, *Empire for Liberty*.

12. Cobbs Hoffman, *American Umpire*. See also Ferguson, *Colossus*; and Suri, *Liberty's Surest Guardian*.

13. On the informal mechanisms of U.S. empire, see Joseph, Legrand, and Salvatore, *Close Encounters of Empire*; de Grazia, *Irresistible Empire*; Hoganson, *Consumers' Imperium*; Sadowski-Smith, *Border Fictions*; Tyrrell, *Reforming the World*; and Bender and Lipman, *Making the Empire Work*. On "soft power" as a variation of informal empire, see Nye, *Soft Power*; and Lundestadt, " 'Empire by Invitation.' "

14. Kramer, "Power and Connection," 1350.

15. On the "new imperial history," see Wilson, "Old Imperialisms and New Imperial Histories"; and Ghosh, "Another Set of Imperial Turns?," 793. See also Kaplan, " 'Left Alone with America.' " For a lucid comparative analysis, see Go, *Patterns of Empire*.

16. Kramer, "Power and Connection," 1353.

17. Kipling, "The White Man's Burden," 79.

18. Springhall, *Youth, Empire, and Society*; Rosenthal, *The Character Factory*; MacDonald, *Sons of the Empire*; Parsons, *Race, Resistance, and the Boy Scout Movement*; and Woollacott, *Gender and Empire*.

19. Wagner, "The Boy Scouts of America"; Macleod, *Building Character in the American Boy*; Rowan, *To Do My Best*; Maher, *Nature's New Deal*, 33–41; Wills, *Boy Scouts of America*; Scott and Murphy, *The Scouting Party*; and Jordan, *Modern Manhood and the Boy Scouts of America*. Mechling, *On My Honor*, offers an anthropological perspective on the BSA. See also Mechling, "Boy Scouts."

20. The term "Boy Scout" reportedly first appeared in a short story published in 1899 in the juvenile magazine *Buffalo Bill Library*. On the significance of military Scouts for U.S. frontier mythology, see Slotkin, *Gunfighter Nation*, 29–62; and Lears, *Rebirth of a Nation*. On the frontier and continental empire building, see Greenberg, *Manifest Manhood*.

21. Jobs, *Riding the New Wave*, 11.

22. See Ariès, *Centuries of Childhood*; Gillis, *Youth and History*, 1–35; Fass, *Children of a New World*, 1–17; Mintz, "Reflections on Age as a Category of Historical Analysis"; and Stearns, *Childhood in World History*, 1–16.

23. Malkki, "Children, Humanity, and the Infantilization of Peace," 60. On the metaphysical politics of youth, see Roy, "International Utopia and National Discipline," 165.

24. See, for instance, Mosse, *The Image of Man*, 120–70; Hüppauf, "The Birth of Fascist Man from the Spirit of the Front"; and Chen, *Creating the "New Man."*

25. For children as focal points of imperial authority, see Pomfret, *Youth and Empire*.

26. Turner, "Address at the Dedication of a New High School Building in Portage, Wisconsin," January 1, 1896, reported in the *Portage Weekly Democrat*, January 3, 1896.

27. Historical research on old age masculinity is still in its infancy. See, for example, Wood, *Retiring Men*; Field and Syrett, *Age in America: The Colonial Era to the Present*; and Harrison, "Aging." On the crisis of old age and the culture of rejuvenation, see Stoff, *Ewige Jugend*, 11–23; and Register, *The Kid of Coney Island*.

28. See Soloway, *Demography and Degeneration*; Kline, *Building a Better Race*; and Bederman, *Manliness and Civilization*, 200–206.

29. My use of the term "boyification" is inspired by Cross, *Men to Boys*. On images of imperial boyhood in turn-of-the-century British culture, see Deane, *Masculinity and the New Imperialism*, 85–114. On changing father-son relationships in U.S. history, see Martschukat, *Die Ordnung des Sozialen*, 209–39.

30. On the "boy-man" ideal in scouting, see Jeal, *Baden-Powell*, 208–9. Late nineteenth-century precedents are examined in Rotundo, *American Manhood*, 256–62.

31. Morefield, *Empires without Imperialism*, 6.

32. The BSA kept an internal file on scoutmasters accused of radical tendencies or "moral perversions." Dee, "Boy Scouts Head Explains 'Red' List," *New York Times*, June 9, 1935. On male-male desire in Western culture, see Sedgwick, *Between Men*. For a lucid discussion of boyhood and sexuality in the BSA, see Mechling, *On My Honor*, 187–98.

33. Bederman, *Manliness and Civilization*, 100. On the racialization of childhood innocence, see Bernstein, *Racial Innocence*, 4–8. On the infantilization of nonwhite races, see Paisley, "Childhood and Race," 240.

34. Forbush, *The Boy Problem*, 41–42; Kidd, *Making American Boys*, 14–17; and Macleod, *Building Character*, 55.

35. On the correlation of violence and national regeneration, see Lears, *Rebirth of a Nation*. See also Frühstück, *Playing War.*

36. On this idea, see Lewis, *The American Adam*, 5.

37. For scholarship on North America, see Fass, *The Damned and the Beautiful*; Kett, *Rites of Passage*; Nasaw, *Children of the City*; Mintz, *Huck's Raft*; Lindenmeyer, *The Greatest Generation Grows Up*; and Comacchio, *The Dominion of Youth*. On twentieth-century student activism, see Klimke, *The Other Alliance*; and Suri, *Power and Protest*. See also Honeck and Rosenberg, "Transnational Generations."

38. Spivak, "Can the Subaltern Speak?" On subalternity and childhood, see Alexander, "Can the Girl Guide Speak?"

39. Mechling, "Children in Scouting and Other Organizations," 428. On youth and moral panics, see Cohen, *Folk Devils and Moral Panics*.

40. On the concept of "Eigen-Sinn," see Lüdtke, *The History of Everyday Life*, 313–14.

41. Skott-Myhre, *Youth and Subculture as Creative Force*, 136, 138.

1. Brothers Together

1. Albert W. Snoke to John W. and Helen Snoke, August 16, 1924, Albert Waldo Snoke Papers. See also Albert W. Snoke, "50th Anniversary: International Scout Jamboree at Copenhagen, Denmark, 1924–1974 (unpublished)," ibid.

2. "Four Texas Boy Scouts Win Privilege of Going Abroad," *San Antonio Express*, August 3, 1924.

3. Hawkins quoted in Snoke, "50th Anniversary."

4. "Coolidge Counsels Reverence in Boys," *New York Times*, July 26, 1924.

5. West, "Around the World with the Boy Scouts," *Rotarian*, April 1926, 56.

6. On West's early life and beginnings in the BSA, see Rowan, *To Do My Best*, 13–34; and Macleod, *Building Character*, 148–59.

7. Ross, "The Causes of Race Superiority," 88. On "race suicide," see Bederman, *Manliness and Civilization*, 200–206.

8. Grant, *The Passing of the Great Race*; Roosevelt, "A Letter from President Roosevelt," 550.

9. Bederman, *Manliness and Civilization*, 5–10. Jordan, *Modern Manhood*, emphasizes the corporatist elements in the recalibration of American manhood after 1900.

10. See Jacobson, *Whiteness of a Different Color*, 39–136; and Shah, *Stranger Intimacy*.

11. Smith-Rosenberg, *Disorderly Conduct*, 245–96.

12. On muscular Christianity, see Putney, *Muscular Christianity*, 99–107.

13. See Hoganson, *Fighting for American Manhood*; and Streets, *Martial Races*.

14. Handford, *Theodore Roosevelt*, 191.

15. See Wallach, *Obedient Sons*, 118–21.

16. Hall, *Adolescence*.

17. On the "scientization of the social," see Raphael, "Die Verwissenschaftlichung des Sozialen," 165–93.

18. Hall, *Adolescence*, 1:52, 2:398. See also Lesko, *Act Your Age!*, 55–61.

19. Hall, *Adolescence*, 1:vii–xiii, 534. See also Savage, *Teenage*, 64–73; and Bender, *American Abyss*, 180–84.

20. Alexander, *Guiding Modern Girls*, 22; Toerpe, "Children's Bureau," 142.

21. BSA, *Handbook for Scout Masters* (1913), 76.

22. Hall quoted in Bederman, *Manliness and Civilization*, 99. See also Putney, *Muscular Christianity*, 99–107.

23. See Kimmel, *Manhood in America*, 87–136; Woollacott, *Gender and Empire*, 75–76, 122–46; and Rotundo, *American Manhood*, 255–62.

24. Rotundo, *American Manhood*, 258.

25. On changing conceptions of childhood and child policies in that period, see Stearns, *Childhood in World History*, 71–83.

26. Rodgers, *Atlantic Crossings*, 229, 244, 300; and Taylor, *Mother-Work*.

27. Key, *Century of the Child*.

28. Addams, *Spirit of Youth*, 161.

29. Michel and Varsa, "Children and the National Interest," 27–49. On juvenile courts, see Mintz, *Huck's Raft*, 176–78; and Dickinson, *The Politics of German Child Welfare*, 100–105.

30. Hermann, *"Mit uns zieht die neue Zeit"*; and Donson, *Youth in the Fatherless Land*, 35–39.

31. Savage, *Teenage*, 101–12.

32. See Fass, *The Damned and the Beautiful*; Mintz, *Huck's Raft*, especially chap. 11; Leslie Paris, *Children's Nature*; and Comacchio, *The Dominion of Youth*.

33. Baden-Powell, *Scouting and Youth Movements*, 23–24.

34. "Boy Scout Leaders Dine with Baden-Powell," *New York Times*, September 24, 1910. See also Scott and Murphy, *The Scouting Party*, 1–4.

35. Jeal, *Baden-Powell*, 396.

36. "Boy Scout Leaders Dine with Baden-Powell."

37. BSA, *Handbook for Scout Masters* (1913), 2–3. See also Jeal, *Baden-Powell*, 488–97.

38. Baden-Powell, *Scouting for Boys*, 14–18, 56–62.

39. MacDonald, *Sons of the Empire*, 135.

40. Ibid., 209; Anderson, "A Boy Who Has Refused to Grow Up," *St. Nicholas Magazine*, February 1920, 304.

41. Baden-Powell, *Aids to Scoutmastership*, 1.

42. Rotundo, *American Manhood*, 261; Deane, *Masculinity*, 85; "Sir Robert Baden-Powell," *Boys' Life*, August 1929, 24.

43. Seton, "The Boy Scouts in America," *Outlook* 95 (1910): 630.

44. Seton, *The Gospel of the Red Man*, 1–2.

45. See Armitage, "'The Child Is Born a Naturalist,'" 43–70; and Deloria, *Playing Indian*, 95–127.

46. See Macleod, *Building Character*, 112–13, 130–32, 151; and Deloria, *Playing Indian*, 109–10.

47. Beard, *Boy Pioneers*, v, 91, 111. On the sexual connotations of the term "mollycoddle," see Murphy, *Political Manhood*.

48. Beard, *Boy Pioneers*; and Macleod, *Building Character*, 132–33.

49. Beard, *Boy Pioneers*, vi.

50. Beard to George J. Fisher, January 13, 1920, Daniel Carter Beard Papers, Box 48. See also Beard to Walter H. Head, March 1, 1929, ibid., Box 60; Beard to Robert Baden-Powell, 1920 (undated) and April 23, 1920, ibid., Box 24.

51. On Beard's criticism of Seton, see Deloria, *Playing Indian*, 95–127.

52. Seton, *Two Little Savages*.

53. Beard, *Hardly a Man Is Now Alive*, 205.

54. "The Magnetic Attraction of the BSA," *Scouting*, June 1919, 9.

55. "Two Boy Scouts Talking to Two Italian Immigrant Boys," February 16, 1915, *Chicago Daily News Photograph Collection*.

56. See Macleod, *Building Character*, 146–87.

57. See Rosen, *Preaching Eugenics*; and Bender, *American Abyss*.

58. Baden-Powell, *Scouting for Boys*, 19; BSA, *Handbook for Boys* (1911), v, 14.

59. West quoted in Macleod, *Building Character*, 148.

60. BSA, *Handbook for Boys* (1911), 219.

61. On Eugene Sandow, see Lears, *Rebirth of a Nation*, 270.

62. BSA, *Handbook for Boys* (1911), 219–36.

63. Ibid., 16, 219–35; "A Physical Training Not Confined to Hard Muscles," *Scouting*, May 15, 1916, 1.

64. Roosevelt, "The American Boy," in *The Strenuous Life*, 155.

65. BSA, *Handbook for Boys* (1911), 233.

66. See Bederman, *Manliness and Civilization*, 84–103; and Lears, *Rebirth of a Nation*, 68–69.

67. Forbush, *The Boy Problem*, 147–51.

68. Murphy, *Political Manhood*, 3. See also Moran, *Teaching Sex*.

69. Gibson, *Camping for Boys*, 14.

70. Richardson and Loomis, *The Boy Scout Movement*, 212, 215–16.

71. For a typology of Victorian manhood, see Adams, *Dandies and Desert Saints*, 183–228. Alternative masculinities are examined in Kimmel, *Manhood in America*, 81–116; Chauncey, *Gay New York*; and Fass, *The Damned and the Beautiful*.

72. On disabled Boy Scouts, see BSA, *Annual Report* (1923), 16 ("1923" refers to the year covered, not the year of publication); "Scouting among Disabled Scouts," *Jamboree*, January 1932, p.1932; and "Handicapped Boys in Scouting," *New York Times*, February 14, 1937.

73. See Macleod, *Building Character*, 148–50, 203.

74. "Ernest Thompson Seton folder (untitled essay)"; Beard to James West, April 10, 1913, and January 7, 1914, Beard Papers, Box 110, 128. The BSA issued a different version, saying that Seton did not resign but was dropped because he was not a U.S. citizen. "Why Mr. Seton Is Not Chief Scout," *Boys' Life*, January 1916, 28.

75. Macleod, *Building Character*, 282.

76. BSA, *Handbook for Scout Masters* (1913), 89.

77. Hall, *Adolescence*, 1:44.

78. BSA, *Annual Report* (1920), 31–32; BSA, *Annual Report* (1921), 1922. See also "Making Americans," *Scouting*, August 1921, 4.

79. "And Again—Grit!," *Boys' Life*, August 1925, 39; and "The Scout World," *Boys' Life*, November 1929, 25, 68.

80. On William Hillcourt, see "Bill Hillcourt: Still Going Strong on the Scout Trail," *Boys' Life*, September 1985, 26, 79.

81. Henry Pratt Fairchild is the author of *Conduct Habits of Boy Scouts*.

82. BSA, *Official Report* (1923), 191.

83. Report of Scout Troop 24, July 15, 1924, Box 6, Chicago Commons Manuscript Collection.

84. KKK (George L. Nye) to West, October 16, 1923, Beard Papers, Box 131.

85. "Extracting the Hyphen," *Scouting*, July 1922, 4.

86. BSA, *Official Report* (1923), 542–43.

87. Mangione, "Growing Up Sicilian," 473.

88. Lee quoted in Jorae, *The Children of Chinatown*, 63.

89. West, "Around the World with the Boy Scouts," 29.

90. "Dan Beard's Scouting Section," *Boys' Life*, May 1933, 24.

91. On the fraternalism of the Victorian and Progressive Eras, see DeVault, *United Apart*; Kane, *Separatism and Subculture*, 69–98; and Skocpol, Liazos, and Ganz, *What a Mighty Power We Can Be*.

92. See Tyrrell, *Woman's World, Woman's Empire*. On the women's suffrage movement in international perspective, see Sneider, *Suffragists in an Imperial Age*.

93. On female gender roles in modern urban America, see Deutsch, *Women and the City*.

94. On the Camp Fire Girls, see Deloria, *Playing Indian*, 111–14; and Miller, *Growing Girls*.

95. See Rosenthal, *Character Factory*, 11; and Proctor, *Scouting for Girls*, 1–10.

96. GSA, *Scouting for Girls*, 1.

97. On Low and the founding of the GSA, see Tedesco, "Making a Girl into a Scout," 19–39.

98. Sara Louise Arnold to Jane D. Rippin (GSA), December 20, 1924, Beard Papers, Box 131; and West to Rippin, January 11, 1925, ibid. See also West to Baden-Powell, January 4, 1922, ibid., Box 129.

99. Gulick quoted in Rowan, *To Do My Best*, 65.

100. BSA, *Policies and Regulations*, 1–3.

101. E. G. Stowell to West, March 12, 1925, Beard Papers, Box 131. See also "Minutes of the Fourth Annual Regional Meeting of Region Two, Boy Scouts of America, December 15, 1923," 8, Beard Papers, Box 210.

102. West to Rippin, January 11, 1925, Beard Papers, Box 131.

103. BSA, *Handbook for Boys* (1911), 15.

104. Ibid., 243–44.

105. BSA, *Handbook for Scout Masters* (1913), 278.

106. Beard, *Boy Heroes of Today*, contains accounts of Boy Scouts who received the gold honor medal for saving lives. It also acknowledges twenty-one boys who died in attempts to rescue others (eight).

107. See Paris, *Children's Nature*, 151–53; and Fass, *The Damned and the Beautiful*. On Boy Scouts' attitudes toward girls, see Mechling, *On My Honor*, 97–103; and Macleod, *Building Character*, 284.

108. Duane Paul to Beard, February 25, 1935, Beard Papers, Box 214.

109. See Macleod, *Building Character*, 288.

110. Snoke to John W. and Helen Snoke, August 1, 1924, Snoke Papers.

111. Baden-Powell, *Boy Scouts beyond the Seas*, 63. See also the accounts of this episode in the *Christian Science Monitor*, May 24 and August 21, 1911; and the *Kansas City Star*, May 27, 1911. These scouts were probably the sons of U.S. servicemen.

112. Tyrrell, *Reforming the World*.

113. Roosevelt quoted in Stratemeyer and Copeland, *American Boys' Life of Theodore Roosevelt*, 297–98.

114. Beveridge, *The Young Man and the World*, 336, 342.

115. Hall, "Universities and the Training of Professors," *Forum* 17 (May 1894): 302–3.

116. See Bederman, *Manliness and Civilization*, 104–20.

117. BSA, *Handbook for Boys* (1911), 333, 338–39.

118. Ibid., 239–40.

119. Ibid., 241. See also BSA, *Handbook for Scout Masters* (1913), 278–87.

120. "Our Country Is at War," *Boys' Life*, May 1918, 3.

121. "Every Boy Scout to Feed a Soldier," *Washington Post*, April 10, 1917; Ames, *Under Boy Scout Colors*, 296. See also Jordan, *Modern Manhood*, 106.

122. "Proclamation by the President of the United States," in BSA, *Annual Report* (1919), 43–44.

123. "Opportunities for Service," *Scouting*, December 1, 1915, 3; "Boy Scouts in Serbia Need Friends," *Scouting*, February 1, 1918, 13; "How Scouts Can Help the Red Cross," *Scouting*, November 14, 1918, 1; and "Boy Scouts of Devastated France," *Boys' Life*, June 1920, 30.

124. "Controversy of Boy Scouts Is Explained," *Christian Science Monitor*, April 20, 1917.

125. Anonymous Scout quoted in Peterson, *The Boy Scouts*, 85.

126. On Boy Scout fiction, see Mechling, "Heroism and the Problem of Impulsiveness," 42–43.

127. Ralphson, *Boy Scouts in the Philippines*. Ralphson wrote eighteen novels between 1910 and 1916 as part of his Boy Scouts adventure series. Many are set in imperial borderlands such as Panama, Mexico, and the Philippines.

128. Wilson, "The Three Young Citizens," *Boys' Life*, October 1924 to March 1925.

129. Roosevelt, *The Strenuous Life*.

130. "Approves Boy Scouts," *Boston Daily Globe*, September 24, 1910; "Roosevelt—Citizen," *Boys' Life*, February 1912, 30. On Roosevelt's brand of imperial manhood, see Bederman, *Manliness and Civilization*, 170–215.

131. "Give Praise to the Boy Scouts," *Baltimore American*, February 15, 1911; "Mr. Roosevelt and President Praise Scouts," *Christian Science Monitor*, February 15, 1911.

132. "Appeal to the American Boy," *Boys' Life*, December 1913, 13.

133. Theodore Roosevelt to James West, July 20, 1911, reprinted in BSA, *Handbook for Boys* (1911), 355. See also Murphy, *Political Manhood*, 1–2.

134. Banta, *Barbaric Intercourse*, 305–15.

135. Roosevelt quoted in "A Man to Be Thankful For," *Life Magazine*, December 2, 1957, 44. See also Rotundo, *American Manhood*, 259.

136. "Roosevelt in Argentina," *New York Times*, November 6, 1913; "Roosevelt Gets a Medal," *New York Times*, November 9, 1913. See also Ornig, *My Last Chance to Be a Boy*, 62.

137. "To Honor Roosevelt in True Scout Fashion," *Boys' Life*, February 1919, 26.

138. "Nation Mourns Roosevelt," *Scouting*, January 16, 1919, 2; "Hold Roosevelt Memorial Meetings," *Scouting*, February 6, 1919. See also "Memorials to Roosevelt to Be Held Soon," *Belleville News Democrat*, February 6, 1919; "Boy Scouts Will Honor Roosevelt," *Anaconda (MT) Standard*, February 8, 1919; "Churches Today Honor Memory of Late Ex-President," *Oregonian*, February 9, 1919.

139. "The Scout World," *Boys' Life*, December 1936, 23. *Boys' Life* covered the Roosevelt pilgrimages from 1920 to 1941. See also "Boy Scouts' Pilgrimage to Roosevelt's Grave," *New York Times*, September 28, 1930; and "Beard Leads 5,000 Scouts on Pilgrimage," *Washington Post*, October 25, 1936.

140. Beard, "Notes for the Roosevelt Pilgrimage, 1928," Beard Papers, Box 221; and "Resolution in Re: American Folk Lore," ibid., Box 127.

141. "The Scout World," *Boys' Life*, January 1931, 25.

142. White quoted in Studlar, *This Mad Masquerade*, 22.

143. Beard quoted Roosevelt's *Strenuous Life* address. "The Scout World," *Boys' Life*, December 1936, 23.

144. Beard, "Address for the 1929 Roosevelt Pilgrimage," Beard Papers, Box 221. Beard's dislike for bureaucrats and intellectuals also resonated in the slur "swivel chair," which he used with

relish. See Beard to Baden-Powell, September 5, 1929, September 9, 1934, and an undated note to George J. Fisher, Beard Papers, Box 24, 48.

145. Beard to Scout Executives, August 28, 1935, Beard Papers, Box 221.

2. From Africa to Antarctica

1. Mangum to West, November 3, 1928, Beard Papers, Box 132.

2. Both books were translated into German: David Martin Jr., Douglas L. Oliver, and Robert Dick Douglas Jr., *Drei Pfadfinder in Afrika*, trans. Felix Beran (Zurich, 1930); Paul Siple, *Mit Byrd zum Südpol*, trans. Felix Beran (Zurich: Orell Füssli, 1933).

3. Turner, "Betwixt and Between." Turner built his observations on the classic study by van Gennep, *The Rites of Passage*.

4. For similar caveats, see Gleason, "Avoiding the Agency Trap," and Miller, "Assent as Agency."

5. Marr, *Into the Frozen South*. On the Mexican Scouts, see Albarrán, "Boy Scouts under the Aztec Sun," 45. On the Venezuelan Scouts, see Scruggs, "Twelve Pairs of Boots," *Boys' Life*, July 1937, 20.

6. Roosevelt, *The Strenuous Life*. On Putnam, see Chapman and Mansfield, *Whistled Like a Bird*.

7. Lindbergh, "*We.*"

8. BSA, *Annual Report* (1927), 11.

9. Imperato and Imperato, *They Married Adventure*, 147–48; Putnam, *David Goes to Baffin Land*; and Putnam, *David Goes to Greenland*. See also Roosevelt Jr., "Scouts on Safari," *Boys' Life*, June 1928, 26; and Roosevelt Jr., "An Unusual Invitation," *Chief Scout Executive Bulletin*, January 30, 1928.

10. Official membership figures for every year can be found in the BSA's annual reports. The number of enrolled Scouts (including Lone Scouts, who do most of their scouting on their own, skyrocketed between 1915 and 1925 from 143,782 to 592,132. Over the next five years, the growth rate dwindled: the annual report for 1930 lists 617,254 active Scouts. BSA *Annual Report* (1930), 290. BSA leaders also worried about "lapsed troops," units that failed to retain enough members to function. BSA, *Chief Scout Executive Bulletin*, September 15, 1927, and March 3, 1928.

11. Lindsey and Evans, *The Revolt of Modern Youth*.

12. Thorp, "This Flapper Age," *Forum* 68 (August 1922): 639–43; "A Jazz Appeal to 'Flaming Youth,'" *Literary Digest*, April 24, 1926, 32. See also Fass, *The Damned and the Beautiful*, 119–67, 228–30. On dating culture, see Bailey, *From Front Porch to Back Seat*, 18. On the flapper, see Lowe, *Looking Good*, 103–34. On the global aspects of young modern femininity, see Weinbaum et al., *The Modern Girl around the World*.

13. Felando, "Hollywood in the 1920s," 82.

14. Holt and Thompson, "Man-of-Action Heroes," 425.

15. Tillery, "Little Babbitts," *Forum*, December 1930, 342.

16. BSA, *Community Boy Leadership*, 471–86. See also Macleod, *Building Character*, 281–86.

17. Richardson and Loomis, *The Boy Scout Movement*, 212; BSA, *Annual Report* (1922), 26; and "Around the World with the Boy Scouts," 56.

18. Hurt, "*Boy Facts*," 47.

19. "Reverence," *Boys' Life*, March 1931, 22.

20. West, "Peace-Time Slackers," *Rotarian*, May 1925, 20–21. See also Willrich, "Home Slackers."

21. Fisher, "The Boy and the Modern World," *Scout Executive*, February 1928, 6.

22. West, "Peace-Time Slackers," 20. See also Macleod, *Building Character*, 181–84.

23. *Boys' Life* during the 1920s regularly featured articles about star pilots and sea captains as well as ads that show Boy Scouts learning the latest consumer-friendly technology. See Haring, *Ham Radio's Technical Culture*, 42–44.

24. Douglas, Martin, and Oliver, *Three Boy Scouts in Africa*, xi.

25. "Scout Adventure," *Boys' Life*, June 1928, 24.

26. "How Would You Like to Go to Africa," *Boys' Life*, March 1928, 43; "Martin Johnson Writes from Africa," *Boys' Life*, April 1928, 46; "Do You Want to Go with Byrd to the Antarctic?," *Boys' Life*, July 1928, 9; Byrd, "The Great Challenge of Pioneering," *Boys' Life*, September 1928, 11, 58–59. See also Siple, *Boy Scout with Byrd*, 153–65.

27. Douglas, *The Best 90 Years of My Life*, 51. See also "Three Boy Scouts in Africa: An Interview with David Martin," Oral History Collection, BSA National Scouting Museum.

28. F. D. Coman to Captain Railey, n.d., Richard E. Byrd Papers, Box 27.

29. Jack Bowman to Byrd, August 15, 1928, Byrd Papers, Box 27; Siple, *Boy Scout with Byrd*, 154–55.

30. "Scouts in Race for Honor of Joining Byrd's Expedition," *New York Herald Tribune*, August 18, 1928.

31. Walter H. Smith to the Committee in Charge of the Selection (Application Materials for Byrd Expedition), Paul A. Siple Family Papers, BSA/Correspondence, Box 10. See also William Spencer to Byrd, July 13, 1928, Byrd Papers, Box 118.

32. Malcolm C. Douglas to West, "Memo. To Mr. West: Re: Choice of Scout for Byrd Expedition," August 18, 1928, Byrd Papers, Box 27.

33. On Siple's support of prohibition, see "Who Will Our Next President Be," Paul Siple Papers, Box 1.

34. See also Siple, *Boy Scout with Byrd*, 158.

35. "Paul Is Typical American Youth," *Erie Dispatch-Herald*, August 21, 1928. Similar reports include "Boy Scout Orderly Is Named for Byrd," *New York Times*, August 21, 1928; "Erie Scout Chosen to Go to Antarctic," *Washington Post*, August 21, 1928; and "Paul Siple, Eagle Scout, to Accompany Byrd to Antarctic," *Berkeley Daily Gazette*, September 3, 1928.

36. West quoted in Siple, *Boy Scout with Byrd*, 164. See also "With Byrd to the Antarctic," *Boys' Life*, October 1928, 17, 66; and "Young America Sees Byrd's Ship off to South Pole," *Sandusky Star Journal*, August 29, 1928.

37. "The Romance of Scouting," *Daily Record* (magazine of the Sixth BSA National Training Conference), March 16, 1936. See also "Boy Scouts and High Adventure," *Scout Executive: Equipment Number* (1928–29): 3.

38. Patzert to Byrd, August 22, 1928, Byrd Papers, Box 27.

39. Frank N. Robinson to West, August 15, 1928, ibid.; and West to Byrd, August 15, 1928, ibid. Several letters sent to Byrd directly from Boy Scouts are filed in Byrd Papers, Box 118. Some applicants were as young as eleven years of age.

40. "Charleston Eagle Scout Qualified to Make South Pole Flight with Commander Byrd," *Charleston Daily Mail*, June 17, 1928.

41. "Diary of Scout Paul A. Siple: Member, Byrd Antarctic Expedition," August 25, September 7, and October 8, 1928, Siple Family Papers, Expedition Records, Box 1.

42. Siple, *Boy Scout with Byrd*, 5. See also "Byrd Crew Is Happy as Ship Rolls South," *Buffalo Evening News*, August 29, 1929; "A Million-Dollar Attack on the South Pole," *Literary Digest*, September 15, 1928, 35–52; "Georgia Negro Is Headed South," *Statesville Landmark*, August 30, 1928. Lanier was forced to leave the ship in Panama because he was deemed unfit for the hardships of mariner life. "Byrd Ship Drops Negro Stowaway," *New York Times*, September 17, 1928.

43. On perceptions of Africa in early twentieth-century U.S. society, see Jones, *In Search of Brightest Africa.*

44. Roosevelt, *African Game Trails*, 3. See also Bederman, *Manliness and Civilization*, 207–13.

45. As a sign of appreciation, TR dedicated his safari book to Kermit.

46. Roosevelt Jr., "Scouts on Safari," 26.

47. Douglas, Martin, and Oliver, *Three Boy Scouts in Africa*, xxv. See also "Three Boy Scouts in Africa: An Interview with David Martin."

48. Siple, *Boy Scout with Byrd*, 163.

49. Byrd, "This Hero Business," *Ladies Home Journal*, January 1927, 21; and Byrd, *Skyward*, 191–95. See also Studlar, *This Mad Masquerade*, 12–75.

50. "Martin Johnson Writes from Africa," 46; "Safari," *Boys' Life*, July 1928, 24. See also Jones, *In Brightest Africa*, 177–210; and Enright, *The Maximum of Wilderness.*

51. "Boy Scout, 16, to Hunt Grizzlies in Alaska," *New York Times*, May 6, 1929. See also Imperato and Imperato, *They Married Adventure*, 147. Martin Johnson recounts that "there had been some objections at home" about whether the Boy Scouts should shoot a lion. Johnson, *Lion*, 234.

52. Johnson, *Camera Trails in Africa*, 197.

53. Douglas, Martin, and Oliver, *Three Boy Scouts in Africa*, viii. See also "Safari," 24.

54. Johnson, *Lion*, 233. See also Douglas, Martin, and Oliver, *Three Boy Scouts in Africa*, 22; and Imperato and Imperato, *They Married Adventure*, 148.

55. See Enright, *The Maximum of Wilderness*, 65–67; and Czech, *With Rifle and Petticoat*, 168–70.

56. On Byrd, see Rose, *Explorer*. Byrd's first Antarctic expedition from 1928 to 1930 is the subject of Rodgers, *Beyond the Barrier*. On the BSA's admiration for Byrd, see the piece Byrd wrote for West, *The Boy Scout's Book of True Adventure*, 122–34.

57. Byrd, "Crusaders," *Saturday Evening Post*, September 22, 1928; "Land Claims in Antarctica Come to the Fore," *New York Times*, January 5, 1930; and "The Conquest of Antarctica by Air," *National Geographic Magazine*, August 1930, 127, 168.

58. "Into the Home of the Blizzard," *New York Times*, September 23, 1928.

59. Byrd quoted in "Scout to Accompany Antarctic Expedition," *Scouting*, July 1928, 4.

60. "Red-Blooded Romance on Byrd Ship," *Zanesville Sunday Times-Signal*, August 26, 1928; "Byrd Is the Born Adventurer," *New York Times*, April 1, 1928.

61. See Byrd, "How I Select My Men," *Saturday Evening Post*, April 21, 1928.

62. "This Boy Goes with Byrd," *Sandusky Star Journal*, August 24, 1928. See also Rodgers, *Beyond the Barrier*, 21.

63. "Scout with Byrd Greets His Mother," *Boys' Life*, July 1929, 29.

64. "Diary of Scout Paul A. Siple," April 13 and 20, 1929.

65. "This Boy Goes With Byrd."

66. Douglas, Martin, and Oliver, *Three Boy Scouts in Africa*, 36–47, 77–93, 108–21.

67. "Daisy Air Rifles" advertisement, *Boys' Life*, March 1927, 2. Companies producing Springfield guns and Benjamin air rifles also advertised regularly in this magazine. Remington manufactured a "Boy Scout Special" rifle. See also Gregg Lee Carter, "Guns," in *Boyhood in America: An Encyclopedia*, 332.

68. Douglas, Martin, and Oliver, *Three Boy Scouts in Africa*, 44, 46–47. The scene is also recounted in Johnson, *Lion*, 237–38.

69. "Three Boy Scouts Return from Battles in Jungle," *San Antonio Express*, September 30, 1928.

70. Johnson, *Lion*, 232, 252; Douglas, Martin, and Oliver, *Three Boy Scouts in Africa*, xiv. See also "Boy Scouts Show Craft in Africa," *New York Times*, October 21, 1928; and "For Fun, Go to Africa," *Sandusky Star Journal*, September 27, 1928.

71. Douglas, *The Best 90 Years of My Life*, 56.

72. Douglas, Martin, and Oliver, *Three Boy Scouts in Africa*, 113. Osa Johnson's prowess as a hunter is acknowledged elsewhere in the book, especially on pp. 27–28. See also Czech, *With Rifle and Petticoat*, 166–71.

73. "3 Boy Scouts Back from Lion Shoot," *New York Times*, September 19, 1928.

74. See Jordan, "'Conservation of Boyhood.'"

75. Johnson, *Lion*, 234–35; and Douglas, Martin, and Oliver, *Three Boy Scouts in Africa*, 31.

76. "For Fun, Go to Africa"; Imperato and Imperato, *They Married Adventure*, 150.

77. Douglas, Martin, and Oliver, *Three Boy Scouts in Africa*, 148.

78. Ibid., 44.

79. Johnson, *Lion*, 241.

80. Siple, "Thoughts on Admiral Byrd," Siple Family Papers, Expedition Records, Box 3. See also Siple, *Boy Scout with Byrd*, 151.

81. "Siple Fights Killer Whales," *Erie Dispatch-Herald*, January 23, 1929; "Siple Aids Rescue in Far South," *Erie Dispatch-Herald*, November 13, 1929, Siple Family Papers, Expedition Records, Box 6; "Siple Drills Through Ice," *New York Times*, December 16, 1929.

82. H. R. Spencer to Siple, August 27, 1928, Siple Family Papers, Expedition Records, Box 4.

83. Malcolm C. Douglas to Siple, September 27, 1928, ibid.

84. West to Siple, May 1, 1930, Siple Family Papers, BSA/Correspondence, Box 2.

85. "Diary of Scout Paul A. Siple," August 28, 1928, and October 25, 1928.

86. Ibid., August 28 and September 15, 1928.

87. Ibid., December 25, 1928. In retrospect, Siple complained that the "filthy language" about him during the expedition had made him "heartsick." "Loose Diary Entry," October 30, 1933, ibid., Box 8.

88. Owen, *South of the Son*, 57–58.

89. "Diary of Scout Paul A. Siple," September 12 and 13, 1928.

90. A cartoon drawn by one of the expedition members, which he titled "'Penguin Paul' at Work," shows Siple sitting in the corner of the mess hall over his penguins. Siple Family Papers, Expedition Records, Box 2.

91. Siple to West, September 28, 1928, Siple Family Papers, Expedition Records, Box 4. At times, Paul was frustrated that Byrd would not let him go on the trail with the sled dogs "because I am a little Boy Scout and the Commander won't let me go." See "Diary of Scout Paul A. Siple," May 3, 1929. See also Siple, *90 Degrees South*, 42.

92. Smith, *By the Seat of My Pants*, 179; "Diary of Scout Paul A. Siple," May 9, 1929: "The sober were sick of it and the drunk were sick with it."

93. "Diary of Scout Paul A. Siple," February 7, 1930: "The confidential letter . . . more or less took the comd off his feet and he called me in for a conference."

94. Ibid., July 21, 1929: "I promised to keep absolute silence and secrecy to what he told me. But I can say this: He has one grand idea and ideal which puts more pep into me for the expedition." "Loyal League Oath" (undated), Byrd Papers, Box 128.

95. "Diary of Scout Paul A. Siple," February 14, 1930.

96. Robinson to Siple, September 27, 1928, Siple Family Papers, BSA/Correspondence, Box 2. Robinson continued, "I was glad to hear intimate stories from you of your life aboard ships. But be careful who gets it—at least, caution them about how eager the newspapers are for sensational stuff about booze—etc., etc. For the same reason, whatever you send me (or Mr. West) you had better mark 'Personal.'"

97. Siple, *Boy Scout with Byrd*, iii; "A Tribute from Admiral Byrd," *Boys' Life*, June 1930, 69. See also "Diary of Scout Paul A. Siple," June 24, 1929.

98. Seminal studies on this topic are Pratt, *Imperial Eyes*; and Clark, *Travel Writing and Empire*.

99. Douglas, Martin, and Oliver, *Three Boy Scouts in Africa*, 26–27.

100. Ibid., 51, 54–56, 68, 142.

101. Homi K. Bhabha coined the concept of mimicry for postcolonial scholarship. See Bhabha, "Of Mimicry and Man."

102. Johnson, *Lion*, 233.

103. Douglas, *The Best 90 Years of My Life*, 56; Johnson, *Lion*, 247–48; Douglas, Martin, and Oliver, *Three Boy Scouts in Africa*, 80.

104. Osa Johnson quoted in Imperato and Imperato, *They Married Adventure*, 353.

105. "Boy Scouts Show Craft in Africa," *New York Times*, October 21, 1928.

106. "Diary of Scout Paul A. Siple," September 16, 1928. See also Siple, *Boy Scout with Byrd*, 7–10.

107. Douglas, Martin, and Oliver, *Three Boy Scouts in Africa*, 51.

108. Ibid., xiv.

109. Douglas, *The Best 90 Years of My Life*, 53–54.

110. "Three Boy Scouts Return from Battles in Jungle," *San Antonio Express*, September 30, 1928.

111. Johnson, *Lion*, 249–50.

112. Siple expressed his abhorrence of cross-racial sexual encounters in racist portrayals of indigenous populations. Tahitian girls are described as "flabby, flatfaced individuals" who had "degenerated to a pitiful degree." Siple, *Boy Scout with Byrd*, 17. See also "Loose diary entries," November 19, 1933, Siple Family Papers, Expeditions/BAE II, Box 8.

113. "Siple Is Lionized during Stay in Canal Zone," *Erie Dispatch-Herald*, June 4, 1930.

114. See, for example, the report "Dans les glaces de l'Antarctique" in the Swiss Scout magazine *L'Eclaireur*, May 1931, 80–84.

115. See Alexander, "The Girl Guide Movement and Imperial Internationalism."

116. "Diary of Scout Paul A. Siple," March 15 and April 1, 1930; "Billiards Limited to Byrd," March 20, 1930, Siple Family Papers, BSA/Correspondence, Box 2.

117. Douglas, Martin, and Oliver, *Three Boy Scouts in Africa*, 9. See also Douglas, *The Best 90 Years of My Life*, 52; and "To Greet Our Boy Scouts," *New York Times*, July 4, 1928.

118. "Three Boy Scouts Return from Battles in Jungle"; Grazia, *Irresistible Empire*.

119. van Gennep, *Rites of Passage*, 20–36.

120. See, for example, "Three Boy Scouts Are Home from Africa, Tell of Shooting Big Lions," *New Castle News*, September 19, 1928; "Three Boy Scouts Return from Battles in Jungle," *San Antonio Express*, September 30, 1928; "An Eagle Scout Back from Africa Talked Here Friday," *Evening Tribune* (Albert Lea, MN), November 26, 1928; Douglas, *The Best 90 Years of My Life*, 61.

121. "My Diary," *Scouting* (jamboree edition), August 8, 1929. On the commercial success of *Three Boy Scouts in Africa*, see Douglas, *The Best 90 Years of My Life*, 61.

122. "The Scout World," *Boys' Life*, August 1930, 25.

123. Amos R. Shields (scout executive) to Siple, December 3, 1930, Siple Family Papers, BSA/Correspondence, Box 2.

124. Alton A. Lindsey, "A Far Way with Paul Siple," 10, Alton A. Lindsey Papers, Box 1.

125. Beard, "Greetings to Paul Siple," March 26, 1929, Paul Siple File, BSA National Archives; and West, "Suggested Outline for an Address on the Occasion of Paul Siple's Return to Erie, Pa.," June 30, 1930, ibid.

126. August Horowitz to Siple, October 12, 1929, Siple Family Papers, Expeditions/BAE I, Box 4.

127. "Honors Awarded Detroit Scouts at Rally," attached to a letter to Siple from H. W. White (a Detroit scout executive), February 17, 1931, ibid., BSA/Correspondence, Box 2; "Eagle Scout Siple Tells of Glamour and Romance on Trip to South Pole," *Manitowoc Herald Times*, January 28, 1936.

128. BSA, "Region Six News Letter," July 30, 1931, Siple Family Papers, Misc. Scout Publications, Box 11.

129. "Lectures and Announcements," ibid., BSA/Correspondence, Box 11.

130. West to Siple, June 9, July 1, and July 11, 1930, Siple Family Papers, BSA/Correspondence, Box 2; Frank N. Robinson to Siple, July 17, 31, and August 7, 1930, ibid.; and August Horowitz to Siple, January 26, 1931, ibid. See "Boy Scout Tells of Expedition," *Marion (OH) Star*, January 24, 1931; "Boy Scout in Book Writes of Byrd Trip," *New York Times*, January 28, 1931; and "Paul Siple Writes," *Buffalo Evening News*, January 31, 1931, for a sample of positive reviews.

131. West did not like that Siple's draft mentioned the lack of sleep on the part of the men, fearing that it cast a negative light on Byrd as a leader. "Paul Siple's book," Memorandum from Chief Scout Executive, October 11, 1930, Paul Siple File.

132. Siple to August Horowitz, July 24, 1930, Siple Family Papers, BSA/Correspondence, Box 1; West to Siple, October 10, 1930, ibid., Box 2.

133. Paul Siple to Remo M. Lombardi, July 29, 1930, ibid., Box 1.

134. These trips resulted in three more books published with Putnam: Douglas, *A Boy Scout in the Grizzly Country*; Martin, *A Boy Scout with the 'Sea Devil'*; and Oliver, *A Boy Scout in the Grand Cavern*.

135. "Paul Siple as Aide Inspects the Camps," *New York Times*, July 2, 1937. Siple wrote daily columns for the *Jamboree Journal* titled "With Siple of Little America at the Big Jamboree."

136. "Obituary: Paul Allman Siple," *Polar Record* 14, no. 93 (1969): 854–55. On Siple's postwar career, see Farish, "Creating Cold War Climates."

3. A Junior League of Nations

1. Beard to Fisher, April 14, 1920, Beard Papers, Box 48; Borah, *Americanism*, 13.

2. Robert Baden-Powell, "League of Youth," *Jamboree*, October 1922, 113; "A Junior League of Nations," *Boys' Life*, September 1924, 3; "The Junior League of Nations," *Jamboree*, January 1925, 407; "Our Great Family of 50,000: Junior League of Nations at the Jamboree," *Derby Daily Telegraph*, August 1, 1929.

3. Historical scholarship on the world jamborees is stunningly meager. One British-centered exception is Proctor, *On My Honour*, 93–106. See also my cursory observations in Honeck, "An Empire of Youth."

4. See Savage, *Teenage*, 181–251; Fass, *Children of a New World*, 202–18; and Rosenberg, "Transnational Currents in a Shrinking World."

5. This distinction is prominent in Proctor, *On My Honour*, 131–50.

6. On the place of children in modern configurations of internationalism and humanitarianism, see Malkki, "Children, Humanity, and the Infantilization of Peace."

7. See Endy, "Travel and World Power"; Rydell, *World of Fairs*; Laqua, *Internationalism Reconfigured*; Gorman, *The Emergence of International Society*; Rupp, *Worlds of Women*; and Green, *The Other Americans*.

8. Carter, "These Wild Young People," *Atlantic Monthly*, September 1920, 302.

9. Barrie, *Courage*, 20.

10. "A League of Youth," *Harvard Crimson*, May 23, 1922.

11. Locke, "Negro Youth Speaks."

12. See Mishler, *Raising Reds*; and Neumann, *The Communist Youth League*.

13. See Weinbaum et al., *The Modern Girl around the World*; and Conor, *The Spectacular Modern Woman*.

14. On the origins of these institutions, see BSIB, *The Jamboree Story*, 9–15; Vallory, *World Scouting*, 7–50; and Jeal, *Baden-Powell*, 510–12.

15. See Mitcham, *Race and Imperial Defence*.

16. McCarthy, "The League of Nations," 118. See also Proctor, *On My Honour*, 93–106.

17. Beard to Fisher, January 13 and April 14, 1920, Beard Papers, Box 48.

18. Macleod, *Building Character*, 151, 183. Recognized for his service to youth and international finance, Schiff appeared on the cover of the February 14, 1927, issue of *Time* magazine. On Schiff, see also Pak, *Gentlemen Bankers*, 125–30.

19. "High Spots at the Jamboree," *Scouting*, September 1920, 8–9; Wilson, *Scouting Round the World*, 45; BSA, *Annual Report* (1920), 38.

20. BSA, *Annual Report* (1920), 37–38, 65; BSA Executive Board Meeting, January 21 and March 24, 1922, Beard Papers, Box 210. See also "Scouting to the Rescue in Devastated France," *Boys' Life*, August 1920, 32; Schiff, "Scouting from Jersey to Japan," *Our World*, October 1922, 110–15. For the French response, see BSA, *Official Report* (1922), 7–9.

21. "What Is a Brother For?" *Scouting*, May 1922, 3; BSA, *Annual Report* (1923), 62–63.

22. "Missionaries of Scouting," *Boys' Life*, November 1925, 21; "Visit of Boy Scouts of America to Cuba," *Jamboree*, April 1930, 1077.

23. Wilson, *Scouting Round the World*, 45; "An International Friendship Fund," *Scouting: World Jamboree Edition*, August 2, 1929; "World-Wide Scouting," *Scouting*, October 1929, 323.

24. Harris, *This Rotarian Age*, 14, 58, 220. On Rotary's origins and global spread, see de Grazia, *Irresistible Empire*, 26–36.

25. Head to Roosevelt Jr., August 4, 1937, The Papers of Theodore Roosevelt Jr., Box 28.

26. Schiff, "Scouting among the Nations," *Jamboree*, October 1930, 1138.

27. Martin, "Scouting in America," *Jamboree*, January 1929, 928–30; "Report to Sir Alfred Pickford, of Mr. John A. Stiles, as British Representative to the Fourth Biannual Conference of the Executives of the Boy Scouts of America," Beard Papers, Box 133. See also J. D. Makgill (British national scout commissioner) to James Storrow (BSA), March 16, 1926, ibid.

28. BSA, *National Conference of Scout Masters and Executives*, 19.

29. Guérin-Desjardins quoted in "From Conference to Conference—III," *Jamboree: Journal of World Scouting*, June 1947, 168. On his last visit to the United States in 1935, Baden-Powell begrudged that he saw too many Scouts "going about their work with long faces." Baden-Powell to Head, July 19, 1935, Beard Papers, Box 60.

30. Lord Hampton, "Summary of Impressions Gained During My Visit to the Boy Scouts of America," ibid., Box 133.

31. Baden-Powell quoted in Jeal, *Baden-Powell*, 489. See also Martin, "Scouting in America"; Rowan, *To Do My Best*, 89–90; and Mcleod, *Building Character*, 136–45.

32. Martin to Baden-Powell, June 22, 1923, Founder's Files, U.S.A. (Visits and General), TC/54.

33. Baden-Powell quoted in Johnston, "Looking Wide?," 65.

34. Schiff to West, June 22, 1924, Beard Papers, Box 132.

35. West to Head, May 15, 1926, ibid., Box 133. See also Jeal, *Baden-Powell*, 488–91.

36. West to Beard, September 14, 1937, Beard Papers, Box 138. See also Rowan, *To Do My Best*, 158–59.

37. Wilson, *Scouting Round the World*, 45.

38. Ibid., 21–22; "World-Wide Scouting," *Scouting*, August 1922, 4; Baden-Powell, "Opening Address to the Delegates," *BSIC Conference Proceedings*, "From Conference to Conference—II," *Jamboree: Journal of World Scouting*, May 1947, 147.

39. "The Third International Conference," *Boys' Life*, December 1924, 55–56; Wilson, *Scouting Round the World*, 69; "Resolutions Adopted by the Third International Scout Conference," *Jamboree*, October 1924, 373.

40. *Jamboree*, October 1924, 373–74.

41. "Minority Scouts," *Jamboree*, October 1926, 660–61; Wilson, *Scouting Round the World*, 69–70.

42. See, for example, Head, "To the Chief Scout of the World," in BSA, *The World Jamboree*, 1.

43. Cecil quoted in Boy Scouts Association (Great Britain), *The Jamboree Book*, 102. See also McCarthy, "League of Nations," 118.

44. League of Nations, "Second General Conference on Communications and Transit: Travel Facilities for Groups of Students, Boy Scouts, and Girl Guides, November 17, 1923," Boy Scouts File, Dossier No. 22650; "Message from the Secretary General of the League of Nations," *Jamboree*, January 1924, 274; Baden-Powell, "League Realizes Value of Scouts," *Christian Science Monitor*, January 24, 1924.

45. Schiff to West, June 22, 1924; Nitobe, "Report to the Secretary General," August 27 and 28, 1924, Boy Scout File, Dossier No. 22650.

46. On efforts to introduce a League of Nations merit badge, see Baden-Powell to Dame Rachel, November 22, 1922, Boy Scout File, Dossier No. 22650; and Christobal Rodriguez to W. Lewis Bailey, August 8, 1924, ibid., Dossier No. 41815.

47. Owen W. Matthews, "How Can America Stay Out of War?" *Boys' Life*, July 1936, 19, 49; "Just Wrote What I Knew, Stunned Youth Explains," *Oregonian*, April 20, 1936. See also West to Beard, April 20, 1936, Beard Papers, Box 135.

48. "U.S. Scouts Entertain Foreigners with 'Flapjacks' and Harmonicas," *Evening Huronite* (Huron, SD), August 17, 1933.

49. "The League of Youth," *Punch Magazine*, August 4, 1920, 91.

50. "Patrols of Peace," *Punch Magazine*, July 31, 1929, 127; "Again—Youth Points the Way," *Jamboree*, June 29, 1937, 5.

51. "The Place of Competitions at the Jamborees," *Jamboree*, October 1926, 666–68; "Resolutions," ibid., 668.

52. "Scouts of 71 Lands in World Jamboree," *New York Times*, July 31, 1929.

53. Baden-Powell quoted in BSIB, *The Jamboree Story*, 36.

54. Ibid., 51.

55. Ibid., 35–38. See also Jeal, *Baden-Powell*, 514.

56. Bookstaber, "Scouting and the 12th Law," *Scouting*, January 1934, 26.

57. Kirkham, *A World Program for Friendship, Brotherhood, and Peace*.

58. Boy Scouts Association (Great Britain), *The Jamboree Book, 1920*, 15; West, *The Scout Jamboree Book*, 24, 71; BSA, *The National and World Jamborees in Pictures*, 169.

59. At Ermelunden, Danish scouter Hartvig Møller recalled seeing "men with tears in their eyes" as boys from different nations rushed forward to gather around Baden-Powell. Knudsen, *Jamboree Denmark*, 2.

60. "The Boy Scouts' Great Jamboree," *Literary Digest*, August 31, 1929.

61. "Diary of Richard Roswell Lyman, 1935–1937," vol. 1, 226, Mormon Missionary Diary Collection.

62. Daniel Carter Beard to Robert Baden-Powell, September 5, 1929, Beard Papers, Box 24.

63. "Boy Scout Founder Attends Jamboree," *New York Times*, August 2, 1933; "Hungary: Fourth Jamboree," *Time Magazine*, August 14, 1933, 78.

64. Anonymous French scouter quoted in BSA, *Third Biennial Conference*, 363.

65. "World Champion Sea Scouts back from Jamboree," *Chicago Daily Tribune*, August 24, 1929; Beard to Baden-Powell, September 5, 1929, Beard Papers, Box 24.

66. Fisher quoted in BSA, *The National and World Jamborees in Pictures*, 130.

67. West and Hillcourt, *The 1933 Scout Jamboree Book*, 6.

68. "Archbishop Conducts Services for Scouts at Birkenhead," *New Castle News*, August 10, 1929.

69. "The Boy Scouts' Great Jamboree."

70. On "minor utopias," see Winter, *Dreams of Peace and Freedom*, 1–7.

71. The World Scout Bureau Archives, in Geneva, Switzerland, has a collection of maps depicting all world jamboree campgrounds since 1924. Some point out the location of each national delegation.

72. West, *The Scout Jamboree Book*, 39.

73. Baden-Powell to Michal Grazynski (undated, probably August 1937), Founder's Files (World Jamborees, Vogelenzang), TC/56.

74. Strunk, *Die Pfadfinder in Deutschland*, 183. On the origins of the Pfadfinder movement in Germany, see Bowersox, *Raising Germans*, 165–211.

75. Wilson, *Scouting Round the World*, 90.

76. "Rückblick und Ausblick," *Neues Deutschland*, March 22, 1947.

77. On twentieth-century female internationalism, see Berkovitch, *From Motherhood to Citizenship*; and Steans, *Gender and International Relations*.

78. On the internationalization of the Girl Guides and Girl Scouts, see Proctor, *Scouting for Girls*, 101–46; and Alexander, *Guiding Modern Girls*.

79. "First Lady Greets World Girl Scouts," *New York Times*, August 11, 1937.

80. "Where Do the Boy Scouts Stand?" *Army and Navy Journal*, December 2, 1922.

81. Baden-Powell, "Education in Love in Place of Fear," *Jamboree*, January 1923, 326.

82. Schiff, "Scouting among the Nations," 1138.

83. Baden-Powell, "World Patriotism," *Jamboree*, October 1923, 231.

84. Schiff, "Scouting from Jersey to Japan," 110, 112.

85. Hungarian Boy Scout Association, *Jamboree 1924*.

86. Deloria, *Playing Indian*, 95–127. See also Huhndorf, *Going Native*, 69–78.

87. Rydell and Kroes, *Buffalo Bill in Bologna*, 29–34. On Indians in the German imagination, see Penny, *Kindred by Choice*; and Lutz, "German Indianthusiasm," 167–84.

88. BSA, *Handbook for Boys* (1928), 538–39.

89. On Hubbard's Boy Scout work, see Yost, *A Man as Big as the West*, 90–122; Snoke, "50th Anniversary: International Scout Jamboree at Copenhagen, Denmark, 1924–1974 (unpublished)," 3, Snoke Papers.

90. On the use of folklore in cultural diplomacy, see Schwartz, "The Regional and the Global"; and Peer, *France on Display*.

91. "High Spots at the Jamboree," *Scouting*, September 16, 1920, 8; "The Leaders," *Boys' Life*, September 1924, 47.

92. Yost, *A Man as Big as the West*, 108; Albert Snoke to John W. and Helen Snoke, July 14, 17, and 22, 1924, Snoke Papers, Box 22.

93. "High Spots at the Jamboree," *Scouting*, 8.

94. Yost, *A Man as Big as the West*, 107–8.

95. Hubbard quoted in BSA, *Third Biennial Conference*, 443.

96. Eastman, *The Indian To-Day*, 164–78.

97. BSA, *Handbook for Scout Masters* (1913), 280.

98. BSA, *Official Report* (1922), 8; "L'Écriture Imagée des Indiens," *Le Journal des Éclaireurs*, February 15, 1925, 53–56; Wu, "'A Life of Make-Believe.'" On the popularity of playing Indian in U.S. scouting, see BSA, *Community Boy Leadership*, 410–20.

99. West, *The Scout Jamboree Book*, 102–3; Schiff, "World Jamboree—1929," *Boys' Life*, August 1929, 8; "Hatchet of War Buried at World Scout Jamboree," *Ludington Daily News*, August 27, 1929.

100. "High Spots at the Jamboree," *Scouting*, September 16, 1920, 9.

101. "South African Dance," *Scouting: World Jamboree Edition*, August 3, 1929; "Fort Sam Houston Boy Believes Jamboree Helps Cause of World Peace," *San Antonio Express*, August 25, 1929.

102. Tomkins, *Universal Indian Sign Language*. See also "A Universal Language for the Jamboree," *Jamboree*, January 1929, 927–28; "Boy Scouts at Jamboree Will Study Indian Signs," *New York Times*, July 14, 1929.

103. "Scouts of 71 Lands in World Jamboree," *New York Times*, July 31, 1929.

104. West, *The Scout Jamboree Book*, 79–83; Schiff, "World Jamboree—1929," *Boys' Life*, August 1929, 8; "Latest News about the Jamboree," *Scouting*, August 1929, 277.

105. British Boy Scout Association, *The Jamboree Book*, 118; West, "The International Jamboree," *Boys' Life*, October 1920, 50.

106. West and Hillcourt, *The 1933 Scout Jamboree Book*, 95, 122–23.

107. Ibid., 31–32.

108. See also Paris, *Children's Nature*; and van Slyck, *A Manufactured Wilderness*.

109. "The Scout World," *Boys' Life*, October 1937, 50.

110. "The Eastman Kodak Awards," *Scouting*, December 1929, 375.

111. West and Hillcourt, *The 1933 Scout Jamboree Book*, 95, 122–23.

112. Snoke, "50th Anniversary," 9–10.

113. "The Scout Jamboree," *Ludington Daily News*, August 29, 1929; "American Luxuries Criticized," *New York Times*, August 1, 1929. Five years earlier, a Danish publication noted that many participants "were of the opinion that the Americans were very pretentious and very reserved compared to the boys of the other nations." Knudsen, *Jamboree Denmark*, 11.

114. "Scouts Have 'Rich Man's Row,'" *Christian Science Monitor*, July 31, 1929; Smith, *Jamboree Joys*, 24.

115. "American Scouters Just 'Softies' to Associates at World Jamboree," *Atlanta Constitution*, September 2, 1937.

116. Herrmann to West, September 29, 1926, Beard Papers, Box 133.

117. "Scout Camp Resembles City with Shops, Cafe, and Banks," *Christian Science Monitor*, July 31, 1937.

118. BSA, *Pre-Jamboree Camp Training Manual for Jamboree Troops*, 10.

119. Beard, "Roosevelt Pilgrimage 1933 (Private Notes)," Beard Papers, Box 221.

120. Baden-Powell, "The Jamboree at Arrowe Park," in *Playing the Game*, 266.

121. Albert Snoke to John W. and Helen Snoke, August 11, 1924; "Brief Daily Log of the American Delegation," August 9, 1924, World Jamboree Collection, Box 1924.

122. "Boy Scout's Letter," *Oak Parker*, August 30, 1929.

123. "Fort Sam Houston Boy Believes Jamboree Helps Cause of World Peace," *San Antonio Express*, August 25, 1929.

124. Douglas Oliver, "As I Saw the Jamboree," *Boys' Life*, October 1929, 20.

125. "Jamboree Scout Tells of Trip," *Idaho Falls Post-Register*, August 16, 1937.

126. Smith, *Jamboree Joys*, 21.

127. "Stowaway Fails to Reach Jamboree," *New York Times*, August 7, 1929; "Boy Scout Stowaway on Liner Will Not Get a Chance to Attend British Jamboree," *Evening Independent* (Massillon, OH), August 6, 1929.

128. West, *The Scout Jamboree Book*, 66; West and Hillcourt, *The 1933 Scout Jamboree Book*, 54–55.

129. Kemp quoted in Townley, *Legacy of Honor*, 17.

130. "Jimmie Ricklefs Tells of Fun at Scout Jamboree," *Monticello Express*, August 22, 1929.

131. "When Johnny Comes Marching Home," *Scouting: World Jamboree Edition*, August 3, 1929.

132. Smith, *Jamboree Joys*, 25; "A Request," *Scouting: World Jamboree Edition*, August 2, 1929.

133. West and Hillcourt, *The 1933 Scout Jamboree Book*, 57–58.

134. William (anonymous) to his parents, August 2, World Jamboree Collection, Box 1929.

135. "One Day at the Scouts' Jamboree," *Evening Telegraph*, August 21, 1929.

136. "Scots Lead to Scout Brotherhood," *Dundee Courier*, August 12, 1929.

137. Hopkins to Ong, 1930–1976, Walter J. Ong Manuscript Collection, Filed Correspondence, Folder 309.

138. "World Brotherhood of Boys," *Boys' Life*, February 1922, 29.

139. BSA, *Handbook for Boys* (1913), 35.

140. See Wilson, *Scouting Round the World*, 89.

141. West, *The Scout Jamboree Book*, 36.

142. West and Hillcourt, *The 1933 Scout Jamboree Book*, 69.

143. "Jamboo and Ree," *Jamboree Journal*, July 6, 1937.

144. "Jimmie Ricklefs Tells of Fun at Scout Jamboree."

145. Smith, *Jamboree Joys*, 29.

146. "Spencer A. Gard Talk at Scout Jamboree Anniv. Reunion, May 18, 1989," Walter J. Ong Manuscript Collection, General Files, Folder 205.

147. "Jamboree Diary by Eugene L. Vickery," August 3, 1929, World Jamboree Collection, Box 1929.

148. "Travel Diary of Walter J. Ong," Walter J. Ong Manuscript Collection, General Files, Folder 202.

149. Jobs, "Youth Movements," 376–404.

150. Nelson quoted in "Three Famous Boy Scouts Recall," *Family Weekly*, July 30, 1967.

151. Albert Snoke to John W. and Helen Snoke, August 22, 1924.

152. Ibid., August 26, 1924.

153. "American Scouters Just 'Softies' to Associates at World Jamboree."

154. "A Street Scene in Brussels Lures Visiting American Scout," *Kansas City Star*, September 1, 1929.

155. "Youthful Odyssey Relived," *Kansas City Star*, May 18, 1979, Walter J. Ong Manuscript Collection, General Files, Folder 205.

156. "Jamboree Diary by Eugene L. Vickery," August 29, 1929.

157. "Boy Scout News," *Oak Parker*, September 12, 1924.

158. Albert Snoke to John W. and Helen Snoke, August 25, 1924.

159. "Diary of Byron Stoothoff," August 12, 1929, World Jamboree Collection, Box 1929.

160. Smith, *Jamboree Joys*, 7.

161. Ibid., 23.

162. Albert Snoke to John W. and Helen Snoke, August 19, 1924.

163. Moore, "Photographs of the first Boy Scout International Jamboree in London, 1920," William C. Moore Collection. See also West, "The Story of the International Scout Jamboree," *Boys' Life*, October 1920, 50.

164. "Bronxville Scouts Tour England," *Bronxville Review*, August 31, 1929.

165. "Travel Diary of Walter J. Ong," August 25, 1929.

166. Ibid., July 29, 1929; Smith, *Jamboree Joys*, 19; "Scotland's Scenery and Food Ranks First with the Scouts," *Kansas City Star*, August 16, 1929.

167. West, *The Scout Jamboree Book*, 54.

168. Westmoreland to Harry D. Thorenson Jr., September 21, 1978, William C. Westmoreland Papers, Personal Papers, Box 16.

169. Snoke, 50th Anniversary, 24.

170. "Portland Scouts at Jamboree Doubt Peace Aid," *Oregonian*, August 27, 1933.

171. Spencer A. Gard to Heart of America Troop, August 1, 1979, Walter J. Ong Manuscript Collection, General Files, Folder 205.

172. Snoke, 50th Anniversary, 24.

173. "International Affairs," *Jefferson City Post-Tribune*, July 10, 1933.

4. A Brother to All?

1. Ono quoted in Fujimoto, "Trans-Pacific Boy Scout Movement in the Early Twentieth Century," 38.

2. Raphael, *Imperiale Gewalt und mobilisierte Nation*.

3. See above all Macleod, *Building Character*, 214–18; and Jordan, *Modern Manhood*, 170–220.

4. Kramer, *The Blood of Government*, 12–14. For an astute early twentieth-century analysis, see Du Bois, "The Present Outlook for the Darker Races of Mankind."

5. Murray, *The History of the Boy Scouts of America*, 539.

6. BSA, *Official Report* (1926), 282–87, 324–30. See also the unpublished thesis by Voss, "Scouting among Primitive Boys," 1939, Kenneth Woltz Badgett Papers.

7. "Europe," *Crisis*, October 1929, 343.

8. Lowe to West, April 24 and May 18, 1918, Beard Papers, Box 130. See also Robinson to West, May 6, 1918, and Beard to Lowe, May 8, 1918, ibid.

9. See, for example, BSA, *Handbook for Boys* (1928), 33; and Baden-Powell, *Scouting for Boys*, 212.

10. Riis, "The Boy Scouts," *Outlook*, October 25, 1913, 413. See also Lyman Beecher Stowe, "The Boy Scouts of the World," *Columbian Magazine*, September 1911, 1095.

11. Schiff quoted in BSA, *Official Report* (1928), 324.

12. Baden-Powell, *Boy Scouts beyond the Seas*, 19.

13. West to D. D. Moore, September 15, 1911, unfiled letter, BSA National Archives.

14. Interview with Stanley Harris, March 12, 1967, BSA National Archives; Beard to Lowe, May 8, 1918; Interview of Mary White Ovington with James West, August 16, 1919, NAACP Papers, Administrative Subject File: Discrimination, Boy Scouts 1919, Box I:C269. See also Jordan, *Modern Manhood*, 187.

15. The 1913 *Handbook for Scout Masters* advised to leave this problem "to the local councils and the Scout Masters who are directly facing the situation." BSA, *Handbook for Scout Masters* (1913), 79.

16. Jordan, *Modest Manliness*, 173–79.

17. For a sample of racist humor in the BSA, see *Boys' Life*, September 1919, 4; November 1919, 26; and August 1921, 27. See also BSA, *Executive Conference Report, 1922*, 3. For minstrel performances of Boy Scouts, see *Boys' Life*, October 1913, 18; "A Minstrel Show for Soldiers," *Boys' Life*, August 1918, 14; "'Putting On' a Minstrel Show," *Boys' Life*, March 1923, 37, 41; and BSA, *Community Boy Leadership*, 409. On the significance of minstrel shows for white identity, see Roediger, *Wages of Whiteness*.

18. See Jordan, *Modern Manhood*, in particular.

19. Baden-Powell, *Boy Scouts beyond the Seas*, 106–23; Wilson, *Scouting Round the World*, 18–23. See also Parsons, *Race, Resistance, and the Boy Scout Movement*, 65–78; and Rosenthal, *The Character Factory*, 252–73. On the situation in India, see Watt, "'The Promise of Character,'" 37–62.

20. On the origins of Scouting in the Philippines, see BSP, *Diamond Jubilee Yearbook*, 41–42; and Isaac, *American Tropics*, 48–49.

21. Kiser to "whom it may concern," August 11, 1966, Sherman L. Kiser File.

22. "Photographs of Sherman Kiser," Sherman L. Kiser File.

23. Kiser quoted in "The Boy Scout Movement," *Labor Digest*, July 1915, 18; and "A Boy's a Boy for A' That," *Outlook*, May 5, 1915, 5. See also "Little Moros of the Boy Scouts Are Quick to Learn," *Christian Science Monitor*, April 12, 1915.

24. "The Moro Boy Scouts," *Outlook*, October 20, 1915, 404.

25. Ibid., 405.

26. "Kiser's Sturdy Brown Boy Scouts of Moroland," *New York Tribune*, February 21, 1915; "A Boy's a Boy for A' That," 6.

27. BSA, *Handbook for Scoutmasters* (1922), 2–3.

28. BSA (Great Britain), *The Jamboree Book*, 34; Wilson, *Scouting Round the World*, 44, 65; "Scouts of the World," *Times*, July 31, 1929.

29. "Resolutions Adopted by the Third International Scout Conference, Copenhagen, August 18–20, 1924," *Jamboree*, October 1924, 373–74; "The Third International Conference," *Boys' Life*, December 1924, 57.

30. BSA, *Annual Report* (1921), 27. West was referencing the popular racist tract by Stoddard, *The Rising Tide of Color*, which predicted the downfall of the white empires because of the superior birth rates of nonwhite people.

31. See Parsons, *Race, Resistance, and the Boy Scout Movement*, 84–91.

32. BSA, Minutes of the Executive Board, January 14, 1918, Beard Papers, Box 211; "Scouting for Negro Boys," *Scout Executive*, August 1920, 3; R. M. Wheat, "Colored Department of the Louisville, KY, Council," *Scout Executive*, February 1924, 4; and "The Louisville Plan for Colored Boys," *Scout Executive*, October 1924, 5. See also Macleod, *Building Character*, 213; and Jordan, *Modern Manhood*, 197–98, 204–5.

33. Bolton Smith to Rose Lowe, May 8, 1918, Beard Papers, Box 130.

34. Smith quoted in BSA, *Official Report* (1928), 325. See also Smith to Beardsley Ruml, January 15, 1925, Laura Spelman Rockefeller Memorial Collection (LSRM), Subseries 3_08: Appropriations—Interracial Relations, Box 96.

35. BSA, *Official Report* (1926), 286–87.

36. BSA, *Official Report* (1928), 325.

37. Ibid.

38. See BSA, *Handbook for Scout Masters* (1913), 89; and BSA, *Community Boy Leadership*, 19–20.

39. Baden-Powell, "White Men in Black Skins," *Elders Review of West African Affairs*, July 1929, 6–7.

40. On Euro-American imperialism and religious mission, see Tyrrell, *Reforming the World*; Porter, *Religion versus Empire*; and White and Daughton, *In God's Empire*.

41. BSP, *Diamond Jubilee Yearbook*, 43–44; and Gleeck, *The Manila Americans*, 121–22.

42. Macfarlane quoted in BSA, *Annual Report* (1925), 73. On Macfarlane's service abroad, see "Alfred S. Macfarlane," *Scout Executive*, January 1958, 10.

43. Voss, "Scouting among Primitive Boys," 4–5; BSA, *Annual Report* (1929), 115.

44. Tyrrell, *Reforming the World*.

45. Macfarlane, "Scouting in the Outlying Possessions of the United States: Part I, The Philippine Islands," *Scout Executive*, June 1927, 4.

46. Fisher quoted in BSA, *Official Report* (1936), 210–11.

47. On the linkage of sports and the civilizing mission, see Hübner, "Muscular Christianity and the Western Civilizing Mission," 532–57.

48. "Scouting in Porto Rico," in *The Boy Scouts' Year Book*, ed. Franklin K. Mathiews (New York, 1922), 179. See also Bary, *Child Welfare in the Insular Possessions: Porto Rico*, 16–20, 51. On infant mortality in the Philippines, see Choy, *Empire of Care*, 24.

49. On Boy Scouts with leprosy in Hawaii and the Philippines, see "The Scout World," *Boys' Life*, November 1925, 21; and "The Scout World," *Boys' Life*, February 1931, 25. Roosevelt quoted in Bator, "Toward Filipino Self-Rule," 169. The leper colony episode is recounted in Collier, *The Roosevelts*, 332.

50. Wilder, "Boy Scouts of Hawaii," *Friend*, March 1916, 64; "Scouting in Hawaii," *Scouting*, December 15, 1915, 5. On Wilder, see Jordan, *Modern Manhood*, 240, 370.

51. Voss, "Scouting among Primitive Boys," 52.

52. "The Significance of Boys' Week," *Rotarian*, July 1925, 15–17, 39. For the "Be His Pal" initiative, see the poster collection in the Boys' Week Scrapbooks, Rotary International Archives. On the spread of Boys' Week to Panama and Puerto Rico, see "Boys' Week and the Boy Problem," *Rotarian*, April 1923, 196; and "Boys' Week in San Juan," *Rotarian*, January 1925, 41–42.

53. "Want Secretary for Porto Rico," *Spokane Daily Chronicle*, July 6, 1911.

54. Macfarlane quoted in BSA, *Official Report* (1928), 330.

55. Voss, "Scouting among Primitive Boys," 268; "Camping," *Philippine Education Magazine*, April 1927, 667; "Memorial Day," *Philippine Education Magazine*, June 1927, 30; "The Scout World," *Boys' Life*, July 1931, 23; West to Voss, March 28, 1932, Beard Papers, Box 133; "Washington Tribute in Philippines," *New York Times*, February 20, 1932.

56. For the development of scouting in Puerto Rico, see BSA, *Annual Report* (1923), 153; *Annual Report* (1925), 284, 286; *Annual Report* (1929), 115–16; and *Annual Report* (1933), 168; "Scouting in the Outlying Possessions of the United States: 2—Scouting in Porto Rico," *Scout Executive*, August 1927, 3; and Macfarlane, "Summary of Progress in Porto Rico," *Scout Executive*, February 1929, 2.

57. See Voss, "Scouting among Primitive Boys," 245. Slightly deviating figures are listed in BSP, *Diamond Jubilee Yearbook*, 147.

58. Voss, "Scouting among Primitive Boys," 264. See also "What Shall I Do with My Boy? A Letter from the Chief Scout of the World to the Parents of Boys of the Philippines," *Philippine Education Magazine*, March 1927, 614; and BSP, *Diamond Jubilee Yearbook*, 44–45.

59. See Macfarlane, "Scouting in the Outlying Possessions," 2–3.

60. Leonard Wood to West, June 9, 1924, Records of the Bureau of Insular Affairs, Record Group (RG) 350.3, Box 26981.

61. "The Annual Meeting of the Council, Boy Scouts of America," *Philippine Education Magazine*, March 1928, 574–75.

62. Macfarlane, "Scouting in the Outlying Possessions," 2–3. See also "Scouting in the Philippines," *New York Times*, October 2, 1927.

63. BSA, *Official Report* (1928), 330.

64. Voss, "Scouting among Primitive Boys," 62, 95; and Macfarlane, "Scouting in the Outlying Possessions," 4.

65. Voss, "Scouting among Primitive Boys," 331–38.

66. Ibid., 335–36.

67. BSA, *Official Report* (1928), 330.

68. "Boy Scouts Active in the U.S. Island Possessions," *Christian Science Monitor*, September 5, 1914.

69. Robley, "Scouting in the Outlying Possessions of the United States—3. The Hawaiian Islands," *Scout Executive*, September 1927, 3. See also "Boy Scouts in Honolulu," *Boys' Life*, July 1912, 22; and "Scouting in Hawaii," *Scouting*, December 15, 1915, 5.

70. "The Scout World," *Boys' Life*, July 1930, 25. On how the BSA's imperial presences paralleled the globalization of British and French Scout organizations, see Voss, "Scouting among Primitive Boys," 358–59.

71. On Harris, see "Stanley A. Harris: Thirty Years of Service with the Boy Scouts of America, 1917–1947," Badgett Papers; Harris, "Early Days of Scouting," 1935, unpublished manuscript, BSA National Archives; and "Pioneers in Scouting: Stanley A. Harris," *Scout Executive*, November 1931, 8.

72. On the KKK's opposition to the Boy Scouts, see Nye to West (undated), Beard Papers, Box 131. For plans to establish a Pathfinder-like organization for African Americans, see BSA, "Minutes of the National Council Annual Meeting, April 30–May 1, 1926," 537, BSA National Archives, unfiled volume.

73. Leonard Outhwaite, "Memorandum of Interview with Stanley Harris," February 19, 1926, LSRM Papers, Box 96; and Will W. Alexander to Outhwaite, March 5, 1926, ibid.

74. See Parmar, *Foundations of the American Century*; and Friedman and McGarvie, *Charity, Philanthropy, and Civility in American History*.

75. Harris, "Conditions Discovered and Action Taken," March 26, 1925, LSRM Papers, Box 96.

76. Smith quoted in BSA, *Official Report* (1928), 328.

77. Harris to Outhwaite, January 6, 1927, LSRM Papers, Box 96.

78. Interview with Stanley Harris, March 12, 1967.

79. Harris, "Conditions Discovered and Action Taken," March 26, 1925; BSA, *Annual Report* (1927), 89. See also John D. Trawick to Harris, March 10, 1925, LSRM Papers, Box 96; Will W. Alexander to Outhwaite, March 5, 1926, ibid.; and Harris to Fisher, December 31, 1926, ibid.

80. Smith, "An Outstanding Need: The Maintaining of the Inter-Racial Service of the Boy Scouts of America," January 17, 1933, Papers of the General Education Board (GEB), Box 217.

81. Outhwaite, "Memorandum of Interview with Stanley Harris," September 30, 1927, ibid. See also Fisher to Outhwaite, October 26, 1927, ibid.

82. Smith to Outhwaite, September 6, 1928, ibid. On Beauchamp's employment, see Harris, "Progress in Work with Negro Boys," (undated, probably late 1927), ibid.; and "Report of Stanley A. Harris, National Director of Interracial Activities," December 14, 1927, ibid.

83. Harris to Outhwaite, January 6, 1927.

84. See Zimmerman, *Alabama in Africa*, 22.

85. "Minutes of the Inter-Racial Relations Committee Meeting, Boy Scouts of America, New York City," February 18, 1927, LSRM Papers, Box 96; "Report of Stanley A. Harris on Hampton School," (undated, probably mid-1927), ibid.; Ray O. Wyland to Fisher, August 26, 1927, ibid.;

and W. H. Evans to Harris, July 20, 1928, ibid.; BSA, *Annual Report* (1928), 76. See also "A Train-ing Innovation," *Scout Executive*, August 1927, 4; and "Hampton Gives Summer Course for Boys' Leaders," *Chicago Defender*, June 23, 1928.

86. "Report of Stanley A. Harris to the Committee of Inter-Racial Relations, New York," February 25, 1927, LSRM Papers, Box 96; BSA, *Annual Report* (1929), 105–8. On white opposi-tion to black scouting in these states, see Harris, "Report of Inter-Racial Work of the Boy Scouts of America," November 23, 1926, LSRM Papers, Box 96.

87. "Report on Membership—Negro Boys," May 17, 1944, GEB Papers, Box 217.

88. Jordan, *Modern Manhood*, 331–32.

89. Smith, "An Outstanding Need." On discrimination in camping and use of the swimming pool, see Wheat, "Colored Department of the Louisville, KY, Council"; and Jordan, *Modern Man-hood*, 204–5.

90. "Minutes of the Meeting of the Committee on Inter-Racial Activities, December 14, 1927," LSRM Papers, Box 96. On the BSA's growing interest in these groups, see BSA, *Annual Report* (1929), 108–9; *Annual Report* (1931), 131–32; *Annual Report* (1933), 161, 167; and BSA, *Executive Conference Report* (1936), 518–32.

91. BSA, *Annual Report* (1929), 109.

92. According to Jordan, Native Americans were represented in the BSA at a rate 1.85 times their population in 1932, while in 1929 blacks in segregated Scout troops were represented at a rate of just 0.28 times their population. Jordan, *Modern Manhood*, 375. For Native American member-ship statistics, see BSA, *Annual Report* (1929), 109; *Annual Report* (1930), 130; and *Annual Report* (1932), 188–89.

93. BSA, *Annual Report* (1929), 109–10. See also "Indian Scout Village," *Boys' Life*, Novem-ber 1930, 69.

94. "Perform Good Turn," *Scouting: World Jamboree Edition*, August 6, 1929. For a photograph of the Muscogee Scouts, see G. Barrett Rich, "1929 World Jamboree Scrapbook," Box 1929, World Jamboree File, BSA National Archives.

95. "Outstanding Events of the World Jamboree," *Scouting*, September 1929, 299; "Scouts Pag-eant of Dixieland Thrills 25,000 D.C. Spectators," *Washington Post*, July 4, 1937.

96. West and Hillcourt, *The 1933 Scout Jamboree Book*, 41–42.

97. West to Hubert Martin, June 11, 1925, Boy Scouts File, Dossier No. 41815, International Committee on Intellectual Cooperation, League of Nations Archives; Hubert Martin to W. Lewis Bailey, June 16, 1925, ibid.

98. Lord Hampton, "Report of the Chief Commissioner on His Visit to America, 12 June, 1931," 3, 6, Founder's Files, U.S.A. (Visits and General), TC/54; Hubert Martin, "Scouting in America: Some Impressions," *Jamboree*, January 1930, 928–30; "Hubert S. Martin on Scouting in America," *Scouting*, March 1929, 77.

99. "A Training Course for Negro Scoutmasters," *Jamboree*, January 1928, 817; "Scouting among Negro Boys," *Jamboree*, July 1929, 991; "American Indian Scouts," *Jamboree*, October 1930, 1143.

100. Smith to Ruml, January 15, 1925.

101. Ibid.

102. Morris, *Puerto Rico*, 38, 70; Lawcock, "Filipino Students in the United States." On Afri-can American activism and youth, see Du Bois, "Negro Education"; Stein, *The World of Marcus Garvey*, 83–85; and Locke, "Negro Youth Speaks."

103. Harris to Outhwaite, January 6, 1927.

104. Smith to Outhwaite, March 9, 1928, LSRM Papers, Box 96.

105. Lewis to West, May 2, 1918, Beard Papers, Box 130; and Beard to West, May 8, 1918, ibid.

106. Smith to Lewis, May 10, 1918, ibid.

107. "Report of Stanley A. Harris, February 25, 1927," 3. See also Harris, "Conditions Discovered and Action Taken"; and "Work of Inter-Racial Activities Committee of the Boy Scouts of America, November 9, 1931," GEB Papers, Box 217; Harris, "Negro Youth and Scouting"; and BSA, *Annual Report* (1928), 77.

108. W. H. Wolcott to Harris (undated, probably January 1927), LSRM Papers, Box 96.

109. BSA, *Annual Report* (1930), 100–101. On preparing Native American Boy Scouts for the modern workplace, see Asbury, "Some Redskin Boy Scouts," *Boys' Life*, March 1917, 21; "First Indian Troop of Boy Scouts in the World," *Carlisle Arrowe*, January 15, 1915; and "Boy Scout Notes," *Carlisle Arrowe*, February 5, 1915.

110. Franklin, *Mirror to America*, 27–28; "We Had to Do a Good Deed Every Day: Interview with John Hope Franklin."

111. Harris, "Early Days of Scouting, Memorandum for Dr. H. W. Hurt," October 14, 1935, unfiled letter, BSA National Archives. See also "Colored Troop of Boy Scouts Formed," *Harrisburg Daily Independent*, April 27, 1911; "Colored Boy Scouts," *Wichita Beacon*, May 5, 1911; "Made Good Showing," *Brooklyn Daily Eagle*, May 31, 1911; and "Colored Boy Scouts," *Galveston Daily News*, August 28, 1911.

112. "Prospective Scouts," *Chicago Defender*, June 10, 1911; "City of Evanston," *Chicago Defender*, October 7, 1911, and June 1, 1912.

113. See "Interview with Thomas W. Chinn," in Tong, *Asian American Children*, 193–95.

114. Chen, *Being Chinese*, 128. See also Jorae, *The Children of Chinatown*, 63. On Chinese American Boy Scouts in New York, see "New York," *Boys' Life*, August 1911, 34.

115. "Boy Scouts," *Chicago Defender*, July 26, 1924. See also "Character Building," *Chicago Defender*, May 26, 1923; "Boy Scouts," *Chicago Defender*, November 17, 1923; and "Boy Scout Idea Progressing with Youth of Race," *Pittsburgh Courier*, January 26, 1929.

116. Photo album, David H. Dwight Sr. File (African American scoutmaster, Jacksonville, 1882–1959), BSA National Archives.

117. Alcantara, "Boy Scouts in the Philippines," *Philippine Education Magazine*, September 1926, 207.

118. Mechling, "Heroism and the Problem of Impulsiveness."

119. Beard, *Boy Heroes of Today*, 80, 103–4. See also "Three Heroes," *Boys' Life*, March 1928, 25; and "Another Scout Receives Carnegie Medal," ibid., July 1929, 58. On celebrations of boy heroism in the African American press, see "Colored Boy Scout Cited for Heroism," *Pittsburgh Courier*, February 19, 1927; and "Honor Boy Scout, 14, for Daring Act of Bravery," *Chicago Defender*, February 16, 1935.

120. John C. Wright to Stanley Harris, July 8, 1928, LSRM Papers, Box 96.

121. Eastman, *Indian Scout Talks*, 7.

122. "Boy Scout Notes," *Carlisle Arrow*, February 12, 1915.

123. R. Kelly Bryant to John Shillady, July 28, 1919, NAACP Papers, Discrimination, Boy Scouts 1919, Box I:C269; Mary White Ovington (NAACP executive secretary) to West, August 9, 1919, ibid.; West to Ovington, August 11, 1919, ibid.; Ovington, "Interview with Mr. James West, Chief Scout Executive, Boy Scouts of America, August 12, 1919," ibid.

124. NAACP Assistant Secretary to BSA National Headquarters, May 6, 1926, NAACP Papers, Discrimination, Boy Scouts 1926, Box I:C269; William E. Bailey to BSA, April 26, 1926, and to James W. Johnson (NAACP field secretary), April 29, 1926, ibid.

125. Wilkins to West, June 4, 1937, NAACP Papers, Discrimination, Boy Scouts 1937, Box I:C269. See also Dorothy Canavan to West, May 15, 1937, and to Charles H. Houston (NAACP litigation director), June 1, 1937, ibid.

126. "Negro Boy Scout Barred from Jamboree," *Pittsburgh Courier*, June 12, 1937; see also NAACP Papers, Discrimination, Boy Scouts 1937, Box I:C269. See also Aria E. Carson to Roy Wilkins, June 25, 1937, ibid.; and Edward P. Lovett to Wilkins, July 25, 1937, ibid.

127. "Another Good Deed," *Chicago Defender*, July 14, 1928; "American Boy Scouts," *Chicago Defender*, February 19, 1929.

128. "Editor Asks Boy Scouts to Oust Mobbers," *Chicago Defender*, August 31, 1929; "American Color Prejudice Finds Hard Time in Holland," *Chicago Defender*, December 14, 1929.

129. "100 Per Cent American Boy Scouts," *Chicago Defender*, September 29, 1928; "My Trip Abroad: The Colored American in Paris," *Chicago Defender*, November 23, 1929.

130. W. E. B. Du Bois, "The Negro Silent Parade," *Crisis*, September 1917, 244–45. See also Hale, *Making Whiteness*, 36.

131. Crucy, "Marcus Garvey, a New Moses, April 17, 1924," 160.

132. "African Youth Inspired Boy Scout Movement," *Chicago Defender*, October 13, 1928.

133. "Boy Scouts Lead Bud's Big Parade," *Chicago Defender*, August 23, 1930; "Billiken Boy Scouts Hold Flag Raising," *Chicago Defender*, February 27, 1932; "Bud Sets Up Hospital Tent for Kiddies," *Chicago Defender*, August 20, 1932; and "75,000 at Billiken Picnic," *Chicago Defender*, August 25, 1934.

134. Paris, *Children's Nature*, 214. See also Deloria, *Playing Indian*, 135–36.

135. "Eagle Scout Trails," *Boys' Life*, December 1928, 85; "Indian Tribal Names for Patrols," *Boys' Life*, October 1931, 37. On the ceremonial induction of Baden-Powell into the Sarcee tribe, see Baden-Powell, *Scouting Round the World*, 154–55.

136. "Indian Troop," *Weekly Bulletin of Boy Scout Activities*, March 29, 1930. See also Jordan, *Modern Manhood*, 217.

137. BSP, *Diamond Jubilee Yearbook*, 44–45; Voss, "Scouting among Primitive Boys," 264–65.

138. "The Annual Meeting of the Council," *Philippine Education Magazine*; Voss, "Scouting among Primitive Boys," 77; "Minutes of the Executive Board Meeting, Philippine Council, Manila, October 6, 1932," Records of the Bureau of Insular Affairs, RG 350.3, Box 26981.

139. Emanuel A. Baja, "The Filipino's Creed," "The Filipino National Flag," 11, and "Laws Protecting the Flag," Records of the Bureau of Insular Affairs, RG 350.3, Box 26981.

140. K. F. Baldwin, "Memorandum for General Parker, Subject: Approval of Philippine Supplement to Boy Scouts Handbook, December 6, 1932," 2, ibid.

141. West to Voss, March 28, 1932, Beard Papers, Box 132; "The Jamboree at Gödöllö," *Boy's Life*, October 1933, 21; "Philippine Fete Staged by Scouts," *New York Times*, August 30, 1935.

142. BSP, *Diamond Jubilee Yearbook*, 45–46; "Philippine Scouts Honor U.S. Leader," *New York Times*, October 27, 1937; "Col. Roosevelt Honored, Philippine Scouts Present Flag at Ceremony Here," *New York Times*, January 28, 1938. On Vargas, see Hübner, *Pan-Asian Sports*, 67.

143. Theodore Roosevelt Jr. to West, December 4, 1937, Papers of Theodore Roosevelt Jr., Box 30.

144. BSP, *Diamond Jubilee Yearbook*, 147.

145. "Sons of Pirates Join Boy Scouts in Philippines," *New York Herald Tribune*, April 28, 1929.

146. See Voss, "Scouting among Primitive Boys," 246–47; and McCoy, *Closer Than Brothers*, 23.

147. Du Bois, "Defensive Military Training," 200.

148. Harris, "Conditions Discovered and Action Taken"; Smith to Outhwaite, September 6, 1928, LSRM Papers, Box 96. See also Myrdal, *An American Dilemma*, 1193; Macleod, *Building Character*, 217; and DuRocher, *Raising Racists*.

149. Some of these instances are mentioned in Harris, "Conditions Discovered and Action Taken"; and Bolton Smith to Outhwaite, February 9, 1929, LSRM Papers, Box 96.

150. On long-distance solidarity with Filipino Scouts, see "A Fine Opportunity," *Scouting*, February 1931, 12; and "Philippines Leper Scouts Send Jamboree Greetings," *Jamboree Journal*, June 29, 1937. On a white boy's perception of scouting in Puerto Rico, see Martin, *A Boy Scout with the 'Sea Devil,'* 122–23.

151. BSA, *Annual Report* (1928), 77. On the uniforms in Mississippi, see A. J. Taylor, "Man with Man in Scouting: Work with Colored Boys," *Southern Workman*, April 1935, 109–10.

152. "Diary of Charles S. Bartlett of the Boy Scout World Jamboree, Moisson, France, July 16–August 30, 1947," 6, unfiled manuscript, BSA National Archives.

153. Cochran, *Be Prepared*, 82–99, 94. "Cochran" was one of Monroe's literary pseudonyms.

154. See Reed, *Fly in the Buttermilk*, 35–37. For another example of interracial solidarity in the BSA, see Taylor, *A History of Troop Thirty*, 15–20.

155. Lawrence L. Stanley, "Negro Scouting (undated, probably 1945)," 2, GEB Papers, Box 218; "Young Sayre Wins Radio for Letter on 'Patriotism,'" *Chicago Defender*, May 17, 1924.

156. This episode is described in Neuman, *Indian Play*, 89.

157. Luis E. Goenago to Beard, December 20, 1931, Beard Papers, Box 134.

158. "Fadden, Ray," in *Native Americans Today*, 96–97.

159. "We Need More of This," *Chicago Defender*, June 22, 1929; "Along the Color Line," *Crisis*, August 1931, 273.

160. On the Chicago episode, see Gilmore, *Defying Dixie*, 42. On James E. Jackson, see Lewis, "James and Esther Jackson," 14–15.

161. P. H. Easom to Harris, January 27, 1941, GEB Papers, Box 217.

162. Bernstein, *Racial Innocence*, 4.

5. Youth Marches

1. On the official membership figures for Scouts, Cubs, and scoutmasters for the years 1933, 1941, and 1945, see BSA, *Annual Report* (1934, 1942, 1946). On Depression-era scouting in the United States, see Jordan, *Modern Manhood*, 327–35. On the popularity of camping, see Paris, *Children's Nature*, 211, 244–45; and Lindenmeyer, *The Greatest Generation Grows Up*, 194–95.

2. See Winslow, *Youth*; Lewis, *Doom of Youth*; Eleanor Roosevelt, "Facing the Problems of Youth"; Davis, *The Lost Generation*; and Rainey, *How Fare American Youth?*

3. Nolan, *The Transatlantic Century*, 124.

4. Blum quoted in Whitney, *Mobilizing Youth*, 3.

5. For regional variations of communist and fascist youth organizing, see Mulready-Stone, *Mobilizing Shanghai Youth*; Ponzio, *Shaping the New Man*; Hwang, "Authority over the Body"; Whitney, *Mobilizing Youth*; and Mangan, *Superman Supreme*.

6. Davis, *The Lost Generation*, 3.

7. See, for example, Patel, *Soldiers of Labor*, and *The New Deal*; Ekbladh, *The Great American Mission*, 40–76; Nolan, *Transatlantic Century*, 104–30; and Rodgers, *Atlantic Crossings*, 409–84.

8. Poling, *Youth Marches*, 6, 7, 12.

9. See Reiman, *The New Deal and American Youth*, 31–54; and Nicholson, "'In America.'"

10. Winslow, *Youth*.

11. Poling, *Youth Marches*, 135.

12. Davis, *The Lost Generation*, 5–6.

13. See Neumann, *The Communist Youth League*, 214–15; Mishler, *Raising Reds*, 41–46; and Savage, *Teenage*, 193.

14. Mishler, *Raising Reds*, 64–73.

15. See Cannistraro, *Blackshirts in Little Italy*.

16. On the Bund's family and youth policies, see Bernstein, *Swastika Nation*, 77–85.

17. Russell, *Education and the Social Order*, 116.

18. "What's the Truth about the Boy Scouts?," *Young Comrade*, November 1927, 2.

19. Baden-Powell quoted in Rosenthal, *The Character Factory*, 274.

20. Krupskaya, "Young Pioneers: How Women Can Help," *Workers' Weekly*, July 3, 1925; U.S. House of Representatives (HR), *Investigation of Communist Propaganda: Hearings*, Part 1 (1930), 3: 81; and HR, *Investigation of Un-American Propaganda* (1938), 3: 2985.

21. "Smash the Boy Scouts," *Young Pioneer*, June 1929, 2. See also Campion, *Who Are the Young Pioneers?*, 26–27.

22. "Boy Communist, 15, Assails Schools," *New York Times*, May 2, 1927.

23. Mickenberg, *Learning from the Left*, 67–72; and deGraffenried, *Sacrificing Childhood*, 2–12.

24. "Reds Riot on Pier as Boy Scouts Sail," *New York Times*, July 20, 1929; "New York Pioneers Hold Demonstration against Boy Scouts Jamboree," *Young Pioneer*, July–August, 1929, 2; Eisman, *An American Boy in the Soviet Union*, 5.

25. Eisman, *An American Boy in the Soviet Union*, 6; HR, *Investigation of Communist Propaganda: Hearings* (1930), 1: 29.

26. Kahn, "Why We Are against the Boy Scouts," *Young Comrade*, March 1924, 5; "Investigations, the Juniors and the Boy Scouts," *Young Comrade*, May 1924, 5; "Pioneers Active in Anti-Boy Scout Campaigns," *Young Pioneer*, April 1929, 3.

27. HR, *Investigation of Un-American Propaganda Activities in the United States: H.Res. 282* (1942), 1453; and Kuhn, "Bund Command #22," June 1, 1939, General Records Seized from the German-American Bund (GAB), RG 131, Box 49.

28. Dinkelacker quoted in Bernstein, *Swastika Nation*, 80.

29. Ibid., 81.

30. Dinkelacker, "Unsere Jugendbewegung in Nordamerika," General Records Seized from the GAB, Box 10. On the Bund's Anglophobia, see "Der Gau Ost des Amerikadeutschen Volksbundes Feiert den Unabhängigkeitstag am 4. Juli im Lager Nordland," ibid., Box 2.

31. "Camp Aflutter with Swastikas Denies It Trains Young Nazis," *Milwaukee Journal*, July 23, 1937. See also "Landesjugendbefehl Nr. 5," September 9, 1939, General Records Seized from the GAB, Box 7; and "10 Jahre deutsche Jugend in Nordamerika," ibid., Box 8.

32. HR, *Investigation of Un-American Propaganda Activities, Part IV*, 1452. On GAB youths calling the Boy Scouts "sissies," see HR, *Investigation of Un-American Propaganda Activities in the United States* (1938), 1: 1135.

33. See Bernstein, *Swastika Nation*, 234–35. On Nationalist Socialist conceptions of reproductive sexuality, see Bialas, *Moralische Ordnungen*, 167–80.

34. See Mishler, *Raising Reds*, 12–13.

35. "Reds Riot on Pier as Boy Scouts Sail."

36. BSA, *Scouting in Less-Chance Areas*, 7. See also Levy, *Building a Popular Movement*, 86–87; and Rosenthal, *The Character Factory*, 88–107.

37. Irons, *Testing the New Deal*, 133.

38. Roman, *Opposing Jim Crow*, 88. See also, for example, the cover illustrations of the May 1931, October 1931, and October 1932 editions of the *New Pioneer*; and Mickenberg, *Learning from the Left*, 77–79.

39. Communist children's stories such as *Pickets and Slippery Slicks* (1931), which shows two white southern brothers overcome the racial prejudice of their elders, or *A Night's Adventure* (1932), also stress the importance of interracial solidarity.

40. "Negro Boy Scout Joins the Young Pioneers," *Young Pioneer*, July–August 1929, 2.

41. HR, *Investigation of Communist Propaganda*, Part 1 (1930), 3: 104. Strickland is also mentioned in Shvarts, *Slet*, 14; and HR, *Investigation of Communist Propaganda, Report: Pursuant to H.Res. 220* (1931), 29.

42. Campion, *Who Are the Young Pioneers?*, 15–20; and Bernstein, *Swastika Nation*, 61–65.

43. See Mishler, *Raising Reds*, 68; and Bernstein, *Swastika Nation*, 68.

44. HR, *Investigation of Communist Propaganda, Report: Pursuant to H.Res. 220* (1931), 28. See also Goodall, "Red Herrings?"

45. See, for instance, HR, *Investigation of Nazi Propaganda Activities* (1934), 175; and HR, *Investigation of Un-American Propaganda Activities in the United States* (1940), 12: 8191. See also Goodall, *Loyalty and Liberty*, 177–224.

46. Campion, *Who Are the Young Pioneers?*, 29.

47. See, for example, "Bill Haywood—Pioneer," *New Pioneer*, May 1931, 8–9. See also Mishler, *Raising Reds*, 49, 60.

48. Ibid., 79.

49. Fritz Kuhn, "Bund Command #13," 25, General Records Seized from the GAB, Box 26.

50. HR, *Investigation of Un-American Propaganda Activities in the United States* (1939), 6: 3721. See also Bernstein, *Swastika Nation*, 1–7, 229–32.

51. Reiman, *The New Deal and American Youth*, 31–44.

52. Boy Scout Foundation of Greater New York, *America's Answer*. A second edition was published in January 1939. See also Beard to Head, March 30, 1939, Beard Papers, Box 60; and "Boy Scouts to Open Patriotic Program," *New York Times*, January 28, 1939.

53. On the redefinition of democracy in U.S. society in World War I, see Capozzola, *Uncle Sam Wants You*, 14, 21–54. For New Deal definitions of democracy, see Wall, *Inventing the "American Way,"* 15–101.

54. See Kimmel, *Manhood in America*, 191–221; Cohen, *Making a New Deal*, 246–49; and Stieglitz, *100 Percent American Boys*, 184–222. For a gendered history of the New Deal, see Mettler, *Dividing Citizens*.

55. See Abbott, "Titans/Planners, Bohemians/Revolutionaries," 464; "Scouting and the Economic Crisis," *Scout Executive*, November 1931, 1; "How Scouts Are Serving," ibid. On the BSA's anti-individualist ethos, see West, "Address at the Fourth International Boys' Work Conference," November 28–30, 1927, Beard Papers, Box 133.

56. BSA, *Annual Report* (1932), 37.

57. BSA, *Chief Scout Executive Bulletin*, September 8, 1933, 1–2; "Boy Scout Week—1934," *Scouting*, February 1934, 3–4; "The Scout World," *Boy's Life*, June 1934, 21.

58. McKenney, *Industrial Valley*, 107. See also "The Scout World," *Boys' Life*, December 1933, 54.

59. West, "Meeting the Situation," *Scouting*, November 1931, 23.

60. American Liberty League quoted in Wolfskill, *The Revolt of the Conservatives*, 132; Minkley quoted in *Madison (WI) Times*, May 1, 1937.

61. On age as a factor in fascist and communist antiliberal rhetoric, see, for example, Evans, *The Third Reich in Power*, 271–81; Kucherenko, *Little Soldiers*, 58–61; Neumann, *The Communist Youth League*, 87–88; and Katznelson, *Fear Itself*, 5–6.

62. Luce quoted in Katznelson, *Fear Itself*, 244.

63. BSA, *The National and World Jamborees in Pictures*; "The National Jamboree," *Boys' Life*, August 1937, 18–19; "Scouts' Pageants Open in Jamboree," *New York Times*, July 2, 1937.

64. On FDR's relationship with the BSA, see Maher, *Nature's New Deal*, 33–41; and Rowan, *To Do My Best*, 137–40. Roosevelt himself acknowledged that he "took a leaf out of the notebook of Scouting" when founding the CCC. BSA, *Annual Report* (1934), 66.

65. "Roosevelt Hails Boy Scouts' Deeds," *New York Times*, February 9, 1935.

66. Fisher quoted in BSA, *The National and World Jamborees in Pictures*, 130–31. See also Fisher, "The Nation's Capital Captured by 25,000 Youth," *Scouting*, September 1937, 3–4, 20–21.

67. Siple, "Boy Scouts and the National Jamboree," undated (probably July 1937), Paul Siple Collection, unfiled, BSA National Archives.

68. "Foreign Units Open Peace Drive," *New York Times*, July 4, 1937.

69. "What's Right with America," *Christian Science Monitor*, January 4, 1939; "National Rededication," *Scouting*, September 1938, 3–4; "You and I—and America," *Boys' Life*, November 1938, 18–19; and BSA, *Annual Report* (1939), 25–26. On the AYC, see Cohen, *When the Old Left Was Young*; and Nicholson, "In America," 4–10.

70. Harold Homann, "The Citizens of 2000 Anno Domini," undated (probably 1941), 2, Harold J. Homann Papers, Box 5.

71. "Address of Dr. James E. West—Chief Scout Executive," April 26, 1938, Beard Papers, Box 137; West, "Do Not Sell America Short—Keep Informed," May 24, 1940, ibid.; "2 Youth Groups Plan Campaign of Patriotism," *Washington Post*, January 30, 1939; "The Paramount Need in National Defense Is the Strengthening and Invigorating of Democracy," *Boys' Life*, September 1940, 11; BSA, *Annual Report* (1940), 37.

72. "Democracy Fight Made Permanent," *New York Times*, August 18, 1939; Pote, "Our 'Bill of Responsibilities,'" *Scout Executive*, February 1939, 1–2.

73. BSA, *Handbook for Boys*, 3rd ed., title cover.

74. Ray O. Wyland, "Prepared for Freedom," March 5, 1940, 3, Harold J. Homann Papers, Box 6.

75. Homann, "The Citizens of 2000 Anno Domini," 6.

76. Dewey, "In Step with Democracy," Beard Papers, Box 139.

77. "Merry Christmas Hans," *Boys' Life*, December 1939, 3–5, 48.

78. Brown, *Youth under Dictators*.

79. Beard, "How to Make and Fly the American Eagle," *Boys' Life*, August 1939, 15.

80. Wyland, "Prepared for Freedom," 3.

81. McNutt, "Scouting's Place in the Nation," *Scouting*, June 1941, 11.

82. West, "Address of Dr. James E. West—Chief Scout Executive: Region Seven Annual Meeting," April 26, 1938, Beard Papers, Box 138; and Beard, "Address by Daniel Carter Beard . . . at the Twentieth Annual Memorial Pilgrimage to the Grave of Theodore Roosevelt, Saturday, October 21, 1939," 5–6, Ray Lyman Wilbur Papers, Box 15.

83. "It Shall All Come to Naught . . . Nazi," *Scouting*, July 1942, 33.

84. Beard, "Address by Daniel Carter Beard . . . at the Twentieth Annual Memorial Pilgrimage to the Grave of Theodore Roosevelt, Saturday, October 21, 1939," 6.

85. BSA, *Annual Report* (1944), 227. On the wartime mobilization of children in the United States, see Tuttle, *"Daddy's Gone to War"*; Ossian, *The Forgotten Generation*; and Mintz, *Huck's Raft*, 254–74.

86. BSA, "National Defense and War Relief Service Opportunities for the Boy Scouts of America in the Present and Possible Future Situations," October 15, 1940, Beard Papers, Box 139.

87. "We, Too, Have a Job to Do," *Boys' Life*, March 1942, cover image. See also "Once Again, We Have a Job to Do," *Boys' Life*, March 1942, 30; and "On Uncle Sam's Team," *Boys' Life*, December 1942, 49.

88. BSA, "Boy Scouts and Civilian Defense," January 4, 1942, World War II Collection; "World War II Items Removed from Official BSA Scrapbook," BSA National Archives. See also BSA, "Boy Scouts on the Home Front" (undated brochure), ibid.

89. BSA, *Annual Report* (1942), 34.

90. BSA, *High School Victory Program and Scouting*. See also Rowan, *To Do My Best*, 186.

91. "It Shall All Come to Naught . . . Nazi," *Scouting*, July 1942, 33; BSA, *Annual Report* (1942), 35; "Executive Committee Meeting: Blackhawk Area Council, B.S.A., June 10, 1943," Homann Papers, Box 5.

92. Sawyer, "A Challenge from the Front," *Scout Executive*, March 1943, 5.

93. West, "What Can We Do About It?" *Boys' Life*, January 1939, 16.

94. Boy Scout Foundation of Greater New York, *America's Answer*, 13.

95. See, for example, "Americans All—United under One Flag," *Chicago Defender*, April 19, 1941.

96. BSA, *Annual Report* (1927), 89.

97. "The State of the Youth of the World," February 11, 1938, Piasa Bird Council, Boy Scouts of America, Alton, Illinois, p. 8, Homann Papers, Box 5.

98. AYC, "The Declaration of the Rights of American Youth."

99. West, "Personal and Confidential: To All Scout Executives," August 12, 1938, Beard Papers, Box 138; and "Confidential: The Role of the Communists in the American Youth Congress," ibid. On black-white cooperation in the AYC and the World Youth Congress, see Bynum, *NAACP Youth*, 23–44.

100. On racial segregation at the 1937 National Jamboree, see Wilkins to West, June 4, 1937, NAACP Papers, Discrimination, Boy Scouts 1937, Box I:C269; and Edward P. Lovett to Wilkins, July 25, 1937, ibid.

101. BSA, *Executive Conference Report* (1936), 125, 518–32. Smith, "An Outstanding Need."

102. See Ellis, "Getting the Message Out."

103. Langston Hughes, "Here to Yonder," *Chicago Defender*, May 22, 1943; "Ala. High Court Justice Tells Waters Race Relations Improving in Southland," *Chicago Defender*, February 27, 1943.

104. HR, *Japanese Immigration*, 710. On Japanese American internment in transnational perspective, see Hayashi, *Democratizing the Enemy*.

105. This photograph is reprinted in Kennedy, Cohen, and Bailey, *The American Pageant*, 876.

106. "Bill Shishima Interview, Segment 05." See also "Scouting in World War II Detention Camps," *Scouting*, November–December 1999, 18–19.

107. "Statement of Joint Policy for Japanese Relocation Centers: Boy Scouts of America—War Relocation Authority," June 15, 1942, Records of the War Relocation Authority (RG 210), Box 325.

108. Andrew J. Roberts to C. J. Carlson, August 14, 1945, ibid., Box 325. See also Robert H. Lamott (BSA) to Harvey M. Coverley, February 22, 1943, ibid.; Coverley to R. B. Cozzens, March 3, 1943, Memorandum on Boy Scout Camping Activities, ibid.; and Coverely to Dillon S. Myer (WRA), April 15, 1943, ibid.

109. Harris to Edward B. Marks, July 21, 1943, ibid.; Harris to Marshall Stalley, April 25, 1944, ibid., Box 325.

110. See HR, *Investigation of Un-American Propaganda Activities in the United States: H.Res. 282* (1943), 9215, 9322.

111. On the presence of fascist youths at the 1933 world jamboree, see Oelrich, *"Sportgeltung—Weltgeltung,"* 268–74; and Proctor, *On My Honor*, 145–46.

112. Wilson, *Scouting Round the World*, 88; Klepper quoted in West, "Home Folks Letter #5," August 18, 1933, Beard Papers, Box 234.

113. "A Jamboree Leader Remembers," *Scouting*, May–June 1991, 12.

114. Cornell, "'A Jamboree without Jam.'"

115. "American Scouters Just 'Softies' to Associates at World Jamboree," *Atlanta Constitution*, September 2, 1937.

116. "Portlanders on Boy Scout Expedition to Berlin," *Oregonian*, September 4, 1937.

117. Brady, "What Can Rotary Do for Youth," 87–93.

118. Diary of H. T. Wickham, entries for "Cologne," "Bingen," "Würzburg," and "Nuremberg," World Jamborees, Founder's Files, TC/73.

119. Baden-Powell quoted in Rosenthal, *The Character Factory*, 274.

120. "Scout Chief, Back from Europe, Found Our Boys, Lead Them All," *New York Times*, August 21, 1935.

121. "Camping—Better Than Usual," *Boys' Life*, June 1942, 1.

122. Baden-Powell to Hubert Martin, October 8, 1937, Founder's Files, TC/50. Baden-Powell's views of the Hitler Youth have been the subject of intense discussions. See the differing accounts of Rosenthal, *The Character Factory*, 276–78; and Jeal, *Baden-Powell*, 543–53.

123. On the attempt to downplay the interest of leading scouters in fascist youth, see Wilson, *Scouting Round the World*, 89–90.

124. Beard to West, April 13, 1929, Beard Papers, Box 134.

125. West, "Neglected Boyhood Breeds Bolshevism," *Scouting*, April 1919, 7.

126. On the Loyalty Day parades, see the following press reports: James Roe, "The Significance of Boys' Week," *Rotarian*, July 1925, 15–17, 39; "The Boys Remind Us," *Chicago Tribune*, May 5, 1921; "Men of Tomorrow Given Ovation by Huge Throng," *San Francisco Chronicle*, May 3, 1924; "Boys' Week Concludes," *Geelong Advertiser* (Australia), May 4, 1929; "La Semana del Niño," *El Merida* (Mexico), May 6, 1930. See also "A Brief Story of New York's 1920 Boys' Week," Boys' Week Scrapbook, 1921, Rotary International Archives; and Haverty-Stacke, *America's Forgotten Holiday*, 118–20.

127. "25,000 Boys Challenge Radicalism," *Kansas City State Journal*, May 2, 1923; "San Francisco's Boys on Parade," *San Francisco Chronicle*, May 3, 1924.

128. Norwood, *Strike-Breaking and Intimidation*, 11; YPA, "Boy Scouts Week: Outline for Speakers" (undated, probably February 1929), Beard Papers, Box 134.

129. "Shorty" to Siple, May 1, 1930, Siple Family Papers, Expedition Records, Box 4.

130. Butcher, "Boys' Week and the Boy Problem," *Rotarian*, April 1923, 195.

131. BSA, *Annual Report* (1922), 27.

132. Martin, "Report of the Director of the Boy Scouts International Bureau to the International Conference," *Jamboree*, October 1924, 368.

133. "Scout Camp Guarded against British Reds," *New York Times*, July 30, 1929; "Red Pamphleteers Seized," *New York Times*, August 2, 1929.

134. "Your Aid Is Asked," *Scouting*, June 1924, 13.

135. Arthur B. Reeve, "The Voice in the Dark," *Boys' Life*, November 1924, 30–31, 60–61; and ibid., December 1924, 16, 37, 81–82.

136. "British 'Blitz' Scouts See the Sights with 'Dead-End' Friends as Guides," *New York Times*, July 7, 1942. See also "'Blitz Scouts' Arrive Today to See Capital," *Washington Post*, July 8, 1942.

137. "Booth Tarkington Writes a Letter to Konstantin Gregorivich Konstantinov," *Boys' Life*, September 1943, 13. See also "Hero of Leningrad," *Edwardsville Intelligencer*, October 21, 1942, and the *Piqua Daily Call*, October 27, 1942.

138. Quentin Reynolds, "Children of Mars," *Collier's Weekly*, June 26, 1943.

139. Ibid. See also "Russian Youth at War," *Christian Science Monitor*, November 16, 1944.

140. McKelway, "Trustworthy, Loyal, Helpful, Friendly . . . ," *New Yorker*, July 25, 1942.

141. BSA, "Boys in Wartime: Special Research Supplement," *Scouting for Facts*, June 1942, 6–8. The survey also contains the point of view that "the boys feel that older people don't consider them seriously enough."

142. BSA, "Gearing Research to Wartime Needs," *Scouting for Facts*, March 1943, 1.

143. BSA, "Boys in Wartime," 14. Another common Boy Scout statement laden with racist stereotypes was that "the Emperor ordered the [Japanese] army to sneak up on Pearl Harbor. We don't sneak up on anyone."

144. Ibid.

145. These numbers are drawn from a current research project by Rebecca Jo Plant and Frances Clark on underage youth in the U.S. military during World War II.

6. Are You a Crusader?

1. Halpern, *Norman Rockwell*, 78.

2. For a selection of Rockwell's Boy Scout paintings, see Csatari, *Norman Rockwell's Boy Scouts of America*; and Bezucha, *The Golden Anniversary Book of Scouting*.

3. Whyte, "How the New Suburbia Socializes," *Fortune Magazine*, August 1953. See also BSA, *A Study of Adolescent Boys*, 1. On childhood and youth in postwar America, see Mintz, *Huck's Raft*, 277, 275–309; Holt, *Cold War Kids*; and Fass and Grossberg, *Reinventing Childhood after World War II*.

4. For official membership figures for the years 1945–75, see the BSA annual reports.

5. See Medovoi, *Rebels*, 25–29. On the origins of the "teenager," see Savage, *Teenage*, 441–65; and Palladino, *Teenagers*. For a perspective from literary studies, see Jonnes, *Cold War American Literature*.

6. See Cuordileone, *Manhood and American Political Culture*; Dean, *Imperial Brotherhood*; Gilbert, *Men in the Middle*; and Martschukat, *Ordnung des Sozialen*, 263–92.

7. Stevenson quoted in Cuordileone, *Manhood and American Political Culture*, 122. On mass society, conformity, and masculinity in the 1850s, see Whyte, *Organization Man*; Riesman, Glazer, and Denney, *The Lonely Crowd*; and the novel by Wilson, *The Man in the Gray Flannel Suit*.

8. May, *Homeward Bound*, 16–17.

9. On the importance of religion in Cold War culture, see Herzog, *The Spiritual-Industrial Complex*; and Kirby, "The Religious Cold War."

10. See BSA, *Handbook for Boys* (1942), 16–26.

11. Lewis, *The American Adam*, 5.

12. Schuck, "Are You a Crusader?," *Scouting*, November 1949, 3.

13. See Fousek, *To Lead the Free Word*; and Belmonte, *Selling the American Way*.

14. "Scouts Stage Atom Drill," *New York Times*, May 25, 1952. See also "Big Scouting Fete Opens Tomorrow," *New York Times*, May 23, 1952.

15. See, for example, Peacock, *Innocent Weapons*; Holt, *Cold War Kids*; Fieldston, *Raising the World*; Jacobs, *The Dragon's Tail*, 99–117; and O'Brien, "Mama, Are We Going to Die?"

16. See Jacobs, *The Dragon's Tail*, 102–6. On Cold War civil defense in the United States, see Oakes, *The Imaginary War*. For a comparison of civil defense planning in the United States, Canada, and Great Britain, see Davis, *States of Emergency*.

17. Ibid., 26.

18. BSA, *Annual Report* (1950), 7–8; Schuck, "Civilian Defense," *Scouting*, November 1950, 2–3.

19. BSA, *Pattern for Survival*; *A Family "Be Prepared" Plan*; *First Aid and Rescue Methods*; and *Collection, Distribution, and Communication Services*.

20. BSA, *Pattern for Survival*, 9.

21. BSA, *Annual Report* (1956), 21; Herzog, *The Spiritual-Industrial Complex*, 155.

22. Davis, *States of Emergency*, 27. See also Peacock, *Innocent Weapons*, 37.

23. Quoted in Scheibach, *"In Case Atom Bombs Fall,"* 121.

24. Engelhardt, *The End of Victory Culture.*

25. For midcentury expressions of the importance of the pal role in scouting, see BSA, *Scouting for Facts with a Local Council,* 5, 13; and BSA, *Scoutmaster's Handbook,* 5th ed., 340.

26. BSA, *Pattern for Survival,* 50.

27. Ibid., 50–54.

28. Ibid., 51.

29. See Mackert, *Jugenddeliquenz;* Wright, *Comic Book Nation;* and Medovoi, *Rebels.* For a comparative perspective, see Poiger, *Jazz, Rock, and Rebels.*

30. Kietzman, *Why I Became a Scoutmaster,* 16–17.

31. BSA Inter-Racial Service (Division of Relationships), *Annual Report for the Year 1959,* 2–3, Division of Relationships File, BSA National Archives; and *Annual Report for the Year 1960,* 46, ibid. See also Peacock, *Innocent Weapons,* 109.

32. The "campfires of democracy" motif appeared on the front page of the April 1949 issue of *Scouting.*

33. Schuck, *Are You a Crusader?,* 3.

34. Houghton, "Strengthen the Arm of Liberty," *Scouting,* February 1949, 3. See also "The Crusade Gets Underway," *Scouting,* March 1949, 2–3; "Strengthen the Arm of Liberty," *Boys' Life,* February 1949, 3; and "To Strengthen Arm of Liberty," *New York Times,* February 13, 1949.

35. "The Crusade Shield—Will Your Flag Fly It?," *Scouting,* June–July 1949, 9.

36. See, for example, BSA, *Annual Report* (1950), vi–vii; and "The Crusade Sweeps the Country," *Scouting,* May 1949, 4–5.

37. See "Crusade Theme for January," *Scouting,* December 1949, 14–15.

38. Leslie A. Stratton, "The Statue of Liberty," *Scout Executive,* July 1950, 1–2. See also, for example, "Beatrice Will Have Its Own 'Statute of Liberty,'" *Beatrice Daily Sun,* February 2, 1950; "Dedication Set for Scouts' Replica of the Statue of Liberty," *Northwest Arkansas Times,* February 6, 1951; "Philippines to Get Model of 'Liberty'," *New York Times,* March 8, 1950; "The Way It Was—The 'Little Sisters of Liberty,'" *Scouting,* October 2007, 14, 44–45.

39. "Scouts Dedicate Replica of Liberty Statue: Governor Warns Freedom Periled," *Wyoming State Tribune,* May 28, 1950; "Statue and Liberty Bell Will Be Featured in Ceremony Today," *Wyoming State Tribune,* May 27, 1950.

40. BSA, *Pattern for Survival,* 1.

41. Hillcourt, "Be Prepared for Emergencies," *Boys' Life,* November 1950, 28.

42. See BSA, *Scoutmaster's Handbook,* 29: "Laugh with your boys and live Scouting with them. Be like an older brother, setting out on an exciting journey with them. And pick up Scouting skills with them as you travel along."

43. Schuck, "He Is My Brother," *Boys' Life,* February 1955, 19.

44. BSA, *Handbook for Boys,* 6th ed., 381.

45. "World Scouts Summoned to Anti-Red Drive," *Philadelphia Inquirer,* July 7, 1950. See also "Scouts Hear Truman Assail Communists' 'Religion of Hate,'" *Washington Post,* July 1, 1950; "Truman Tells Boy Scouts Need for 'Burning Faith,'" *Christian Science Monitor,* July 1, 1950.

46. "World Scouts Summoned to Anti-Red Drive."

47. On the Girl Scouts and civil defense, see Scheibach, *Atomic Narratives and American Youth,* 101; and Peacock, *Innocent Weapons,* 39–40. See also the GSA pamphlet *How to Be Prepared.*

48. "Dominating Delilah," *Scouting,* October 1952, 5; "Dominating Delilah," *Scouting,* November 1953, 9.

49. Castledine, *Cold War Progressives,* 68.

50. See McEnaney, *Civil Defense Begins at Home.*

51. Dunbar, "Be Prepared for Anything," *Boys' Life*, April 1951. 23–24. See also Dunbar, "Family First Aid," *Boys' Life*, June 1951, 22–23; "Ready at Home," *Boys' Life*, September 1951, 28; and "Scouting and Civil Defense: Prepare Your Unit Now," *Scouting*, March 1951, 2–3.

52. Eisenhower quoted in Oakes, *The Imaginary War*, 105–6.

53. Kietzman, *Why I Became a Scoutmaster*, 9. See also BSA, *Scoutmaster's Handbook*, 29.

54. See Monteyne, *Fallout Shelter*, 15.

55. John Limehouse, "Aircraft Flash," *Boys' Life*, May 1955, 65.

56. "Think and Grin," *Boys' Life*, February 1961, 78.

57. Cochran, *Be Prepared*, 213. See also Cochran, "Confessions of a Jamboree Scoutmaster," *Harper's Magazine*, February 1951, 59–66.

58. On the growth of science fiction literature and the comic book industry, see Wright, *Comic Book Nation*.

59. The first episode of "Space Conquerors" appeared in the September 1952 issue of *Boys' Life*; the final episode appeared in the magazine's October 1972 issue.

60. Roy Gallant, "Escape from Earth," *Boys' Life*, part 1, September 1954, 12, 73–77; Roy Gallant, "Escape from Earth," *Boys' Life*, part 2, October 1954, 16, 68–71.

61. "Space Conquerors," *Boys' Life*, August 1956, 34.

62. Robert A. Heinlein, "Satellite Scout," *Boys' Life*, August–November, 1950.

63. The first episode of "Time Machine" appeared in the December 1959 issue of *Boys' Life*; the final episode appeared in the magazine's September 1989 issue. A collection of these stories was published separately as *Mutiny in the Time Machine* (New York, 1963).

64. See also Onion, Innocent Experiments, 113–42.

65. Rodney Carver joins the "Time Machine" patrol in the episode featured in *Boys' Life*, February 1965, 25, 51–53.

66. Martone, "The Boy Who Saved the World," *Boys' Life*, December 1956, 30–31, 96–97.

67. Seltzer, "Maybe, We'll Wake Up," *Scouting*, May–June 1958, 2–3; Speedy, "Today's Challenge for Leaders of Youth," *Scouting*, May–June 1958, 6.

68. Seltzer, "Maybe, We'll Wake Up," 2–3.

69. Driscoll, "Space Travel," *Boys' Life*, May 1957, 64.

70. "Tailored to a Need: The New Exploring Program," *Scouting*, October 1958, 4–5. For the new Exploring symbol, see the front page of the December 1958 issue of *Scouting*.

71. BSA, "Rockets, Rocks, Rhythm."

72. "The First Merit Badge in Space," *Scouting*, March 1966, 6–7; "Gemini Astronauts," *Boys' Life*, April 1966, 16.

73. "Heroes of Our Time," *Bulletin of the Atomic Scientists*, May 1962, 25–26; "John Glenn, Youth's Finest Hero," *New York Times*, August 23, 1962; "Let's 'Go' with Glenn," *Scouting*, November 1962, 10. On the figure of the heroic male astronaut, see Llinares, *The Astronaut*.

74. Troutner, "Space Isn't Easy."

75. Von Braun, "Statement before Boy Scouts of America."

76. BSA, "Astronauts and the BSA."

77. Ibid.

78. Barclay, "Brothers Together," *Scouting*, January 1945, 2. See also West to Luther Gulick, February 4 and May 1, 1944, United Nations Relief and Rehabilitation (UNRRA) Collection, Rec. No. S-1267-0000-0089.

79. Cotter, "Scouting Far From Home," *Scouting*, September 1945, 7.

80. See BSA, *Annual Report* (1945), 11–12; BSA, *Annual Report* (1946), 29–30; "Scouts Will Raise a Friendship Fund," *New York Times*, February 11, 1945; BSA, "Scouts of the World—Building Together, Boy Scout Week, February 8–14, 1946," World Friendship File, BSA National Archives;

"Scouts of the World—Building for Tomorrow: Boy Scout Week, February 7 to 13, 1947," ibid.; "A World Friendship Fund," *Scouting*, February–March 1945, 4; Howard R. Patton, "The World Friendship Fund of the Boy Scouts of America," *Jamboree*, April 1949, 108, 117–120; Schuck, "The Good Turn with the Long Reach," *Boys' Life*, February 1957, 11.

81. This figure is from Boy Scouts of America, "The World Friendship Fund," accessed August 19, 2015, http://www.scouting.org/scoutsource/International/InformationSheets/22-329.aspx.

82. See BSA, *Annual Report* (1952), 31; and Peacock, *Innocent Weapons*, 114. The world brotherhood badge was discontinued in 1972.

83. On the "Shirts Off Our Back" campaign, see BSA, *Annual Report* (1947), 30; BSA, "Scouts of the World—Building Together, Boy Scout Week, February 8–14, 1946"; "Shirt-Off-Our-Back Campaign," *Milwaukee Journal*, February 7, 1946; and "Scouts Send Aid Abroad," *New York Times*, September 1, 1947.

84. "Troop 1 Goes 'Round the World,'" *Scouting*, October 1946, 5, 23.

85. See, for example, Fieldston, *Raising the World*; Oh, *To Save the Children of Korea*; and Fieldston, "Little Cold Warriors," 240–50.

86. "Culver City Boy Scouts 'Adopt' Philippine Troop," *Boys' Life*, February 1950, 61.

87. "Report of a Meeting with Cub Scouts," February 10, 1948, in Bland, Stoler, et al., *The Papers of George Catlett Marshall*, 354–56.

88. Fieldston, *Raising the World*; Zahra, *The Lost Children*.

89. "Report of a Meeting with Cub Scouts," 355.

90. A. Zemgals to Harry K. Eby, January 9, 1947, in Eby, "Scouting in D.P. Camps: Memo to Mr. J. S. Wilson, International Bureau," UNRRA Collection, Rec. No. S -1267-0000-0084.

91. Celier, "Thank You, America," *Scouting*, December 1945, 5; "They're Counting on Us," *Scouting*, September 1946, 5.

92. "10-Minute Talk by Boy Scout," in "Scouts of the World—Building Together," World Friendship File, BSA National Archives.

93. "French Boy Scouts Secretly Harbor Group of 17 Young German Visitors at Jamboree," *New York Times*, August 17, 1947. See also "Moisson: Jamboree Mondial De La Paix," *Jamboree*, September 1947, 297–321.

94. "Scenes Change for Boy Scouts," *Rockford Register-Republic*, August 13, 1951.

95. "The World, Too," 6; Wes H. Klusmann, "Jamboree Friend," *Scouting*, December 1951, 2–3; BSIB, *The Jamboree Story*, 82; "Boy Scout Jamboree," *European Stars and Stripes*, August 12, 1951.

96. "46 Nations' Flags Raised by Scouts—Colors of Japan Are Included," *New York Times*, July 1, 1950.

97. BSA, *Jamboree Public Relations*, 3, 4, World Jamboree File, BSA National Archives.

98. See Fieldston, *Raising the World*, 54–77. On Eisenhower's People-to-People initiative, see Klein, *Cold War Orientalism*, 49–56. On the "model United Nations," see Nicholson, "Apprentices to Power," 152–54.

99. See Chatelain, "International Sisterhood," 261–70; Swafford, "The Challenge and Promise of Girl Scout Internationalism," 105–24; and Helgren, *American Girls and Global Responsibility*.

100. LeFevre quoted in Sheenan, "The Girl Scouts, the United Nations, and Our Own Constitution," A4941–A4942.

101. American Legion Department of Illinois, "Resolution No. 33: Girl Scouts of America."

102. Fieldston, *Raising the World*, 87–88.

103. Eby, "Where There's a Will," *Scouting*, May 1947), 2–3, 23; Eby, "Scouting with Displaced Persons (D.P.s)," *Jamboree*, May 1947, 155–57. On DP scouting, see Wilson, *Scouting Round the World*, 145–56; and Wyman, *DPs*, 103–5.

104. Eby, "Scouting with Displaced Persons (D.P.s)," 155; Eby, "Scouting in D.P. Camps: Memo to Mr. J. S. Wilson," 12.

105. "Moisson: Jamboree Mondial De La Paix," 304–5; "D.P. Scouts," *Jamboree*, January 1949, 23–24; J. R. Monnet, "D.P. Scouting," *Jamboree*, February 1950, 33–40. The BSIB established the D.P. Scout Division with separate national chapters in 1947; see "The D.P. Scout Division of the International Bureau, 1947–1950," *Jamboree*, June 1950, 161–72.

106. On the World Youth Festivals, see Rutter, "Enacting Communism." On the 1957 rally in Moscow, see Rupprecht, *Soviet Internationalism after Stalin*, 51–57.

107. "Red Youths Mass for Berlin Rally," *New York Times*, August 5, 1951; "2,200 Stranded," *Christian Science Monitor*, August 6, 1951. See also Rutter, "The Western Wall," 78–106.

108. "Scout Executive Sees World Hope in Youth's Hands," *Christian Science Monitor*, October 3, 1950. See also "Three Youth Rallies," *New York Times*, August 7, 1951.

109. "His Holiness Hears Boy Scouts Sing," July 27, 1951, *Associated Press Photo Collection*; "American Boy Scouts Sing Their Hymn for the Pope," *New York Times*, July 31, 1951.

110. Truman quoted in BSA, *Jamboree Public Relations*, 2; "Text of Truman Address to Boy Scouts," *New York Times*, July 1, 1950.

111. "Scouting Makes for Freedom," *Scouting*, July–August 1956, front matter; "Youth, 1951," *New York Times*, August 14, 1951. See also Zarah, *The Lost Children*, 17.

112. "If You Lived in Russia," *Scouting*, April 1950, 2–3; "Communists Will Train Our Youth," *Scouting*, November 1953, 5; Thompson, "What's Happening to the Soviet School Child," *Scouting*, September 1956, 2–3, 23; Schuck, "Our Answer to Brainwashing," *Scouting*, September 1956, 3–4, 20.

113. Lodge, "Toward a Free World," *Scouting*, November 1957, 2–3; "Catholic Boy Scouts Pray for Hungarians," *Washington Post*, November 13, 1956.

114. See Van Zandt, "Remarks at the Boy Scout Court of Honor, Tyrone, Pa., August 10, 1950," A5759.

115. "Britons Debate 'Red Scout,'" *Christian Science Monitor*, February 12, 1954; "British Scouts Order Red's Resignation," *Washington Post*, February 13, 1954; "Little Red Eagle Scout," *Time Magazine*, February 22, 1954. See also Mills, "Be Prepared," 429–50.

116. "Red Plot on Youth Revealed," *Pacific Stars and Stripes*, August 14, 1952; "British Scout Who's Red Told He Cannot Be Both," *New York Times*, February 11, 1954.

117. "Strengthen the Arm of Liberty," *Boys' Life*, February 1949, 3.

118. "Escape to Freedom," *Boys' Life*, March 1957, 11, 73, 75.

119. "Kansas Scouts Help Czech Friend Escape from Red-Ruled Homeland," *Boys' Life*, March 1951, 61. See also Tom MacPherson, "Soon I Can Vote!" *Boys' Life*, April 1952, 36–37.

120. "World Brothers," *Scouting*, January 1951, 5; "Scout Edits 'World' Paper," *Boys' Life*, May 1951, 60; "U.S.A.," *World Scouting/Scoutisme Mondial*, May 1955, 246–48; Sanzare, "A Bridge of Friendship," *World Scouting/Scoutisme Mondial*, November 1956, 546.

121. Nguyen, *The Gift of Freedom*, xii, 1–8, 13–14.

122. "Help 'Em Come Back: World Friendship Fund," Scout Executives World Friendship Fund Kit, World Friendship File.

123. Ibid. See also Peacock, *Innocent Weapons*, 115–16; and BSA, *World Jamboree 1967 Program Guidebook*.

124. See, for example, BSA, "Scouts of the World—Building for Tomorrow," February 1947, World Friendship File.

125. "Scouts of the World—Building for Tomorrow: Plans for 1947 Scout Week," *Scouting*, November 1947, 13.

126. See IRS (Division of Relationships), "Annual Bulletin, July 31, 1953," 2, 9–10; "History of the Interracial Service (probably 1959)," 13–15, Division of Relationships File; and Peacock, *Innocent Weapons*, 111–13.

127. IRS (Division of Relationships), "Annual Report for the Year 1960," 32–33, Division of Relationships File; and IRS (Division of Relationships), "Annual Report for the Year 1959," 4–15.

128. BSA, *Annual Report* (1961), 84.

129. "Seventy-Three and Still Prepared," *Ebony*, July 1968, 80.

130. Ford, "Remarks to Scout Leaders (October 1966)," The Ford Congressional Papers, Box D21, Press Secretary and Speech File, Gerald R. Ford Presidential Library.

131. Marie Wynne Clark, "The Changing World of Youth Groups," *Scouting*, November 1968, 9.

132. Simanga, *Amiri Baraka and the Congress of African People*, 14–15.

133. "Boy Scouts Returning from Nigeria," January 8, 1965, *New York World-Telegram & Sun Collection*, Prints and Photographs Division, Library of Congress; Welch quoted in "Building Bamboo Fires and Brotherhood," *Carolina Times* (Durham, NC), October 9, 1965.

134. "Hungarian Exile Warns Africans," *New York Times*, September 11, 1960. See also Glant, *Remember Hungary, 1956*, 41. On the Soviet-African student exchange of the late 1950s and 1960s, see Guillory, "Culture Clash in the Socialist Paradise," 271–81.

135. "Gen. William C. Westmoreland, TIME Magazine's 'Man of the Year,'" *Scouting*, October 1966, 2.

136. Fulbright, *The Arrogance of Power*, 15.

7. Innocents Abroad

1. "Dramatize It! A Play and a Ceremony for Anniversary Use," *Scouting*, January 1945, 13–14. On the popularity of U.S.-centric cartography, see Barney, *Mapping the Cold War*, 61–95.

2. Höhn and Moon, *Over There*, 19, 25. See also Höhn, *GIs and Fräuleins*; Gillem, *America Town*; Green, *Black Yanks in the Pacific*; Höhn and Klimke, *A Breath of Freedom*; and Maulucci and Junker, *GIs in Germany*.

3. See also Bright and Geyer, "Where in the World Is America?," 72.

4. Höhn and Moon, *Over There*, 11.

5. BSA, *Annual Report* (1954), 212; *Annual Report* (1958), 226; *Annual Report* (1965), 252.

6. BSA, *Annual Report* (1954), 212; *Annual Report* (1958), 226; *Annual Report* (1965), 252.

7. The BSA *Annual Report* for 1972 lists a total of 31,778 boys served by the Transatlantic and Far East Councils. BSA, *Annual Report* (1972), 84. Subsequent reports fail to provide membership figures for both councils. On U.S. military redeployments in the 1970s, see Zilian, "The Shifting Military Balance in Central Europe," 158–59; and Vazansky, "Army in Crisis."

8. Stoler, *Haunted by Empire*, 1–22.

9. Alvah, *Unofficial Ambassadors*, 1–13.

10. Mechling, *On My Honor*, 128. See also Smith, Oral History Report 2006.056.007, October 27, 2006, Oral History Collection, BSA National Archives.

11. See Hogan, *A Cross of Iron*. For a gendered perspective, see Dean, *Imperial Brotherhood*.

12. R. A. Dague, "Is the Boy Scout Movement of a Military Nature?," *Railway Carmen's Journal*, December 1911, 673–74.

13. "Baden-Powell Aim of Socialist Hisses," *Oregonian*, March 10, 1912.

14. Pyne quoted in Peterson, *The Boy Scouts*, 85, 91. See also Macleod, *Building Character*, 253–54.

15. Examples of this cross-generational dispute between parents wary of the dangers of militarism and children who wanted to join the Boy Scouts are contained in letters that boys addressed to Daniel Carter Beard, in Beard Papers, Boxes 213–15.

16. "'Boy Scouts' and the War Spirit," *Literary Digest*, November 26, 1910, 986. See also Macleod, *Building Character*, 147.

17. Beard to West, August 31, 1936, Beard Papers, Box 209. See also Scott and Murphy, *The Scouting Party*, 170.

18. Nitobe, "Commentary on the Boy Scouts," August 5, 1924, Boy Scout File, Dossier No. 22650.

19. West to William H. Kilpatrick, March 18, 1931, Beard Papers, Box 131.

20. The International Scout Conference of 1922 in Paris recommended these changes. See also "The Story of the International Scout Jamboree," *Boys' Life*, October 1920, 9; and BSA, *Official Report* (1922), 7.

21. BSA, *Annual Report* (1923), 60–61. See also West to Baden-Powell, February 28, 1928, Beard Papers, Box 133.

22. Roosevelt quoted in West and Hillcourt, *The 1933 Scout Jamboree Book*, vi.

23. Theodore Roosevelt to West, November 30, 1915, Beard Papers, Box 129.

24. Leonard Wood to West, November 9, 1914, The Papers of Theodore Roosevelt, Box 276, ser. 1.

25. BSA, *Handbook for Boys*, 2nd ed. (1916), 12; BSA, *Annual Report* (1920), 7. See also Macleod, *Building Character*, 179–80.

26. "American Legion Backs Scouts," *Scouting*, December 11, 1919, 7; U.S. Congress, "Loan of War Department Equipment for Use at the World Jamboree of the Boy Scouts of America, May 16, 1929"; U.S. Congress, "Lend Army Equipment for Use at the World Jamboree to the Boy Scouts of America to Be Held in the Netherlands, March 16, 1937"; John J. Pershing to Colin H. Livingston, July 25, 1918, in *The Boy Scouts Year Book* (1919), 59.

27. "Report of the Commission on the Underprivileged Boy," in BSA, *Executive Conference Report* (1922), 365. See also Jordan, *Modern Manhood*, 221.

28. Clarke, "Transatlantic Friendship: Scout-to-Scout," *Scouting*, May–June 1962, 12, 28.

29. On the intersections of childhood and military culture, see Marten, "Children and War," 142–57; and Honeck and Marten, *War and Childhood*.

30. According to Alvin Townley, Eagle Scouts make up less than 1 percent of the U.S. population but regularly represent between 12 and 16 percent of the student bodies at U.S. military academies. Townley, *Spirit of Adventure*, 98.

31. BSA, *Annual Report* (1948), 45; Wilson to Harry A. Wann (Office of Military Government for Hesse), April 1, 1948, Office of Military Government for Germany (OMGUS), RG 260, Youth Activities Section, Box 135.

32. "Report of W.C. Wessel, Part II, Observations and Recommendations," OMGUS, Youth Activities Section, Box 135, 1–2; "Report of W.C. Wessel, Part III, Boy Scouting," ibid., 10.

33. Kage, *Civic Engagement in Postwar Japan*, 28.

34. See Koshiro, *Trans-Pacific Racisms*, 21–22.

35. Wilson, *Scouting Round the World*, 248–49; "Good Scouts," *Pacific Stars and Stripes*, November 22, 1953.

36. "Military Government Policy on Re-establishment of Boy Scout and Girl Scout Activities," September 13, 1946; L. E. Norrie (OMGUS, Office Adult & Youth Education), "Boy Scout Report," undated (probably 1946), OMGUS, Youth Activities Section, Box 135. On the British ban on German scouting, see "Statement on German Scouting and Guiding," August 1947, OMGUS, Bremen, Records of the Education Division, Box 32; and "Future Policy in Regard to

German Scouting in the British Zone," May 11, 1948, OMGUS, Baden-Wuerttemberg, Education & Cultural Relations Division, Box 963.

37. John W. Taylor, "Plan for Utilization of Boy Scout Executives, September 10, 1945," OMGUS, Education and Cultural Relations Division, Box 17; BSA, *Annual Report* (1946), 32.

38. On the transmittal of BSA literature to the U.S.-occupied parts of Germany, see the correspondence between WFF Director Howard Patton and OMGUS officials, Youth Activities Section, Box 135. See also "The World Too," *Scouting*, March 1949, 6.

39. "Pfadfinders," *Scouting*, January 1954, 16.

40. OMGUS (Education and Cultural Relations Division), *German Youth between Yesterday and Tomorrow*, 15.

41. See Puaca, *Learning Democracy*; and Blessing, *The Antifascist Classroom*.

42. See, for example, "Telephone Conversation between Mr. Cozart, OMG Berlin Sector, and Mr. Strong, OMGUS," August 13, 1947, OMGUS, Youth Activities Section, Box 135.

43. "Aus dem 'Bund Deutscher Pfadfinder' (Interkonfessioneller Pfadfinderbund Bayerns," June 7, 1949, OMGUS Bavaria, Records of the Intelligence Division, 1946–49, Box 4.

44. Werner Hübert (Bündische Freischar) to Jugendamt Bremen, Jugendpflege, February 18, 1948, OMGUS, Youth Activities Section, Box 135.

45. S. M. Lee, "Plan for Unesco Youth Work in Japan for 1951," Records of the Allied Operational and Occupation Headquarters, World War II, RG 331, Civil Information & Education Section, General Subject File, 1945–52, Box 5935.

46. Elizabeth P. Lam (OMGUS, Youth Activities Section, Nuremberg) to Howard Patton, October 25, 1948, OMGUS, Youth Activities Section, Box 135.

47. Robert P. Martin, "Why Korean Liberals Are So Few—Because It's Safer at Extremes," ibid.

48. Dwight P. Griswold to Colonel A. W. Jacobs, May 22, 1947, ibid.

49. OMGUS, *German Youth between Yesterday and Tomorrow*, 11–18. See also Nawyn, "'Striking at the Roots of German Militarism,'" 450; and Swafford, "The Challenge and Promise of Girl Scout Internationalism."

50. For an institutional history of the GYA, see U.S. Army, Europe, *The U.S. Armed Forces German Youth Activities Program*. For a critical perspective, see Goedde, *GIs and Germans*, 127–65.

51. On the uniform ban in occupied Germany, see Jarausch, *After Hitler*, 29. Such a ban also existed in Japan; see, for example, "GI Social Life in Japan Stifled," *Daily Pacifican*, May 12, 1946.

52. On German Boy Scouts wearing Hitler Youth uniforms, see Protsch, *Be All You Can Be*, 64.

53. Leon A. Shelnutt to Deputy Director, November 8, 1948, OMGUS Baden-Württemberg, Education and Cultural Relations Division, Box 973. See also Nawyn, "'Striking at the Roots of German Militarism,'" 311–12.

54. See, for example, "Antrag des Bundes Deutscher Pfadfinder für sein Abzeichen," May 31, 1947, OMGUS, Bavaria, Education and Cultural Relations Division, Box 48; and Helmut Nohlen to Military Government Württemberg-Baden, October 17, 1948, OMGUS Baden-Wuerttemberg, Education and Cultural Relations Division, Box 963.

55. Lion to General Walther J. Muller (OMGUS Bavaria), September 16, 1946, OMGUS, Bavaria, Education and Cultural Relations Division, Box 48.

56. "Perennial Boy Scout," *European Stars and Stripes*, July 25, 1948; "MG Warns on Boy Scout Uniforms," *European Stars and Stripes*, July 25, 1948.

57. See John P. Steiner, "Illegal Wearing of Boy Scout Uniforms," September 9, 1948, OMGUS Baden-Wuerttemberg, Education and Cultural Relations Division, Box 963; and "MG Again Warns German Youth on Scout Uniforms," *European Stars and Stripes*, September 19, 1948.

58. Goedde, *GIs and Germans*, 128.

59. BSA, *Annual Report* (1950), 49; and Walter Kunkel, "Scouting in Germany," *Scouting*, April 1952, 3.

60. "Area Leader Explains American Scouting to Ex-Hitler Youth," *Red Feather Facts* 4 (1952), Homann Papers, Box 5.

61. C. M. Finnell, "Japan Honestly Wants Help," *Scouting*, November 1953, 24.

62. L. E. Norrie to Commanding General, U.S. Constabulary, Berlin, undated (probably 1946), OMGUS, Youth Activities Section, Box 135.

63. Steiner is quoted in Nawyn, " 'Striking at the Roots of German Militarism,' " 312.

64. Wilson, "Light and Shade," *Jamboree*, December 1948, 363.

65. UNESCO Youth Work Office, "Report of Survey on Japanese Youth (April–May 1951)," 1, Records of the Allied Operational and Occupation Headquarters, World War II, Box 5935. See also Fousek, *To Lead the Free World*, 72–73.

66. Wolfgang Plewe, "The Actual State of German Youth," December 28, 1945, Report of Youth Activities Survey in the American Zone, 579.8, World Scout Bureau Archives.

67. "Solche Kerle wie die Makefinger," *Der Spiegel*, May 15, 1948, 7.

68. Office of Military Government for Bremen, "Meeting on Boy Scouts, Bremen Youth Center, May 3, 1947," 3, OMGUS, Youth Activities Section, Box 135.

69. These quotes are taken from Nawyn, " 'Striking at the Roots of German Militarism,' " 459. On social-democratic youth groups such as the Falken opposing the Boy Scouts, see "Report on the German Scout Conference held at Barsbüttel, on the 4th, 5th, and 6th May 1948," 6, OMGUS, Youth Activities Section, Box 135.

70. Quoted in Swafford, "Democracy's Proving Ground," 189.

71. George C. King to John J. McCloy, March 23, 1951, 2, Records of the High Commissioner for Germany, RG 466, Security General Records, 1949–52, Box 133.

72. On the British and U.S. role in the founding of the Ring Deutscher Pfadfinder, see Keyler, "Auslandsbeziehungen," 282–83.

73. "Scouting behind the Iron Curtain with Freedom Outpost's Troop 46," *Berlin Observer*, October 24, 1958.

74. Ibid.

75. Swafford, "Democracy's Proving Ground," 22; and Alvah, *Unofficial Ambassadors*, 1–13.

76. See, for example, Swafford, "The Challenge and Promise of Girl Scout Internationalism."

77. "B.S.A. in Japan," *Pacific Stars and Stripes*, September 24, 1949.

78. "Man among Boys," *European Stars and Stripes*, February 27, 1957.

79. "Scouts Learn Gun Safety," *Berlin Observer*, April 13, 1957; "Scouts Given WAB Jaunt," *Wiesbaden Post*, March 13, 1953; "Sky's the Limit for Burtonwood Cubs," *European Stars and Stripes*, February 21, 1956; "F.E. Explorer Scouts Set Air Encampment," *Pacific Stars and Stripes*, November 28, 1955.

80. See, for example, the interviews with Joseph Mait, Daniel Cheung, and Chip Pierce.

81. "70 Honored at Wiesbaden Fete," *European Stars and Stripes*, February 15, 1955; "Scouts 'Command' Army Units in Ulm," *European Stars and Stripes*, March 6, 1956; "Explorer Scouts 'Take Over' Command," *Berlin Observer*, February 3, 1961; "Scouts Simulate Command Control during Week-Long Celebration of 51st Anniversary," *Berlin Observer*, February 10, 1961.

82. "Scout Leaders Needed by Local Organizations," *Stuttgart Post News*, April 13, 1951; "Scoutmaster Deficit Threatens American Boy Scouts in Tokyo," *Pacific Stars and Stripes*, November 5, 1951; "At Scout Banquet," *Wiesbaden Post*, March 21, 1952; "Dinner, Exhibit Mark 45th Year of Boy Scouts," *Wiesbaden Post*, February 4, 1955; "Troop 46 Looks Forward to Father-Son Banquet," *Berlin Observer*, February 13, 1959.

83. "Wiesbaden Boy Receives Eagle Award," *Wiesbaden Post*, June 17, 1955; "We're Proud of You, Son," *Berlin Observer*, February 25, 1956; "From General to Duke," *Berlin Observer*, July 27, 1957.

84. On the "pal ideal" in modern discourses on American fathering, see Martschukat, *Die Ordnung des Sozialen*, 225–27; and Cross, *Men to Boys*, 82–83.

85. Alvah, *Unofficial Ambassadors*, 223.

86. See, for example, Alexander Vazansky, "'Army in Anguish'"; and Höhn and Klimke, *A Breath of Freedom*, 144, 216.

87. Interview with Tom Tippins.

88. Interview with Bruce W. Doole.

89. Interview with Joseph Mait.

90. Interview with Walter Hamscher.

91. Interview with Winston R. Davis.

92. Interview with Joseph E. Boling.

93. Taylor quoted in Eisenhuth and Krause, "Inventing the 'Outpost of Freedom,'" 196.

94. Edward P. Black, "Scouting 19 Miles from Russia," *Scouting*, September 1964, 23.

95. J. Edgar Gamble, "Camping in the Far East," preface, unfiled, BSA National Archives.

96. See, for instance, "Westward Ho!" *Berlin Observer*, April 18, 1958.

97. Interview with Don Atwood.

98. David Teska, Oral History Report 2006.056.060, September 25, 2009, Oral History Collection.

99. "Camp Freedom: A Tribute to Determination," *European Stars and Stripes*, July 29, 1956.

100. "Lemnitzer Cites 'Duty to Youth,'" *Pacific Stars and Stripes*, February 7, 1956.

101. Interview with Joseph Mait.

102. Interview with Chip Pierce. See also Hamscher, interview.

103. Atwood, interview.

104. Hamscher, interview.

105. Kidd, "Moving Experience."

106. Hamscher, interview. See also Boling, interview.

107. Ballard, "Memories of Clark Air Base 1959/1960."

108. "Scouting," *Mediterranean Stars and Stripes*, January 3, 1946.

109. For the first quote, see Höhn and Moon, *Over There*, 112; for the second quote, see Kniptash, *On the Western Front*, 56.

110. Cf. note 81.

111. Davis, *Men of Schiff*, 120.

112. BSA, *Annual Report* (1960), 240; for the figure for military dependents, see Alvah, *Unofficial Ambassadors*, 11. See also Browder, "Appendix." In 347–52.

113. "U.S. Scouts Termed 'Best Ambassadors,'" *Pacific Stars and Stripes*, March 12, 1958.

114. Peacock, *Innocent Weapons*; Fieldston, *Raising the World*; Oh, *To Save the Children of Korea*.

115. Vernon A. Gifford to Mr. Thurman, December 19, 1944, Boy Scouts, July 1944–February 1945, Records of the Allied Operational and Occupation Headquarters, Box 4865.

116. On early interactions between U.S. soldier-scoutmasters and German boys, see GYA, "Desirability of Joint Scout Organizations," OMGUS, Youth Activities Section, Box 311; "Democratic Youth Groups Fostered by Troops," ibid.; Norrie, "Boy Scout Report; and "Perennial Boy Scout."

117. Fieldston, *Raising the World*, 42–47.

118. "Scouts Learn New Knots," *Pacific Stars and Stripes*, June 22, 1948; "U.S., Japan Youths in Boy Scout Meet," *Pacific Stars and Stripes*, December 29, 1948; "Okinawa Youths Form First Boy Scout Troop," *Pacific Stars and Stripes*, January 6, 1950.

119. "Memorial Service for Chief Scout," *Pacific Stars and Stripes*, July 14, 1948; "Scout Leaders Attend Services," *Pacific Stars and Stripes*, November 5, 1948.

120. "Easter Train," *European Stars and Stripes*, April 3, 1948; "Women's Club and Girl Scouts Present Easter Gifts to Berlin's Orphan Children," *Berlin Observer*, March 30, 1951. For reports on German American and Japanese American Boy Scout camps, see "American, German Scouts Conduct Summer Camp," *Wiesbaden Post*, July 24, 1951; "International Boy Scout Camporee in Grunewald," *Berlin Observer*, April 18, 1952; "Itami Scouts Host Japanese in Camp-Out," *Pacific Stars and Stripes*, October 14, 1956; "U.S., Japanese Scouts Wind Up 3-Day Camporee," *Pacific Stars and Stripes*, May 6, 1962. See also Pinl, *Im Zeichen der Rautenlilie*, 114.

121. "Neun Tag mit den Amerikanern," *Frankfurter Allgemeine Zeitung*, April 30, 1964; "Mit Hamburger und Pingpong," *Frankfurter Allgemeine Zeitung*, April 7, 1967. For similar events in the Far East Council, see "Scout Pageantry Ranges from Dances to Karate," *Pacific Stars and Stripes*, May 15, 1962.

122. "Japanese-American Scouts Swap Flags," *Pacific Stars and Stripes*, March 28, 1952; "Japanese, American Boy Scouts Trade Flags at Pershing Heights," *Pacific Stars and Stripes*, November 19, 1956; "American, Ryukyuan Scouts Hold Camporee," *Pacific Stars and Stripes*, January 3, 1963.

123. This is according to Francis H. Guess, Oral History Report 2011.006.168, December 15, 2010, Oral History Collection.

124. "Troop 46 and German Scouts Fly to England This Month to Attend American Jubilee," *Berlin Observer*, August 12, 1960; "A Jolly Good Trip," *Berlin Observer*, September 2, 1960.

125. "Ambassadors of World Friendship," *Scouting*, December 1955, 4–5; Kid Magid, "Exploring Japan," *Boys' Life*, February 1957, 14, 71. See also "1956 Pacific Airlift from the United States of America," Pacific Airlift, Division of Relationships File, BSA. For Operation Kinderlift, see Alvah, *Unofficial Ambassadors*, 73, 160.

126. "Ambassadors of World Friendship," 5.

127. U.S. Department of the Army, *Ambassadors All*, 12–13. See also Alvah, *Unofficial Ambassadors*, 199–200.

128. Boling, interview.

129. Atwood, interview.

130. Joe Dodson, "Airlift Questionnaire," Pacific Airlift. Division of Relationships File, BSA.

131. "Boy Scouts to Assist with Clothing Drive," *Wiesbaden Post*, April 13, 1951; "Cub Scout Pack Entertain Boys from Orphanage," *Wiesbaden Post*, January 6, 1956; "Neubiberg Troops Collect Clothes for German Needy," *European Stars and Stripes*, March 15, 1956; "Tapei Orphans Clothed by Boy Scouts," *Pacific Stars and Stripes*, January 9, 1959.

132. "American Legion Commander to Distribute 'Tide of Toys,'" *Berlin Observer*, March 23, 1951; "A Gift Is Given," *Berlin Observer*, December 2, 1955; "A Generous Boost," *Berlin Observer*, November 24, 1956; "Cub Scouts Collect Gifts for Refugee Camps," *European Stars and Stripes*, December 15, 1958; "Boy Scouts Back 'Toys for Tots,'" *Pacific Stars and Stripes*, November 17, 1959.

133. "Santa-san Comes to Japan," *Pacific Stars and Stripes*, December 29, 1948. See also "Guam Scouts Play Santa to Tropical Island," ibid., January 2, 1959.

134. GYA, "Desirability of Joint Scout Organizations."

135. Alvah, *Unofficial Ambassadors*, 222.

136. "Report of W. C. Wessel, Part II," 4.

137. Kurt Garke to Kajus Roller, January 18, 1950, in *Straßen sind wie Flüsse zu überqueren*, 76, 77.

138. Roller, "Rundschreiben 1/49 BFM," September 5, 1949, ibid., 69.

139. Phillips's narrative is based on a questionnaire prepared by Donna Alvah; see Alvah, *Unofficial Ambassadors*, 201, 223–24.

140. J. R. Bader (BSA Director International Service), *Travel Tips for Scouts*, 1–2, 5–6, November 9, 1959, Division of Relationships File.

141. Jerry Solberg, "Airlift Questionnaire," Pacific Airlift. Division of Relationships File, BSA.

142. Interview with Daniel Cheung.

143. See, for example, Larry Herbert, Richard Maule, and Carl Linde, "Airlift Questionnaire," Pacific Airlift. Division of Relationships File, BSA. See also Ballard, "Memories of Clark Air Base 1959/1960."

144. Fiege and Huthmann, *Weltpfadfindertum und Imperialismus*, 37.

145. Ibid., 37, 44–63.

146. Hübner, *Straßen sind wie Flüsse zu überqueren*, 350.

Epilogue

1. "A Great Mark of Our Times," *Scouting*, September 1976, 16–17, 82. See also "Boy Scouts of America Adopt Name of Scouting/USA," *New York Times*, February 23, 1977; "Boy Scouts: Now 'Scouting-USA,'" *Washington Post*, February 24, 1977.

2. "Boy Scouts—A Formula for Survival," *New York Times*, October 17, 1976. See also Wills, *Boy Scouts of America*, 164.

3. BSA, *Annual Report* (1968), 5.

4. Applebome, *Scout's Honor*, xiii–xiv.

5. See Yankelovich, *Is Scouting in Tune with the Times?*, 102–7.

6. MacDonald, "Why the Boy Scouts Work," *City Journal* (Winter 2000): 26.

7. Borstelmann, *The 1970s*, 7.

8. Putnam, *Bowling Alone*, 54–55, 438. For a critical assessment of Putnam's thesis, see Foley and Edwards, "The Paradox of Civil Society," 38–52.

9. Despite their outspoken progressive policies, the Girl Scouts fared no better, losing almost 30 percent of their members from 1970 to 1980. Robert Calvert, "The BSA in Our Changing Society," *Scouting*, May–June 1971, 8.

10. "Scouting Blazes a Trail into the Ghetto," *Life Magazine*, June 4, 1971, 39. On the BSA's inner-city program, see BSA, *Annual Report* (1965), 8–9; BSA, *Annual Report* (1972), 22; and Wills, *Boy Scouts of America*, 154–61.

11. Mac Donald, "Why the Boy Scouts Work," 14–27.

12. BSA, *Annual Report* (1968), 5; Calvert, "The BSA in Our Changing Society," 8–9; Yankelovich, *Is Scouting in Tune with the Times?*, 102–7.

13. "Letters to the Editor: America at Odds with Boy Scout Values," *Portland Press Herald*, August 25, 2012. See also Rudd, *Underground*, 10.

14. Rush quoted in Leffler, *Black Leaders on Leadership*, 125.

15. Yankelovich, *Is Scouting in Tune with the Times?*, 12, 15.

16. Wills, *Boy Scouts of America*, 177–78. On changing hairstyles and fashion in the BSA, see "Hitchin' Rack," *Boys' Life*, July 1973, 4; "Growing Up: Looking Good," *Boys' Life*, December 1976, 80–81; and "Scouting Blazes a Trail into the Ghetto."

17. "Madame Scoutmaster? The Long Battle Continues?" *New York Times*, February 1, 1983; "Woman Still Fighting to Be a Scoutmaster," *New York Times*, July 8, 1984.

18. "Boy Scouts of America Adopt New Name of 'Scouting/USA'"; "Boy Scouts: Now 'Scouting-USA.'"

19. See Peterson, *The Boy Scouts*, 196–99. See also "Scouting for the 1970s," *Scouting*, March–April 1972, 2–5, 61; BSA, *Scout Handbook*, 8th ed. (1972).

20. Quoted in Peterson, *The Boy Scouts*, 197.

21. BSA and Hillcourt, *The Official Boy Scout Handbook*, 9th ed. (1979).

22. Wills, *Boy Scouts of America*, 196–200; Peterson, *The Boy Scouts*, 209–24.

23. Macleod, "Original Intent," 24–25.

24. On the culture-war controversies affecting the BSA, see Mechling, *On My Honor*, xvii–xix, 35–48, 207–36.

25. For a collection of stories about Eagle Scouts who served in Afghanistan and Iraq, see Townley, *Spirit of Adventure*.

26. Mechling, *On My Honor*, xviii.

27. A ruling of the Oregon Supreme Court in June 2012 required the BSA to disclose child abuse records dating from 1965 to 1985. "Boy Scout Files Give Glimpse into 20 Years of Sex Abuse," *New York Times*, October 18, 2012.

28. Boyle, *Scout's Honor*. On Baden-Powell's presumed homosexuality, Boyle references Rosenthal, *The Character Factory*; and Jeal, *Baden-Powell*.

29. Jeal, *Baden-Powell*, 57.

30. "Boy Scouts End Ban on Gay Leaders, over Protests by Mormon Church," *New York Times*, July 27, 2015; David A. Graham, "Robert Gates: America's Unlikely Gay-Rights Hero," *Atlantic*, July 28, 2015.

31. "Boy Scouts, Reversing Century-Old Stance, Will Allow Transgender Boys," *New York Times*, January 30, 2017.

32. "After Trump Injects Politics Into Speech, Boy Scouts Face Blowback," July 25, 2017.

33. Levine, *Gender and Empire*, 1.

34. Jennifer Weiner, "The Men Who Never Have to Grow Up," *New York Times*, July 20, 2017.

Bibliography

Archival Collections

British Scout Association Archives, Gilwell Park, Great Britain
    Founder's Files
BSA National Scouting Museum and Archives, Irving, Texas
    David H. Dwight Sr. File
    Division of Relationships File
    Paul Siple File
    Sherman L. Kiser File
    World Friendship File
    World Jamboree File
    World War II File
    Miscellaneous Unfiled Documents and Photographs
Chicago Historical Society Research Center, Chicago
    Chicago Commons Manuscript Collection
    Chicago Daily News Photograph Collection
Gerald R. Ford Presidential Library, Ann Arbor, Michigan
    Press Secretary and Speech File
Harold B. Lee Library, Brigham Young University, Salt Lake City
    Mormon Missionary Diary Collection
Hoover Institution Archives, Stanford University, Stanford, California
    Ray Lyman Wilbur Papers
    William C. Moore Collection
League of Nations Archives, Geneva, Switzerland
    Boy Scouts File (International Committee on Intellectual Cooperation)

Library of Congress, Manuscript Division, Washington, DC
    Daniel Carter Beard Papers
    NAACP Papers
    The Papers of Theodore Roosevelt
    The Papers of Theodore Roosevelt Jr.
Library of Congress, Prints and Photographs Division, Washington, DC
    Associated Press Photo Collection
    New York World-Telegram & Sun Collection
National Archives (NARA) I, 700 Pennsylvania Avenue, NW, Washington, DC
    Records of the U.S. House of Representatives, RG 233, Special Committee on
        Un-American Activities
National Archives (NARA) II, College Park, Maryland
    General Records Seized from the German-American Bund, RG 131
    Office of Military Government for Germany (OMGUS), RG 260, Youth Activities
        Section
    Paul A. Siple Family Papers
    Records of the Allied Operational and Occupation Headquarters, World War II,
        RG 331, Civil Information & Education Section
    Records of the Bureau of Insular Affairs, RG 350.3, Records Relating to the
        Philippine Islands (1898–1939)
    Records of the High Commissioner for Germany, RG 466, Security General
        Records, 1949–52
    Records of the War Relocation Authority, RG 210
Ohio State University Library Archives, Columbus, Ohio
    Alton A. Lindsey Papers
    Paul Siple Papers
    Richard E. Byrd Papers
Rockefeller Archive Center, Sleepy Hollow, New York
    Laura Spelman Rockefeller Memorial Collection
    Papers of the General Education Board
    Welfare/Youth Collection
Rotary International Archives, Lincolnwood, Illinois
    Boys' Week Scrapbooks
St. Louis University Library, Special Collections, St. Louis, Missouri
    Walter J. Ong Manuscript Collection
South Caroliniana Library, University of South Carolina, Columbia, South Carolina
    William C. Westmoreland Papers
United Nations Archives, New York
    United Nations Relief and Rehabilitation Collection
Wilson Special Collections Library, University of North Carolina, Chapel Hill
    Kenneth Woltz Badgett Papers
Wisconsin State Historical Society Archives, Madison, Wisconsin
    Harold J. Homann Papers
World Scout Bureau Archives, Geneva, Switzerland

BSIC Conference Proceedings.
Miscellaneous Unfiled Documents
Yale University Library, New Haven, Connecticut
    Albert Waldo Snoke Papers

Newspapers and Periodicals

Australia

Geelong Advertiser

France

Le Journal des Éclaireurs

Germany

Berlin Observer
Der Spiegel
European Stars and Stripes
Frankfurter Allgemeine Zeitung
Neues Deutschland
Stuttgart Post News
Wiesbaden Post

Great Britain

Derby Daily Telegraph
Dundee Courier
Elders Review of West African Affairs
Evening Telegraph
Jamboree
Punch Magazine
Times
Workers' Weekly
World Scouting/Scoutisme Mondial

Denmark

Jambo

Italy

Mediterranean Stars and Stripes

Japan

Pacific Stars and Stripes

Mexico

El Merida

Switzerland

L'Eclaireur
World Scouting/Scoutisme Mondial

The Philippines

Daily Pacifican

United States

Anaconda Standard
Army and Navy Journal
Atlanta Constitution
Atlantic Monthly
Baltimore American
Beatrice Daily Sun
Belleville News Democrat
Berkeley Daily Gazette
Boston Daily Globe
Boy Scouts' Yearbook (BSA)
Boys' Life (BSA)
Bronxville Review
Brooklyn Daily Eagle
Buffalo Evening News
Bulletin of the Atomic Scientists
Carlisle Arrowe
Carolina Times
Charleston Daily Mail
Chicago Daily Tribune
Chicago Defender
Chief Scout Executive Bulletin (BSA)
Christian Advocate
Christian Science Monitor
Collier's Weekly
Columbian Magazine

Crisis
Ebony
Edwardsville Intelligencer
Erie Dispatch-Herald
Evening Huronite
Evening Independent
Evening Tribune
Family Weekly
Fortune Magazine
Forum
Friend
Galveston Daily News
Harrisburg Daily Independent
Harvard Crimson
Idaho Citizen
Idaho Falls Post-Register
Jamboree Journal (BSA)
Jefferson City Post-Tribune
Kansas City Star
Kansas City State Journal
Ladies Home Journal
Life Magazine
Literary Digest
Ludington Daily News
Madison Times
Manitowoc Herald Times
Marion Star
Milwaukee Journal
Monticello Express
National Americanism Commission Newsletter
National Geographic Magazine
New Castle News
New Pioneer
New Yorker
New York Herald Tribune
New York Times
Northwest Arkansas Times
Oak Parker
OklaHomann
Oregonian
Our World
Outlook
Philadelphia Inquirer
Philippine Education Magazine

Piqua Daily Call
Pittsburgh Courier
Portage Weekly Democrat
Portland Press Herald
Post Register
Railway Carmen's Journal
Region Six Newsletter (BSA)
Rockford Register-Republic
Rotarian
San Antonio Express
Sandusky Star Journal
San Francisco Chronicle
Saturday Evening Post
Scout Executive (BSA)
Scouting (BSA)
Southern Workman
Spokane Daily Chronicle
Statesville Landmark (North Carolina)
St. Nicholas Magazine
Time Magazine
Washington Post
Weekly Bulletin of Boy Scout Activities (BSA)
Wichita Beacon
Wyoming State Tribune
Young Comrade
Young Pioneer
Zanesville Sunday Times-Signal

Oral Histories

Interviews with Former Scouts and Scoutmasters based on Author's Questionnaire (see Appendix)

Atwood, Don. September 19, 2014.
Boling, James M. December 12, 2015.
Boling, Joseph E. December 16, 2015.
Cheung, Daniel. November 22 and December 23, 2015.
Davis, Winston R. December 10, 2015.
Doole, Bruce W. July 15, 2015.
Hamscher, Walter. November 23, 2015.
Mait, Joseph. November 22, 2015.
Pierce, Chip. July 8, 2015.
Tippins, Tom. September 24, 2014.

Oral History Collection, BSA National Archives

Guess, Francis. Oral History Report 2011.006.168, December 15, 2010.

Smith, Roscoe. Oral History Report 2006.056.007, October 27, 2006.

Teska, David. Oral History Report 2006.056.060, September 25, 2009.

"Three Boy Scouts in Africa: An Interview with David Martin."

Primary Sources

Printed

Addams, Jane. *The Spirit of Youth and the City Streets*. New York: Macmillan, 1909.

Ames, Joseph B. *Under Boy Scout Colors*. New York: Grosset & Dunlap, 1917.

Applebome, Peter. *Scout's Honor: A Father's Unlikely Foray into the Woods*. Orlando, FL: Harcourt, 2003.

AYC. "The Declaration of the Rights of American Youth." In *Reading the Twentieth Century: Documents in American History*, edited by Donald W. Whisenhunt, 111–13. Lanham, MD: Rowman & Littlefield, 2009.

Baden-Powell, Robert. *Aids to Scoutmastership: A Guidebook for Scoutmasters on the Theory of Scout Training*. London: H. Jenkins, 1920.

———. *Boy Scouts beyond the Seas: My World Tour*. London: C. Arthur Pearson, 1913.

———. *Playing the Game: A Baden-Powell Compendium*. Edited by Mario Sica. London: Macmillan, 2007.

———. *Scouting and Youth Movements*. London: Ernest Benn, 1929.

———. *Scouting for Boys: A Handbook for Instruction in Good Citizenship*. Edited by Elleke Boehmer. New York: Oxford University Press, 2004. First published in 1908.

———. *Scouting round the World*. London: H. Jenkins, 1935.

Barrie, James M. *Courage: The Rectorial Address Delivered at St. Andrews University, May 3, 1922*. New York: Charles Scribner's Sons, 1922.

Bary, Helen V. *Child Welfare in the Insular Possessions of the United States: Part I, Porto Rico*. Washington, DC: Government Printing Office, 1923.

Beard, Daniel Carter. *Boy Heroes of Today*. New York: Brewer Warren & Putnam, 1932.

———. *The Boy Pioneers; Sons of Daniel Boone*. New York: Charles Scribner's Sons, 1909.

———. *Hardly a Man Is Now Alive: The Autobiography of Dan Beard*. New York: Doubleday, 1939.

Beveridge, Albert J. *The Young Man and the World*. New York: D. Appleton & Co., 1906.

Bezucha, R. D., ed. *The Golden Anniversary Book of Scouting*. New York: Golden Press, 1959.

Borah, Willam E. *Americanism: Speech of Hon. William E. Borah of Idaho in the Senate of the United States*. Washington, DC: Government Printing Office, 1919.

Bourne, Randolph S. *Youth and Life*. Boston: Houghton & Mifflin, 1913.

Boy Scouts Association (Great Britain). *The Jamboree Book*. London: Boy Scouts Association, 1920.

Boy Scout Foundation of Greater New York. *America's Answer*. New York: Boy Scout Foundation of Greater New York, 1938.

Brady, Darrel. "What Can Rotary Do for Youth." In *Proceedings of the Thirtieth Annual Convention of Rotary International, Cleveland, Ohio, U.S.A., June 19–23, 1939*, 87–93. Chicago: Rotary International, 1939.

Brown, Oril. *Youth under Dictators: A Study of the Lives of Fascist and Communist Youth*. Evanston, IL: Row, Peterson, 1941.

BSA. *Annual Reports of the Boy Scouts of America*. Washington, DC: Government Printing Office, 1918, 1920–77.

——. "Boys in Wartime: Special Research Supplement," *Scouting for Facts: A Bulletin of Information and Interpretation* (June 1942): 2–16.

——. *Collection, Distribution, and Communication Services*. New York: BSA, 1951.

——. *Community Boy Leadership: A Manual for Scout Executives*. New York: BSA, 1922.

——. *Executive Conference Report of the Boy Scouts of America*. New York: BSA, 1936.

——. *Executive Conference Report of the Boy Scouts of America, Atlanta, 1922*. New York: BSA, 1922.

——. *A Family "Be Prepared" Plan*. New York: BSA, 1951.

——. *First Aid and Rescue Methods*. New York: BSA, 1951.

——. "Gearing Research to Wartime Needs," *Scouting for Facts: A Bulletin of Information and Interpretation* (March 1943): 1–8.

——. *Handbook for Boys*. Garden City, NY: Doubleday, 1911.

——. *Handbook for Boys*. 2nd ed. New York: BSA, 1916.

——. *Handbook for Boys*. 3rd ed. New York: BSA, 1928.

——. *Handbook for Boys*. 4th ed. New York: BSA, 1942.

——. *Handbook for Boys*. 6th ed. New Brunswick, NJ: BSA, 1961.

——. *Handbook for Scout Masters: Boy Scouts of America*. New York: BSA, 1913.

——. *Handbook for Scoutmasters*. 2nd ed. New York: BSA, 1922.

——. *Handbook for Scoutmasters*. 3rd ed. New York: BSA, 1944.

——. *High School Victory Program and Scouting: Issued by the Boy Scouts of America in Cooperation with the Committee on Scouting in Schools*. New York: BSA, 1943.

——. *Jamboree Public Relations*. New York: BSA, 1951.

——. *The National and World Jamborees in Pictures: The First National Jamboree of the Boy Scouts of America and the Fifth World Jamboree of Scouting*. New York: BSA, 1937.

——. *National Conference of Scout Masters and Executives, September 15 to 22, 1920: Verbatim Stenographic Report*. Vol. 1. New York: BSA, 1920.

——. *Official Report of the Second Biennial Conference of Boy Scout Executives, September 12th to 19th, 1922*. New York: BSA, 1923.

——. *Official Report of the Third Biennial Conference of Scout Executives, September 6th to 15th, 1924*. New York: BSA, 1924.

——. *Official Report of the Fourth Biennial Conference of Scout Executives, September 22nd to 28th, 1926*. New York: BSA, 1926.

——. *Official Report of the Fifth National Training Conference of Scout Executives, September 5th to 12th, 1928*. New York: BSA, 1928.

——. *Pattern for Survival: A Guide for Unit Leaders*. New York: BSA, 1951.

———. *Policies and Regulations of the Boy Scouts of America: Relationship of Boy Scouts of America and Girl Scouts*. New York: BSA, 1918.

———. *Pre-Jamboree Camp Training Manual for Jamboree Troops: National Jamboree, Washington DC, August 21–30, 1935*. New York: BSA, 1935.

———. *Scout Handbook*. 8th ed. New Brunswick, NJ: BSA, 1972.

———. *Scouting for Facts with a Local Council: Straight from the Boy—Why Scouts Drop*. New York: BSA, 1949.

———. *Scouting in Less-Chance Areas: A Descriptive Statement Developed in Cooperation with the Local Councils at Buffalo, Cleveland, Chicago, and the Chicago Institute for Juvenile Research, State of Illinois*. New York: BSA, 1939.

———. *Scoutmaster's Handbook*. 5th ed. New Brunswick, NJ: BSA, 1959.

———. *A Study of Adolescent Boys*. New Brunswick, NJ: BSA, 1955.

———. *The World Jamboree*. New York: BSA, 1929.

———. *World Jamboree 1967 Program Guidebook: "For Friendship."* New Brunswick, NJ: BSA, 1967.

BSA and William Hillcourt. *The Official Boy Scout Handbook*. 9th ed. Irving, TX: BSA, 1979.

BSIB. *The Jamboree Story: The Full Story of the Eight World Jamborees of the Boy Scout Movement, 1920–1955*. London: BSIB, 1957.

Byrd, Richard E. *Skyward: Man's Mastery of the Air as Shown by the Brilliant Flights of America's Leading Air Explorer*. New York: G. P. Putnam's Sons, 1928.

Campion, Martha. *Who Are the Young Pioneers?* New York: New Pioneer Pub. & Co., 1934.

Cochran, R. E. *Be Prepared: The Life and Illusions of a Scoutmaster*. New York: Sloane, 1952.

———. "Confessions of a Jamboree Scoutmaster." *Harper's Magazine*, February 1951, 59–66.

Crucy, François. "Marcus Garvey, A New Moses, April 17, 1924." In *The Marcus Garvey and Universal Negro Improvement Association Papers: African for the Africans, 1923–1945*, edited by Robert A. Hill. Vol. 10, 159–61. Berkeley: University of California Press, 2006.

Daniel Yankelovich, Inc. *Is Scouting in Tune with the Times? A Research Report Conducted for Boy Scouts of America*. New York: Daniel Yankelovich, 1968.

Davis, Maxine. *The Lost Generation: A Portrait of American Youth Today*. New York: Macmillan, 1936.

Douglas, Robert Dick, Jr. *A Boy Scout in the Grizzly Country*. New York: G. P. Putnam's Sons, 1929.

———. *The Best 90 Years of My Life*. Greensboro, NC: Battleground Printing & Publishing, 2007.

Douglas, Robert Dick, Jr., David Martin Jr., and Douglas L. Oliver. *Three Boy Scouts in Africa: On Safari with Martin Johnson*. New York: G. P. Putnam's Sons, 1928.

Du Bois, W. E. B. "Defensive Military Training." In *The World of W. E. B. Du Bois: A Quotation Sourcebook*, edited by Meyer Weinberg. Westport, CT: Greenwood Press, 1992.

———. "Negro Education." In *W. E. B. Du Bois: A Reader*, edited by David Levering Lewis, 261–69. New York: H. Holt, 1995.

———. "The Present Outlook for the Darker Races of Mankind," *A. M. E. Church Review* 17 (1900): 95–110.

Eastman, Charles A. *Indian Scout Talks: A Guide for Boy Scouts and Camp Fire Girls.* Boston: Little, Brown, 1915.

———. *The Indian To-Day: The Past and Future of the First American.* New York: Doubleday, 1915.

Eisenhower, Dwight D. *Crusade in Europe.* Garden City, NY: Doubleday, 1948.

Eisman, Harry. *An American Boy in the Soviet Union.* New York: Youth Publishers, 1934.

Fairchild, Henry Pratt. *Conduct Habits of Boy Scouts.* New York: BSA, 1931.

Fiege, Jürgen, and Rainer Huthmann. *Weltpfadfindertum und Imperialismus: Dokumente und Analysen—Materialien zur Theorie und Praxis demokratischer Jugendarbeit 4/5.* Frankfurt: Bund Deutscher Pfadfinder, 1973.

Forbush, William B. *The Boy Problem: A Study in Social Pedagogy.* Boston: Pilgrim Press, 1902.

Franklin, John Hope. *Mirror to America: The Autobiography of John Hope Franklin.* New York: Farrar, Straus & Giroux, 2005.

Fulbright, J. William. *The Arrogance of Power.* New York: Random House, 1966.

Gibson, H. W. *Camping for Boys.* New York: Association Press, 1911.

Grant, Madison. *The Passing of the Great Race, or The Racial Bias of European History.* New York: Charles Scribner's Sons, 1916.

GSA. *How to Be Prepared: The Girl Scout Motto in Action.* New York: Girl Scouts, 1951.

———. *Scouting for Girls: Official Handbook of the Girl Scouts.* 3rd ed. New York: Girl Scouts, 1922.

Hall, Granville Stanley. *Adolescence: Its Psychology, and Its Relations to Physiology, Anthropology, Sociology, Sex, Crime, Religion, and Education.* 2 vols. New York: Hesperides Press, 1904–5.

Handford, Thomas W. *Theodore Roosevelt: The Pride of the Rough Riders, an Ideal American.* Chicago: Donohue, 1899.

Harris, Paul. *This Rotarian Age.* Chicago: Rotary International, 1935.

Harris, Stanley A. "Negro Youth and Scouting: A Character Education Program." *Journal of Negro Education* 9 (July 1940): 372–78.

Hübner, Axel, Rolf Klatta, and Herbert Swoboda, eds. *Straßen sind wie Flüsse zu überqueren: Ein Lesebuch zur Geschichte des Bundes Deutscher Pfadfinder (BDP).* Frankfurt: Jugend & Politik, 1991.

Hungarian Boy Scout Association. *Jamboree 1924: Pencil- and Color-Drawings of Lewis Márton, with Some Articles of Jamboree-Visitors.* Leipzig, Germany: Offsetverlag, 1924.

Hurt, H. W. *"Boy Facts": A Study from Existing Sources.* New York: BSA, 1924.

Johnson, Martin. *Camera Trails in Africa.* New York: Century, 1924.

———. *Lion: African Adventure with the King of Beasts.* New York: G. P. Putnam's Sons, 1929.

Keith, Donald. *Mutiny in the Time Machine.* New York: Random House, 1963.

Key, Ellen. *The Century of the Child.* New York: G. P. Putnam's Sons, 1909.

Kietzman, August F. *Why I Became a Scoutmaster: Forty-Eight Years of Youth Work.* New York: Comet Press Books, 1958.

Kipling, Rudyard, "The White Man's Burden." In *The Five Nations*, edited by Rudyard Kipling, 78. London: Methuen, 1903.

Kirkham, Oscar A. "Three Great Words." In *Conference Report, October 1951*, edited by Church of Jesus Christ of Latter-Day Saints. Salt Lake City, UT: Church of Jesus Christ of Latter-Day Saints, 1951.

———. *A World Program for Friendship, Brotherhood, and Peace*. Salt Lake City, UT: Church of Jesus Christ of Latter-Day Saints, 1937.

Knudsen, Sven V., ed. *Jamboree Denmark, 1924: Det Danske Spejderkorps*. Copenhagen: Kbh., 1924.

Levy, Harold P. *Building a Popular Movement: A Case Study of the Public Relations of the Boy Scouts of America*. New York: Russell Sage Foundation, 1944.

Lewis, Wyndham. *Doom of Youth*. New York: R. M. McBride, 1932.

Lindbergh, Charles A. *"We."* New York: G. P. Putnam's Sons, 1927.

Lindsey, Benjamin Barr, and Wainwright Evans. *The Revolt of Modern Youth*. New York: Boni & Liveright, 1925.

Locke, Alain. "Negro Youth Speaks." In *The New Negro: Voices of the Harlem Renaissance*, edited by Alain Locke, 47–53. New York: Albert & Charles Boni, 1925.

Marr, James W. S. *Into the Frozen South: Scout Marr of the Quest Expedition*. London: Cassell, 1923.

Marshall, George. C., Larry I. Bland, Mark A. Stoler, Sharon Ritenour Stevens, Daniel D. Holt, Anne S. Wells, Mame Warren, Wesley B. O'Dell, Seth R. Bullard, and Gregory C. Franke, eds. *The Papers of George Catlett Marshall*. Vol. 6. Baltimore: Johns Hopkins University Press, 2013.

Martin, David R., Jr. *A Boy Scout with the "Sea Devil."* New York: G. P. Putnam's Sons, 1930.

McKenney, Ruth. *Industrial Valley*. New York: Harcourt, Brace, 1939.

Murray, William D. *The History of the Boy Scouts of America*. New York: BSA, 1937.

Myrdal, Gunnar. *An American Dilemma: The Negro Problem and Modern Democracy*. New York: Harper, 1944.

Oliver, Douglas L. *A Boy Scout in the Grand Cavern*. New York: G. P. Putnam's Sons, 1930.

OMGUS (Education and Cultural Relations Division). *German Youth between Yesterday and Tomorrow*. Berlin: OMGUS, 1948.

Owen, Russell. *South of the Son*. New York: John Day, 1934.

Poling, Daniel A. *Youth Marches*. Philadelphia: Judson Press, 1937.

Protsch, Dieter H. B. *Be All You Can Be: From a Hitler Youth in World War II to a US Army Green Beret*. Victoria, BC: Trafford, 2004.

Putnam, David Binney. *David Goes to Baffin Land*. New York: G. P. Putnam's Sons, 1927.

———. *David Goes to Greenland*. New York: G. P. Putnam's Sons, 1926.

Rainey, Homer P. *How Fare American Youth?* New York: Appleton-Century, 1938.

Ralphson, George Harvey. *Boy Scouts in the Philippines, or, the Key to the Treaty Box*. Chicago: M.A. Donohue, 1911.

Reed, Cecil. *Fly in the Buttermilk: The Life Story of Cecil Reed*. Iowa City: University of Iowa Press, 1993.

Richardson, Norma E., and Ormond E. Loomis. *The Boy Scout Movement, Applied by the Church*. New York: Charles Scribner's Sons, 1916.

Riesman, David, Nathan Glazer, and Reuel Denney. *The Lonely Crowd: A Study of the Changing American Character*. New Haven, CT: Yale University Press, 1950.

Roosevelt, Eleanor. "Facing the Problems of Youth," *Journal of Social Hygiene* 21 (October 1935): 393–94.

Roosevelt, Theodore. *African Game Trails*. New York: Charles Scribner's Sons, 1910.

———. "A Letter from President Roosevelt on Race Suicide." *American Monthly Review of Reviews* 35 (May 1907): 550–51.

———. *The Strenuous Life: Essays and Addresses*. New York: Century, 1905.

Ross, Edward A. "The Causes of Race Superiority." *Annals of the American Academy of Political and Social Science* 18 (July 1901): 67–89.

Rotary International. *Proceedings: Eighteenth Annual Convention of Rotary International: Ostend, Belgium, June 5–10, 1927*. Chicago: Rotary International, 1927.

Rudd, Mark. *Underground: My Life with SDS and the Weathermen*. New York: William Morrow, 2009.

Russell, Bertrand. *Education and the Social Order*. London: G. Allen & Unwin, 1932.

Seton, Ernest Thompson. *The Birch-Bark Roll of the Woodcraft Indians: Containing Their Constitution, Laws, Games, and Deeds*. New York: Doubleday, 1907.

———. *The Gospel of the Red Man: An Indian Bible*. Garden City, NY: Doubleday, 1936.

———. *Two Little Savages: Being the Adventures of Two Boys Who Lived as Indians and What They Learned*. New York: Grosset & Dunlap, 1903.

Sheenan, Timothy P. "The Girl Scouts, the United Nations, and Our Own Constitution," July 2, 1954. In *Congressional Record*—Appendix, A4941–A4942. Washington, DC: Government Printing Office, 1954.

Shvarts, Oleg. *Slet*. Moscow: Gos. izd-vo, 1930.

Siple, Paul. *A Boy Scout with Byrd*. New York: G. P. Putnam's Sons, 1931.

———. *90 Degrees South: The Story of the American South Pole Conquest*. New York: Putnam, 1959.

Smith, Dean C. *By the Seat of My Pants: A Pilot's Progress from 1917 to 1930*. Boston: Little, Brown, 1961.

Smith, William E. *Jamboree Joys*. Kansas City, Kansas: William Embry Smith, 1930.

Stoddard, Lothrop. *The Rising Tide of Color: The Threat against White World-Supremacy*. New York: Charles Scribner's Sons, 1920.

Stratemeyer, Edward, and Charles Copeland. *American Boys' Life of Theodore Roosevelt*. Boston: Lee & Shepard, 1904.

Taylor, Leon W. *A History of Troop Thirty of the Boy Scouts of America of the Dayton Valley Area Council*. Dayton, Ohio: Taylor, 1945.

Tomkins, Williams. *Universal Indian Sign Language: American Indian Souvenir Edition, Boy Scout World Jamboree, England 1929*. San Diego: W. Tomkins, 1929.

U.S. Army, Europe. *The U.S. Armed Forces German Youth Activities Program, 1945–1955*. Wiesbaden, Germany: U.S. Army, Europe, 1956.

U.S. Congress. "Lend Army Equipment for Use at the World Jamboree to the Boy Scouts of America to be held in the Netherlands, March 16, 1937" *75th Congress, 1st Session, Serial Set No. 10083, Session Vol. 1.*

——. "Loan of War Department Equipment for Use at the World Jamboree of the Boy Scouts of America, May 16, 1929," *71st Congress, 1st Session, Serial Set No. 9185, Session Vol. 1.*

U.S. Department of the Army. *Ambassadors All.* Washington, DC: Government Printing Office, 1952.

U.S. House of Representatives, 66th Congress. *Investigation of Communist Propaganda: Hearings before a Special Committee to Investigate Communist Activities in the United States of the House of Representatives, 71st Congress, Second Session.* Vols. 1 and 3. Washington, DC: Government Printing Office, 1930.

——. *Investigation of Communist Propaganda, Report: Pursuant to H.Res. 220.* Washington, DC: Government Printing Office, 1931.

——. *Investigation of Nazi Propaganda Activities: Special Committee on Un-American Activities.* Washington, DC: Government Printing Office, 1934.

——. *Investigation of Un-American Propaganda Activities in the United States.* Vols. 1 and 3. Washington, DC: Government Printing Office, 1938.

——. *Investigation of Un-American Propaganda Activities in the United States.* Vol. 6. Washington, DC: Government Printing Office, 1939.

——. *Investigation of Un-American Propaganda Activities in the United States.* Vol. 12. Washington, DC: Government Printing Office, 1940.

——. *Investigation of Un-American Propaganda Activities in the United States: H.Res. 282, Appendix—Part IV: German-American Bund.* Washington, DC: Government Printing Office, 1942.

——. *Investigation of Un-American Propaganda Activities in the United States: H.Res. 282.* Washington, DC: Government Printing Office, 1943.

——. *Japanese Immigration: Hearings before the Committee on Immigration and Naturalization.* Vols. 1 and 2. Washington, DC: Government Printing Office, 1921.

Van Zandt, James E. "Remarks at the Boy Scout Court of Honor, Tyrone, Pa., August 10, 1950," *Congressional Record: Proceedings and Debates of the 81st Congress, 2nd Session* (Washington, DC: Government Printing Office, 1950), A5759.

Voss, Ernest E. "Scouting among Primitive Boys." Unpublished thesis, 1939.

Webb, Sidney. "The Decline in the Birth-Rate." *Fabian Society Tract* 131 (March 1907): 1–19.

West, James E., *The Boy Scout's Book of True Adventure.* New York: G. P. Putnam's Sons, 1931.

——, ed. *The Scout Jamboree Book: American Scouts at the 3rd World Jamboree.* New York: G. P. Putnam's Sons, 1930.

West, James E., and William Hillcourt. *The 1933 Scout Jamboree Book: American Scouts at the 4th World Jamboree.* New York: G. P. Putnam's Sons, 1933.

Whyte, William H. *Organization Man.* New York: Simon & Schuster, 1956.

Wilson, John S. *Scouting Round the World.* London: Blandford Press, 1959.

Wilson, Sloan. *The Man in the Gray Flannel Suit.* New York: Simon & Schuster, 1955.

Winslow, W. Thatcher. *Youth: A World Problem.* Washington, DC: Government Printing Office, 1938.

Online

American Legion Department of Illinois. "Resolution No. 33: Girl Scouts of America." 36th Annual Department Convention, August 5–8, 1954. Accessed October 4, 2015. http://gshistory.com/2014/08/07/the-girl-scout-red-scare-part-three.

Ballard, Terry. "Memories of Clark Air Base 1959/1960." Accessed December 17, 2015. http://www.terryballard.org/clark.htm.

"Bill Shishima Interview, Segment 05." Accessed March 16, 2017. https://archive.org/details/ddr-densho-1011-1-5.

Braun, Wernher von. "Statement before Boy Scouts of America, Raymond Jones Armory, Huntsville, Alabama," April 5, 1963. *NASA History Program Office.* Accessed August 15, 2015. https://historydms.hq.nasa.gov/sites/default/files/DMS/e0000 41266.pdf.

BSA. "Astronauts and the BSA." Accessed August 15, 2015. http://www.scouting.org/FILESTORE/pdf/02-558.pdf.

——. "Rockets, Rocks, Rhythm." Accessed August 15, 2015. http://blog.scoutingmagazine.org/2015/04/30/rocks-rockets-rhythm-1958-flier-tells-of-new-exploring-program.

——. "The World Friendship Fund." Accessed August 19, 2015. http://www.scouting.org/scoutsource/International/InformationSheets/22-329.aspx.

Cornell, Douglas. "'A Jamboree without Jam': South African Scouts Enjoyed Themselves, but Oh! the Food." Accessed April 7, 2015. http://www.scouting.org.za/capewest/heritage/Overseas_Jamborees/1933_WJ4_Hun_Report.pdf.

Gates, Robert M. "Boy Scout Jamboree, Fort A.P. Hill, Virginia, Wednesday, July 28, 2010." Accessed August 29, 2014. http://www.defense.gov/Speeches/Speech.aspx?SpeechID=1494.

Kidd, James. "Moving Experience." Accessed December 17, 2015. http://militarybratlife.com/moving-experience.

The Scout Association. "World Scouting." Accessed March 14, 2017. http://members.scouts.org.uk/supportresources/2194/world-scouting-fs260010.

Troutner, Brent. "Space Isn't Easy." Accessed September 2, 2015. http://blog.utahscouts.org/boy-scouting/space-isnt-easy.

"We Had to Do a Good Deed Every Day: Interview with John Hope Franklin." Accessed August 15, 2014. http://storycorps.org/listen/john-hope-franklin-with-his-son-john-w-franklin.

Secondary Literature

Abbott, Philip. "Titans/Planners, Bohemians/Revolutionaries: Male Empowerment in the 1930s." *Journal of American Studies* 40, no. 3 (2006): 463–85.

Adams, James Eli. *Dandies and Desert Saints: Styles of Victorian Masculinity.* Ithaca, NY: Cornell University Press, 1995.

Adelman, Jeremy, and Stephen Aron. "From Borderlands to Borders: Empires, Nation-States and the Peoples in North American History." *American Historical Review* 104, no. 3 (1999): 814–41.

Albarrán, Elena Jackson. "Boy Scouts under the Aztec Sun: Mexican Youth and the Transnational Construction of Identity." In Jobs and Pomfret, *Transnational Histories of Youth in the Twentieth Century,* 45–69.

Alexander, Kristine. "Can the Girl Guide Speak? The Perils and Pleasures of Looking for Children's Voices in Archival Research." *Jeunesse: Young People, Texts, Cultures* 4 (Summer 2012): 132–45.

——. "The Girl Guide Movement and Imperial Internationalism during the 1920s and 1930s." *Journal of the History of Childhood and Youth* 2 (Winter 2009): 37–63.

——. *Guiding Modern Girls: Imperialism, Internationalism, and the Girl Guide Movement in Interwar England, Canada, and India.* Vancouver: University of British Columbia Press, 2017.

Alvah, Donna. *Unofficial Ambassadors: American Military Families Overseas and the Cold War, 1946–1965.* New York: New York University Press, 2007.

Ariès, Philippe. *Centuries of Childhood.* Translated by Robert Baldick. New York: Alfred A. Knopf, 1962.

Armitage, Kevin C. " 'The Child Is Born a Naturalist': Nature Study, Woodcraft Indians, and the Theory of Recapitulation." *Journal of the Gilded Age and Progressive Era* 6, no. 1 (January 2007): 43–70.

Bailey, Beth L. *From Front Porch to Back Seat: A History of Dating in America.* Baltimore: Johns Hopkins University Press, 1988.

Banta, Martha. *Barbaric Intercourse: Caricature and the Culture of Conduct, 1841–1936.* Chicago: University of Chicago Press, 2003.

Barney, Timothy. *Mapping the Cold War: Cartography and the Framing of America's International Power.* Chapel Hill: University of North Carolina Press, 2015.

Bator, Stefanie. "Toward Filipino Self-Rule: American Reform Organizations and American Colonialism in the Philippines, 1898–1946." PhD diss., Northwestern University, Evanston, IL, 2012.

Bayly, C. A., Sven Beckert, Matthew Connelly, Isabel Hofmeyr, Wendy Kozol, and Patricia Seed. "AHR Conversation: On Transnational History." *American Historical Review* 111, no. 5 (2005): 1440–64.

Bederman, Gail. *Manliness and Civilization: A Cultural History of Race and Gender in the United States, 1880–1917.* Chicago: University of Chicago Press, 1996.

Belmonte, Laura A. *Selling the American Way: U.S. Propaganda and the Cold War.* Philadelphia: University of Pennsylvania Press, 2009.

Bender, Daniel E. *American Abyss: Savagery and Civilization in the Age of Industry.* Ithaca, NY: Cornell University Press, 2009.

Bender, Daniel E., and Jana K. Lipman, eds. *Making the Empire Work: Labor and United States Imperialism.* New York: New York University Press, 2015.

Bender, Thomas, ed. *Rethinking American History in a Global Age.* Berkeley: University of California Press, 2002.

Bender, Thomas, and Michael Geyer. "Empires: Might and Myopia." In *The United States and Germany during the Twentieth Century: Competition and Convergence*, edited by Christof Mauch and Kiran Klaus Patel, 12–31. New York: Cambridge University Press, 2010.

Berkovitch, Nitza. *From Motherhood to Citizenship: Women's Rights and International Organizations*. Baltimore: Johns Hopkins University Press, 1999.

Bernstein, Arnie. *Swastika Nation: Fritz Kuhn and the Rise and Fall of the German American-Bund*. New York: St. Martin's Press, 2013.

Bernstein, Robin. *Racial Innocence: Performing American Childhood from Slavery to Civil Rights*. New York: New York University Press, 2011.

Bhabha, Homi K. "Of Mimicry and Man: The Ambivalence of Colonial Discourse." In *The Location of Culture*, 85–92. London: Routledge, 1994.

Bialas, Wolfgang. *Moralische Ordnungen des Nationalisozialismus*. Göttingen, Germany: Vandenhoeck & Ruprecht, 2014.

Blessing, Benita. *The Antifascist Classroom: Denazification in Soviet-Occupied Germany, 1945–1949*. New York: Palgrave Macmillan, 2006.

Block, Nelson R., and Tammy M. Proctor, eds. *Scouting Frontiers: Youth and the Scout Movement's First Century*. Newcastle upon Tyne, UK: Cambridge Scholars Publishing, 2009.

Borstelmann, Thomas. *The 1970s: A New Global History from Civil Rights to Economic Inequality*. Princeton, NJ: Princeton University Press, 2011.

Bowersox, Jeff. *Raising Germans in the Age of Empire: Youth and Colonial Culture, 1871–1914*. New York: Oxford University Press, 2013.

Boyle, Patrick. *Scout's Honor: Sexual Abuse in America's Most Trusted Institution*. Rocklin, CA: Prima Publishing, 1994.

Bright, Charles, and Michael Geyer. "Where in the World Is America? The History of the United States in the Global Age." In *Rethinking American History in a Global Age*, edited by Thomas Bender, 63–100. Berkeley: University of California Press, 2002.

Browder, Dewey A. "Appendix: Population Statistics on the U.S. Military in Germany, 1945–2000," In *GIs in Germany: The Social, Economic, Cultural, and Political History of the American Military Presence*, edited by Thomas W. Maulucci, Jr. and Detlef Junker, 347–52. New York: Cambridge University Press, 2013.

BSP. *Diamond Jubilee Yearbook: Boy Scouts of the Philippines, 1936–1996*. Manila: BSP, 1996.

Bynum, Thomas. *NAACP Youth and the Fight for Black Freedom, 1936–1965*. Chapel Hill: University of North Carolina Press, 2013.

Cannistraro, Philip V. *Blackshirts in Little Italy: Italian Americans and Fascism*. West Lafayette, IN: Bordighera, 1999.

Capozzola, Christopher. *Uncle Sam Wants You: World War I and the Making of the Modern American Citizen*. New York: Oxford University Press, 2008.

Carter, Greg Lee. "Guns." In *Boyhood in America: An Encyclopedia*, edited by Priscilla Ferguson Clement and Jacqueline S. Reinier, 330–35. Santa Barbara, CA: ABC Clio, 2001.

Castledine, Jaqueline L. *Cold War Progressives: Women's Interracial Organizing for Peace and Freedom*. Urbana: University of Illinois Press, 2012.

Chapman, Sally Putnam, and Stephanie Mansfield. *Whistled Like a Bird: The Untold Story of Dorothy Putnam, George Putnam, and Amelia Earhart*. New York: Warner Books, 1997.

Chatelain, Marcia. "International Sisterhood: Cold War Girl Scouts Encounter the World." *Diplomatic History* 38, no. 2 (2014): 261–70.

Chauncey, George. *Gay New York: Gender, Urban Culture, and the Making of the Gay Male World, 1890–1940*. New York: Basic Books, 1994.

Chen, Shehong. *Being Chinese, Becoming Chinese-American*. Urbana: University of Illinois Press, 2002.

Chen, Yinghong. *Creating the "New Man": From Enlightenment Ideals to Socialist Realities*. Honolulu: University of Hawaii Press, 2009.

Choy, Catherine Cenzia. *Empire of Care: Nursing and Migration in Filipino American History*. Durham, NC: Duke University Press, 2003.

Clark, Steven H., ed. *Travel Writing and Empire: Postcolonial Theory in Transit*. London: Zed Books, 1999.

Cobbs Hoffman, Elizabeth. *American Umpire*. Cambridge, MA: Harvard University Press, 2013.

Cohen, Lizabeth. *Making a New Deal: Industrial Workers in Chicago, 1919–1939*. New York: Cambridge University Press, 1990.

Cohen, Robert. *When the Old Left Was Young: Student Radicals and America's First Mass Student Movement, 1929–1941*. New York: Oxford University Press, 1993.

Cohen, Stanley. *Folk Devils and Moral Panics: The Creation of the Mods and Rockers*. London: Routledge, 2002.

Collier, Peter. *The Roosevelts: An American Saga*. New York: Simon & Schuster, 1994.

Comacchio, Cynthia. *The Dominion of Youth: Adolescence and the Making of Modern Canada, 1920 to 1950*. Waterloo, Ontario: Wilfrid Laurier University Press, 2006.

Connell, R. W., and James W. Messerschmidt. "Hegemonic Masculinity: Rethinking the Concept." *Gender & Society* 19, no. 6 (December 2005): 829–59.

Conor, Liz. *The Spectacular Modern Woman: Feminine Visibility in the 1920s*. Bloomington: Indiana University Press, 2004.

Cross, Gary. *Men to Boys: The Making of Modern Immaturity*. New York: Columbia University Press, 2008.

Csatari, Joseph. *Norman Rockwell's Boy Scouts of America*. New York: DK Publishers, 2009.

Cuordileone, K. A. *Manhood and American Political Culture in the Cold War*. New York: Routledge, 2005.

Czech, Kenneth. *With Rifle and Petticoat: Women as Big Game Hunters*. Lanham, MD: Rowman & Littlefield, 2002.

Davis, Tracy C. *States of Emergency: Cold War Nuclear Civil Defense*. Durham, NC: Duke University Press, 2007.

Davis, Winston. *Men of Schiff: A History of the Professional Scouters Who Built the Boy Scouts of America*. Lulu Online, 2013.

Dean, Robert D. *Imperial Brotherhood: Gender and the Making of Cold War Foreign Policy*. Amherst: University of Massachusetts Press, 2003.

Deane, Bradley. *Masculinity and the New Imperialism: Rewriting Manhood in British Popular Literature, 1870–1914*. New York: Cambridge University Press, 2014.

DeGraffenried, Julie K. *Sacrificing Childhood: Children and the Soviet State in the Great Patriotic War*. Lawrence: University Press of Kansas, 2014.

Deloria, Philip J. *Playing Indian*. New Haven, CT: Yale University Press, 1998.

Deutsch, Sarah. *Women and the City: Gender, Space, and Power in Boston, 1870–1940*. New York: Oxford University Press, 2000.

DeVault, Ileen A. *United Apart: Gender and the Rise of Craft Unionism*. Ithaca, NY: Cornell University Press, 2004.

Dickinson, Edward R. *The Politics of German Child Welfare from the Empire to the Federal Republic*. Cambridge, MA: Harvard University Press, 1996.

Donson, Andrew. *Youth in the Fatherless Land: War Pedagogy, Nationalism, and Authority in Germany, 1914–1918*. Cambridge, MA: Harvard University Press, 2010.

DuRocher, Kristina. *Raising Racists: The Socialization of White Children in the Jim Crow South*. Louisville: University Press of Kentucky, 2011.

Eisenhuth, Stefanie, and Scott H. Krause. "Inventing the 'Outpost of Freedom': Transatlantic Narratives and Historical Actors Crafting West Berlin's Postwar Political Culture." *Zeithistorische Forschungen/Studies in Contemporary History* 2 (2014): 188–211.

Ekbladh, David. *The Great American Mission: Modernization and the Construction of an American World Order*. Princeton, NJ: Princeton University Press, 2010.

Ellis, Robert. "Getting the Message Out: The Poster Boys of World War II—Part 2." *Prologue Magazine* 37, no. 2 (Summer 2005): 8–10.

Endy, Christopher. "Travel and World Power: Americans in Europe, 1890–1917." *Diplomatic History* 22, no. 4 (1998): 565–94.

Engelhardt, Tom. *The End of Victory Culture: Cold War America and the Disillusioning of a Generation*. New York: Basic Books, 1995.

Enright, Kelly. *The Maximum of Wilderness: The Jungle in the American Imagination*. Charlottesville: University of Virginia Press, 2012.

Evans, Richard J. *The Third Reich in Power*. New York: Penguin Press, 2005.

Farish, Matthew. "Creating Cold War Climates: The Laboratories of American Globalism." In *Environmental Histories of the Cold War*, edited by J. R. McNeill and Corinna Unger, 51–84. New York: Cambridge University Press, 2010.

Fass, Paula S. *Children of a New World: Society, Culture, and Globalization*. New York: New York University Press, 2007.

——. *The Damned and the Beautiful: American Youth in the 1920s*. New York: Oxford University Press, 1977.

Fass, Paula S., and Michael Grossberg, eds., *Reinventing Childhood after World War II*. Philadelphia: University of Pennsylvania Press, 2012.

Felando, Cynthia. "Hollywood in the 1920s: Youth Must Be Served." In *Hollywood Goes Shopping*, edited by David Desser and Garth S. Jowett, 82–107. Minneapolis: University of Minnesota Press, 2000.

Ferguson, Niall. *Colossus: The Price of America's Empire*. New York: Penguin Books, 2004.

Field, Corinne T., and Nicholas L. Syrett, eds., *Age in America: The Colonial Era to the Present*. New York: New York University Press, 2015.

Fieldston, Sara. "Little Cold Warriors: Child Sponsorship and International Affairs." *Diplomatic History* 38, no. 2 (2014): 240–50.

——. *Raising the World: Child Welfare in the American Century.* Cambridge, MA: Harvard University Press, 2015.

Foley, Michael W., and Bob Edwards. "The Paradox of Civil Society." *Journal of Democracy* 7, no. 3 (1996): 38–52.

Fousek, John. *To Lead the Free Word: American Nationalism and the Cultural Roots of the Cold War.* Chapel Hill: University of North Carolina Press, 2000.

Friedman, Lawrence J., and Mark D. McGarvie, eds. *Charity, Philanthropy, and Civility in American History.* New York: Cambridge University Press, 2003.

Frühstück, Sabine. *Playing War: Children and the Paradoxes of Modern Militarism in Japan.* Oakland: University of California Press, 2017.

Fujimoto, Shigeo. "Trans-Pacific Boy Scout Movement in the Early Twentieth Century: The Case of the Boy Scout Movement in Osaka, Japan." *Australasian Journal of American Studies* 27, no. 2 (December 2008): 29–43.

Gabbacia, Donna R. "Is Everywhere Nowhere? Nomads, Nations, and the Immigrant Paradigm of United States History." *Journal of American History* 86, no. 3 (1999): 1115–34.

Gennep, Arnold van. *The Rites of Passage.* Chicago: University of Chicago Press, 1960.

Ghosh, Dubra. "Another Set of Imperial Turns?" *American Historical Review* 117, no. 3 (2012): 772–93.

Gilbert, James B. *Men in the Middle: Searching for Masculinity in the 1950s.* Chicago: University of Chicago Press, 2005.

Gillem, Mark L. *America Town: Building the Outposts of Empire.* Minneapolis: University of Minnesota Press, 2007.

Gillis, John R. *Youth and History: Tradition and Change in European Age Relations, 1770–Present.* New York: Academic Press, 1974.

Gilmore, Glenda. *Defying Dixie: The Radical Roots of Civil Rights, 1919–1950.* New York: W. W. Norton, 2009.

Glant, Tibor. *Remember Hungary, 1956: Essays on the Hungarian Revolution and War of Independence in American Memory.* Boulder, CO: Social Science Monographs, 2007.

Gleason, Mona. "Avoiding the Agency Trap: Caveats for Historians of Children, Youth, and Education." *Journal of the History of Education* 45, no. 4 (2016): 446–59.

Gleeck, Lewis E., Jr. *The Manila Americans: 1901–1961.* Manila: Carmelo & Bauemann, 1977.

Go, Julian. *Patterns of Empire: The British and American Empires, 1688 to the Present.* New York: Cambridge University Press, 2011.

Goedde, Petra. *GIs and Germans: Culture, Gender, and Foreign Relations, 1945–1949.* New Haven, CT: Yale University Press, 2003.

Goodall, Alex. *Loyalty and Liberty: American Countersubversion from World War I to the McCarthy Era.* Urbana: University of Illinois Press, 2013.

——. "Red Herrings? The Fish Committee and Anti-Communism in the Early Depression Years." In *Little 'Red Scares': Anti-Communism and Political Repression in the United States, 1921–1946,* ed. Robert Justin Goldstein, 71–104. Burlington, VT: Ashgate, 2014.

Gorman, Daniel. *The Emergence of International Society in the 1920s*. New York: Cambridge University Press, 2012.

Grazia, Victoria de. *Irresistible Empire: America's Advance through Twentieth-Century Europe*. Cambridge, MA: Belknap Press of Harvard University Press, 2005.

Green, Michael Cullen. *Black Yanks in the Pacific: Race in the Making of American Military Empire after World War II*. Ithaca, NY: Cornell University Press, 2010.

Green, Nancy L. *The Other Americans in Paris: Businessmen, Countesses, Wayward Youth, 1880–1941*. Chicago: University of Chicago Press, 2014.

Greenberg, Amy. *Manifest Manhood and the Antebellum American Empire*. New York: Cambridge University Press, 2005.

Guillory, Sean. "Culture Clash in the Socialist Paradise: Soviet Patronage and African Students' Urbanity in the Soviet Union, 1960–1965." *Diplomatic History* 38, no. 2 (2014): 271–81.

Hale, Grace Elizabeth. *Making Whiteness: The Culture of Segregation in the South*. New York: Pantheon Books, 1998.

Halpern, Richard. *Norman Rockwell: The Underside of Innocence*. Chicago: Chicago University Press, 2006.

Haring, Kristen. *Ham Radio's Technical Culture*. Cambridge, MA: MIT Press, 2007.

Harrison, James. "Aging." In *Men and Masculinities: A Social, Cultural, and Historical Encyclopedia*, edited by Michael Kimmel and Amy Aronson, 9–15. Santa Barbara, CA: ABC Clio, 2004.

Haverty-Stacke, Donna T. *America's Forgotten Holiday: May Day and Nationalism, 1867–1960*. New York: New York University Press, 2009.

Hayashi, Brian Masary. *Democratizing the Enemy: The Japanese American Internment*. Princeton, NJ: Princeton University Press, 2004.

Helgren, Jennifer. *American Girls and Global Responsibility: A New Relation to the World during the Early Cold War*. New Brunswick, NJ: Rutgers University Press, 2017.

Hermann, Ulrich, ed. *"Mit uns zieht die neue Zeit": Der Wandervogel in der deutschen Jugendbewegung*. Munich: Juventa, 2006.

Herzog, Jonathan P. *The Spiritual-Industrial Complex: America's Religious Battle against Communism in the Early Cold War*. New York: Oxford University Press, 2011.

Hogan, Michael J. *A Cross of Iron: Harry S. Truman and the Origins of the National Security State, 1945–1954*. New York: Cambridge University Press, 1996.

Hoganson, Kristin L. *Consumers' Imperium: The Global Production of American Domesticity, 1865–1920*. Chapel Hill: University of North Carolina Press, 2007.

——. *Fighting for American Manhood: How Gender Politics Provoked the Spanish-American and Philippine-American Wars*. New Haven, CT: Yale University Press, 1998.

Höhn, Maria. *GIs and Fräuleins: The German-American Encounter in 1950s West Germany*. Chapel Hill: University of North Carolina Press, 2002.

Höhn, Maria, and Martin Klimke. *A Breath of Freedom: The Civil Rights Struggle, African American GIs, and Germany*. New York: Palgrave Macmillan, 2010.

Höhn, Maria, and Seungsook Moon, eds. *Over There: Living with the U.S. Empire from World War Two to the Present*. Durham, NC: Duke University Press, 2010.

Holt, Douglas B., and Craig J. Thompson. "Man-of-Action Heroes: The Pursuit of Heroic Masculinity in Everyday Consumption." *Journal of Consumer Research* 31, no. 2 (September 2004): 425–40.

Holt, Marilyn Irvin. *Cold War Kids: Politics and Childhood in Postwar America, 1945–1960*. Lawrence: University Press of Kansas, 2014.

Honeck, Mischa. "An Empire of Youth: American Boy Scouts in the World, 1910–1960." *Bulletin of the German Historical Society* 52 (Spring 2013): 95–112.

Honeck, Mischa, and James Marten, eds. *War and Childhood in Era of the Two World Wars*. New York: Cambridge University Press, forthcoming.

Honeck, Mischa, and Gabriel Rosenberg. "Transnational Generations: Organizing Youth in the Cold War." *Diplomatic History* 38, no. 2 (2014): 233–39.

Hübner, Stefan. "Muscular Christianity and the Western Civilizing Mission: Elwood S. Brown, the YMCA, and the Idea of the Far Eastern Championship Games." *Diplomatic History* 39, no. 3 (2015): 532–57.

——. *Pan-Asian Sports and the Emergence of Modern Asia, 1914–1974*. Singapore: NUS Press Singapore, 2016.

Huhndorf, Shari M. *Going Native: Indians in the American Cultural Imagination*. Ithaca, NY: Cornell University Press, 2001.

Hunt, Lynn, and Victoria L. Bonnell, eds. *Beyond the Cultural Turn: New Directions in the Study of Society and Culture*. Berkeley: University of California Press, 1999.

Hüppauf, Bernd. "The Birth of Fascist Man from the Spirit of the Front: From Langemarck to Verdun." In *Fascism: Critical Concepts in Political Science*, edited by Roger Griffin and Matthew Feldman, 264–92. London: Routledge, 2004.

Hwang, Jinlin. "Authority over the Body and the Modern Formation of the Body." In *Creating Chinese Modernity: Knowledge and Everday Life, 1900–1940*, edited by Peter Zarrow, 183–212. New York: Peter Lang, 2007.

Immerman, Richard H. *Empire for Liberty: A History of American Imperialism from Benjamin Franklin to Paul Wolfowitz*. Princeton, NJ: Princeton University Press, 2010.

Imperato, Pascal James, and Eleanor M. Imperato. *They Married Adventure: The Wandering Lives of Martin and Osa Johnson*. New Brunswick, NJ: Rutgers University Press, 1992.

Iriye, Akira. "The Internationalization of History." *American Historical Review* 94, no. 1 (1989): 1–10.

Irons, Janet. *Testing the New Deal: The General Textile Strike of 1934 in the American South*. Urbana: University of Illinois Press, 2000.

Isaac, Allan Punzalan. *American Tropics: Articulating Filipino America*. Minneapolis: University of Minnesota Press, 2006.

Jacobs, Robert A. *The Dragon's Tail: Americans Face the Atomic Age*. Amherst: University of Massachusetts Press, 2010.

Jacobson, Matthew Frye. *Whiteness of a Different Color: European Immigrants and the Alchemy of Race*. Cambridge, MA: Harvard University Press, 1999.

Jarausch, Konrad H. *After Hitler: Recivilizing Germans, 1945–1995*. New York: Oxford University Press, 2006.

Jeal, Tim. *Baden-Powell: Founder of the Boy Scouts*. New Haven, CT: Yale University Press, 2001.

Jobs, Richard Ivan. *Riding the New Wave: Youth and the Rejuvenation of France after the Second World War*. Stanford, CA: Stanford University Press, 2007.

———. "Youth Movements: Travel, Protest, and Europe in 1968." *American Historical Review* 114, no. 2 (2009): 376–404.

Jobs, Richard Ivan, and David M. Pomfret, eds. *Transnational Histories of Youth in the Twentieth Century*. New York: Palgrave Macmillan, 2015.

Johansen, Bruce Elliott, ed. *Native Americans Today: A Biographical Dictionary*. Santa Barbara: ABC Clio, 2010.

Johnston, Scott. "Looking Wide? Imperialism, Internationalism, and the Boy Scout Movement, 1918–1939" (MA thesis, University of Waterloo, Ontario), 2012.

Jones, Jeannette Eileen. *In Search of Brightest Africa: Reimagining the Dark Continent in American Culture, 1884–1936*. Athens: University of Georgia Press, 2010.

Jonnes, Denis. *Cold War American Literature and the Rise of Youth Culture: Children of Empire*. New York: Routledge, 2015.

Jorae, Wendy R. *The Children of Chinatown: Growing Up Chinese-American in San Francisco*. Chapel Hill: University of North Carolina Press, 2009.

Jordan, Benjamin R. "'Conservation of Boyhood': Boy Scouting's Modest Manliness and Natural Resource Conservation." *Environmental History* 15 (2010): 612–42.

———. *Modern Manhood and the Boy Scouts of America: Citizenship, Race, and the Environment, 1910–1930*. Chapel Hill: University of North Carolina Press, 2016.

Joseph, Gilbert M., Catherine C. Legrand, and Ricardo D. Salvatore, eds. *Close Encounters of Empire: Writing the History of U.S.-Latin American Relations*. Durham, NC: Duke University Press, 1998.

Kage, Rieko. *Civic Engagement in Postwar Japan: The Revival of a Defeated Society*. New York: Cambridge University Press, 2011.

Kane, Paula M. *Separatism and Subculture: Boston Catholicism, 1900–1920*. Chapel Hill: University of North Carolina Press, 1994.

Kaplan, Amy. *The Anarchy of Empire in the Making of U.S. Culture*. Cambridge, MA: Harvard University Press, 2002.

———. "'Left Alone with America': The Absence of Empire in the Study of American Culture." In *Cultures of United States Imperialism*, edited by Amy Kaplan and Donald Pease, 3–21. Durham, NC: Duke University Press, 1994.

Katznelson, Ira. *Fear Itself: The New Deal and the Origins of Our Time*. New York: Liveright Publishing, 2013.

Kennedy, David M., Lizabeth Cohen, and Thomas A. Bailey. *The American Pageant*. Vol. 2, *Since 1865*. Boston: Wadsworth Cengage Learning, 2010.

Kett, Joseph F. *Rites of Passage: Adolescence in America, 1790 to the Present*. New York: Basic Books, 1977.

Keyler, Hartmut. "Auslandsbeziehungen." In *Kreuz und Lilie: Christliche Pfadfinder in Deutschland von 1909 bis 1972*, edited by Ulrich Bauer, Hartmut Keyler, and Klaus Meier, 281–89. Berlin: Wichern-Verlag, 2014.

Kidd, Kenneth B. *Making American Boys: Boyology and the Feral Tale*. Minneapolis: University of Minnesota Press, 2004.

Kimmel, Michael. *Manhood in America: A Cultural History*. New York: Free Press, 1996.

Kirby, Dianne. "The Religious Cold War." In *The Oxford Handbook of the Cold War*, edited by Richard H. Immerman and Petra Goedde, 540–64. New York: Oxford University Press, 2013.

Klein, Christina. *Cold War Orientalism: Asia in the Middle-Brow Imagination*. Berkeley: University of California Press, 2003.

Klimke, Martin. *The Other Alliance: Student Protest in West Germany and the United States in the Global Sixties*. Princeton, NJ: Princeton University Press, 2010.

Kline, Wendy. *Building a Better Race: Gender, Sexuality, and Eugenics from the Turn of the Century to the Baby Boom*. Berkeley: University of California Press, 2001.

Kniptash, Vernon E. *On the Western Front with the Rainbow Division: A World War I Diary*. Norman: University of Oklahoma Press, 2009.

Koshiro, Yuiko. *Trans-Pacific Racisms and the U.S. Occupation of Japan*. New York: Columbia University Press, 1999.

Kramer, Paul A. *The Blood of Government: Race, Empire, the United States, and the Philippines*. Chapel Hill: University of North Carolina Press, 2006.

———. "Power and Connection: Imperial Histories of the United States in the World." *American Historical Review* 116, no. 5 (December 2011): 1348–91.

Kucherenko, Olga. *Little Soldiers: How Soviet Children Went to War, 1941–1945*. New York: Oxford University Press, 2011.

Laqua, Daniel, ed. *Internationalism Reconfigured: Transnational Ideas and Movements between the World Wars*. London: Palgrave Macmillan, 2011.

Lawcock, Larry A. "Filipino Students in the United States and the Philippines Independence Movement." (PhD thesis, University of California, Berkeley, 1975).

Lears, Jackson. *Rebirth of a Nation: The Making of Modern America, 1877–1920*. New York: HarperCollins, 2009.

Leffler, Phyllis. *Black Leaders on Leadership: Conversations with Julian Bond*. New York: Palgrave Macmillan, 2014.

Lesko, Nancy. *Act Your Age! A Cultural Construction of Adolescence*. New York: Routledge, 2001.

Levine, Philippa, ed. *Gender and Empire*. New York: Oxford University Press, 2004.

Lewis, David Levering. "James and Esther Jackson: A Historical Assessment." In *Red Activists and Black Freedom: James and Esther Jackson and the Long Civil Rights Revolution*, edited by David L. Lewis, Michael H. Nash, and Daniel J. Leab, 11–20. New York: Routledge, 2010.

Lewis, R. W. B. *The American Adam: Innocence, Tragedy, and Tradition in the Nineteenth Century*. Chicago: University of Chicago Press, 1955.

Lindenmeyer, Kriste. *The Greatest Generation Grows Up: American Childhood in the 1930s*. Chicago: Ivan R. Dee, 2005.

Llinares, Dario. *The Astronaut: Cultural Mythology and Idealized Masculinity*. Newcastle upon Tyne, UK: Cambridge Scholars Publishing, 2011.

Lowe, Margaret A. *Looking Good: College Women and Body Image, 1875–1930*. Baltimore: Johns Hopkins University Press, 2006.

Lüdtke, Alf, ed. *The History of Everyday Life: Reconstructing Experiences and Ways of Life*. Princeton, NJ: Princeton University Press, 1995.

Lundestadt, Geir. "'Empire by Invitation' in the American Century." *Diplomatic History* 23, no. 2 (Spring 1999): 189–217.

Lutz, Hartmut. "German Indianthusiasm: A Socially Constructed German National(ist) Myth." In *Germans and Indians: Fantasies, Encounters, Projections*, edited by Colin G. Calloway, Gerd Gemünden, and Susanne Zantop, 167–84. Lincoln: University of Nebraska Press, 2002.

MacDonald, Heather. "Why the Boy Scouts Work." *City Journal* 10, no. 1 (Winter 2000): 14–27.

MacDonald, Robert H. *Sons of the Empire: The Frontier and the Boy Scout Movement, 1890–1918*. Toronto: University of Toronto Press, 1993.

Mackert, Nina. *Jugenddeliquenz: Die Produktivität eines Problems in den USA der späten 1940er bis 1960er Jahre*. Konstanz, Germany: UVK, 2014.

MacLeod, David I. *Building Character in the American Boy: The Boy Scouts, YMCA, and Their Forerunners, 1870–1920*. Madison: University of Wisconsin Press, 1983.

——. "Original Intent: Establishing the Creed and Control of Boy Scouting in the United States." In Block and Proctor, *Scouting Frontiers*, 13–27.

Maher, Neil M. *Nature's New Deal: The Civilian Conservation Corps and the Roots of the American Environmental Movement*. New York: Oxford University, 2007.

Maier, Charles S. *Among Empires: American Ascendency and Its Predecessors*. Cambridge, MA: Harvard University Press, 2006.

Malkki, Liisa. "Children, Humanity, and the Infantilization of Peace." In *In the Name of Humanity: The Government of Threat and Care*, edited by Ilana Feldman and Miriam Ticktin, 58–85. Durham, NC: Duke University Press, 2010.

Mangan, J. A., ed. *Superman Supreme: Fascist Body as Political Icon—Global Fascism*. London: Frank Cass, 2000.

Mangione, Jerre. "Growing Up Sicilian." In *The Italian American Reader: A Collection of Outstanding Fiction, Memoirs, Journalism, and Poetry*, edited by Bill Tonelli, 471–78. New York: HarperCollins, 2003.

Marten, James. "Children and War." In *The Routledge History of Childhood in the Western World*, edited by Paula Fass, 142–57. London: Routledge, 2013.

Martschukat, Jürgen. *Die Ordnung des Sozialen: Väter und Familien in der amerikanischen Geschichte seit 1770*. Frankfurt: Campus, 2013.

May, Elaine Tyler. *Homeward Bound: American Families in the Cold War Era*. New York: Basic Books, 2008.

McCarthy, Helen. "The League of Nations, Public Ritual, and National Identity in Britain, c.1919–56." *History Workshop Journal* 70, no. 1 (2010): 108–32.

McCoy, Alfred W. *Closer Than Brothers: Manhood at the Philippine Military Academy*. New Haven, CT: Yale University Press, 1999.

McEnaney, Laura. *Civil Defense Begins at Home: Militarization Meets Everyday Life in the Fifties*. Princeton, NJ: Princeton University Press, 2000.

Mechling, Jay. "Boy Scouts." In *Men and Masculinities: A Social, Cultural, and Historical Encyclopedia*, edited by Michael Kimmel and Amy Aronson, 99–101. Santa Barbara, CA: ABC Clio, 2004.

——. "Children in Scouting and Other Organizations." In *The Routledge History of Childhood in the Western World*, 419–33.

——. "Heroism and the Problem of Impulsiveness for Early Twentieth-Century American Youth." In *Generations of Youth: Youth Cultures and History in Twentieth-Century America*, edited by Joe Austin, 36–49. New York: New York University Press, 1998.

——. *On My Honor: Boy Scouts and the Making of American Youth*. Chicago: University of Chicago Press, 2001.

Medovoi, Leerom. *Rebels: Youth and the Cold War Origins of Identity*. Durham, NC: Duke University Press, 2005.

Mettler, Suzanne. *Dividing Citizens: Gender and Federalism in New Deal Public Policy*. Ithaca, NY: Cornell University Press, 1998.

Michel, Sonya, and Eszter Varsa. "Children and the National Interest." In *Raising Citizens in the Century of the Child: The United States and German Central Europe in Comparative Perspective*, edited by Dirk Schumann, 27–49. New York: Berghahn Books, 2010.

Mickenberg, Julia L. *Learning from the Left: Children's Literature, the Cold War, and Radical Politics in the United States*. New York: Oxford University Press, 2006.

Miller, Susan A. *Growing Girls: The Natural Origins of Girl Organizations in America*. New Brunswick, NJ: Rutgers University Press, 2007.

——. "Assent as Agency in the Early Years of the Children of the American Revolution," *Journal of the History of Childhood and Youth* 9, no. 1 (Winter 2016): 49.

Mills, Sarah. "Be Prepared: Communism and the Politics of Scouting in 1950s Britain." *Contemporary British History* 25, no. 3 (2011): 429–50.

Mintz, Steven. *Huck's Raft: A History of American Childhood*. Cambridge, MA: Harvard University Press, 2004.

——. "Reflections on Age as a Category of Historical Analysis." *Journal of the History of Childhood and Youth* 1 (Winter 2008): 91–94.

Mishler, Paul C. *Raising Reds: The Young Pioneers, Radical Summer Camps, and Communist Political Culture in the United States*. New York: Columbia University Press, 1999.

Mitcham, John C. *Race and Imperial Defence in the British World, 1870–1914*. New York: Cambridge University Press, 2016.

Monteyne, David. *Fallout Shelter: Designing for Civil Defense in the Cold War*. Minneapolis: University of Minnesota Press, 2011.

Moran, Jeffrey. *Teaching Sex: The Shaping of Adolescence in the 20th Century*. Cambridge, MA: Harvard University Press, 2000.

Morefield, Jeanne. *Empires without Imperialism: Anglo-American Decline and the Politics of Deflection*. New York: Oxford University Press, 2014.

Morris, Nancy. *Puerto Rico: Culture, Politics, and Identity*. Westport, CT: Praeger, 1995.

Mosse, George L. *The Image of Man: The Creation of Modern Masculinity*. New York: Oxford University Press, 1996.

Mulready-Stone, Kristin. *Mobilizing Shanghai Youth: Ccp Internationalism, Gmd Nationalism, and Japanese Collaboration*. London: Routledge, 2015.

Münkler, Herfried. *Imperien: Die Logik der Weltherrschaft—vom Alten Rom bis zu den Vereinigten Staaten*. Berlin: Rowohlt Verlag, 2005.

Murphy, Kevin P. *Political Manhood: Red Bloods, Mollycoddles, and the Politics of Progressive Era Reform*. New York: Columbia University Press, 2010.

Nasaw, David. *Children of the City: At Work and at Play*. Garden City, NY: Doubleday, 1985.

Nawyn, Kathleen J. "'Striking at the Roots of German Militarism': Efforts to Demilitarize German Society and Culture in American-Occupied Württemberg-Baden" (PhD dissertation, University of North Carolina, Chapel Hill, 2008).

Neuman, Lisa K. *Indian Play: Indigenous Identities at Bacone College*. Lincoln: University of Nebraska Press, 2013.

Neumann, Matthias. *The Communist Youth League and the Transformation of the Soviet Union, 1917–1932*. New York: Routledge, 2011.

Nguyen, Mimi Thi. *The Gift of Freedom: War, Debt, and Other Refugee Passages*. Durham, NC: Duke University Press, 2012.

Nicholson, Bryan W. "Apprentices to Power: The Cultivation of American Youth Nationalism" (PhD diss., University of Illinois, 2012).

——. "'In America, the Young Men and Women Would Be Taught HOW, Not WHAT, to Think': Transnational Exchanges That Shaped U.S. Youth Politics, 1932–43." *New Global Studies* 4, no. 3 (2010): 1–29.

Nolan, Mary. *The Transatlantic Century: Europe and America, 1890–2010*. New York: Cambridge University Press, 2012.

Norwood, Stephen H. *Strike-Breaking and Intimidation: Mercenaries and Masculinity in Twentieth-Century America*. Chapel Hill: University of North Carolina Press, 2002.

Nye, Joseph S. *Soft Power: The Means to Succeed in World Politics*. New York: Public Affairs, 2004.

Oakes, Guy. *The Imaginary War: Civil Defense and American Cold War Culture*. New York: Oxford University Press, 1994.

O'Brien, Chris. "Mama, Are We Going to Die? America's Children Confront the Cuban Missile Crisis." In *Children and War: A Historical Anthology*, edited by James Marten, 75–86. New York: New York University Press, 2002.

Oelrich, Harald. "*Sportgeltung—Weltgeltung*": *Sport im Spannungsfeld der deutsch-italienischen Außenpolitik von 1918 bis 1945*. Münster, Germany: LIT, 2003.

Oh, Arissa H. *To Save the Children of Korea: The Cold War Origins of International Adoption*. Stanford, CA: Stanford University Press, 2015.

Onion, Rebbeca. *Innocent Experiments: Childhood and the Culture of Popular Science in the United States*. Chapel Hill: University of North Carolina Press, 2016.

Ornig, Joseph R. *My Last Chance to Be a Boy: Theodore Roosevelt's South American Expedition of 1913–1914*. Mechanicsburg, PA: Stackpole Books, 1994.

Ossian, Lisa L. *The Forgotten Generation: American Children and World War II*. Columbia: University of Missouri Press, 2011.

Paisley, Fiona. "Childhood and Race: Growing Up in the Empire." In *Gender and Empire*, edited by Philippa Levine, 240–59. Oxford: Oxford University Press, 2010.

Pak, Susie J. *Gentlemen Bankers: The World of J.P. Morgan*. Cambridge, MA: Harvard University Press, 2013.

Palladino, Grace. *Teenagers: An American History*. New York: Basic Books, 1996.

Paris, Leslie. *Children's Nature: The Rise of the American Summer Camp*. New York: New York University Press, 2008.

Parmar, Inderjeet. *Foundations of the American Century: The Ford, Carnegie, & Rockefeller Foundations in the Rise of American Power*. New York: Columbia University Press, 2011.

Parsons, Timothy H. *Race, Resistance, and the Boy Scout Movement in British Colonial Africa*. Athens: Ohio University Press, 2004.

Patel, Kiran Klaus. *The New Deal: A Global History*. Princeton, NJ: Princeton University Press, 2016.

———. *Soldiers of Labor: Labor Service in Nazi Germany and New Deal America, 1933–1945*. New York: Cambridge University Press, 2005.

Peacock, Margaret. *Innocent Weapons: The Soviet and American Politics of Childhood in the Cold War*. Chapel Hill: University of North Carolina Press, 2014.

Peer, Shanny. *France on Display: Peasants, Provincials, and Folklore in the 1937 Paris World's Fair*. Albany: State University of New York Press, 1998.

Penny, H. Glenn. *Kindred by Choice: Germans and American Indians since 1800*. Chapel Hill: University of North Carolina Press, 2013.

Perry, Rick. *On My Honor: Why the Values of the Boy Scouts of America Are Worth Fighting For*. Macon, GA: Stroud & Hall, 2008.

Peterson, Robert. *The Boy Scouts: An American Adventure*. New York: American Heritage, 1984.

Pinl, Harald. *Im Zeichen der Rautenlilie: Der Bund Deutscher Pfadfinder in Erlangen von 1949 bis 1971*. Norderstedt, Germany: Books on Demand, 2014.

Poiger, Uta G. *Jazz, Rock, and Rebels: Cold War Politics and American Culture in a Divided Germany*. Berkeley: University of California Press, 2000.

Pomfret, David M. *Youth and Empire: Trans-Colonial Childhoods in British and French Asia*. Stanford, CA: Stanford University Press, 2015.

Ponzio, Alessio. *Shaping the New Man: Youth Training Regimes in Fascist Italy and Nazi Germany*. Madison: University of Wisconsin Press, 2015.

Porter, Andrew. *Religion versus Empire? British Protestant Missionaries and Overseas Expansion, 1700–1914*. Manchester: Manchester University Press, 2004.

Pratt, Mary Louise. *Imperial Eyes: Travel Writing and Transculturation*. London: Routledge, 1992.

Proctor, Tammy M. "Building an Empire of Youth: Scout and Guide History in Perspective." In *Scouting Frontiers: Youth and the Scout Movement's First Century*, edited by Nelson R. Block and Tammy M. Proctor, xxvi–xxxviii. Newcastle, UK: Cambridge Scholars Publishing, 2009.

———. *On My Honour: Guides and Scouts in Interwar Britain*. Philadelphia: American Philosophical Society, 2002.

———. *Scouting for Girls: A Century of Girl Guides and Girl Scouts*. Santa Barbara, CA: Praeger, 2009.

Puaca, Brian M. *Learning Democracy: Education Reform in West Germany, 1945–1965.* New York: Berghahn Books, 2009.

Putnam, Robert. *Bowling Alone: The Collapse and Revival of American Community.* New York: Simon & Schuster, 2001.

Putney, Clifford. *Muscular Christianity: Manhood and Sports in Protestant America, 1880–1920.* Cambridge, MA: Harvard University Press, 2001.

Raphael, Lutz. "Die Verwissenschaftlichung des Sozialen als methodische und konzeptionelle Herausforderung für eine Sozialgeschichte des 20. Jahrhunderts." *Geschichte und Gesellschaft* 22 (1996): 165–93.

——. *Imperiale Gewalt und mobilisierte Nation: Europa, 1914–1945.* Munich: Beck, 2011.

Register, Woody. *The Kid of Coney Island: Fred Thompson and the Rise of American Amusements.* New York: Oxford University Press, 2001.

Reiman, Richard A. *The New Deal and American Youth: Ideas and Ideals in a Depression Decade.* Athens: University of Georgia Press, 1992.

Rodgers, Daniel T. *Atlantic Crossings: Social Politics in a Progressive Age.* Cambridge, MA: Harvard University Press, 1998.

Rodgers, Eugene. *Beyond the Barrier: The Story of Byrd's First Antarctic Expedition.* Annapolis, MD: Naval Institute Press, 1990.

Roediger, David. *Wages of Whiteness: Race and the Making of the American Working Class.* New York: Verso, 1991.

Roman, Meredith L. *Opposing Jim Crow: African Americans and the Soviet Indictment of U.S. Racism.* Lincoln: University of Nebraska Press, 2012.

Rose, Lisle A. *Explorer: The Life of Richard E. Byrd.* Columbia: University of Missouri Press, 2008.

Rosenberg, Emily S. "Transnational Currents in a Shrinking World." In *A World Connecting, 1870–1945,* edited by Emily S. Rosenberg, 815–996. Cambridge, MA: Harvard University Press, 2012.

Rosenberg, Gabriel N. *The 4-H Harvest: Sexuality and the State in Rural America.* Philadelphia: University of Pennsylvania Press, 2015.

Rosenthal, Michael. *The Character Factory: Baden-Powell's Boy Scouts and the Imperatives of Empire.* New York: Pantheon Books, 1986.

Rotundo, E. Anthony. *American Manhood: Transformations in Masculinity from the Revolution to the Modern Era.* New York: Basic Books, 1993.

Rowan, Edward L. *To Do My Best: James E. West and the History of the Boy Scouts of America.* Exeter, NH: PublishingWorks, 2005.

Roy, Franziska. "International Utopia and National Discipline: Youth and Volunteer Movements in Interwar South Asia." In *The Internationalist Moment: South Asia, Worlds, and World Views, 1917–39,* edited by Ali Raza, Franziska Roy, and Benjamin Zachariah, 150–87. New Delhi: SAGE Publications, 2015.

Rupp, Leila J. *Worlds of Women: The Making of an International Women's Movement.* Princeton, NJ: Princeton University Press, 1997.

Rupprecht, Tobias. *Soviet Internationalism after Stalin: Interaction and Exchange between the USSR and Latin America during the Cold War.* Cambridge, UK: Cambridge University Press, 2015.

Rutter, Nick. "Enacting Communism: The World Youth Festival, 1945–1975" (PhD dissertation, Yale University, 2013).

——. "The Western Wall: The Iron Curtain Recast in Midsummer 1951." In *Cold War Crossings: International Travel and Exchange across the Soviet Bloc, 1940s–1960s*, edited by Patryk Babiracki and Kenyon Zimmer, 78–106. Arlington: Texas A&M University Press, 2014.

Rydell, Robert W. *World of Fairs: The Century-of-Progress Expositions*. Chicago: University of Chicago Press, 1993.

Rydell, Robert W., and Rob Kroes. *Buffalo Bill in Bologna: The Americanization of the World, 1869–1922*. Chicago: University of Chicago Press, 2005.

Sadowski-Smith, Claudia. *Border Fictions: Globalization, Empire, and Writing at the Boundaries of the United States*. Charlottesville: University of Virginia Press, 2008.

Savage, Jon. *Teenage: The Prehistory of Youth Culture, 1875–1945*. New York: Viking, 2007.

Scheibach, Michael. *"In Case Atom Bombs Fall": An Anthology of Governmental Explanations, Instructions and Warnings from the 1940s to the 1960s*. Jefferson, NC: Macfarland, 2009.

Schwartz, Angela. "The Regional and the Global: Folk Culture at World's Fairs and the Reinvention of the Nation." In *Folklore and Nationalism in Europe during the Long Nineteenth Century*, edited by Timothy Baycroft and David Hopkin, 99–112. Leiden: Brill, 2012.

Scott, David C., and Brendan Murphy. *The Scouting Party: Pioneering and Preservation, Progressivism and Preparedness in the Making of the Boy Scouts of America*. Garland, TX: Red Honor Press, 2010.

Sedgwick, Eve Kosofsky. *Between Men: English Literature and Male Homosocial Desire*. New York: Columbia University Press, 1985.

Shah, Nayan. *Stranger Intimacy: Contesting Race, Sexuality, and the Law in the North American West*. Berkeley: University of California Press, 2011.

Simanga, Michael. *Amiri Baraka and the Congress of African People: History and Memory*. New York: Palgrave Macmillan, 2015.

Skocpol, Theda, Ariane Liazos, and Marshall Ganz. *What a Mighty Power We Can Be: African American Fraternal Groups and the Struggle for Racial Equality*. Princeton, NJ: Princeton University Press, 2006.

Skott-Myhre, Hans Arthur. *Youth and Subculture as Creative Force: Creating New Spaces for Radical Youth Work*. Toronto: University of Toronto Press, 2008.

Slotkin, Richard. *Gunfighter Nation: The Myth of the Frontier in Twentieth Century America*. Norman: University of Oklahoma Press, 1998.

Slyck, Abigail A. van. *A Manufactured Wilderness: Summer Camps and the Shaping of American Youth*. Minneapolis: University of Minnesota Press, 2010.

Smith-Rosenberg, Caroll. *Disorderly Conduct: Visions of Gender in Victorian America*. New York: Alfred A. Knopf, 1985.

Sneider, Allison. *Suffragists in an Imperial Age: U.S. Expansion and the Woman Question, 1870–1929*. New York: Oxford University Press, 2008.

Soloway, Richard A. *Demography and Degeneration: Eugenics and the Declining Birth Rate in Twentieth-Century Britain*. Chapel Hill: University of North Carolina Press, 1995.

Spivak, Gayatri C. "Can the Subaltern Speak?" In *Marxism and the Interpretation of Culture*, edited by Carry Nelson and Larry Grossberg, 271–313. Urbana: University of Illinois Press, 1988.

Springhall, John. *Youth, Empire, and Society: British Youth Movements, 1883–1940*. Hamden, CT: Archon Books, 1977.

Steans, Jill. *Gender and International Relations*. 3rd ed. Malden, MA: Polity Press, 2013.

Stearns, Peter N. *Childhood in World History*. London: Routledge, 2011.

Stein, Judith. *The World of Marcus Garvey: Race and Class in Modern Society*. Baton Rouge: Louisiana State University Press, 1986.

Stieglitz, Olaf. *100 Percent American Boys: Disziplinierungsdiskurse und Ideologie im Civilian Conservation Corps, 1933–1942*. Stuttgart: Franz Steiner Verlag, 1999.

Stoff, Heiko. *Ewige Jugend: Konzepte der Verjüngung vom späten 19. Jahrhundert bis ins Dritte Reich*. Cologne: Böhlau, 2004.

Stoler, Ann Laura, ed. *Haunted by Empire: Geographies of Intimacy in North American History*. Durham, NC: Duke University Press, 2006.

Streets, Heather. *Martial Races: The Military, Race and Masculinity in British Imperial Culture, 1857–1914*. Manchester: Manchester University Press, 2004.

Strunk, Piet. *Die Pfadfinder in Deutschland, 1909–2009*. Neckenmarkt, Germany: Novum Pro Verlag, 2010.

Studlar, Gaylin. *This Mad Masquerade: Stardom and Masculinity in the Jazz Age*. New York: Columbia University Press, 1996.

Suri, Jeremi. *Liberty's Surest Guardian: American Nation-Building from the Founders to Obama*. New York: Simon & Schuster, 2011.

——. *Power and Protest: Global Revolution and the Rise of Détente*. Cambridge, MA: Harvard University Press, 2003.

Swafford, Emily. "The Challenge and Promise of Girl Scout Internationalism: From Progressive-Era Roots to Cold War Fruit." *Bulletin of the German Historical Institute* 55 (Fall 2014): 105–24.

——. "Democracy's Proving Ground: U.S. Military Families in West Germany, 1946–1961" (PhD diss., University of Chicago, 2014).

Taylor, Molly-Ladd. *Mother-Work: Women, Child Welfare, and the State, 1890–1930*. Urbana: University of Illinois Press, 1994.

Tedesco, Laureen. "Making a Girl into a Scout: Americanizing Scouting for Girls." In *Delinquents and Debutantes: Twentieth-Century American Girl Cultures*, edited by Sherrie A. Inness, 19–39. New York: New York University Press, 1998.

Thelen, David. "The Nation and Beyond: Transnational Perspectives on United States History." *Journal of American History* 86, no. 3 (1999): 965–75.

Toerpe, Kathleen. "Children's Bureau." In *The United States in the First World War: An Encyclopedia*, edited by Anne Cipriano Venzon, 141–42. New York: Routledge, 2012.

Tong, Benson, ed. *Asian American Children: A Historical Handbook and Guide*. Westport, CT: Greenwood Press, 2004.

Townley, Alvin. *Legacy of Honor: The Values and Influence of America's Eagle Scouts*. New York: St. Martin's Press, 2007.

——. *Spirit of Adventure, Eagle Scouts and the Making of America's Future*. New York: St. Martin's Press, 2009.

Turner, Victor W. "Betwixt and Between: The Liminal Period in *Rites des Passage*." *Proceedings of the American Ethnological Society* (1964): 4–20.

Tuttle, William M., Jr. *"Daddy's Gone to War": The Second World War in the Lives of America's Children*. New York: Oxford University Press, 1993.

Tyrrell, Ian. *Reforming the World: The Creation of America's Moral Empire*. Princeton, NJ: Princeton University Press, 2010.

——. *Transnational Nation: The United States in Global Perspective since 1789*. Basingstoke, UK: Palgrave Macmillan, 2007.

——. *Woman's World, Woman's Empire: The Woman's Christian Temperance Movement in International Perspective*. Chapel Hill: University of North Carolina Press, 1991.

Vallory, Eduard. *World Scouting: Educating for Global Citizenship*. New York: Palgrave Macmillan, 2012.

Vazansky, Alexander. "'Army in Anguish': The U.S. Army, Europe, in the Early 1970s." In Maulucci and Junker, *GIs in Germany*, 273–95.

——. "Army in Crisis: The United States Army, Europe, 1968–1975" (PhD diss., Heidelberg University, 2009).

Wagner, Carol Ditte. "The Boy Scouts of America: A Model and a Mirror of American Society" (PhD diss., Johns Hopkins University, 1979).

Wall, Wendy. *Inventing the "American Way": The Politics of Consensus from the New Deal to the Civil Rights Movement*. New York: Oxford University Press, 2008.

Wallach, Glenn. *Obedient Sons: The Discourse of Youth and Generations in American Culture, 1630–1860*. Amherst: University of Massachusetts Press, 1997.

Watt, Carey. "'The Promise of Character' and the Specter of Sedition: The Boy Scout Movement and Colonial Consternation in India." *South Asia* 22, no. 2 (1999): 37–62.

Weinbaum, Alys Eve, Lynn M. Thomas, Priti Ramamurthy, Uta G. Poiger, Madeleine Yue Dong, Tani E. Barlow, eds. *The Modern Girl around the World: Consumption, Modernity, and Globalization*. Durham, NC: Duke University Press, 2009.

Westfahl, Gary. *Science Fiction, Children's Literature, and Popular Culture: Coming of Age in Fantasyland*. Westport, CT: Greenwood Press, 2000.

White, Owen, and J. P. Daughton, eds. *In God's Empire: French Missionaries and the Modern World*. New York: Oxford University Press, 2012.

White, Richard. *The Middle Ground: Indians, Empires, and Republics in the Great Lakes Region, 1650–1815*. New York: Cambridge University Press, 1991.

Whitney, Susan. *Mobilizing Youth: Communists and Catholics in Interwar France*. Durham, NC: Duke University Press, 2009.

Willrich, Michael. "Home Slackers: Men, the State, and Welfare in Modern America." *Journal of American History* 87, no. 2 (2000): 460–89.

Wills, Chuck. *Boy Scouts of America: A Centennial History*. New York: DK Publishers, 2009.

Wilson, Kathleen. "Old Imperialisms and New Imperial Histories: Rethinking the History of the Present." *Radical History Review* 95 (2006): 211–34.

Winter, Jay M. *Dreams of Peace and Freedom: Utopian Moments in the Twentieth Century.* New Haven, CT: Yale University Press, 2006.

Wolfskill, George. *The Revolt of the Conservatives: A History of the American Liberty League, 1934–1940.* Cambridge, MA: Houghton Mifflin, 1962.

Wood, Gregory. *Retiring Men: Manhood, Labor, and Growing Old in America, 1900–1960.* Lanham, MD: Rowman & Littlefield, 2012.

Woollacott, Angela. *Gender and Empire.* New York: Palgrave Macmillan, 2006.

Wright, Bradford W. *Comic Book Nation: The Transformation of Youth Culture in America.* Baltimore: Johns Hopkins University Press, 2001.

Wu, Jialin Christina. "'A Life of Make-Believe': Being Boy Scouts and 'Playing Indian' in British Malaya (1910–1940)." In *Gender, Imperialism, and Global Exchanges,* edited by Stephan F. Mitscher, Michel Mitchelle, and Naoko Shibusawa, 205–35. Malden, MA: Polity Press, 2015.

Wyman, Mark. *DPs: Europe's Displaced Persons, 1945–1951.* Ithaca, NY: Cornell University Press, 1998.

Yost, Nellie Snyder. *A Man as Big as the West.* Boulder, CO: Pruett Pub., 1979.

Zahra, Tara. *The Lost Children: Reconstructing Europe's Families after World War II.* Cambridge, MA: Harvard University Press, 2011.

Zeiger, Hans. *Get off My Honor: The Assault on the Boy Scouts of America.* Nashville, TN: Broadman & Holman, 2005.

Zilian, Frederick, Jr. "The Shifting Military Balance in Central Europe." In *The United States and Germany in the Era of the Cold War, 1968–1990: A Handbook.* Vol. 2., edited by Detlef Junker, 155–62. New York: Cambridge University Press, 2004.

Zimmerman, Andrew. *Alabama in Africa: Booker T. Washington, the German Empire, and the Globalization of the New South.* Princeton, NJ: Princeton University Press, 2010.

Index

Note: Page numbers in italics indicate illustrations.